CONTEMPORARY ECONOMIC PROBLEMS 1977

aei studies
CONTEMPORARY ECONOMIC PROBLEMS 1977
william fellner, editor

American Enterprise Institute for Public Policy Research
Washington, D.C.

ISBN 0-8447-1326-0

Library of Congress Catalog Card No. 77-89065

© 1977 by American Enterprise Institute for Public Policy Research, Washington, D.C. Permission to quote from or to reproduce materials in this publication is granted when due acknowledgment is made.

Printed in the United States of America

CONTRIBUTORS

William Fellner—*Editor*

> Sterling professor of economics emeritus at Yale University, former member of the Council of Economic Advisers, and past president of the American Economic Association. Resident scholar with the American Enterprise Institute.

Phillip Cagan

> Professor of economics at Columbia University, research staff of the National Bureau of Economic Research, and former senior staff economist for the Council of Economic Advisers. Adjunct scholar with the American Enterprise Institute.

Barry R. Chiswick

> Senior Fellow at the Hoover Institution, Stanford, California, and former senior staff economist for the Council of Economic Advisers.

Gottfried Haberler

> Galen L. Stone professor of international trade emeritus at Harvard University, and past president of the American Economic Association and International Economic Association. Member of the Academic Advisory Board and resident scholar with the American Enterprise Institute.

D. Gale Johnson

Eliakim Hastings Moore distinguished service professor of economics and provost at the University of Chicago, and past president of the American Farm Economics Association. Member of the Academic Advisory Board and adjunct scholar with the American Enterprise Institute.

Marvin Kosters

Former associate director for economic policy at the Cost of Living Council. Director of research of the Center for the Study of Government Regulation and resident scholar with the American Enterprise Institute.

Geoffrey H. Moore

Director of business cycle research for the National Bureau of Economic Research, senior research fellow at the Hoover Institution, Stanford University, and former U.S. commissioner of labor statistics. Adjunct scholar with the American Enterprise Institute.

Herbert Stein

A. Willis Robertson professor of economics at the University of Virginia, former chairman of the Council of Economic Advisers, and former vice president and chief economist of the Committee for Economic Development. Adjunct scholar with the American Enterprise Institute.

Marina v. N. Whitman

Distinguished public service professor of economics at the University of Pittsburgh, and former member of the Council of Economic Advisers and National Price Commission. Adjunct scholar with the American Enterprise Institute.

CONTENTS

GUIDE TO THE VOLUME

William Fellner

The Contemporary Economic Problems project of the American Enterprise Institute was started in 1976; hence, our 1977 volume is the second in the series. This year again we met several times as a group to discuss our work with each other.

While all our studies were directed at problems of significance for contemporary economic policy, they were written by economists with a general analytical interest. In several papers, the reader will find quite a bit of elaboration on the analytical background of the topical part of the discussion. There is a general tendency in these studies to look at policy problems with a reasonable time span in mind—a longer time span than that to which our policy practices have often been oriented. In the final section of my paper in this volume, I tried to express myself on the advantages of taking such a point of view and on the serious risks involved in policies attempting to shape the events of each successive short period.

The purpose of this introduction is to describe the main theme in which all participants have shown an interest in our meetings and which connects our studies. Something should be said in these opening pages about this connecting theme and the relation of the studies to it, because the authors were asked not to limit themselves merely to what would fit into a book written on a single theme but to cover broader areas in a generally informative manner.

The theme of common interest may be described as the dependence of the sustainable level of resource utilization in the United States on structural and institutional factors. These factors include the *modus operandi* of our monetary and fiscal authorities, the composition of our labor force, competitive and competition-limiting forces in our various markets, our system of transfer payments, gov-

1

ernment regulation in general, and the arrangements under which exchange rates and trade and payments relations become established among countries.

A sustainable level of resource utilization and a sustainable growth path can be achieved only without resort to inflationary stimuli, which after a while have always backfired and would backfire in the future in an even shorter time. They backfire because the public learns from experience, with the result that the inflationary process must be stepped up more and more if it is to continue to provide stimulus, and before long it becomes imperative to suppress such a process. This is why a measured unemployment rate that, given the relevant structural and institutional factors, is too low will not prove sustainable: after a while it will shoot up.

Those structural and institutional factors which reduce the sustainable level of utilization and increase the sustainable level of unemployment are frequently referred to as "rigidities." No objection can be raised to this terminology as long as it is realized that some of these rigidities were built into the system as expressions of widely held value judgments—income transfers to the poor provide one illustration. In these cases, it would be misleading to suggest that the problem is simply that of freeing ourselves from the rigidities in question. In such cases, the problem is partly that of finding the least rigidifying arrangement compatible with the accepted value judgments, and it is partly a problem of making allowances for the accepted rigidifying elements in setting other goals, including our employment-policy goals. At the same time, many rigidities cannot be reasonably said to express widely shared value judgments, and these call for a concentrated effort at removal, despite the resistance likely to be put up by interest groups. In any event, it is necessary to recognize that some of the institutional and structural factors on which the sustainable growth path depends fall in the category of "rigidities." The theme so described has played a prominent role in our thinking, though in our limited number of papers we could not, of course, pay equal attention to all aspects of the problem at hand.

I now turn to a brief elaboration on the relevance of the core of our individual studies to the common theme.

Barry Chiswick's paper, appearing as the last in this volume, lends itself particularly well to making the point I have in mind in a few simple words. The paper may well contain the most competent and up-to-date discussion of our entire income-transfer system, and the reader would have lost much valuable information if the author had limited himself to elements tying in directly with propositions developed in the other papers. At the same time, the significance of the properties of the transfer system for the problem of reaching a sustainable growth path will hardly be overlooked. Explicit statements will, of course, also be found on this in several other studies.

The studies prepared by Phillip Cagan, by Herbert Stein, and by myself are directed at employment policy and inflation (Cagan), at a crucial aspect of fiscal policy (Stein), and (as concerns my own study) at demand-management policies in general, including both monetary and fiscal policy, with a focus on the pursuit of desirable targets for total effective demand.

The Stein study explores, in addition to the trends in fiscal expenditures taken as a whole, the composition or "structure" of these expenditures, which has changed significantly over time, with income transfers acquiring more and more prominence. The author suggests that the automatic increase of tax payments in relation to incomes—over the past decade mainly a result of inflation—biases the political decision process in favor of increased fiscal expenditures. By periodic reductions of tax rates the impression can be given that the tax burden is reduced even if, given the tax-raising effect of inflation, the whole fiscal dividend (or more than that) expresses itself in increasing government expenditures of various sorts rather than in any true lightening of the tax burden. This ties in with the case made in my paper for correcting the tax structure for inflation. As was suggested in an earlier study, that case rests on longer-run considerations; it does not derive from the view that additional fiscal stimulus would be required at present in order to add further force to the current recovery process and to the movement toward lower unemployment rates in an as yet dangerously inflationary situation.

The main thrust of my paper reflects the conviction that among the structural and institutional factors on which the sustainable unemployment rate depends, two play a particularly large role. First, the composition of the labor force has been changing to a substantial extent toward adult women and teenagers, these being groups in which new entrants and reentrants into the labor force are heavily represented and which, largely for this reason, have high specific unemployment rates; and income transfer entitlements have been greatly expanded. The second factor, discussed in detail in Barry Chiswick's study, reduces significantly the pressure on workers to accept jobs they consider inferior to those they hope will become available to them. Our measured unemployment rate for 1976—a rate not far below 8 percent, with an average duration of about fifteen weeks for those counted as unemployed—was clearly a supernormal rate, reflecting the difficulties of an adjustment period after steep inflation, yet even this unemployment did not lead to any under-bidding of a rising money and *real* wage trend by those counted as unemployed. Nevertheless, inflation did decelerate in 1976. Recent wage trends are discussed in some detail in Marvin Kosters's study to which I shall return.

Cagan applies quantitative analysis to the problem of the measured unemployment rate along a sustainable future path of the American economy—a path not destabilized by inflationary policies. Whereas he would not recommend committing ourselves to any specific number in the present circumstances, he shows that one method of estimating the conventionally measured unemployment rate at which inflation would not accelerate leads to the presumption that that rate is about 6 percent. The conclusion would then be that decelerating the present inflation rate would call for allowing unemployment to remain temporarily above 6 percent.

The author suggests that the advantages and drawbacks of a slow rather than rapid deceleration of inflation depend largely on the properties of a function which he defines in his study. At the present time practically all American economists stressing the need for anti-inflationary policies favor a gradualist program. It is unclear how far conditions would have to be allowed to deteriorate before the conviction started spreading that gradualism would not work and that the shock associated with a sudden move to noninflationary demand management was inevitable. It is unclear also how widespread the conviction is that in practice it is impossible to stabilize a significant rate of inflation and that therefore it is necessary to reduce inflation gradually to a negligible rate—say, the rate that prevailed in the United States in the period 1951 to 1965. At least some of us do hold this conviction strongly, as indeed Cagan too is focusing on the condition of *reducing* the inflation rates of the recent past, even if he does not specify the precise characteristics of the price trend which in his appraisal could be stabilized.

Cagan clearly recognizes, as we all do, that numerical estimates based on regression analysis may be suggestive but cannot claim to be definitive in identifying the sustainable measured unemployment rate. It will be necessary gradually to feel out the level of utilization that can be established without reliance on inflationary stimuli—the level that can be achieved, after the present adjustment period, without exposing the economy subsequently to painful disturbances. But, in spite of all the qualifications attaching to the use of regression analysis for arriving at tentative estimates of the sustainable unemployment rate, and with all the modifications readers may wish to apply to Cagan's specific assumptions, his results do remain consistent with reasonable conjectures. In the mid-1950s the normal unemployment rate—the rate implying no inflationary instability—is often said to have been 4 percent, but it probably was a good many decimal points higher even at that time. In the present circumstances, the rate may well be in the general neighborhood of 6 percent. This was suggested also in the paper I contributed to our 1976 collection of studies, and it is consistent with Geoffrey Moore's views expressed in the same collection.

Moore's paper in the present volume carries the suggestion, based on tendencies observed in past business cycles, that at some stage of an expansion the rate of price increase is very likely to accelerate. The conclusion would be that it will take longer than the duration of the present recovery to bring the inflation rate down to insignificance. This is likely to be the case, though I believe that very much depends on whether a consistent line of demand-policy restraint will be adopted, so that the decision makers in the markets will face a well-understood constraint to which they expect other decision makers to adjust their wage and price-setting practices, and to which they themselves will therefore also adjust. This is what occurred in many past cases when stabilization came after major inflationary developments. How much optimism one is entitled to concerning the adoption of a consistent and credible policy of this kind is another question, but in any event we should remain aware of the fact that success in gradually reducing inflation to insignificance does not necessarily imply success in preventing oscillations in the inflation rate on the way down. On the other hand, getting into a phase of renewed steepening is, of course, a disturbing experience. At the present writing, about one year and a half after the cyclical upturn which occurred in the late part of 1975, inflation does show signs of reacceleration from its reduced rate of 1976; and it does so at an overall unemployment rate of 7 percent.

Moore's work is not limited to the exploration of the relationship between ups and downs in the inflation rate and phases of conventionally dated business cycles. Relationships that express the effect of labor-market tightness on inflation are also stressed, and this part of Moore's analysis comes nearer to tying in with Cagan's approach. Yet while in his similar attempt Cagan links acceleration and deceleration of inflation to a measure of *unemployment*, Moore links the variation of the inflation rate to the *employment ratio*. Relating the observed movements of the inflation rate to the *overall* rate of unemployment requires explaining why an upward trend in this overall rate has been associated with upward trending (rather than weakening) inflation. Aside from changes in the unemployment compensation system, divergent trends in the unemployment rates of specific labor groups play a large role in the explanation, and Cagan's technical analysis places the relation between prime-age male unemployment and inflation in the foreground. On the other hand, even the *overall* employment ratio stressed in Moore's work has been moving in a direction suggesting that demand has been rising rapidly enough to secure employment for a rising proportion of the population.

The employment ratio expresses the employed fraction of the entire noninstitutional population aged sixteen and over, regardless of who among those not employed is counted as unemployed. The unemployment rate, on the other hand, is a ratio relating those counted as unemployed to the "labor force" consisting of the employed plus the unemployed. The unemployed are those persons without employment who are available for work and were looking for a job some time during the past four weeks or expect to report to a job within the next four weeks. To translate a given employment ratio into the corresponding unemployment rate, we must therefore know the proportion of the noninstitutional population aged sixteen years or over which either is employed or is counted as unemployed, this percentage being defined as the labor-force participation rate.

The overall employment ratio has shown a rising trend, as has inflation. At the same time this ratio has shown lessening cyclical instability because, as Moore also demonstrates, employment is more stable in the service industries than in the goods-producing industries, and the weight of services in the output mix has been growing substantially.

When we compare cyclically similar periods, the overall unemployment rate as well as the overall employment ratio have shown a rising trend. The reason why the overall unemployment rate could show an upward trend along with an upward trend in the overall employment ratio is that the labor-force participation rate of women has increased very greatly, and this increase has more than offset the decline in the participation rate of adult males. If the participation rate rises, a rising proportion of the population may become employed, and at the same time a rising proportion of the population may satisfy the requirements of being counted as unemployed, mainly the requirement of looking for a job. This is what resolves the "paradox" that the overall employment ratio as well as the overall unemployment rate have been trending upward. Meanwhile money wage and price increases have become steeper despite the higher unemployment rates. However, our present difficulties have also further causes connected with recent antecedents.

The coexistence of inflation rates with unemployment rates as high as those recently observed results from commitments and expectations built into the wage structure, and into the cost structure in general, during a preceding period in which inflationary demand-management policies were keeping markets very tight. For example, the specific unemployment rate for prime-age males (ages twenty-five to fifty-four), which rose significantly after 1973, was lower in the entire period from 1965 to 1973 than in comparable years from 1953 through 1965. Any estimate or guess concerning the sustainable unemployment rate should therefore be interpreted as applying to conditions that can become established only after a period of adjustment, the costs of which are unavoidable after years of accelerating inflation.

From Marvin Kosters's analysis of wage developments, we may conclude that increases in current-dollar average hourly earnings in the private nonfarm sector have somewhat decelerated from their 1974 peak quarterly rates, which exceeded 10 percent on an annual basis. They decelerated to the 6 to 7 percent range in the late part of 1976. It would be difficult to relate this deceleration directly to movements in unemployment rates or in the employment ratio— at least without introducing lags and other variables—because the money wage trend, after having accelerated in much of the period of rising unemployment during the recession, continued to decelerate during the period following the 1975 business-cycle upturn when unemployment rates were declining to some extent and the employment ratio was rising. However, the first-quarter 1977 data suggest some degree of *reacceleration* in hourly earnings. It is too early to appraise the prospects for 1977, all the more because the wage-rate figures are influenced by the bargaining calendar and by the market power of the parties involved in the successive bargaining rounds. Also, as Kosters shows, in many sectors wages have been rising much less than in the highly unionized sector, and general trends depend in part on how these differentials will behave in the future. Kosters presents a thorough analysis of the past behavior of these differentials. He believes that they may well narrow in the period for which we are heading. However, the rising differentials do not tell the *full* story of average-wage deceleration from 1974 to 1975 and then from 1975 to 1976, because for those years Kosters's data also show some deceleration of effective wage increases under major collective bargaining settlements.

Part of this wage deceleration cannot serve as an explanation of the deceleration of the price trend from 1974 through 1976 since, in view of rapidly spreading escalator clauses, part of the wage deceleration of these years is the result of price deceleration. The deceleration of prices—slowing of inflation—during most of 1975 and 1976 took place in part because specific prices not directly related to the wage trend behaved much better than before, and also because productivity trends were recovering. This raises the chicken-and-egg problem involved in wage-price acceleration and deceleration.

Yet, leaving aside the complexities of this interaction, I feel convinced of the validity of the thesis that the constraints which Federal Reserve policy placed on the economy played a large role in bringing about both the cost and the price deceleration. Given the other relevant variables, the rate of increase in the money supply—I believe that the emphasis belongs on the M_2 supply—was kept significantly below that which would have "financed" the inflation rate of 1974 or that of early 1975 in addition to a recovery process from the early 1975 trough-level of real activity. The Federal Reserve was not intimidated by the prophecy voiced by some of its critics that its "exaggerated" restraint would strangle the recovery process while exerting only a relatively small anti-inflationary influence. Instead, the Federal Reserve rightly trusted that market behavior would fall in line with its policy to a sufficient extent to result in recovery at reduced inflation rates. In the early part of 1977 the price trend accelerated again, but, as in the case of wages, it is too early to tell what this implies for the future. One can only hope that, despite the pressures exerted by its critics, the Federal Reserve will avoid "accommodating" any acceleration of inflation and that, on the contrary, its policies will be consistent with the objective of gradual deceleration. From our own experience as well as from that of many countries abroad we know enough about the aftermath of policies of accommodation.

The wage trends explored by Kosters thus give rise to the problem of the effect of demand policy on cost and price developments. In particular, it gives rise to the problem usually referred to as that of the choice between "accommodation" and "nonaccommodation." Accommodation in the sense relevant to this discussion describes a policy that generates more nominal demand—more demand measured in current dollars—when the authorities observe or anticipate a rise in the general money-cost and price level. In general, a policy of accommodation will be easily "figured out" by the markets and, given the role of expectations and also of imperfections of competition in our economies, such a policy is exceedingly likely to lead to further increases in the steepness of cost trends and in the rate of inflation in successive rounds. This is why it is so dangerous to adopt an accommodating policy in relation to inflationary money-wage trends and cost trends in general, even after a period in which the mistake of accommodating was in fact made on a major scale, the circumstances may call for "gradualism" in putting an end to it (that is, may call for a consistently diminishing degree of accommodation, leading finally to persistent nonaccommodation).

These remarks were focused on general cost and price trends, but essentially the same distinction between accommodation and non-accommodation bears closely on the question how the authorities should behave if the prices of specific goods entering into the costs of other goods or services rise in response to events over which the demand-management authorities have no control. Raw-material price increases, originating in domestic events or in events abroad, may confront demand-management policy with this question, as has repeatedly been the case in the past. The question of accommodating or nonaccommodating specific cost increases comes to mind particularly in connection with problems discussed by Gale Johnson (agriculture), but also in connection with some of the problems in international economics covered by Gottfried Haberler and by Marina v. N. Whitman. The question comes to mind also, of course, in connection with the energy problem, since this cannot be solved without allowing market forces to bring about a significant rise in energy prices and without allowing both the demand-constraining and the supply-increasing effect of these price adjustments to materialize. But this year's volume contains no paper on energy and among the studies included, it is mainly those mentioned above which give rise to the question of specific cost changes and of the appropriate demand-policy attitudes to these.

Given our market structures, it should probably be taken for granted that events resulting in major specific cost increases will show in an increase in the general price level over some period *even if* demand policy is nonaccommodating, in the sense of not promoting an increase in effective demand to make room for the price increase. However, in the event of a nonaccommodating policy, the increase in the price level will be smaller even during the period of the specific cost increase, and (what matters mainly) under a nonaccommodating policy such an inflationary effect observed over a period will not touch off an inflationary *process* that would accelerate and subsequently have to be suppressed at great cost. On the other hand, a policy that adjusts aggregate effective demand to major specific cost increases *will* touch off such an accelerating process unless cost-raising and cost-reducing developments should cancel each other over periods of brief duration and the adjustment of aggregate demand to these developments should be undertaken symmetrically in the two directions.

While the accommodation of specific cost-raising events lasts, it has the harmful consequence of creating the false impression that the sellers of goods can perform the miracle of getting rid of an inevitable real burden by passing the increase in money costs on to the next buyer without loss of sales volume. The result of such a policy is that the sellers of goods and services will notice in each successive round that in real terms they have not gotten rid of the cost burden because their pricing practices will increasingly lead also to a rise in the prices of the goods and services which they are buying. This, of course, is the usual scenario for accelerating inflation. The somewhat delayed consequences of such a process are much worse than those of nonaccommodation, that is, of facing the markets with an inevitable fact right from the outset, even if it should turn out that the burden will be accepted by the market participants only in the course of a cyclical setback. Hence, there is a strong case against accommodating cost increases resulting from specific price movements.

We all have reason to remember the disturbing consequences of the steep farm and food price increases in 1973 and 1974, but the Johnson study helps us place that experience in perspective. The study demonstrates that in the longer run the worrisome phenomenon here is the significant instability of farm prices rather than any sustained upward trend in the "real" price (relative price) of farm products. As for the trend in relative farm prices—say, the so-called parity ratios—the events of 1973 caused a temporary spurt but did not reverse a downward trend. By now these ratios are back to their pre-1973 level or are slightly lower. Turning to the instability of relative farm prices, Johnson suggests that this becomes significantly magnified by the fact that countries consuming jointly about one-half of farm products in general—and consuming significantly more of important specific products, including grains—follow a policy of adjusting their foreign trade in such a way as to achieve domestic price stabilization. This, of course, greatly enlarges the price fluctuations required for demand-supply equilibrium in all other countries, including the United States.

Quite a bit of price instability is likely to persist as long as the state of the international markets remains as described above. Johnson discusses the measures we could adopt domestically to reduce these fluctuations, but he expects at best very modest results from them. The price support policies introduced in the United States several decades ago were implemented over an extended period in such a way as to delay needed adjustments, which, however, have by now nevertheless largely taken place. This period was associated with a downward trend in "real" farm prices, but we must avoid confusing that trend with the trend in the real *income* of farmers. In spite of the decline in relative prices, the real income of the farm population has risen significantly by the measures applicable to such an analysis—that is, with adjustment for the size of the farm population or for the number of farms. This is by no means exclusively the result of the increased share which incomes earned in nonfarm activities have acquired in the farm population's total income, although the increase of that share is also a well-established fact.

The magnification of the instability of agricultural prices through the policies of many nations has uncomfortable implications, all the more because these prices enter into costs on a major scale and the successive swings may last for some time, even if the long-run downward trend in relative farm prices may well continue. Partly at least, because of prospective policy attitudes, the problems created by the cost of energy materials and also by that of health services are more likely to become felt through long-run trends in the relative prices of these materials and services. All these problems call for placing a good deal of emphasis on the dangers involved in accommodating specific cost increases by demand policies which can cover up real burdens only temporarily with very painful aftereffects.

The transmission of cost changes across the borders has all along played an important role in international economics—the area in which the papers of Gottfried Haberler and Marina v. N. Whitman move. We had the benefit of Haberler's advice in all our meetings, and we received his permission to include in this volume, along with the eight papers prepared for the present project, an appreciably expanded version of his recent article in the *Weltwirtschaftliches Archiv* (1977, no. 1).

The problems covered by our two papers in international economics include, among others, an analysis of the reasons why the present exchange-rate regime of managed floating has replaced the Bretton Woods par-value system and of the process by which this change has taken place (Haberler); and they include an analysis of how the evolution toward managed floating as well as changes in trade relations reflect changes in the relative importance of the "organizing principles" governing the contacts of countries with each other (Whitman).

Haberler was one of the forceful advocates of flexible exchange rates well before the Bretton Woods system collapsed. Exchange-rate flexibility has an important bearing on the main theme I have stressed in this introduction. Unless all major countries are determined to move toward a growth path which is free from inflationary disturbances, and thus is sustainable, an American effort to achieve this objective clearly requires exchange-rate flexibility. However, even flexibility of exchange rates will not remove all disturbances originating abroad when there are substantial disparities between national inflation rates. Hence the most desirable setting would be one in which all major countries would become coordinated in the sense of establishing noninflationary growth. But at present this kind of international coordination is a utopian conception, and coordination resulting in a destabilization of all economies through equalized inflation rates is clearly not a desirable objective. It is understandable therefore that both Haberler and Whitman should be concerned in their analyses with the distinction between types of international coordination to be considered desirable and those to be considered undesirable in the present circumstances.

Recently this question has attracted public attention mainly in the context of a specific policy debate. Countries with a relatively good record of keeping inflation down while achieving a level of domestic prosperity they consider satisfactory were placed under pressure in international negotiations to adopt a more expansionary line than they had intended. This, it was argued on one side of the debate, would serve the interests of other countries by enabling them to diminish their current-account deficits in the present era in which large "oil deficits" must inevitably develop for the aggregate of oil-consuming nations. The West German economy with its moderate inflation rate provides perhaps the most notable illustration of an oil-consuming economy that has had a current-account *surplus*, and the West German authorities have in large part resisted the pressure to "coordinate" their policies in the sense of raising their intended rate of expansion.

The mere fact that one or the other oil-importing country is running a current-account surplus does not, of course, establish a case for placing the country under pressure to become more expansionary and thereby to turn its surplus into a deficit. The forces of competition may make an oil-importing country a "natural" net exporter of goods and services, and then *also* of capital, in spite of the fact that the aggregate of the oil-consuming countries cannot at present avoid running a current-account deficit. Haberler and Whitman agree on the proposition that if in such circumstances the authorities of a country, motivated by justified fears of destabilizing their domestic economy, resist engaging in more than some intended rate of expansion, then their resistance to coordination toward more expansion serves the interests of the other countries as well as their own.

At the same time, the authors agree on the need for positive and effective coordinating efforts in various other respects. These include collaborative efforts to achieve liberalization of trade relations and to avoid interventions in currency markets that would suppress equilibrating market forces. The coordination at which these efforts need to be directed reflects, in Whitman's terminology, a different "organizing principle" if action by an international agency is envisaged than if parallel actions by national authorities are considered. But it seems proper to speak of "coordination" in either case, and thus to include here also the activities of international agencies by which they assist countries in overcoming temporary difficulties with reliance on funds provided by the members of these organizations.

There is, of course, general agreement also on the value of achieving international coordination in the sense of exchanging information and of thereby ensuring mutual consistency of the assumptions which countries make about each other's policies. Whitman has repeatedly called attention to the possibility that, in the absence of sufficient information about prospects in the rest of the world, individual countries may base their policies on wrong assumptions concerning their export potential. Yet we must remember that in policy negotiations the authorities of countries will often find it difficult to tell whether they are asked to modify merely their assumptions or their judgment as to what it is desirable to achieve. A corollary of this is that even economists who, like our two contributors, agree on the foregoing general propositions, may well have different reactions to specific efforts at coordination in individual instances.

Given the uncertainties of economic forecasting, it is often difficult to draw a sharp distinction between legitimate questioning of the realism of a country's forecasts concerning the demand which its monetary and fiscal policies will create and attempts to make the country fall in line with the undesirable overexpansionary policies of others. We must be prepared to witness some attempts of the latter undesirable type. This is partly because of the genuine difficulties of drawing the required distinction. It is partly also because there still

13

are many adherents of the belief that Western countries should use ambitious expansionary policies for achieving an arbitrarily defined state of full employment and should worry less about inflation, or should try to suppress it by administrative controls. Among economists and in the world of politics there has been an increase in the number of those who feel convinced that this conception has caused great harm, but the conception continues to have many supporters and there is no reason to believe that we have passed the danger point in this regard.

THE REDUCTION OF INFLATION AND THE MAGNITUDE OF UNEMPLOYMENT

Phillip Cagan

Summary

Inflation in the United States has declined from the double-digit rates of 1973–1974, but an annual rate of 5 to 6 percent persists despite the excess productive capacity that remains from the recession of 1973–1975. Inflation persists because firms continue to pass on rising costs from past price and wage increases and because many prices and wages are raised in anticipation of future inflation. The competitive conditions fostered by slack demand work to hold down price increases, but do so slowly. The excess capacity squeezes profit margins and stimulates cost cutting, with the result that unit costs eventually begin to rise less rapidly, expectations of inflation weaken, and the upward pressure on prices moderates. Past experience suggests that the excess capacity prevailing in 1977 can reduce the annual rate of inflation during the year by 1 percentage point. Achievement of even this modest reduction, however, is made uncertain by the renewed strength of inflationary pressures in the early part of 1977.

Although monetary and fiscal policies have imposed three periods of restraint on aggregate demand since 1965, the trend of inflation has still been upward. One basic reason for the failure to control inflation is the commitment of national economic policy to avoid excess unemployment by trying to guide the economy along a path at or just

I wish to acknowledge the helpful comments of Solomon Fabricant, Lucas Papademos, Alvin Marty, Jacob Mincer, Alfred Tella, and the members of the AEI panel whose papers appear in this volume. I am particularly indebted to Mincer, Tella, and Barry Chiswick for letting me share their knowledge of unemployment. None of these people necessarily agrees with everything said here.

below full employment. The present objective of policy is to remove the recession-induced slack in the economy and to achieve near-full employment while at the same time dampening inflationary pressures. At near-full employment, however, the restraint exerted on the inflationary momentum is not great, and little room is provided for the risks of a resurgence of inflation from overshooting the target or from unforeseen disturbances as originated with grains and petroleum in 1973. Continuation of the old policy guidelines which so far have failed to subdue inflation no longer inspires confidence that they will now succeed.

Effective policies are thwarted by an outmoded interpretation of full employment based on a 1950s definition that is badly in need of revision. For over a decade, an unemployment rate of 4 percent or less has been the unquestioned full-employment goal, but estimates of an unemployment rate consistent with no increase in the rate of inflation are higher by almost a full percentage point. In addition, structural changes in the labor supply, in part due to expanding programs designed to alleviate the distress of unemployment, have raised this noninflationary rate of unemployment since the 1950s by another 1 to 1½ percentage points, putting it now at around 6 percent. Moreover, economic slack sufficient to reduce inflation is accompanied by unemployment in excess of that level. Hence, an effective policy against current inflation gives little leeway for reducing unemployment much below the mid-1977 rate of 7 percent.

A major policy principle has been to avoid periods of strong restraint in combating inflation (breaches of this principle have been unintentional) on the grounds that the commitment to minimize unemployment supposedly requires that the reduction of inflation be slow and gradual. Such gradualist policies, however, not only have failed to subdue inflation but also have failed to keep unemployment rates low. Not only has the rate of inflation been rising since 1965, but also it has become increasingly variable and unpredictable, resulting in greater dislocations in the economy and greater departures from full employment. Long disposed to view unemployment as the greater and inflation as the lesser concern, we have adopted policies which have increased both.

Recent experience has raised new questions about the longstanding view that policies can be chosen to trade off unemployment against inflation. In that view the "Phillips curve" describes an inverse relationship between inflation and unemployment in the short run, while expected rates of inflation are seen as tending to approach actual rates, causing the trade-off available in the short run to be nonexistent in the long run. An assumed property of the short-run relationship—namely, convexity—supports gradualist policies, because convexity implies that additional increases in unemployment result in successively smaller reductions in inflation. But this property also has important implications for the long run. When the average rate of inflation is higher, the variability of inflation rates in the short run is shown by experience to be greater. The greater variability implies larger movements along the short-run Phillips curve; and, because of convexity, such movements produce a higher average level of unemployment over the long run. Although the convexity of the curve is widely assumed, however, it is, in fact, not firmly established by the data. If the curve is not convex, the preceding implication that higher and more variable inflation rates increase long-run average unemployment does not hold, but at the same time gradualist policies lose their justification, because firmer anti-inflationary measures can be pursued along a linear Phillips curve without increasing the total worker-months of unemployment incurred in reducing inflation.

Experience with high and unpredictable rates of inflation and their implications for long-run levels of unemployment justify a reexamination of present policies of dealing with inflation.

Progress in Reducing Inflation

The economy in 1977 is in the stage of the business cycle midway between recovery from a previous contraction and the high demand of a boom. It is at the stage where monetary and fiscal policy need to set a course that can avoid an excessive speedup of the cyclical expansion. The 1973–1975 recession was the third time that restraint was imposed on the rapid inflation which began in 1965. The two previous restraints were imposed by the mini-recession of 1967 and the mild recession of 1970. These recessions failed to subdue the inflation effectively because the ensuing rebounds in business activity became strong enough to cause a resurgence of inflationary pressures. Public impatience with the slow process of reducing inflation and with the persistence of slack in the economy bring political demands to hasten economic recovery. At the same time, the difficulty of controlling the speed of recovery makes overexpansion a major risk. During this most recent period, policy makers have shown an admirable reluctance to overstimulate the economy, but the real policy test will occur over the next year as the economy approaches the danger zone in which new inflationary pressures develop.

This essay reviews the slow progress made so far in reducing inflation and discusses three longstanding propositions that weaken the case for the maintenance of a firm anti-inflationary policy in the management of aggregate demand. The first proposition is that current unemployment rates of 7 percent are excessively high according to the full-employment standard. The second is that inflation is the cost we incur to keep unemployment lower than it would otherwise be. And the third is that the total amount of unemployment produced by a reduction in the inflation rate is less if inflation is reduced slowly. The first proposition requires revision in the light of new estimates of the full-employment rate. The second two propositions are based on the assumed shape of the Phillips curve, but it can support only one or the other of them, not both.

By early 1977 the rate of inflation had come down dramatically from the high rate of 1974. The consumer price index (CPI), which rose 12.2 percent in 1974, rose 7.1 percent in 1975 and only 5.0 percent in 1976. Economic activity, which began to recover in the second quarter of 1975 from the severe contraction of the previous five quarters, has remained relatively slack causing the reduction in inflation to be greater than many had expected. At the end of 1975 professional forecasters predicted that the GNP deflator would rise 6 percent during 1976, whereas the actual increase was only 4.7 percent.[1]

Much of this decline in the rate of inflation reflected the end of temporary pressures on the world prices of certain basic commodities (mainly feed grains, oil, and metals) that erupted in 1973 and largely faded away during 1974. Perhaps one-third to one-half of the total 10.5 percent annual rise in the CPI in 1973–1974 reflected these world pressures on the prices of basic commodities, while the remainder reflected pressures from the domestic business expansion.[2] Although the recession of 1970 led to a decline in the inflation rate to 3 percent by mid-1972 (see Figure 1), monetary policy at the time supported a business expansion that turned out to be too strong. Consequently, by the end of 1972, just when commodity prices began to erupt, the domestic expansion began to overheat. The recession of 1973–1975

---

[1] "ASA/NBER Business Outlook Survey: Fourth Quarter 1975," *Explorations in Economic Research*, vol. 3 (Winter 1976), Table 1, p. 151. The changes cited in the text pertain to fourth-quarter 1975 to fourth-quarter 1976.

[2] Phillip Cagan, "Monetary Problems and Policy Choices in Reducing Inflation and Unemployment," *Contemporary Economic Problems*, William Fellner, ed. (Washington, D.C.: American Enterprise Institute, 1976), pp. 20-27. To some extent the foreign price increases reflected earlier U.S. monetary influences and consequently did not occur independently. Moreover, these domestic price increases in response to foreign price increases could not have been sustained without sufficient monetary growth.

Figure 1

RATE OF CHANGE OF CONSUMER PRICE INDEX

MONTHLY AND CENTERED SEVEN-MONTH AVERAGE,

1969–1977

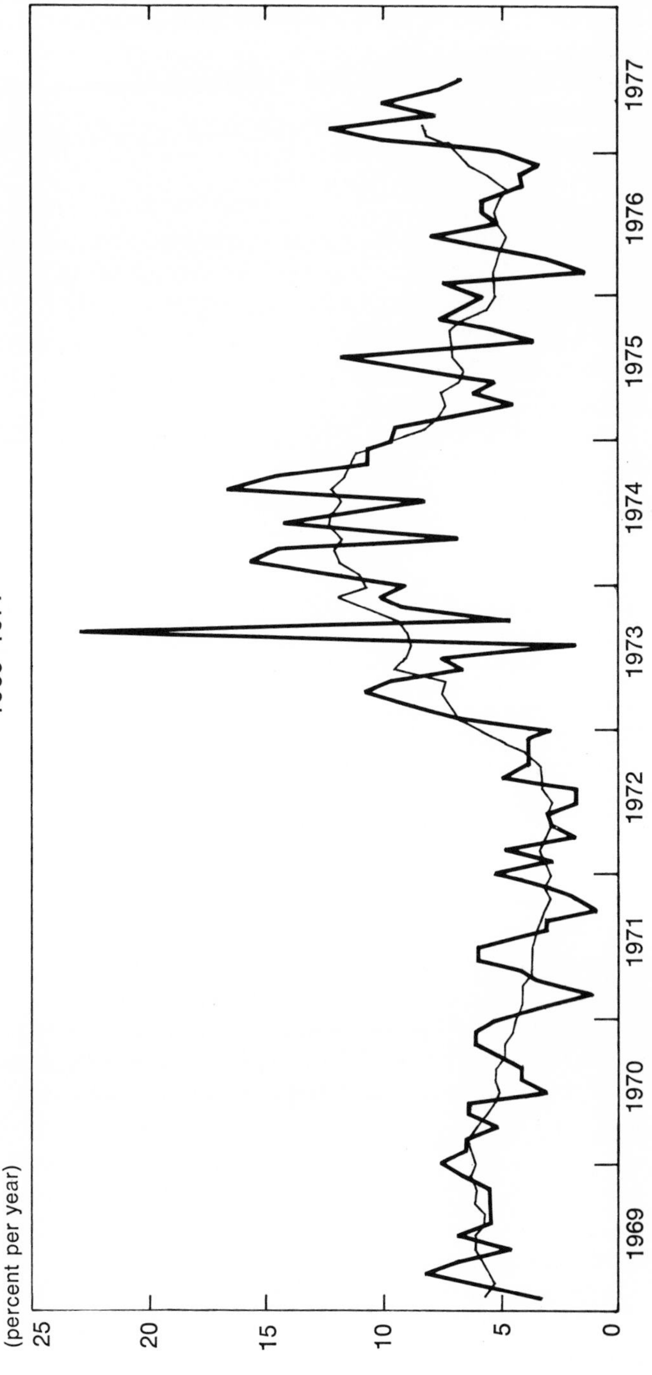

(percent per year)

Source: U.S. Department of Labor, Bureau of Labor Statistics.

skimmed away the inflationary bulge, but the resulting excess capacity in the economy has barely begun to chip away at a persistent inflation rate of 5 to 6 percent.

Consistent with the experience of recent years, an inflation rate of about 5 percent seems to be widely expected for the future. This expected rate of inflation is increasingly built into wage and price contracts, interest rates, price decisions of regulatory commissions, and the setting of list prices in general. These built-in increases raise costs to every business and are passed from one stage of production to the next, a process which gears the entire economy to a continuing rate of inflation of 5 percent.[3] With costs rising, businesses react to a slackening of demand partly by cutting price markups, but this holds down price increases to a limited extent because of the resulting squeeze on profit margins. While prices in basic commodity markets and in highly competitive industries weaken perceptibly, other prices appear to be little affected by slack demand, because businesses adjust to it in the short run mainly by curtailing output.

Slack demand eventually does cause a reduction in inflation, but does so indirectly and slowly. When businesses curtail output, productive capacity becomes idle, adding temporarily but substantially to the ongoing rise in costs per unit of output. This adds to the squeeze on profit margins from the competitive pressures on selling prices. The standard business response to this situation is to trim costs, largely by finding ways to produce at normal output levels with less labor. Recessions also dampen the frenetic conditions of cyclical peak demand that are inhospitable to productivity growth. While output is depressed during a recession, output per hour of labor remains low because the retention of experienced workers holds the work force above immediate needs. When demand recovers, however, cost trimming allows output to expand with less than proportional increases in labor. Unit labor costs then rise less rapidly in comparison not only with the preceding period of declining output, but also with the pre-recession period of high demand and tight markets. The slowing of increases in unit labor costs bolsters profit margins and reduces the upward pressure on prices. As prices rise less rapidly, expectations of inflation moderate and reduce the pressure of anticipatory price increases built into price and wage contracts and into general price-setting decisions.

---

[3] The process is not a smooth one, because not all nominal economic variables inflate proportionately. For example, nominal increases in the value of capital assets are taxed, disturbing their equilibrium values.

Despite the continuing rise in costs and prices during the 1973–1975 recession and the ensuing recovery, cost trimming was vigorous and slowed the advance in unit labor costs appreciably. Labor productivity as measured by output per hour of labor began to rise even before the business upturn in the second quarter of 1975 and passed its previous peak by the first quarter of 1976. During 1976 it rose 2.7 percent in the nonfarm business sector. As a result, unit labor costs in that sector rose only 4.8 percent even though the advance in worker compensation at 7.7 percent was largely unchanged from the previous year. As Figure 2 shows, unit labor costs and prices in the nonfarm business sector were in close alignment during 1976. In the first quarter of 1977 unit labor costs spurted ahead as worker compensation accelerated and labor productivity continued to grow at a trend rate of 2¾ percent per year. Consequently, prices will have to grow faster in subsequent quarters to cover the spurt in costs.

Inflation trends for the next year will be determined in large part by the trend in unit labor costs. The stimulating effect of the 1973–1975 recession on productivity growth had largely played out during 1976, and a growth rate greater than the trend rate of 2¾ percent per year sustained in the first quarter of 1977 seems unlikely. Further deceleration in unit labor costs, therefore, requires a slowing of wage advances, but the prognosis of most commentators is for little change during 1977. For example, the Council of Economic Advisers predicted a rise of 7½ percent in compensation for 1977 and of 5 percent in unit labor costs.[4] Consequently, unit labor costs and prices may be expected to continue to inflate at a rate of at least 5 percent, subject to any increases in the rate which may develop from supply or demand disturbances.

Another view is that inflation will gradually decline so long as excess productive capacity exists in the economy. Under these conditions the competitive pressures of slack labor and materials markets lead to smaller price increases, which in turn reduce the momentum of anticipatory increases in wages and prices.

This effect can be estimated by regressing the change in the inflation rate $\dot{P}$ on the excess unemployment rate:

$$\dot{P}_t - \dot{P}_{t-1} = -a \left(\frac{U_t + U_{t-1}}{2} - U_f \right).$$

The first term in the parentheses is the average unemployment rate concurrent with the change in the inflation rate. U_f is the rate of un-

---

[4] Council of Economic Advisers, *Annual Report*, 1977, p. 41.

Figure 2

INDEX OF UNIT LABOR COSTS AND OF PRICES, NONFARM
BUSINESS SECTOR, QUARTERLY, 1969–1977

(1972 = 100)

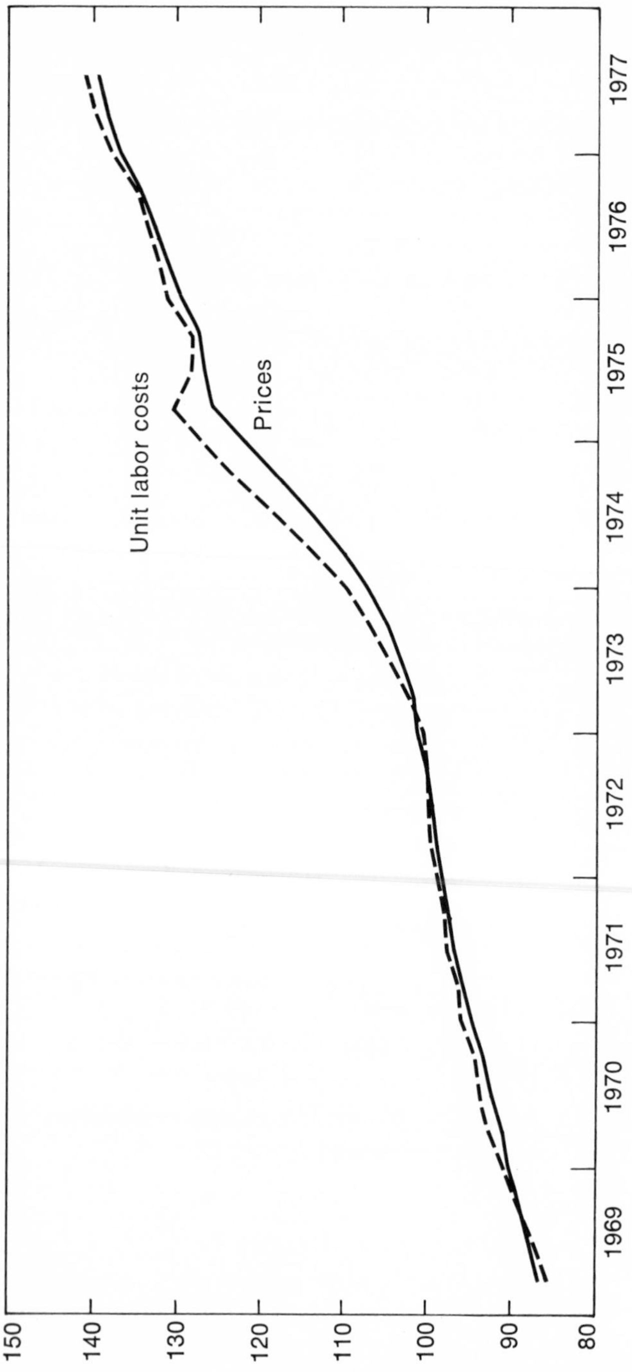

Source: U.S. Department of Commerce, Bureau of Economic Analysis.

22

employment at which the inflation rate does not change; it is assumed to be a constant, and is estimated from the constant term of the regression. The equation supposes that inflation will increase when unemployment is below U_f and will decrease when unemployment is above U_f. Unemployment in relation to U_f is an indicator here of aggregate demand.

The equation makes no allowance for lags or for the effect on the inflation rate of monetary and fiscal policy and of foreign influences not also affecting unemployment. The equation is not the most complete one available for forecasting inflation, but it is consistent with the current practice of relating changes in the inflation rate mainly to the level of excess capacity as reflected by the unemployment rate. It may be interpreted as a version of the Phillips curve under certain conditions.[5]

---

[5] A general form of the Phillips curve is

$$P_t = F(U_t - U_f) + P_t^e$$

where P_t^e is the expected rate of inflation at time t and the function F of the excess unemployment rate $U_t - U_f$ has a negative first derivative. The coefficient of unity for P_t^e assumes that there is no long-run trade-off between inflation and unemployment. It is also assumed that P_t can deviate from P_t^e in the short run, which makes possible corresponding deviations of U_t from U_f.

This general form implies the equation in the text if the expected price change is based on the change in prices during the previous period, $P_t^e = P_{t-1}$, and if the F function is linear. (For recent contributions to the literature see "The Phillips Curve and Labor Markets," Carnegie-Rochester Conference Series on Public Policy, supplement to *Journal of Monetary Economics*, vol. 1, 1976.)

The preceding may be a poor estimate of expected price changes, and many other assumptions about the formation of expectations can be made. Except for the assumption that expectations are "rational," most imply that expectations depend upon past price changes. For present purposes of estimating the effect of excess unemployment on the inflation rate, the particular assumption made (barring "rationality") does not appear critical. For example, a commonly made assumption is that the expected inflation rate is formed by an adaptive system,

$$\frac{dP_t^e}{dt} = b(P_t - P_t^e).$$

We may incorporate this assumption by differentiating the above Phillips curve,

$$\frac{dP_t}{dt} = \frac{dF}{dt} + \frac{dP_t^e}{dt}$$

and substituting for the change in price expectations to obtain

$$\frac{dP_t}{dt} = \frac{dF}{dt} + bF.$$

If the F function is linear and the differentials are represented by first differences, we have

$$P_t - P_{t-1} = -a(U_t - U_{t-1}) - ba\left(\frac{U_t + U_{t-1}}{2} - U_f\right).$$

The fit of this alternative equation to the data is reported in footnote 7.

The *overall* unemployment rate, which is often used in such equations, is not a good indicator of aggregate demand, because it has been subject to unrelated "structural" influences. As will be discussed later, the level of overall U_f has been rising. Consequently, estimation of the equation uses the unemployment rate for men in the prime ages of twenty-five to fifty-four. Although the rate for this group has also been subject to structural influences, the low points of its fluctuations show no clear trend (see Figure 3). Among the rates for major groups it appears to be the least contaminated indicator of aggregate demand.

The equation was fit to quarterly U.S. data from the first quarter of 1953 to the first quarter of 1976. The consumer price index (all items, seasonally adjusted) was used for prices.[6] The value of "a" is estimated to be 0.23, which means that an unemployment rate of 1 percentage point above U_f reduces the annual rate of inflation by 0.9 percentage points in a year. The estimate of U_f is 3.5 percent. These estimates are subject to a considerable range of error because of the many other influences on the inflation rate that are disregarded by the equation.[7] The estimates are, however, consistent with others current in the literature.

Fluctuations in the unemployment rate for men between the ages of twenty-five and fifty-four have been only slightly smaller in recent

---

[6] The inflation rate is the annual rate of change in the CPI between successive quarterly averages. Corresponding to the inflation rate for a given pair of calendar quarters, the unemployment rate is a three-month average centered on the final month of the first quarter of the pair. That is, if P_t is for quarters I and II of a particular year, U_t is an average of February through April of that year. With this dating of the data, the dependent and independent variables of the regression are centered at approximately the same points in time.

[7] These estimates, based on ordinary least squares, are on the borderline of statistical significance at the 5 percent level (both t statistics are 1.94). When the regression is corrected for negative serial correlation in the dependent variable (a characteristic of first differences) by the Cochrane-Orcutt method, the estimates are virtually the same but are statistically significant (both t statistics are 2.35).

In an unpublished memorandum, John Taylor ran the regression with the same underlying data for roughly the same period using a first-order moving-average error term, which is applicable to the kind of disturbances to be expected here. His estimate of the annual effect of excess unemployment on the change in the inflation rate was -1.2 ($t = 3.7$), and of U_f was 3.6 percent.

The equation at the end of footnote 5 was also estimated. Based on the Cochrane-Orcutt method, the regression coefficients were $a = .88$ ($t = 3.7$) and $ba = .20$ ($t = 2.4$), and $U_f = 3.7$ percent. The coefficient ba for excess unemployment is practically the same here as in the regression reported in the text, and so implies the same rate of decline in the inflation rate for a given level of excess unemployment. The similarity of this result to that reported for the text regression suggests that, for present purposes, the method of taking account of price expectations is not critical.

Figure 3

UNEMPLOYMENT RATE OF ALL WORKERS AND OF PRIME AGE MEN, CIVILIAN LABOR FORCE

(monthly, 1948–1977)

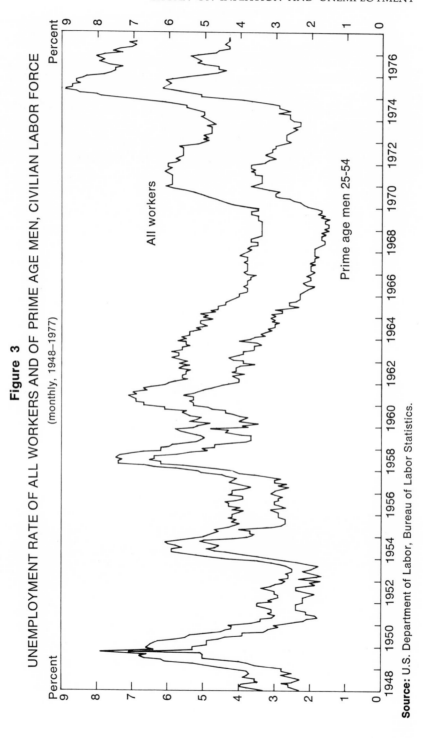

Source: U.S. Department of Labor, Bureau of Labor Statistics.

25

years than the fluctuations in the overall rate. Hence the implied effect of overall excess unemployment on changes per year in the inflation rate is also 0.9 or almost unity. Excess unemployment in mid-1977 was about 1 percentage point above U_f, as discussed later. Excess unemployment during 1977 as a whole will likely average also about 1 percentage point. If it does, the equation implies that the inflation rate will decline by 0.9 percentage points during 1977. That means that the 5 percent inflation rate at the end of 1976 will fall to 4 percent by the end of 1977. The inflation rate would fall still further to 3½ percent by the end of 1978 if excess unemployment of ½ percentage points prevails during that year.

At the beginning of 1977 the Council of Economic Advisers predicted 7 percent unemployment by the end of the year, which can be interpreted to imply that excess unemployment would average above 1 percentage point for the entire year. However, the Council predicted that inflation would remain unchanged at 5 to 6 percent throughout the year.[8] A basis for the Council's prediction can be found in the estimates of the regression equation reported at the end of footnote 7. In addition to the decline in inflation due to excess unemployment, that regression equation also contains a sizable separate effect due to reductions in unemployment. If unemployment decreases by about 1 percentage point during 1977, as appears likely, the estimated coefficient of changes in unemployment implies that the inflation rate will increase by 0.88 percentage points, which offsets the decline in the rate due to the effect of the assumed average excess unemployment level of 1 percentage point in the other variable of the regression. The net effect, therefore, is that the inflation rate will remain approximately unchanged during 1977.

The effect of decreases in unemployment on the inflation rate ceases and inflation eventually declines if excess unemployment subsequently remains constant and positive. This is consistent with the current theory that excess unemployment, if allowed to persist, will reduce inflation over a period of years. In the light of such a slow reduction, a danger exists that, as the business recovery speeds up and progress against inflation is still unclear and undramatic in the eyes of the public, impatience with attempts to restrain the expansion will intensify, particularly since the unemployment rate will, by old standards, still seem inordinately high. At that time the nation's commitment to subdue inflation by braking the expansion will be severely tested.

---

[8] CEA, *Annual Report*, 1977, p. 41.

Reassessment of the Unemployment
Produced by Reducing Inflation

Why Is the Unemployment Rate So High? The overall unemployment rate declined from a high of 8.9 percent in May 1975, remained at about 7.9 percent during the second half of 1976, and fell by mid-1977 to 7 percent. From an historical perspective these rates are high (see Figure 3). In 1948 the overall unemployment rate was between 3½ and 4 percent, and during the Korean War period it fell as low as 2½ percent. Since then its trend has been upward. In the early 1960s, when the rate varied between 5 and 6 percent except during the 1960–1961 recession, the Kennedy administration chose a 4 percent rate as its interim target.[9] This level of unemployment was thought at that time to reflect a conservative definition of prosperity, since a 3½ percent rate had been surpassed in the early 1950s and had almost been achieved at the cyclical peak of 1957. In fact, the 3½ percent rate was often spoken of as the full-employment rate to be achieved after reaching the interim target. The economy finally achieved a 4 percent rate in December 1965 (along with the first signs of inflation) and then a 3½ percent rate in the second half of 1968, though by then inflation had become rampant.

The 4 percent rate was enshrined as the goal of public policy despite an inability to attain it without inflation or since January 1970 even with inflation. Federal budget projections made at the beginning of 1975 targeted a decline in unemployment to 4 percent over the ensuing four-year period. The government based projections of potential output and of revenues on the 4 percent rate. In fact, as late as 1976, the proposed Humphrey-Hawkins bill debated in Congress would have reaffirmed the government's commitment to 4 percent or less unemployment. Not until this year did the Council of Economic Advisers publicly acknowledge that the full-employment rate had changed. In its annual report for 1977, the Council reviewed the evidence and said that the full-employment rate was now at least 4.9 percent and perhaps as high as 5.5 percent. Until very recently professional economists outside the government had also been reluctant to become bearers of the unpopular tidings that the full-employment rate is higher than had been thought.

Unemployment is a focus of public concern and the most widely publicized indicator of economic conditions. It is important to set and pursue policies which keep the social waste of undesired unemployment at a minimum. But unemployment is also central to the control

---

[9] CEA, *Annual Report,* 1962, p. 46.

of inflation through the management of aggregate demand, because the unemployment rate cannot be pushed below a critical level without creating additional inflationary pressures. The level at which the inflation rate begins to rise may be considered a practical definition of full employment. The critical level changes over time because of demographic trends and government manpower programs. It might be reduced through programs to help those seeking work qualify for the jobs available or find new jobs more quickly, but it cannot be reduced permanently by stimulating aggregate demand. Unfortunately, manpower programs have been largely unsuccessful in reducing unemployment, and efforts to achieve the elusive 4 percent goal have fallen by default upon demand management without much consideration of feasibility.

The Noninflationary Rate of Unemployment in 1956. An unemployment goal of 4 percent was chosen because that was the rate attained in the 1950s when inflationary pressures were purportedly absent. However, the rate of unemployment at which inflation tends to be unchanging has been consistently higher than 4 percent. The regressions reported above estimate the unemployment rate for prime-age men that corresponds to an unchanging rate of inflation to be from 3.5 to 3.7 percent. This can be translated into a 1950s rate for overall unemployment: In the period May 1955 to August 1957, when both rates were roughly constant, the overall rate averaged 1.1 percentage points higher than the rate for prime-age men. Therefore, a noninflationary unemployment rate of 3.5 to 3.7 percent for the latter group corresponds to an overall unemployment rate of 4.6 to 4.8. A similar estimate was obtained by Modigliani and Papademos using a conventional Phillips curve with the inflation rate as the left-side variable.[10] They estimated the overall unemployment rate which is noninflationary to be 4.8 percent in 1956. Consequently, the 4 percent target rate turns out to be too low even for 1956 if full employment is to be noninflationary. It should be emphasized that, at this noninflationary rate of unemployment, the inflation rate, while neither increasing nor decreasing, may be at any level.

---

[10] Franco Modigliani and Lucas Papademos, "Monetary Policy for the Coming Quarters: The Conflicting Views," *New England Economic Review*, Federal Reserve Bank of Boston (March/April 1976), p. 10. Their regression used annual data 1953-1971 and allowed for an independent effect on the inflation rate of import prices. The unemployment rate was adjusted for every year to hold constant the composition of the labor force in 1956.

Most other estimates of the full-employment rate of unemployment simply *assume* that it was equal to the actual unemployment rate in 1956, though allowance is usually made for increases since then.

Based on a 4 percent or even a 4¾ percent rate, the 1976 unemployment rates close to 8 percent appeared to be unusually excessive. Yet evidence indicates that the full-employment rate of unemployment is now much higher than the rate applicable to 1956. The explanation is twofold: first, the proportion of people who frequently move in and out of the labor force has grown; second, the government has expanded programs which encourage workers to remain unemployed longer or discourage employers from hiring inexperienced workers.

Changes in the Composition of the Labor Force. Women and young workers have altered the composition of the labor force. The proportion of women in the labor force has increased from 31 percent in 1956 to 40 percent in 1976. This increase reflects a rise in their participation rate from 37 to 48 percent and a decline in this rate for older men. The proportion of young workers aged sixteen to twenty-four in the labor force has increased from 17 percent in 1956 to 24 percent in 1976 because of demographic trends. Both women and young workers tend to experience frequent periods of unemployment as they enter, leave, and reenter the labor force and shift between jobs in search of better opportunities. In the high-employment year of 1973, men between the ages of twenty-five and fifty-four had an unemployment rate of 2.5 percent, whereas women had a 6.0 percent rate and young workers had a 10.5 percent rate. The overall unemployment rate has therefore been rising with the relative growth of those groups in the labor force subject to higher unemployment. As noted in Figure 3, the unemployment rate for prime-age men has a more or less flat trend.

If we compare the data for 1956 and 1973, both years of strong demand and vigorous business activity, the unemployment rate was higher in 1973 by 0.7 percentage points, not only because the groups with high unemployment rates had grown in relative size, but also because their respective unemployment rates had increased relative to those for prime-age men. To focus solely on the change in composition of the labor force, we may calculate the 1973 rate supposing that subgroups classified by sex and age had the same unemployment rates as in 1956. This hypothetical 1973 rate is higher than the 1956 rate by 0.46 percentage points, attributable to the change in the composition of the labor force.[11]

---

[11] A change in the overall unemployment rate U can be decomposed as follows: For 1956, $U^{56} = \Sigma w_i^{56} U_i^{56}$ where i denotes the various sex and age subgroups and w_i is their relative weight in the labor force. (The age subgroups are 16-19, 20-24, 25-54, 55-64, and 65 and over.) For a later year t, where the change in

Women and young workers also account for a greater fluctuation in the size of the labor force.[12] As job prospects decline during a period of business contraction, many of these workers leave the labor force, to return en masse when conditions improve. This phenomenon results in the "hidden" unemployment which is not included in the regular unemployment rate, though many workers may intend to make such periodic withdrawals from employment and synchronize them with fluctuations in labor demand. In any event, this makes the labor-force participation rate fluctuate more over the course of the business cycle. One reason for the high unemployment rates in 1974–1975 is that women did not withdraw from the labor force to the same degree that they had during previous business contractions. It is an open question whether these greater fluctuations in the size of the labor force have affected the average rate of measured unemployment over the length of the business cycle. They nonetheless seem unimportant so far as changes in the full-employment rate are concerned.

---

the subgroup rates and weights from 1956 to year t is denoted by Δ_t,

$$U^t = \sum_i (w_i^{56} + \Delta_t w_i)(U_i^{56} + \Delta_t U_i) = U^{56} + \sum_i (w_i^{56} \Delta_t U_i + U_i^{56} \Delta_t w_i + \Delta_t w_i \Delta_t U_i).$$

For $t = 1973$, these quantities are, in percent,
$$4.85 = 4.13 + .04 + .46 + .22.$$
The compositional change given in the text for $t = 1973$ is
$$\sum_i U_i^{56} (w_i^{56} + \Delta_{73} w_i) - U^{56} = \sum_i U_i^{56} \Delta_{73} w_i = .46.$$
The constant-weight unemployment rate used by Modigliani and Papademos (see footnote 10) was calculated by the CEA (1975, p. 95) and for 1973 is
$$\sum_i w_i^{56} (U_i^{56} + \Delta_{73} U_i) = 4.17.$$
When this amount is subtracted from U^{73}, the remainder shows the implied effect of changes in composition:
$$\sum_i U_i^{56} \Delta_{73} w_i + \sum_i \Delta_{73} w_i \Delta_{73} U_i = .46 + .22.$$
This is greater than the first figure for compositional change above by the amount of the interaction term, $\sum_i \Delta_{73} w_i \Delta_{73} U_i = .22$.

The interaction term is important here because of the rise in unemployment rates of youths and women combined with their growing importance in the labor force. The rising proportion of these groups in the labor force can itself cause their unemployment rates to increase because of the time necessary for the demand for labor to adjust to the expansion of labor supply groups which are not perfect substitutes for other groups. Because of the difficulty of measuring this effect, the interaction term may be kept separate from the direct effect of changes in composition.

[12] See Jacob Mincer, "Labor-Force Participation and Unemployment: A Review of Recent Evidence," *Prosperity and Unemployment*, Robert A. Gordon and Margaret S. Gordon, eds. (New York: John Wiley & Sons, 1966), pp. 73-112; and N. J. Simler and Alfred Tella, "Labor Reserves and the Phillips Curve," *Review of Economics and Statistics*, vol. 50 (February 1968), pp. 32-49.

In addition to compositional changes in the labor force, long-run increases in the unemployment rates of the various subgroups have also affected the overall rate. Most of these long-run increases appear not to be related to aggregate demand but instead to be related to changes in the behavior of workers. In part they reflect changes in life styles which are difficult to quantify, and in part they reflect the introduction and expansion of government programs which have quantifiable effects on unemployment.

Unemployment Insurance. This is one of the largest programs affecting unemployment. Expansions of the insurance program to cover more workers or to add benefits or to allow more lenient acceptance of claims has tended to raise unemployment in various ways: First, such expansions make it easier for more workers to search longer for attractive jobs. Second, covered industries that meet cyclical or seasonal demands tend to hire more workers at the same pay (the industries do not bear the full cost of the insurance), then to lay them off more frequently for temporary periods.[13] Third, sporadic workers such as students and seasonally employed workers can claim unemployment benefits during nonworking periods and be counted as unemployed, whereas previously they either took jobs or dropped out of the labor force at such times. Fourth, the earned-income limitation of social security increases the number of retired people who work part of the year and claim unemployment benefits for the remainder (social security payments are not affected by unemployment benefits, and only thirteen states reduce or deny unemployment benefits to retired persons on social security).

These effects of unemployment insurance will be greatest when take-home earnings forgone are lowest relative to unemployment compensation (which is not taxed), that is, in the case of low-paid workers and of those in high marginal tax brackets, such as married workers with well-paid spouses. Thus the greater number of women in the labor force increases unemployment as they take advantage of unemployment insurance to accept and leave jobs and be unemployed more often, and as their husbands remain longer between jobs.

---

[13] Martin Feldstein, "The Effect of Unemployment Insurance on Temporary Layoff Unemployment," Discussion Paper 520, Harvard Institute of Economic Research, November 1976, processed. The author finds that unemployment insurance accounts for half the volume of job layoffs. Such temporary or seasonal layoffs add to the average amount of unemployment.

Barry Chiswick, "The Effect of Unemployment Compensation on a Seasonal Industry: Agriculture," *Journal of Political Economy*, vol. 84 (June 1976), pp. 591-602. The author estimates that unemployment insurance increased the average unemployment rate in agriculture in 1975 by one percentage point.

Lacking comprehensive studies of these effects on unemployment rates, we may make rough estimates of the changes from 1956 to 1973. The effects of increases in coverage and benefits alone have been fairly small. The proportion of the labor force covered by unemployment insurance was 64.2 percent in 1956 and 78.8 percent in 1973, an increase of 14.6 percentage points.[14] Estimates of the effect on unemployment of this increase in coverage can be derived from the effect on the duration of unemployment, which can then be translated into unemployment rates. One estimate of this effect is that the duration of unemployment in 1968 increased 1.1 weeks for each $10.00 of additional benefits.[15] The $10.00 was 7.9 percent of gross weekly earnings in covered employment in 1968. The same 7.9 percent of weekly earnings of covered workers in 1973 was $12.95, when average weekly benefits were $59.00 or 4.6 times greater. According to the cited effect for the group surveyed in 1968, therefore, average benefits in 1973 would increase the duration of unemployment for the newly covered unemployed by (1.1 × 4.6) five weeks. In 1973 an average of 101,000 workers began receiving unemployment payments each week under state programs. Hence, the estimated increase in the 1973 unemployment rate due to the expansion of coverage since 1956 is:

$$\frac{\left(\begin{array}{c}\text{average weekly}\\\text{number beginning}\\\text{payments in 1973}\end{array}\right) \times \left(\begin{array}{c}\text{increase in}\\\text{coverage}\\\text{since 1956}\end{array}\right) \times \left(\begin{array}{c}\text{increase in}\\\text{duration of}\\\text{unemployment}\end{array}\right)}{\text{total labor force}}$$

[14] Coverage and benefits are for all federal and state programs. CEA, *Annual Report*, 1975, pp. 281 and 122.

[15] Kathleen Classen, "The Effects of Unemployment Insurance: Evidence from Pennsylvania," The Public Research Institute of the Center of Naval Analyses, April 1975, processed. This study is based on an analysis of survey data collected by the Pennsylvania Department of Labor and Industry. The period 1967-1968 was chosen because the maximum weekly benefits in Pennsylvania increased on January 1, 1968 from $45.00 to $60.00. It was possible to measure the effect of benefits on the duration of unemployment because of substantial differences in dollar benefits among similar claimants over a short period. This study might even understate the effect, because higher benefits also foster more temporary layoffs which tend to be of short duration.

Two other studies which give different results may be cited. A recent study of four subgroups of the labor force using the National Longitudinal Survey for the second half of the 1960s (see Ronald G. Ehrenberg and Ronald L. Oaxaca, "Unemployment Insurance, Duration of Unemployment, and Subsequent Wage Gain," *American Economic Review*, vol. 66 [December 1976], pp. 754-66) found the increase in the duration of unemployment due to unemployment insurance to be from two and one-half to six weeks, and for one subgroup nineteen weeks. From a comparison of insured and uninsured workers in 1969, Stephen R. Marston concluded in "The Impact of Unemployment Insurance on Job Search," *Brookings Papers on Economic Activity*, 1975, vol. 1, pp. 13-48, that the duration of unemployment increased by from one-half to one and one-half weeks.

$$= \frac{(101 \text{ thousand}) \times (14.6 \text{ percent}) \times (5 \text{ weeks})}{88.7 \text{ million}}$$

$$= 0.08 \text{ percentage points.}[16]$$

This small effect would be reduced to insignificance if we took the increase in duration to be less than five weeks (as suggested by some other studies cited in footnote 15).

Increases in benefits had an even smaller effect on the unemployment rate. The ratio of benefits to average earnings increased only 2.7 percentage points from 1956 to 1973, and had a negligible effect. The duration of unemployment benefits, however, has at times increased appreciably. The time limit for receiving benefits for each episode of unemployment has generally been twenty-six weeks except in the case of special thirteen week extensions during recessions. Legislation passed in December 1974 and March 1975 increased the time limit temporarily to sixty-five weeks. This allowed workers who would otherwise have exhausted their benefits after the initial thirty-nine weeks to continue receiving them longer. Such an incentive to remain unemployed increases the overall unemployment rate, but since the extensions generally occur during periods of high unemployment, their effect on the full-employment rate when the actual rate is low will be minor.[17]

In December 1974 federal legislation also extended coverage to 12 million more workers, and by further legislation in 1976 about three-quarters of these workers will be able to receive permanent coverage under regular state programs.[18] According to the preceding formula and to 1973 figures, this additional coverage will increase the unemployment rate at full employment by 0.06 percentage points. This may be an overestimate because these newly covered workers are subject to fewer episodes of unemployment than are the previously covered workers.

These estimates do not take into account the incentive that unemployment insurance gives to workers to incur temporary or seasonal layoffs. The estimates take the incidence of unemployment as given

---

[16] The number of workers receiving benefits are from the U.S. Department of Labor, *Unemployment Insurance Statistics*, various monthly issues. Nonstate unemployment programs, which comprise 8 percent of the total, are excluded here.

[17] One estimate of the effect of lengthening the duration of benefits by thirteen weeks is an increase in the unemployment rate of 0.4 percentage points (David O'Neill, Kathleen Classen, and Arlene Holen, "Effects of the 1974 UI Extensions on Unemployment," Public Research Institute of the Center for Naval Analyses, December 1974, processed).

[18] CEA, *Annual Report*, 1977, p. 50.

and show only the additions to the overall rate induced by extended coverage and duration. Also, eligibility requirements for unemployment insurance have probably been enforced more leniently in recent years than before, particularly for newly covered workers.[19] These two effects increase unemployment; however, there exists no accurate estimate of how much they increase it.

A special development occurred in 1975 with the extension of coverage to educational institutions and other seasonal industries. Employees took advantage of a provision that allowed unemployment benefits in off months (except for teachers and administrators who had a work contract for the next season). It has been estimated that this development added 0.2 percentage points to the unemployment rate.[20]

The Minimum Wage. This law discourages employers from hiring low-skilled or inexperienced workers, particularly new entrants into the labor force. In 1956 the federal minimum wage was increased to $1.00 per hour or 55.6 percent of average hourly earnings in the private nonfarm sector. By 1973 it had risen to $1.60 and by 1975 to $2.00 per hour, but had declined as a percentage of average hourly earnings in the private nonfarm sector. If we take an average of hourly earnings in major sectors of the economy (excluding the low-wage farm sector), weighted according to the proportion of workers in each sector covered by the minimum wage, we find that the minimum wage as a percentage of this average rose from 30.7 percent in 1956 to 42.6 percent in 1968.[21] This percentage tends to fall from year to year, as nominal and real wage advances whittle away its importance, and to increase in particular years when the minimum wage is raised. The increase in this percentage over the past two decades is probably understated because it does not allow for the rising proportion of young workers in the labor force, a shift in relative supplies of labor which has tended to reduce the average wage of this group relative to that of older workers and to the minimum wage.

For various reasons the effect of the minimum wage is not easy to estimate. First, it affects labor-force participation as well as employment, thus complicating the net effect on unemployment. Second, local minimum wages in some states and cities extend the coverage and

---

[19] Arlene Holen and Stanley A. Horowitz, "The Effect of Unemployment Insurance and Eligibility Enforcement on Unemployment," *Journal of Law and Economics*, vol. 17 (October 1974), pp. 403-31.

[20] Alfred Tella, "Analyzing Joblessness," *New York Times*, October 27, 1976, op-ed page.

[21] When the weighting takes into account the proportion of covered teenage employment in each sector, the increase is from 21.0 percent to 40.1 percent. See Thomas W. Gavett, "Introduction," *Youth Unemployment and Minimum Wages*, Bureau of Labor Statistics Bulletin 1657 (1970), Table 1.6, p. 12.

in some cases impose a minimum above the federal level. Third, special groups of covered workers can be hired below the minimum wage through exemptions issued by the U.S. Department of Labor.[22] Fourth, compliance with the law is not complete. Fifth, an increase in the minimum wage may take more than a year to have its full impact.

Despite these difficulties, numerous studies in recent years have examined the evidence. Although supporters of the minimum wage used to deny that it increases unemployment, the large rise in the unemployment of young workers is increasingly difficult to disregard as prima facie evidence of such an effect.

In a recent study, Jacob Mincer examined the effect of the minimum wage on employment and labor-force participation separately.[23] He ran time-series regressions from 1954 to 1969 for major subgroups of the labor force. In the regressions various influences on employment and participation are held constant to isolate the effect of minimum wages. We may use Mincer's results to estimate the effects of increases in the ratio of the minimum to average wages from 1956 to 1973. The estimated increase in the unemployment rate was 3.0 percentage points for white teenagers (ages sixteen to nineteen), 5.7 for nonwhite teenagers, 0.8 for young white men (ages twenty to twenty-four), 1.6 for young nonwhites, and 0.2 for white women twenty years of age and over. With the increase in the minimum wage to $2.00 per hour in 1974 the cumulative effects on unemployment were larger.[24] These groups were the only ones for whom Mincer found statistically significant effects. Considering only these groups, the combined effect on the overall unemployment rate was to raise it from 1956 to 1973 by 0.43 percentage points and to 1974 by 0.63 points.[25]

---

[22] In 1976 certificates were issued for about 600,000 students working in educational institutions and for 200,000 other youths. CEA, *Annual Report*, 1977, p. 142.

[23] Jacob Mincer, "Unemployment Effects of Minimum Wages," *Journal of Political Economy*, vol. 84 (August 1976), Part 2, pp. 87-104.

[24] These estimates are based on the change from 1956 to 1973 and to 1974 in the ratio of the minimum wage to average hourly earnings in private nonfarm sectors, weighted by the proportion of all workers or of teenagers covered by the minimum wage in each sector. This variable, used by Mincer in the regressions, was published for the years up to 1968 by the Bureau of Labor Statistics in *Youth Unemployment and Minimum Wages*, Bulletin 1657, p. 12.

For 1973 and 1974 the ratio was approximated using the industrial distribution of covered workers in 1974 (Peyton Elden, "The 1974 Amendments to the Federal Minimum Wage Law," *Monthly Labor Review*, July 1974, Table 2, p. 35) and of teenagers in 1968 (BLS Bulletin 1657). For 1973, when the minimum wage was $1.60 per hour, the ratio was 34.6 percent for covered workers and 34.9 percent for teenagers. For 1974, when the minimum wage was $2.00 per hour, it was 40.0 and 42.1 percent, respectively.

[25] These figures weight the increases in unemployment for each subgroup according to the composition of the labor force in 1973 and 1974. As weighted by the

Although Mincer's estimates for employment are similar to those of other studies,[26] his estimates for unemployment are not comparable with those of other studies. Most other studies do not analyze the effect of the minimum wage on labor-force participation separately as Mincer does, an effect which counteracts the employment effect of the minimum wage on unemployment. Other studies examined unemployment directly and did not find an important influence. Mincer's method seems more reliable than those of the other studies,[27] but it could lead to overestimates of the effect of minimum wages. Mincer's estimates may have spuriously incorporated many other influences on young workers which were not allowed for separately. These other influences include increases in job turnover due to less job experience, which results when longer schooling delays permanent work until an older age;[28] increased seasonal employment of the student population induced by the expansion of unemployment insurance; and so forth. Since all of these influences, together with the minimum wage, raise the full-employment rate of unemployment, it is not inappropriate to include them here. Indeed, it is not unreasonable to conclude that all of the rise in unemployment rates of young workers and women relative to the rate for prime-age men occurred for reasons other than a change in aggregate demand. The lower figures given above, however, have the virtue of being estimates of a specified effect.

Other Effects on Unemployment. Other special effects on the unemployment rate may be noted. First, legislation in 1972 required welfare mothers who were able to work to register for work. Some found jobs, but many were added to the unemployment rolls. Subsequent to this legislation their measured unemployment rate increased

---

1956 composition, the increases are 0.30 and 0.45 percentage points, respectively. The difference between the use of weights for 1956 and 1973 or 1974 can be attributed to the interaction between the effects of compositional changes and the minimum wage (see footnote 11).

[26] R. S. Goldfarb, "The Policy Content of Quantitative Minimum Wage Research," *Proceedings of the Twenty-Seventh Annual Meeting*, Industrial Relations Research Association, 1974, pp. 261-68.

[27] Similar results were found for the 1963-1972 period by James F. Ragan, Jr., "Minimum Wage Legislation and the Youth Labor Market," *Review of Economics and Statistics*, vol. 59 (May 1977), pp. 129-36. Edward Gramlich ("Impact of Minimum Wages on Other Wages, Employment, and Family Incomes," *Brookings Papers on Economic Activity*, 1976, vol. 2, pp. 409-51) reported that the extension of minimum wage coverage has had no effect on unemployment, but this finding is open to question. See Robert J. Gordon, "Structural Unemployment and the Productivity of Women," supplement to *Journal of Monetary Economics*, vol. 5 (1977), pp. 181-229, esp. pp. 207-08.

[28] Jacob Mincer has emphasized the importance of the inverse relationship between work experience and the frequency of job turnover.

by 5.8 percentage points.[29] This increase added 0.2 percentage points to the overall unemployment rate. Also, work registration requirements for various other programs, such as food stamps, have become potentially important in raising the measured unemployment rate, but it is not yet possible to determine the magnitude of their effect.[30]

Affecting unemployment in the other direction, federal manpower programs administered by the Department of Labor had an average monthly enrollment of 700,000 in 1973. The effect on unemployment is not clear, since many of the enrollees would otherwise have had jobs or have remained out of the labor force. We might suppose that 25 percent of this number would otherwise have been unemployed. If so, this effect would have reduced the overall unemployment rate in 1973 by 0.2 percentage points. This reasoning underlies Alfred Tella's estimate that such an effect accounted for a reduction in unemployment in 1976 by 0.3 points.[31]

Finally, the measurement of unemployment is subject to response error. Tella has examined response error in the unemployment survey and concludes that the reported unemployment rate understates the rise during periods of high unemployment, recently by as much as ¾ percentage points, but in times of low unemployment the reported rate shows much less error. His estimate of this understatement is 0.2 percentage points for 1956 and 0.3 points for 1973; consequently, the net effect over two decades has been to reduce the reported rate by 0.1 percentage points.[32]

Summary of Structural Effects on Unemployment. Table 1 lists the influences on unemployment for which estimates, however rough, were made above. It indicates that the unemployment rate is now 1.2 percentage points higher than it was in 1956 for comparable levels of aggregate demand. The 4.1 percent average for 1956 would today be 5.3 percent. It should be emphasized that this is an estimate of the full-employment rate, that is, it does not take into account any additional effects that occur in periods of less than full employ-

---

[29] CEA, *Annual Report*, 1976, pp. 97-98.

[30] Kenneth W. Clarkson and Roger E. Meiners, *Inflated Unemployment Statistics, The Effects of Welfare Work Registration Requirements* (Coral Gables: Law and Economics Center, University of Miami School of Law, March 1977). The authors suggest that the magnitude may have already become very large.

[31] Tella, "Analyzing Joblessness."

[32] Alfred Tella, *Cyclical Behavior of Bias-Adjusted Unemployment*, Methods for Manpower Analysis 11 (Kalamazoo, Mich.: W. E. Upjohn Institute for Employment Research, April 1976), Table 5.

Table 1

ESTIMATES OF STRUCTURAL CHANGES IN THE FULL-EMPLOYMENT UNEMPLOYMENT RATE, 1956–1977
(in percentage points)

Source of Change	To 1973	Change 1974–1977
Change in composition of labor force [a]	+.46	
Extension of unemployment insurance		
Coverage to 1973 [b]	+.08	
Seasonal workers in 1975 [c]		+.2
Nine million new workers in 1976 [d]		+.06
Increase in minimum wage [e]	+.30	+.15
Interaction with composition [f]	+.13	+.05
Work registration of welfare mothers [g]	+.2	
Manpower programs [h]	−.2	−.1
Response error [i]	−.1	
Total	+.87	+.36
Combined total	+1.23	

Note: For details see the following text footnotes: (a) footnote 11, (b) footnote 16, (c) footnote 20, (d) footnote 18, (e) footnote 24, (f) footnote 25, (g) footnote 29, (h) footnote 31, (i) footnote 32.
Source: Based on data cited in text.

ment because of extensions of unemployment benefits and special manpower programs. For example, the time limit extension of unemployment benefits in 1975 by twenty-six weeks added, according to the estimate cited in footnote 17, over ½ percentage points to the unemployment rate.

The 1.2 percentage point increase in the full-employment rate since 1956 is probably an understatement. The potential magnitude of yet unestimated influences can be gauged by considering the unemployment rate for prime-age men twenty-five to fifty-four as the indicator of aggregate demand. This rate was lower in 1973 than in 1956 by an average of 0.42 percentage points. In 1973 the overall unemployment rate was 0.72 percentage points higher than it was in

1956, which, when adjusted for the lower prime-age rate, results in an increase since 1956 of (0.72 + 0.42) 1.14 percentage points in the overall rate due to influences other than aggregate demand. That figure is 0.37 percentage points higher than the figure for changes up to 1973 noted in Table 1. If added to the changes up to 1977, the total increase is (1.23 + 0.37) 1.60 percentage points. Even this figure could be an underestimate, because it still omits a possible structural increase in the unemployment rate for prime-age men, and because it does not consider subsequent developments, such as the increased importance of work registration requirements. It is consistent, however, with other recent estimates which treat the increases for the other groups as due to structural developments.[33]

The fact that labor market developments and federal programs have served to raise the unemployment rate does not make them undesirable. Their overall value is usually assessed on other grounds. The programs are mainly intended to supplement the income of the unemployed. The growing participation of women in the labor force is widely viewed as desirable and, in any case, reflects social developments over which the government of a free society has no control. Even if the resultant increases in unemployment are viewed as undesirable, the management of aggregate demand cannot appropriately provide a remedy. The purpose of demand management is to regulate aggregate demand so that all workers have job opportunities. Long-term influences on the measured unemployment rate unrelated to deficiencies in aggregate demand should be identified and dealt with in other ways.

The Current Noninflationary Rate of Unemployment. The earlier estimate of a 3½ percent noninflationary rate of unemployment for prime-age men in 1956 was shown to be equivalent to a rate for all

---

[33] See Robert E. Hall, "The Process of Inflation in the Labor Market," *Brookings Papers on Economic Activity*, 1974, vol. 2, p. 345; Michael L. Wachter, "The Changing Cyclical Responsiveness of Wage Inflation," *Brookings Papers on Economic Activity*, 1976, vol. 1, pp. 115-59; Wachter, "The Demographic Impact on Unemployment: Past Experience and the Outlook for the Future," *Demographic Trends and Full Employment*, National Commission for Manpower Policy, Special Report No. 12 (December 1976), pp. 27-99; Gordon, "Structural Unemployment and the Productivity of Women." Also see CEA, *Annual Report*, 1977, p. 51. In "Analyzing Joblessness," Tella gives a total increase of 2 percentage points or more, but he includes additional influences which occur mainly in the high-unemployment stages of the business cycle.

All the studies which estimate the rise in the full-employment unemployment rate since the 1950s accept the actual 1956 rate as representing the full-employment level.

workers of 4.7 percent. Table 1 indicates that this rate has increased since then by 1.2 percentage points, and, allowing for omitted influences, it may have increased by 1.6 percentage points. Therefore, the present rate of unemployment at which inflation neither increases nor decreases is 5.9 and perhaps 6.3 percent.

In future years the noninflationary rate of unemployment will probably decline because of a declining proportion of youths in the labor force, and because of a more permanent attachment of women to the labor force that will reduce their job turnover. The measured rate of unemployment could also decline through changes in government programs; for example, tighter administration of unemployment benefits, reduced minimum real wages for youths, and increased enrollment in manpower programs. The rate also might increase in the future through, for example, expanded government programs that are designed to alleviate the distress of joblessness but tend to raise the amount of recorded unemployment.

The overall unemployment rate has more often than not been above the noninflationary rate as well as the 4 percent target rate for the past two decades. Since the low target made the unemployment rates of the past appear to be excessively high, some economists attributed the accompanying prevalence of inflation to an "inflationary bias," by which wage increases push up prices at a moderate rate even when excess unemployment exists.[34] But it is now also clear that we have clung to a goal of full employment which, though more relevant in 1956 than it is today, was unrealistic even then, and which can be achieved only with accelerating inflation. The increase in unemployment to 8.9 percent in the first quarter of 1975 was seen as the worst cyclical increase since the catastrophic 1930s. Measured from a noninflationary level of 5.9 percent, the excess increase was 3.0 percentage points. Yet the increase in unemployment during the 1957–1958 recession to 7.5 percent was a comparable 2.8 points in excess of the noninflationary rate then of 4.7 percent. The mid-1977 unemployment rate of 7 percent is in excess of the current noninflationary rate by only one point. The current excess cannot be reduced much further if sufficient restraint to reduce inflation is to be maintained.

The above estimate of excess unemployment may appear to be too small in view of the fact that capacity utilization in manufacturing

---

[34] James Tobin, "Inflation and Unemployment," *American Economic Review*, vol. 62 (March 1972), p. 10; and Albert Rees, "The Phillips Curve as a Menu for Policy Choices," *Economica*, vol. 37 (August 1970), pp. 227-38.

was 80.4 percent in the fourth quarter of 1976.[35] From past experience, inflationary pressures are encountered when capacity utilization is at only 86 percent.[36] Therefore, excess capacity in the fourth quarter of 1976 was (86/80.4) 6.6 percent. Excess capacity was thought to be greater only in comparison with past peaks of utilization which had exceeded the noninflationary level. The excess of 6.6 percent was nevertheless greater than that indicated by the unemployment rate for the whole economy. Capacity utilization in manufacturing exhibits fluctuations that are about two and one-half times larger than those of the manufacturing unemployment rate; hence, if the excess overall unemployment rate of (8–6) 2 percent existing in the fourth quarter of 1976 were eliminated, capacity utilization in manufacturing would increase 5 percent but still be 1.6 percent below the inflationary level. It therefore appears that stimulation of aggregate demand which resulted in a reduction of overall unemployment to less than 6 percent would not bring about major capacity limitations in manufacturing and would not at first exert inflationary pressures in that sector. But such stimulation would appear to be inflationary for the economy as a whole.

If inflation is to continue to decline, unemployment will have to remain above 6 percent to maintain sufficient slack in the economy. Trends in the labor force and programs designed to alleviate the distress of unemployment have made the former target of 4 percent inappropriate.[37] Future developments in the labor force and government programs may affect the noninflationary full-employment rate, but for the near term they are as likely to raise as to lower it.

Does Inflation Make Unemployment Higher in the Long Run? One of the regularly extolled triumphs of modern economics is the development of aggregate demand policies to control business activity. Since World War II the government has pursued monetary and fiscal policies to moderate fluctuations in aggregate demand with a view

---

[35] "New Estimates of Capacity Utilization: Manufacturing and Materials," *Federal Reserve Bulletin*, November 1976, pp. 892-905, and March 1977, p. A47.

[36] CEA, *Annual Report*, 1977, p. 52. But see Robert H. Rasche and John A. Tatom, "The Effects of the New Energy Regime on Economic Capacity, Production, and Prices," *Review*, Federal Reserve Bank of St. Louis, vol. 59 (May 1977), pp. 2-12, where it is argued that the rise in the relative cost of energy has reduced capacity, in which case much of the apparent excess capacity in manufacturing is illusory.

[37] The price stability and declining unemployment of the early 1960s suggest that the inflationary pressure set off by rising aggregate demand may be less when expected price changes are very low. Hence it may be possible to achieve lower unemployment after a period of price stability than after a period of prolonged inflation.

toward keeping the economy at full employment. The avoidance of a severe depression like the one experienced during the 1930s has been an indication of success, while recurring business recessions with associated fluctuations in unemployment are passed off as due to the difficulties of forecasting and of timing policy actions which improvements in technique will gradually overcome.

During the 1950s it became apparent that stimulation of the economy could result in rising prices and to that extent fail to have the desired effect of reducing unemployment. Nevertheless, for some time inflation was viewed as an annoyance to be endured for the sake of keeping unemployment low. That view was formulated in the famous "Phillips curve" trade-off, wherein lower unemployment would require higher inflation. While such a trade-off has been apparent in the short run, *both* inflation and unemployment rates have been rising in the long run. This anomaly forces a change in how the trade-off is viewed.

Part of the new view is a recognition that continuing inflation comes to be expected and thereby gets built into the price system. The expected rate of inflation determines the trend rate, which then becomes the base rate for further expansions and contractions. For example, if 5 percent is the expected rate of inflation, prices rise 5 percent at normal levels of production; stimulation of aggregate demand raises the rate above, and recessions reduce it below, 5 percent, but 5 percent remains the average rate of inflation. The expected rate changes slowly as experience suggests a different trend rate. Of course, the trend rate cannot persist unless policy accommodates it by producing corresponding growth on the average in nominal aggregate demand. Policy does so or is expected to do so, because any deficiency in demand results in a short-run increase in unemployment with little initial effect on the inflation rate. While continued restraint eventually reduces inflation, this involves the economy in a long and painful adjustment to slower growth in nominal aggregate demand. The present period of slack is part of such an adjustment.

The rising trend of inflation since World War II has reflected, in its simplest terms, the adoption of stimulative policies designed to attain low unemployment that ran the economy up to and too often across the threshold of rising inflationary pressures. Periods of over-stimulation resulted in bursts of more rapid price increases and successively raised the trend rate of inflation. As the economy adjusted to higher trend rates, the same unemployment rates were associated with higher inflation rates.

This history helps explain the rising rate of inflation but not that of unemployment. According to the revised view of the Phillips curve, overstimulation reduces unemployment in the short run but has no effect in the long run. The Phillips curve expresses the inflation rate as a function of excess unemployment and, as revised, also the expected inflation rate:

$$\dot{P} = F(U - U_f) + \dot{P}^e$$

(see footnote 5). For an initial expected rate of inflation, excess unemployment leads to a lower actual inflation rate, which slowly reduces the expected inflation rate. The reduction in the expected rate implies a downward shift in the curve relating the inflation rate and excess unemployment. To avoid the necessity of shifting the curve, the expected rate may be transferred to the left side of the equation to obtain an unshifting relationship between excess unemployment and the deviation between the actual and expected inflation rates (see Figure 4). Excess unemployment is zero when the actual inflation rate equals the expected rate. Deviations of the actual inflation rate from the expected rate trace a downward sloping curve, showing that restraints on aggregate demand initially increase unemployment and reduce inflation below the expected rate. According to the revised view, although the expected rate changes slowly and is not immediately affected by excess unemployment, a reduction in inflation does lead gradually to a lower expected rate, whereupon actual and expected inflation rates can both be lower and equal when unemployment returns to the full-employment level. Therefore, changes in the inflation and unemployment rates are still viewed as inversely related, but only in the short run. The curve is also usually drawn convex to the bottom axis, which means that for further equal increases in excess unemployment the short-run reductions in the inflation rate are successively smaller. That is, the first 1 percentage point increase in unemployment may reduce the inflation rate by 1 percentage point (say), but an additional one point of unemployment further reduces the inflation rate by well less than one point, and so on.

Some changes in the inflation rate, of course, reflect changes in materials costs due to international developments (such as the 1973 increase in oil prices) or to domestic deregulation of a controlled price. These effects on prices do not originate from changes in aggregate demand and so affect unemployment, if at all, in a way different from that described by the Phillips curve. Such effects would be reflected in a discrepancy from the relationship in Figure 4 that would last until they abated or until the expected rate adjusted to the new rate of inflation.

Figure 4

THE PHILLIPS CURVE AS THE DEVIATION BETWEEN ACTUAL
AND EXPECTED INFLATION RATES

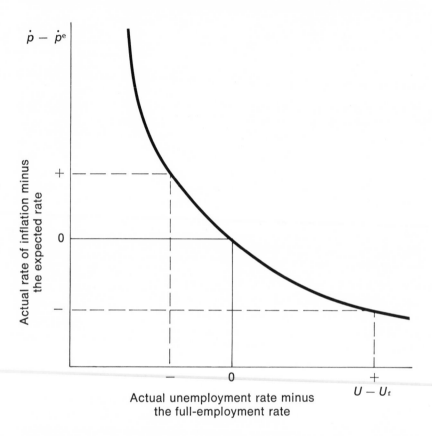

Actual unemployment rate minus
the full-employment rate

Since such disturbances to prices do not directly affect unemployment, and since the inverse relationship depicted in Figure 4 applies to the short run only, higher rates of inflation which are eventually accompanied by corresponding increases in the expected rate will be associated with the *same* level of unemployment. It is disconcerting, therefore, to note that higher inflation rates since World War II have been accompanied by higher average unemployment rates. Upward trends in unemployment and inflation have also been noted in other Western countries over the past two decades.[38] In the United States

[38] In his Nobel lecture Milton Friedman presented evidence of such a relationship for several countries ("Inflation and Unemployment," *Journal of Political Economy*, vol. 85 [June 1977], pp. 451-472).

changes in the labor force and in government programs are responsible for a rising trend in the full-employment rate.[39] But it is not certain that they account for the entire rise in the average rate of unemployment. Reductions of unemployment after recent recessions have occurred more slowly than after previous recessions. Compare the reductions after 1970 and so far after 1975 in Figure 3 with those after 1949, 1954, 1958, and 1960. Unemployment rates during recent business recoveries remain near the high levels of the preceding business recession for longer periods. Such sluggish cyclical recoveries of unemployment tend to make the average unemployment rate over the business cycle higher even if the peak and trough levels reached during the cycle are the same as before. However, recent experience suggests that, even after adjustments are made for structural changes, the peak unemployment rates may be getting higher as well.

The reduction of inflation has probably become more difficult than it was two decades ago because expectations of inflation are now firmer and thus force policy makers to impose greater restraint on aggregate demand. In theory, however, firmer expectations do not explain the rising trend of unemployment, because short-run periods of excess unemployment are balanced by periods of low unemployment.

But there is reason to suspect that inflation does result in increased unemployment in the long run, contrary to the short-run relationship. The reason has to do with the observation that higher average rates of inflation have greater variability. This characteristic was typically disregarded in the earlier theoretical literature on inflation in which fluctuations in the rate of inflation were viewed as unimportant. According to that viewpoint, the economy gradually adjusts to the average rate of inflation and is not affected by the magnitude of the rate. Full adjustment of the economy means that the inflation rate is anticipated, that all contracts allow for it, and that inflation itself produces no expected gains or losses, only surprises if the anticipated rate is not realized. Yet experience demonstrates that actual inflation rates are not so easily anticipated. In a cross-section analysis of many countries, a higher average inflation rate is associated with larger short-run fluctuations in the rate.[40] This association has also been apparent in the United States in recent decades.

---

[39] To some extent these programs were introduced because of the inability of demand management to reduce unemployment as much as was desired. Consequently, they are not entirely independent developments but are indirectly related to the inflation resulting from the efforts of demand management to reduce unemployment further.

[40] See Arthur M. Okun, "The Mirage of Steady Inflation," *Brookings Papers on*

The increase in the variability of inflation has occurred, despite the intention of governments to avoid or to reduce inflation, because the policies actually pursued have varied considerably with economic circumstances. As a result, the public has come to expect a wide range of possible outcomes, and the behavior of prices is no longer constrained by expectations that actual trends will remain within any particular range. The lack of constraint on expectations affects the complex adjustment system by which prices respond to disturbances and makes the system less stable. Therefore, although monetary and fiscal policies since World War II have been increasingly devoted to stabilizing the economy, they have been less successful in the past decade either because policies were pursued too vigorously and became a source of instability, or because intensifying inflation changed the response of the economy to disturbances. It is not clear whether the disturbances themselves became larger, or whether the response of prices to similar disturbances became larger, or both. Whatever the explanation, the present inflationary environment is volatile with wide swings in the rate of inflation from period to period, where the higher the average rate the wider are the swings.

The higher variability of inflation rates increases uncertainty and lessens the efficiency of the price system in guiding the allocation of resources.[41] Less efficiency means less total output of goods and services. This undesirable effect of inflation is disregarded in much of the literature by the invalid assumption that inflation will gradually be anticipated and adjusted to and then will have no disadvantages. Nevertheless, a reduction in efficiency would not necessarily raise unemployment.

Yet, if the Phillips curve is convex, as is usually assumed, greater variability in inflation rates will produce higher average unemployment. If the inflation rate fluctuates more at higher average rates, and if these fluctuations reflect changes in aggregate demand which also affect unemployment, the increase in unemployment associated with a one-point decline in the inflation rate will be greater than the decrease in unemployment associated with a one-point increase in the inflation rate. This is illustrated by the dotted lines in Figure 4. Thus, when fluctuations in aggregate demand and the inflation rate

Economic Activity, 1971, vol. 2, pp. 485-98. Okun's results are supported by Dennis E. Logue and Thomas D. Willett, "A Note on the Relation Between the Rate and Variability of Inflation," *Economica*, vol. 43 (May 1976), pp. 151-58.
[41] Higher inflation rates are also associated with greater fluctuations in relative prices. See Daniel R. Vining, Jr. and Thomas C. Elwertowski, "The Relationship Between Relative Prices and the General Price Level," *American Economic Review*, vol. 66 (September 1976), pp. 699-708.

are larger, not only are fluctuations in the unemployment rate larger,[42] but the shape of the curve also implies that the *average* unemployment rate will be higher.[43]

Crucial to this argument is the assumed convexity of the Phillips curve. In fact, however, there is little empirical support for any particular shape of the curve. For the regression equations reported above, the addition of a quadratic term or reciprocal form of the unemployment rate to show convexity does not add to the explanatory power of the regressions, indicating that the data do not reveal curvature in the relationship.[44] These tests are not conclusive, since the expected

---

[42] The evidence is mixed whether the amplitudes of fluctuation in unemployment and inflation are correlated in recent U.S. experience. The cyclical rise in unemployment was larger than usual in 1974-1975 but smaller than usual in 1967 and 1970, while the inflation rate fluctuated substantially in those cycles. Greater variability in the inflation rate might not, however, produce a larger swing in the unemployment rate from peak to trough of business cycles, because of lags in unemployment. Lags might delay the return of the unemployment rate to the full-employment level during business recoveries. This would raise the average level of unemployment over the course of the cycle and still be consistent with larger cyclical fluctuations. As noted earlier, such a pattern seems to characterize recent U.S. cycles.

[43] Richard G. Lipsey, "The Relation Between Unemployment and the Rate of Change of Money Wage Rates in the United Kingdom, 1862-1957: A Further Analysis," *Economica*, vol. 27 (February 1960), pp. 1-31, points out that convexity in the Phillips curve and fluctuations in demand among sectors of the economy affect aggregate unemployment.

Greater variability of inflation rates could cause firms to attribute most shifts in demand to nominal rather than real effects, and thus to respond largely by changing prices rather than by changing output and employment. The effect is to reduce the slope of the Phillips curve (see Robert E. Lucas, "Some International Evidence on Output-Inflation Tradeoffs," *American Economic Review*, vol. 68 [June 1973], pp. 326-34). It is not clear, however, how this would affect the convexity of the curve. If a steeper curve also had less convexity (as seems plausible), the greater variability of higher average inflation rates might, after the period of transition to a steeper curve, produce little increase in average unemployment. At the same time, there would be less fluctuation in unemployment despite the greater fluctuation in inflation rates. We do not observe smaller fluctuations in unemployment in the United States, but such effects might yet occur if inflation continues to be highly variable.

[44] See footnote 7. A linear function fits the data slightly better than a convex function does, though not significantly according to the usual statistical criteria. Although the previous regressions are not an exact representation of the Phillips curve, they are derived from it as shown in footnote 5 and can be used to deduce its shape.

Lucas Papademos ("Optimal Aggregate Employment Policy and Other Essays," MIT dissertation, 1977) tested the shapes of various versions of the Phillips curve and found that none is statistically superior to the linear form.

In an earlier study, George Perry (*Unemployment, Money Wage Rates, and Inflation* [Cambridge, Mass.: MIT Press, 1966], p. 55) found the reciprocal form of the unemployment rate to fit slightly better than the linear form. His data ended with 1960. Conceivably, convexity exists but the data after 1960 do not reveal it because of greater statistical "noise."

inflation rate can be respresented in other ways, and since more complicated equations allowing for lagged effects may finally reveal some convexity. Nevertheless, for the range of data observed over the post-World War II period, the shape of the relationship is uncertain.

If convexity could be established, it would suggest that greater inflation has increased the long-run average unemployment rate and that future policy should be conducted more cautiously to avoid producing inflation in the long run. However, the lack of evidence as to the convexity of the Phillips curve leaves uncertain whether the variability of higher average inflation rates has contributed to a long-run rise in unemployment. If the Phillips curve is not convex, the rising trend of unemployment may simply reflect recent policies to reduce inflation and may not be a permanent result of higher inflation rates.

I am inclined to believe that, despite the lack of clear evidence, the Phillips curve is characterized by some convexity. But even without convexity and the implied increase in long-run average unemployment, the costs of inflation are major. The variability of inflation increases uncertainty and interferes with the efficient operation of the economic system. Yet, despite the desirability of reducing inflation, Phillips curve analysis has supported the argument that inflation should be reduced gradually to avoid making the total worker-months of unemployment incurred larger than is necessary. If the curve is not convex, this long-standing policy prescription can be questioned. The convexity of the Phillips curve bears on this issue of policy as well.

Is Gradualism the Best Policy? Policies to subdue the inflation which began in 1965 have been guided by the principle of gradualism.[45] This principle calls for the imposition of mild restraint on the growth in aggregate demand in order to produce a little slack in the economy, and the endurance of the resulting excess unemployment, until inflation is subdued.[46] In a business recession like that of 1973–1975,

---

Since the definition of unemployment does not admit negative values, the Phillips curve must show convexity as unemployment approaches zero. But that arithmetical constraint does not mean that the curve cannot be linear within the usual range of experience.

[45] Although the term "gradualism" was coined by the Council of Economic Advisers in 1969 to describe administration policy (which as a staff member at the time I fully agreed with) and then dropped when the 1970 recession ensued, the criterion of policy described by it has persisted.

[46] "Subdued" inflation has never been precisely defined. In practice it does not mean a zero rate of inflation but a rate that, by the standards of the day, is not "excessive." It is easy to forget that, in the late 1950s, 3 percent appeared excessive.

when the slack in the economy is considered to be far too much, gradualism is consistent with a rapid recovery to reduce economic slack to the desired small amount. Gradualism has been difficult to achieve. Policies designed to produce mild restraint on aggregate demand resulted in a mini-recession in 1967, a mild recession in 1970, and a severe recession in 1973–1975. These declines in economic activity were all larger than policy makers considered to be desirable. Gradualism called for smaller declines in economic activity and, consequently, slower reductions of inflation, though the actual reductions of inflation were much slower than was generally expected at the time.

A theoretical justification for the reduction of inflation to be gradual is based on a convex Phillips curve. In Figure 4, to reduce P, a policy of restraint holds U above U_f, and P falls relative to P^e. A lower actual inflation rate eventually leads to a lower expected rate. If the expected rate adjusts slowly, however, the excess unemployment needed to hold the inflation rate below the expected rate must be endured for a long time. The total unemployment endured can be measured by the time and the amount by which U exceeds U_f. Even after P is reduced to the desired level, U must still exceed U_f until P^e also declines to the desired level. The reduction in P is not permanent until P^e is also reduced by the same amount. At that point U can return to the level of U_f.

If P^e adjusts more rapidly, the entire process can be accomplished with less total unemployment. That is why the credibility of a policy to subdue inflation, which can affect P^e, is important to the success and costs of the policy. The time required to reduce inflation and the optimal policy to adopt depend upon the adjustment speed of expectations and the rate at which excess unemployment dampens inflation. If the inflation rate is held at a given level, changes in the unemployment rate are largely determined by the adjustment speed of expectations and are beyond the control of public policy. But the rate at which policy reduces the inflation rate, given the lags in the system, will influence the amount of unemployment to be incurred in the process.

If the Phillips curve is convex, each successive increase in unemployment is accompanied by a smaller reduction in the inflation rate. A given reduction in the inflation rate can then be achieved with a smaller cost in total unemployment if a mild restraint is applied for a long period than if a strong restraint is applied for a short period. Theoretically, since the least total unemployment is produced by the mildest restraint, the time needed to achieve a desired reduction in inflation approaches infinity. Realistic policy makers must select a reasonable time period in which the desired reduction in inflation is to be achieved. A time schedule for reducing inflation is selected which weighs the disadvantages of unemployment against the advantages of reduced inflation.[47] The public concern over unemployment inherited from the 1930s and expressed in the Employment Act of 1946 has until recently outweighed the more remote dangers of uncontrolled inflation. We have therefore tried to subdue inflation gradually by policies of restraint on aggregate demand that were mild in intention if not always in outcome.

If the evidence does not show that the Phillips curve is convex, no basis exists for believing that each successive increase in unemployment is accompanied by a smaller reduction in the inflation rate. If the curve is linear, a given reduction in the inflation rate will result in worker-months of unemployment that sum to the same total whether the reduction is achieved rapidly or slowly, so long as changes in the expected rate of inflation are proportional to the difference between the actual and the expected rate. Then a rapid reduction is preferable, since the disadvantages of inflation are removed sooner.

To be sure, the speed at which we might prefer to reduce inflation has limits even if the Phillips curve is linear over its entire range. A severe depression would be undesirable as a means of subduing inflation, because it could not be properly controlled by policy and the severe unemployment would hit a high proportion of heads of households and become intolerable. However, that is not to say that the recent recession and current slow recovery may not be a desirable means of reducing inflation as compared with a prolonged period of mild slack in the economy. The latter policy requires an interminable time to reduce inflation and risks setbacks if unforeseen disturbances override the mild restraint and unleash new inflationary pressures. Moreover, the slow rate at which gradualism brings results can cause the public to lose patience and to clamor for other measures which are ultimately ineffective and, in the case of wage and price controls, counterproductive. Based on these arguments, the best anti-inflation policy available lies somewhere between very mild restraint and the opposite extreme.

---

[47] The optimal path calls for a constant rate of unemployment until the inflation rate reaches the desired level. The reason for a constant unemployment rate is that a higher rate of unemployment in one quarter does not produce a sufficiently greater reduction in inflation to justify the lower rate of unemployment then possible in a later quarter. However, in a more sophisticated analysis, with discounting of the disadvantages of future inflation and unemployment, a constant unemployment rate may no longer be the optimal path.

Lucas Papademos in "Optimal Aggregate Employment Policy" analyzes the optimal path of inflation reduction under a variety of assumptions.

Assessment of the Policy Alternatives

Post-World War II policies designed to manage aggregate demand have not in general adopted strong anti-inflationary measures in the belief that some inflation had to be allowed in order to keep unemployment low. The first major reassessment of these policies came with the recognition of the role of inflationary expectations. It was realized that a given rate of inflation could not be counted on to stimulate aggregate demand in real terms and increase output and employment. A nominal rise in aggregate demand which is expected has little real effect on the economy. Because output and employment are determined by the expected level of prices and wages in real terms, an effective stimulation of economic activity requires an increase in nominal aggregate demand above the expected increase. An unexpected increase in prices, if continued, will in turn come to be expected, and increasing rates of actual and expected inflation will result from a policy designed to keep unemployment lower than the level at which it settles when actual and expected inflation rates remain equal.

If inflation has no lasting benefit in reducing unemployment, the costs of inflation cannot be so readily brushed aside as they had been when a little inflation was thought to provide considerable benefits. To be sure, if the inflation rate is constant and widely expected, and if the economy adjusts to it completely, the only disadvantage appears to be the inability to compensate holders of currency for the losses in purchasing power due to inflation, which can be dismissed as minor. Inflation might not be a serious concern if it were completely anticipated. But since actual rates of inflation are too volatile to be anticipated with any degree of accuracy, the uncertainty of inflation rates imposes major costs in reduced efficiency of production and resource allocation and in suboptimal saving and investment decisions.

The Phillips curve has served as the theoretical justification for trading off unemployment against inflation in the short run. It is not clear that the objective of keeping unemployment low over the long run is served by focusing on its short-run departures from the full-employment level to the neglect of the long-run consequences, and by primary reliance on the control of aggregate demand to achieve short-run employment targets. Implications of the Phillips curve for long-run unemployment have been disregarded. The curve is usually thought to be convex, implying that greater variability of inflation rates *increases* average unemployment in the long run—which is a good reason, given the tendency of higher average inflation rates to have greater variability, for avoiding policies that result in long-run inflation.

The evidence on convexity of the Phillips curve is in fact unclear, and the curve may be linear within the range of past experience. A linear curve implies that the long-run average level of unemployment is not affected by the average rate of inflation and its degree of variability. Still, there are other costs of inflation to be avoided, and policy makers remain committed to subduing inflation. Policies have generally been designed to reduce inflation gradually, but they have been pursued erratically and have made disappointing progress. These gradualist policies have been justified by a convex Phillips curve. A linear curve puts a different light on the appropriate degree of restraint. Linearity implies that the cost of reducing inflation in terms of unemployment is the same whether the reduction is rapid or slow. Consequently, a policy that reduced inflation sooner rather than later would be attractive.

The recovery from the 1973–1975 recession has been widely deplored as being too slow to reduce unemployment. As its first order of business the new administration proposed additional stimulus to aggregate demand to remove excess unemployment. While the risk of pushing the economy into the zone of increasing inflationary pressures was recognized (and the stimulus was subsequently considered to be unnecessary), strong stimulus was justified at the time by arguing that unemployment was much higher than was needed to reduce inflation. The rationale for this view is based partly on an unrealistically low estimate of the full-employment level of unemployment. But it is also based on the proposition that, while some economic slack serves to reduce inflation slowly, additional slack is comparatively ineffective in reducing it more rapidly.

It is often cynically said that inflation has become inevitable for political reasons because the task of incurring unemployment for the sake of reducing inflation is repeatedly put off for future office holders to face. What makes that such an unattractive economic policy is that the costs of delaying a reduction of inflation are not compensated by lower overall costs of unemployment. If the Phillips curve is linear, the total unemployment incurred is not reduced by putting it off. If the curve is convex, average unemployment is increased over the long run. Either a convex or a linear Phillips curve justifies, for different reasons, an effective anti-inflationary policy.

SPENDING AND GETTING

Herbert Stein

Summary

*Total government spending—federal, state, and local—rose from
24.8 percent of GNP to 31.0 percent between 1956 and 1973, both
years of fairly high employment. This happened despite a decline
of defense spending as a proportion of GNP from 9.7 percent to
6.0 percent. There was an approximately equal rise of total government revenues in relation to GNP.*

*Much of the rise of nondefense spending was in social insurance
programs, and much of the increase of the revenues consisted of contributions to those funds. But other nondefense expenditures, and
other revenues, also increased relative to the GNP, especially at the
state and local levels.*

*It is not possible to make any conclusive judgment about this
rise of total expenditures and taxes relative to the national income
without an examination of particular programs, and this has not been
attempted here. On the other hand, the significance of the general
trend cannot be evaluated simply by looking at particular programs.
In fact, decisions about government spending are, and should be,
the outcome of a synthesis of judgments about the appropriate level
of overall expenditures and about the needs for particular programs.*

*The common argument that rising government expenditure, rela-
tive to the GNP, causes inflation and retards growth is difficult to
validate with confidence from the U.S. experience of the period 1956–
1973. Except for the period of increased spending for the Vietnam
War, spending needs did not force deficits on the country; on the
contrary, spending and tax reduction were caused by the desire to
generate deficits and stimulate the economy—perhaps mistakenly.
Moreover, it is uncertain whether these deficits would have been significantly inflationary without the accompanying monetary expansion,*

and doubtful that the monetary expansion was forced either by the spending or by the deficits.

Any connection between rising government expenditures and the retardation of growth is even harder to demonstrate because there was continued growth during the period. Real GNP grew as rapidly from 1965 to 1973 as from 1956 to 1965, and in both periods more rapidly than in earlier decades. The proportion of the population in the labor force did not diminish, and only small adverse effects of the tax-transfer system on the labor supply have been found in empirical studies. The ratios of private saving and private investment to the GNP in years of high employment have not fallen. It may be that more refined analysis would show that the government budgets had an adverse effect on growth at this time, which was offset by some other factor, but that conclusion must be regarded as speculative.

What does seem possible to say is that the growth of expenditures during the period was the outcome of a decision-making process in which the claims for tax reduction were not evenly balanced against the claims for expenditure increase. In the social insurance programs, increasing commitments for future benefits always seemed a bargain because the present generation of workers and taxpayers was not asked to pay for them. In the other federal accounts, increased expenditures seemed a bargain because it was not necessary to legislate new taxes; growth and inflation automatically poured in more money. In state and local governments, increasing expenditure was a bargain because that was a way to get federal aid.

We should move toward a condition in which the decision to spend more, or to make a commitment to spend more, involves an equal and explicit decision to tax more. One step toward this goal would be to index the federal tax system against inflation, so that inflation would not automatically increase real federal revenue without a deliberate decision to raise taxes. Another step would be to restore and expand the accumulation of reserves in the social insurance programs, so that current workers and taxpayers paid a larger share of the obligations that are being built up for the future. It would also be desirable to de-emphasize federal grants to the states and localities, especially matching grants, in order to bring the taxing and spending decisions closer together.

Introduction

In 1956 total government expenditures in the United States—federal, state, and local—were $104.5 billion. In 1973 the total had risen to

$404.9 billion. (I use these particular years, and sometimes 1965, because they were years in which real GNP was within 1 percent of potential, as recently estimated by the Council of Economic Advisers. This is a crude way of abstracting from cyclical influences. I also use expenditures as calculated for the national income accounts as the only practical way to measure federal, state, and local expenditures in terms comparable to each other and to the GNP statistics.)

This was a period of substantial inflation. A rough adjustment for the rise of prices would show that government expenditures in 1973 were 2.3 times as high as in 1956 in real terms. A further adjustment for the growth of population would bring the real per capita expenditures in 1973 to 1.8 times the 1956 figure. Total government expenditures in 1956 were 24.8 percent of the GNP. By 1973 the figure had risen to 31.0 percent.

There are a number of possible ways to react to these figures, or any variants of them that show the increase of government spending during the past two decades:

(1) *Dismay and horror*—The rise of government spending might be seen as a source of great harm that has befallen the country, or will befall it, if the trend continues. One way to dramatize this view is to calculate that if government expenditures continue to rise as a percent of GNP as fast as they did from 1956 to 1973, they would equal 100 percent of GNP by the year 2057. And while that is not an arithmetically impossible situation, since government transfer payments are not included in the GNP, it is probably an economically unsustainable situation as long as most transfer payments are exempt from taxation.

(2) *Indifference*—One might take the position that government expenditure, as such, is not a relevant category. Because it includes such a variety of activities, no sound value judgment can be made about the total. Programs must be appraised one by one in terms of their own benefits and costs. There is no presumption that a big budget is better or worse than a smaller one.

(3) *Acceptance*—The increase of government expenditures has come about through a democratic process, and it represents the will of the people. There is no higher authority competent to judge it good or bad. The increase of government expenditures as a percent of GNP is no more a problem than the increase of consumers' expenditures for services as a percent of GNP during the same period.

(4) *Understanding*—There are people who look back to an old German economist, Adolph Wagner, finding sympathy with his law, which says that as societies rise in affluence, individuals will want to spend more on government services, just as they will want to eat more beefsteak and less rice. To these people, the rise of government expenditures is not only an actual expression of the people's will but also an understandable and intelligent expression of their wishes.

(5) *Gratification*—Then there are those who regard the political process as inherently superior to the market process for determining the distribution and use of the national income, perhaps because they believe people to be more fairly represented in the political process. Therefore, they welcome the increase of government spending relative to the national income and even look forward to a continuation of that trend.

I propose in this essay to discuss these different attitudes to the recent and prospective trend of government spending. Before doing that, it will be helpful to review what has happened in the past twenty years or so.

A review of spending is not the same as a review of all government actions affecting the economy. It omits, for example, a large volume of regulatory activity, much of which has effects like government spending. For example, if a firm is required to install antipollution equipment, that is like a tax on the firm and a government expenditure. However, despite the fact that my category does not include everything, what I, following convention, call spending is a large enough category to *deserve* attention.

A Brief Survey of Government Spending

The period under review, from the end of the Korean War to the present, was a period of great increase in the national income, in real terms and even more in nominal terms. From 1956 to 1973, real GNP increased by 85 percent and nominal GNP by 210 percent. With the tax system in effect at the beginning of the period, this increase of the GNP would have generated a large increase of revenue.

For all levels of government combined, and including the social insurance systems, the rise of revenue would not have been more than proportional to the rise of GNP. The federal income tax was the only important tax whose yield would rise faster than GNP, and in 1956 that tax accounted for a little less than one-third of combined receipts.

The federal corporate profits tax was approximately proportional to book profits, and since book profits tended to decline relative to GNP during the past two decades, the yield of this tax, at a stable rate, would have declined relative to GNP. Without an increase in the ceiling on wages subject to social insurance contributions, collections from that source would have fallen relative to payrolls and the GNP. Yield of the property tax would have lagged behind GNP, especially in a period of inflation, and the assortment of selective excises and general sales taxes would not have done much more than keep up with GNP.

So it was not the case that the yield to governments as a whole from the existing tax system would rise relative to GNP, although the federal government was in a different position from the states and localities in this respect. However, the governments were faced with a large increase in absolute revenues, in real terms, and could use this "fiscal dividend" to increase expenditures, to reduce tax rates or to increase their budget surpluses and thereby reduce their debts.

These options were broadened with the decline of defense spending relative to GNP that occurred during this period. In 1956 defense expenditures were 9.7 percent of GNP; by 1973 the figure had fallen to 6.0 percent. This meant more room for increasing nondefense spending, cutting taxes, or increasing surpluses.

The decision was simple. The money was spent. There was, on balance, no tax reduction. Total taxes, including social insurance contributions, drifted up as a percentage of GNP during the period, from about 26 percent in 1956 to 31 percent in 1973. Nor was any part of the increased revenue devoted to debt reduction. In 1956 the combined governments had a surplus of $5.2 billion; in 1973 it was only $6.3 billion. Between those dates government receipts had increased by $301.5 billion and expenditures by $300.4 billion. Total nondefense expenditures rose by $262.7 billion, or from 15 percent of GNP to 25 percent.

It is revealing to divide the combined governments into three sectors—the federal sector, excluding the social insurance funds; the state and local sector, with the same exclusion; and the social insurance funds. (Note that "social insurance funds" as used here includes not only OASDI and Medicare but also civilian employees retirement, railroad retirement, veterans life insurance, and unemployment compensation.)

Three characteristics of the social insurance system are especially relevant. First, the system had a strong built-in tendency for expenditures to increase not only absolutely but also relative to the GNP, as the proportion of the population entitled to benefits rose and as the time of participation in the system lengthened, thereby raising average benefits relative to average incomes. Second, during this period there was a strong belief that the social insurance funds should at least balance, in the sense that the annual collection of contributions should equal the concurrent costs of benefits and administration. This condition was met in every one of the years from 1952 through 1975 except in the two years of serious unemployment, 1958 and 1975. The condition was met not simply by the automatic increase of collections as the economy expanded; rate increases and increases of coverage were needed and were forthcoming. Third, there was an unusual willingness to expand the system and to meet the costs of doing so by raising the earmarked taxes. Social insurance costs rose during the two decades not only in fulfillment of the obligations existing at the outset but also because of benefit increases and the installation of entirely new programs, notably Medicare.

Social insurance expenditures rose from 2.5 percent of GNP in 1956 to 6.4 percent in 1973. All other nondefense spending rose from 12.6 percent to 18.6 percent. The rise in social insurance spending relative to GNP was 150 percent; for other nondefense spending less than 50 percent. In fact, the role of social insurance in government spending during this period can hardly be exaggerated. In 1956 social insurance amounted to 10 percent of total government expenditures, including defense. But the rise of social insurance accounted for 62 percent of the rise of total government spending relative to GNP between 1956 and 1973.

Even greater was the relative contribution of social insurance to rising government receipts. Between 1956 and 1973, total government receipts rose from 26 percent of GNP to 31.5 percent, or about 21 percent. Social insurance receipts as a fraction of GNP rose 128 percent and all other receipts rose 6 percent as a proportion of GNP. Social insurance accounted for 73 percent of the rise in total receipts as a percentage of GNP.

What we experienced, then, was a large rise of social insurance expenditures and receipts relative to GNP, with other expenditures and receipts drifting up only slowly. Within spending as a whole other than social insurance, there were two parallel movements. Defense spending fell relative to the GNP and nondefense spending absorbed that decline and a little more. Similarly, federal revenues declined relative to the GNP and state and local revenues absorbed that decline and a little more.

Table 1

GOVERNMENT EXPENDITURES AND REVENUES AS PERCENT OF GNP

	1956 (percent)	**1973** (percent)
Expenditures		
Total	24.8	31.0
Social insurance	2.5	6.4
All other	22.3	24.6
Defense	9.7	6.0
Nondefense	12.6	18.6
Revenues		
Total	26.1	31.5
Social insurance	3.1	7.0
All other	23.0	24.5
Federal	16.0	13.7
State and local	7.0	10.8

Note: Federal grants-in-aid are excluded from federal expenditures and state and local receipts. Interest receipts of the social insurance funds are excluded from social insurance revenues and deducted from nondefense expenditures. These receipts equalled 0.4 percent of GNP in 1956 and 0.8 percent in 1973. The table could be put on a gross basis for the interest transactions by adding these amounts to the amounts shown for total expenditures, all other expenditures, nondefense expenditures, total revenues, and social insurance revenues.

Source: Calculated from *National Income and Product Accounts of the United States, 1929-74, Statistical Tables* (U.S. Department of Commerce, Bureau of Economic Analysis), and *Survey of Current Business*, July 1976.

The federal government (excluding now the social insurance system) had an elastic revenue source, and it also had a relatively declining defense burden. Therefore it had a big "fiscal dividend"— and funds either for tax reduction, for increases of nondefense expenditures, or for generation of surpluses. The government did some of the first two of these things and none—indeed, less than none— of the third. Federal revenues, other than social insurance contributions, fell from 16 percent of GNP in 1956 to 13.7 percent in 1973. But, of course, 13.7 percent of the 1973 GNP was much more than 16 percent of the 1956 GNP.

Joseph Pechman and Emil Sunley have estimated that federal individual income tax liabilities in 1973 were $35.5 billion less than they would have been if the tax law had remained as it was in 1960.[1] Since there was no important change in the law between 1956 and 1960, that figure can be used as a rough estimate of the reduction in tax revenue from changes in the income tax law between 1956 and 1973. If we further assume that without changes in the law federal corporate tax liabilities would have remained the same proportion of book profits as in 1956, and indirect business taxes would have remained the same proportion of GNP, we get a $56 billion reduction in 1973 federal taxes resulting from changes in the law. That was about 4.25 percent of 1973 GNP. Putting it another way, about one-third of the additional revenue that growth and inflation would have yielded was returned to the taxpayers.

This need not be interpreted as an act of extraordinary generosity or self-restraint on the part of the government. Federal taxes, excluding social insurance contributions, increased by $110 billion between 1956 and 1973, or by about 60 percent in real terms. Roughly, about one-half of the *real* increase in revenues that would have been obtained from unchanged tax laws was returned to the taxpayers. The rest—and more than the rest since there was a moderate swing from surplus to deficit between 1956 and 1974—was spent. Whether anything can be said about this distribution of the fiscal dividend is the main subject to be discussed in this paper—the implications of the fiscal dividend and its distribution.

Although I intend no program-by-program analysis of government spending, a general description of where the money went is useful. Quite obviously, a major fact was the decline of defense spending relative to the GNP in the period from 1956 to 1973. The decline is important in explaining the rise of other expenditures in that period. The fact that defense spending, relative to the GNP and to total spending, is at a much lower level today than in 1956 and may not decline further is also important in explaining why a continued rise of nondefense spending would create many more problems than it did in the past two decades.

Total defense spending rose from $40.8 billion in 1956 to $78.6 billion in 1973. But in real terms it did not rise at all and, in fact, declined a little over that period. Federal defense purchases of goods and services, roughly deflated (by the GNP deflator for total federal purchases, in which defense is the dominant component), declined by almost 8 percent. Total defense spending, deflated in the same way,

---

[1] Joseph Pechman and Emil M. Sunley, Jr., "Inflation Adjustment for the Individual Income Tax," in Henry J. Aaron, ed., *Inflation and the Income Tax* (Washington, D.C.: Brookings Institution, 1976), p. 159.

declined less, by about 3 percent, because of the strong rise of retirement pensions.

As a share of GNP in current dollars, defense spending declined from 9.7 percent in 1956 to 6.0 percent in 1973. This decline was, of course, irregular, and was interrupted by the Vietnam War. But even at the height of the Vietnam War, the defense share of GNP was still lower than it had been in 1956.

The decline in the defense share of GNP was equal to almost 40 percent of the rise of nondefense spending as a share of GNP. That is, if defense spending had not fallen relative to GNP, the rise of nondefense spending as a share of GNP would have had to be 40 percent smaller than it actually was unless there had been higher taxes or bigger deficits. In 1956 defense spending was about two-thirds as large as nondefense spending. Thus, cutting defense spending in half would have permitted an increase of one-third in nondefense spending without any increase in total spending. By 1973 defense spending had declined to only one-fourth of nondefense spending; cutting defense spending in half from that level would only permit an increase of one-eighth in nondefense spending. The possibilities of financing increases in nondefense spending out of declining defense spending had obviously diminished greatly.

Expenditures for social insurance rose from $10.7 billion in 1956 to $83.5 billion in 1973, accounting for 24 percent of the rise in total spending and 28 percent of the rise in nondefense spending. Even allowing for the rise of prices, social insurance expenditures were four and one-half times as high in 1973 as in 1965. They had risen from 2.5 percent of GNP to 6.4 percent and from 10.2 percent to 20.6 percent of total government spending.

The largest part of the increase in social insurance spending was in the largest program—Old-Age, Survivors, and Disability Insurance (OASDI). Expenditures for OASDI were already over 50 percent of all social insurance expenditures in 1956 and rose faster than the rest combined so that by 1973 OASDI accounted for over 60 percent of total social insurance spending. The big increase in OASDI, as already noted, was partly the result of the aging of the program, and partly the result of new legislation raising benefits, some of which were intended to keep up with the cost of living and some of which went beyond it. There were two other major elements in the rise of social insurance expenditures. One was a new program, Medicare, which began in 1966 and had exceeded $10 billion by 1973 (and $16 billion by 1975). The other was civil employees pensions and other insurance benefits, which rose from about $2 billion to about $14 billion.

The big rise of social insurance expenditures was more than matched by an increase in the receipts of social insurance funds. In 1956 these funds had an excess of receipts—from contributions and investment income—of about $4 billion. By 1973 that surplus had increased to almost $18 billion. When we look at all government funds combined we see only a slight increase in the surplus from 1956 to 1973—from $5.2 billion to $6.3 billion. But this was the result of a large increase in the surplus of the social insurance funds, just noted, and a swing of the other funds from a surplus of $1.3 billion to a deficit of $11.7 billion.

The surpluses of the insurance funds accumulated during this period and earlier were invested in securities (mainly government securities) which provided substantial income. The rise of investment income accounted for more than half of the increase in the social insurance surplus in the period under review. But even without this revenue there would have been an increase in the surplus from $2.3 billion to $8.0 billion.

During the entire period 1956 through 1973, the social insurance funds ran a surplus of $129 billion while the other government funds ran a deficit of $179 billion. But the truth is that both the social insurance funds and the other funds were in deficit. While the social insurance funds collected as much as they paid out, and more, they did not collect enough to take care of the liabilities they were incurring for future benefit payments. Benefit levels were being promised for the future that could only be financed, when the future came, by much higher tax rates on the generation then employed. The fact that the insurance funds operated on a pay-as-you-go basis concealed the fact that benefit increases were enacted without having to pass the test of the willingness of the prospective beneficiaries to pay for them. At the same time, the consolidation of the social insurance funds with other government accounts, at least at the federal level, concealed the size of the deficits being run in the other funds.

Although social insurance expenditures rose more, in percentage terms, than other nondefense expenditures, the latter category was initially much bigger and contributed more to the increase of total spending. From 1956 to 1973, nondefense spending, other than for social insurance, equalled 63 percent of the increase in total spending and 72 percent of the increase in total nondefense spending.

One critical aspect of the rise in nondefense spending outside the social insurance funds was the changing relation between the federal government and the states and localities. The share of these expenditures made by the federal government directly declined from 35 percent to 29 percent. The share that the federal government paid for rose from 41 percent to 46 percent. The difference, of course, was in federal grants-in-aid to the states and localities. These grants increased from $3.2 billion in 1956, to $10.8 billion in 1965 and $40.2 billion in 1973. They amounted to 9.3 percent of total general fund expenditures of state and local governments in 1956, 15.0 percent in 1965 and 23.2 percent in 1973.

Before 1972 these federal grants were all allotted to programs specified by the federal government and they almost all required matching funds by the recipient governments, in proportions varying from program to program. General revenue sharing, which provided federal money to states and localities without strings or matching requirements, began in 1972 and accounted for $7.1 billion in funds in 1973. But in that year conventional grants-in-aid by the federal government still provided 19.1 percent of all state and local general fund expenditures.

As already noted, the combined federal, state, and local governments, excluding the social insurance funds, had a total deficit of $179 billion from 1956 through 1973. Of this total deficit, $136 billion was the deficit of the federal government and $43 billion that of the states and localities. The states and localities ran deficits in every year from 1956 through 1971. They were usually small and showed no strongly rising trend. In thirteen of those sixteen years, the combined state and local deficit was between $2 billion and $4 billion, and the largest deficit was $5.8 billion. The average annual deficit for the period was $3.3 billion. Then in 1972 and 1973, the state and local governments swung into surplus—$5.6 billion in 1972 and $4.1 billion in 1973. These were years of large increases in federal grants-in-aid, from $29 billion in 1971, to $37.5 billion in 1972 and $40.6 billion in 1973 (including small amounts of grants for national defense). The unusual surpluses of 1972 and 1973 may reflect a lag in keeping up with this flow of money, which included untied revenue sharing.

The federal deficits were much more variable in size than those of the state and local governments, and responded more to economic fluctuations and to the Vietnam War. There was also a trend to larger deficits. In 1956 there was a surplus (excluding social insurance funds) of $3.7 billion. By 1965 this had turned into a deficit of $1.5 billion, and by 1973 the deficit had grown to $15.8 billion. This $19.5 billion swing from deficit to surplus was partly offset in the consolidated accounts by an increase of $7 billion in the surplus in the federal social insurance funds.

While the federal government was running a deficit of $136 billion (excluding social insurance funds) it was making grants to states and localities totalling $273 billion. There was widespread support for this action at that time. It was thought that since the federal government had the growing revenue sources and the states and localities had the growing expenditure requirements, the federal government ought to share some of its increasing revenues with the lower levels of government. The federal government did that and more. It transferred to the states and localities not only part of its increasing revenues but also part—or all—of its increased borrowing. Thus, the federal government took over much of the burden of borrowing from the states and localities. This was significant, because if the lower levels of government had been required to do their own borrowing, they would have run into problems of credit worthiness (as some of them did anyway). The federal government encountered no such limit, at least if credit worthiness is defined as the assured ability to convert debt into dollars.

Education was the largest single object of nondefense expenditures, outside the social insurance funds, during this period, and its share increased from about 25 percent to about 30 percent. If expenditures for public assistance, relief and other welfare, health and hospitals (including Medicaid), and housing and community development are lumped together as assistance mainly directed to low-income people, they constituted a major category, rising more rapidly than education and beginning to rival it in size by 1973. At the same time some of the "old"—that is, early postwar—programs, such as transportation (mainly highways), veterans benefits, and international affairs, were clearly declining in share of the total spending. These changes are shown in Table 2.

The changing distribution of government expenditures among functions was mirrored in the changing distribution among recipients, notably in the division between expenditures for the purchase of goods and services and expenditures for transfers to persons. The relative decline in defense spending was especially important in this respect because over 90 percent of defense expenditures was for the purchase of goods and services as compared with about 20 percent

Table 2

FEDERAL, STATE AND LOCAL EXPENDITURES BY
FUNCTION AS PERCENT OF TOTAL NONDEFENSE,
NON-SOCIAL-INSURANCE EXPENDITURES

	1956 (percent)	1973 (percent)
Education	24.7	30.2
Public assistance, relief, et cetera	7.2	11.8
Health and hospitals	5.9	8.5
Housing and community development	a	1.5
Space	—	1.3
Central administration	7.4	8.6
Transportation	13.7	8.8
Interest[b]	9.7	6.3
Veterans benefits	8.9	5.3
International affairs	4.1	1.4
Agriculture	4.7	1.8
All other	13.7	14.5
Total	100.0	100.0

[a] Less than 0.05 percent.

[b] These figures are net of interest received, including interest received by social insurance funds. If the interest received by the social insurance funds were added back to the interest total, and to total expenditures, the share of interest would be 12.4 percent in 1956 and 10.0 percent in 1973, and all the other shares would be slightly reduced.

Source: Calculated from *National Income and Product Accounts of the United States, 1929-74, Statistical Tables* (U.S. Department of Commerce, Bureau of Economic Analysis), and *Survey of Current Business,* July 1976.

of all other federal expenditures. A very large percentage of all state and local expenditures—over 90 percent—was for the purchase of goods and services.

Between 1956 and 1973, purchases of goods and services declined from 76.0 percent to 66.6 percent of total government spending. This decline was concentrated in the federal government, where purchases fell from 66.9 percent to 45.5 percent of the total (excluding grants-in-aid). In this period total federal, state, and local government purchases (in nominal terms) rose from 18.9 percent of GNP to 20.6 percent, as the decline of defense purchases relative to GNP was matched by a rise in state and local purchases. Federal nondefense purchases also rose relative to GNP but remained small throughout the period—1.4 percent of GNP in 1956 and 2.2 percent in 1973. This included the cost of the entire nondefense federal payroll, which in 1973 amounted to only 1.2 percent of GNP.

Transfer payments to persons rose sharply, from 4.1 percent of GNP in 1956 to 8.7 percent in 1973, and almost all of this increase was in the social insurance programs. Transfer payments through other programs rose from 1.7 percent of GNP to 2.5 percent. (In the national income amounts, state expenditures for Medicaid are considered a purchase rather than a transfer payment. These expenditures amounted to about 0.6 percent of GNP in 1973.)

Government is a producer of output, or at least is so reckoned in the national income accounts. Of course, to measure the value of the output of government is difficult since the output is not sold. By convention the output of government is valued at its cost, which is essentially the cost of the government payroll. Looked at in that way, the output of government rose from 8.7 percent of GNP in 1956 to 9.8 percent in 1965 and 11.4 percent in 1973. All of the increase was in the payrolls of state and local governments. In constant dollars the output of government declined a little relative to GNP, from 12.9 percent in 1956 to 11.2 percent in 1973. This is because the conventional assumption in the national income accounts is that, except for changes in the composition of employment by grades, productivity in the government sector is constant, rather than rising as in most other sectors.

As noted above (Table 1) the rise in total government spending was almost exactly matched by a rise in government receipts during the 1956-1973 period. One-fourth of the increase in receipts came from additional social insurance contributions but these accounted for almost all of the increase in receipts relative to GNP. That is, whereas other receipts combined rose only a little faster than GNP, social insurance receipts rose much faster.

Personal taxes rose relative to the GNP, from 9.4 percent in 1956 to 11.5 percent in 1973, or in terms of earned personal income (personal income less transfers plus social security contributions) they rose from 12.5 percent to 15.5 percent in those years. Most of this increase was at the state level, and resulted from increases in tax rates and the adoption of the income tax by additional states as well as the process of growth and inflation. At the federal level, there was only a slight increase, from 11.1 percent of earned personal income in 1956 to 11.7 percent in 1973. This was entirely due to the impact of growth and inflation on the progressive tax system, as rates were reduced during the period and a number of other revenue-reducing changes were made in the law.

Corporate profits taxes fell during this period, from 5.2 percent of GNP in 1956 to 3.7 percent in 1973. This was mainly the result of the decline in profits as a share of the GNP, but the effective tax rate on book profits also declined slightly, from 45.2 percent in 1956 to 42.1 percent in 1973. This is explained by changes in the federal tax laws, which lowered the nominal tax rate, increased depreciation allowances and introduced the investment tax credit. State and local corporate profits taxes, although always quite small compared with the federal corporate taxes, rose a little relative to the GNP and to profits. Adjusting profits for inflation in inventory valuations and depreciation would have had little effect up to 1973. But in 1974 and 1975 these adjustments made a substantial difference as corporate taxes rose sharply as a proportion of inflation-adjusted profits but not of book profits as conventionally reported.

The Significance of Rising Expenditures

With this background let us now return to the attitudes expressed at the outset regarding this trend of rising government expenditures. One view was that no defensible opinion could be formed about government expenditures in terms of aggregates, as presented in the preceding pages. On the contrary, one must consider each program on its own merits, deciding whether its benefits are worth its costs, and allowing the total budget to be determined by the addition of all of the programs which, when considered individually, pass the cost-benefit test.

It seems to me that this is an unnecessarily and impossibly restrictive view, and not one with which we can or do operate. I would not maintain the converse, that a satisfactory judgment can be made about the total level of expenditures without consideration of the separate programs composing this total. It is neither satisfactory nor practical to consider each program individually without reference to the total budget. Each expenditure decision, if of significant size, has economic, social, and ethical implications that are not peculiar to the particular decision, and that depend on the overall size of the government's budget.

The more general considerations might, in principle, be factored into each particular decision. In that case, it would still be necessary to formulate some general view of the costs involved in expanding the budget in total, and judgments on that subject would be relevant. But in practice it is not realistic to operate in that way. There has to be a division of labor between the people who make the specific decisions and those who evaluate the overall situation. The people who do the former are not capable of the latter or indeed responsible for it. In fact, budget making proceeds from both directions, from the general and from the particular. Guidelines are set for total expenditures, on the basis of some judgments about the appropriate size of the total. Decisions are made about particular programs within the limits set by those guidelines, and cost-benefit analysis used, as far as it will go, in comparing the relative merits of different programs within that total. If, as often happens, programs for which there seems to be a strong case cannot be accommodated within the specified total, then both the total and the programs should be reevaluated.

This two-way approach has been standard in the executive branch of the federal government for a long time. One of the merits of the recent reform of the congressional budget process was to introduce such an approach at that level of government. Congress now makes a decision about total expenditures, and expenditures for major categories, before it examines all the claims for specific programs. This means not that the contents of the budget are ignored at that point, but only that a preliminary judgment is made about the total, as such, with only general information about the individual programs. Thereafter, a strong presumption exists against exceeding the targets for the total, although the total may be exceeded if examination of the specifics reveals a compelling case for doing so.

Another example of this kind of thinking was Mr. Carter's statement during the 1976 campaign that he intended to prevent total federal spending from growing to a point where it represented a bigger share of the GNP. He was obviously not summarizing his conclusions about every item in the budget. Nevertheless, the statement revealed a position that was helpful to the voters in judging him.

It does, therefore, appear to be highly relevant to reach an opinion about the trend of total government spending, while recognizing that such an opinion by itself would not be conclusive in deciding on the claims of particular government functions. For example, I might decide that the rise of spending from 25 percent to 31 percent of GNP was unfortunate, and a further rise would be still more unfortunate, but I might be quick to support a rise to 50 percent if that seemed reasonably productive in defending the nation against foreign enemies.

The fact that expenditure decisions, in total and in particular, are made in a "democratic process" is not a reason for accepting them as immune from evaluation, let alone criticism. In the end there is no defensible appeal from the democratic process, but it is always open to question whether the process has been guided by accurate information and analysis, and then to try to improve the situation in that respect. We also have to ask whether the decision-making process has actually been democratic in the sense of evaluating all the interests and opinions that have a legitimate claim to representation. That is the kind of question that gave rise to the reform of the executive budget process sixty years ago, and of the congressional budget process three years ago. But surely these reforms did not exhaust the possibilities for improvement.

One of the most serious issues about the trend of government spending is whether it came out of a process that was truly democratic, and whether there is in fact, any process that would be democratically accepted and that would yield a different outcome. Probably that is the only discussable issue in the end. If an economist could show that the increase of government spending in the past twenty years had reduced the real income of every individual in the country by 10 percent, that would still not be conclusive evidence against it unless it could also be shown that the people had not taken the information into account in making their decision to increase spending. Much of the discussion that follows will focus on the processes that affect the total spending outcome.

Not much sustenance is to be derived today from Wagner's Law of the rising share of government spending in the national income. Even if it were a law that as societies grow and interdependence and externalities increase, the need for government intervention rises, that would tell us little about where we stand today. Wagner did not tell us what our ultimate destination is—it is presumably not a government which spends 100 percent of the GNP—or how fast we should get there. In 1929 government expenditures in the United States were 10 percent of GNP. While Wagner's Law might tell us that they should now be more than 10 percent, it does not tell us whether they should be 11 percent, 30 percent, or 50 percent.

Moreover, Wagner's Law may not be relevant to us at all. As affluence and educational attainment rise one might expect a coincident rise in the ability of individuals to do for themselves what was once the function of government. Much of the increase of government spending in the past twenty years—for example, for social insurance and education—has been of a kind that might have been more and more within the scope of private budgets as average incomes rise.

The Economic Consequences of Increased Spending

The foregoing arguments for accepting the increase of government spending are not, in my opinion, convincing. On the other hand, the common arguments about the adverse economic consequences of an increase in the fraction of the national income devoted to government spending are hard to verify, at least from American experience of the past two decades.

The classical proposition about the economic evils of large government spending is that of Colin Clark. He argued, in the early 1950s, that dire consequences would follow if government expenditures exceeded 25 percent of the gross national product. The particular dire consequence he had in mind was inflation. This result was to be expected whether or not the enlarged budget was kept in balance.

Writing in 1965, Professor James Buchanan, no enthusiast for big budgets, appraised this proposition as follows:

> Since the Korean War, total public spending, federal and state-local, in the United States has remained reasonably stable as a percentage of national product, at approximately 30 percent. Inflationary results have not been observed. Any modern treatment of the critical limit hypothesis would, therefore, have to revise the figure upwards from the 25 percent initially suggested. The institutions and the behavior pattern in the United States have, at least in part, adjusted to the current share of GNP taken up collectively.
>
> The useful content of the hypothesis seems to lie in its concentration on the institutional adjustment process in the socio-political structure that must be taken into account in any long-range predictions of the effects of changes in budgetary size. If, for example, there should take place a sudden or dramatic shift from a 30 percent to a 40 percent share of GNP utilized by government, the very institutional fabric would undergo changes, and the inflationary consequences predicted in the hypothesis would be likely to occur. [2]

---

[2] James M. Buchanan, *The Public Finances* (Homewood, Ill.: Richard D. Irwin, Inc., 1965), p. 83.

Since this was written, of course, we have had a further increase in government's share of GNP and we have had substantial inflation. Does this mean that Clark's prediction, as amended by Buchanan, has come true?

Actually, our experience has not been sufficient to test the proposition that a big increase in expenditures balanced by increased revenues would be inflationary. Although there was a surplus of $6.3 billion in all governments combined in 1973, the terminal year for most of my comparisons, there were large deficits in most of the inflationary years that followed 1965. This raises a number of questions. Were the deficits the result of the rise of expenditures? Would the deficits have caused the inflation without the accompanying speed-up in the growth of the money supply? Did the deficits cause the inflationary increase of the money supply?

I discussed these questions in last year's volume of these essays,[3] and while the conclusions of that discussion were tentative, I can do no better than summarize them here.

Except during the years of rising expenditures for the Vietnam War, the growth of expenditures did not cause the deficit. The Vietnam War expenditures rose so fast, and the political obstacles to acknowledging the cost and mobilizing support to raise the required taxes were so great, that it was difficult to keep the budget in balance. That there would have been deficits of anything like the size we experienced from 1966 through 1968 without the Vietnam War is extremely unlikely. But the reverse of this situation occurred in 1971, 1972, 1975, and 1976. In those years it was nearer the truth to say that we had the spending because we wanted the deficits rather than that we had the deficits because we wanted the spending. The deficits were wanted to stimulate the economy, and spending was a way to get the deficits. (Political officials would not have put the matter just this way, but that was the implication of their position.) Nor did the deficits occur because of an inability to raise taxes to cover urgently needed expenditures. On the contrary, taxes were also being cut. If these deficits were inflationary it was because of a miscalculation of the value of deficits under the circumstances, not because of runaway expenditures.

Whether the deficits would have been inflationary without the accompanying monetary expansion raises persistently unsolved questions of economic theory. On the principle that everything matters,

---

[3] Herbert Stein, "Fiscal Policy: Reflections on the Past Decade," in William Fellner, ed., *AEI Studies on Contemporary Economic Problems, 1976* (Washington, D.C.: American Enterprise Institute, 1976).

my own view is that the deficits themselves—or, more precisely, the increases in the deficits—would have been inflationary but not persistently so, and that they probably would not have been on a very large scale except during the Vietnam War when the economy was at a high level.

The monetary expansion of the past ten years was not necessitated by, or even strongly motivated by, the contemporary deficits. Except possibly in early 1966, the Federal Reserve was not under pressure from the administration to help finance its deficits. The most rapid monetary expansion came when interest rates were relatively low and the Federal Reserve was not required to expand the money supply in order to maintain a desirable pattern of rates. If monetary and fiscal policies were overexpansive at the same time, it was because both the monetary and the fiscal authorities were looking at the same information and making the same mistakes, not because the fiscal policy was forcing the monetary policy. Our experience in 1975 showed the ability of the Federal Reserve to restrain monetary growth in the presence of an enormous budget deficit.

There is nothing in economic theory, or in the experience of the past twenty years, to suggest that if the ratio of government expenditures to GNP had risen steadily at the average rate of 1956 to 1973, and if the government surplus had been steady except for automatic variations due to economic fluctuations, this course of events would have been inflationary because of the creation of excess demand. Of course, we did not follow that course. We had some sharp increases of expenditure, as in the period of the Vietnam War, and we had some highly variable deficits, due either to these sharp increases or to an excessively ambitious attempt to deal with recessions. Whatever inflationary consequences were created should not be attributed either to the level, or average rate of increase, of government spending.

There is another view about the relation between budgetary growth and inflation that finds the connection on the side of supply rather than demand. One version of this view raises the possibility of "tax push," a phenomenon in which an increase in taxes leads workers and other suppliers of resources to insist upon increases in pretax earnings to compensate for any increase in their taxes. If the government in its turn insists upon maintenance of the real value of its taxes, this could lead to an endlessly inflationary process.

This kind of theory, in which any reduction in the rate of increase of real incomes causes a round of inflation, may have some explanatory value but only for a temporary period until expectations become adapted to the new reality. Unless expectations do become adjusted we cannot explain why our present expectations are not still dominated by the countless millenia in which real incomes did not rise at all.

If the proportion of real income taken in taxes continuously rises, and the rate of growth of productivity—or real income before taxes—is constant, the rate of growth of real income after taxes would be continuously diminishing. The attempt to maintain the recently experienced rate of growth of after-tax incomes could be continuously inflationary. But if that went on for long, people would come to recognize that the rate of growth of after-tax real incomes was declining and would accept that.

In any case, the theory has little relevance to the United States experience of the past two decades because the rise in tax burdens was relatively small. From 1956 to 1965, real weekly spendable earnings, as estimated by the Bureau of Labor Statistics, rose at an annual rate of 1.4 percent (in private nonagricultural employment). In the period 1965 to 1973, the average annual increase was 0.5 percent. On the theory just discussed the attempt of workers to make up some of the lost 0.9 percent per annum may have contributed to the inflation of the second period. But of the lost 0.9 percent, only 0.2 percent was due to the increase of taxes and social security contributions. And almost all of that was in social security contributions, which the worker may not regard as a total loss since it helps to buy future benefits. So if the attempt of workers to continue their earlier rate of real wage increase was a factor in the inflation of 1965-1973, it was a relatively minor factor.

Another view connecting the growth of government spending and inflation has to do with the presumed effects of spending on production. The argument is that the expansion of government spending slows the growth of real output and that this causes inflation. Why a slower growth of real output should cause inflation is not clear, unless it is assumed that the growth of nominal demand is unaffected, which is an unrealistic assumption. After all, countries can have a lot of inflation with a rapid rate of growth—Japan, for example—and other countries can have little inflation with little growth.

A temporary connection between a lower growth rate and inflation can be sought in the theory discussed above. In this case, society might attempt to continue rates of real income increase, which had existed during an earlier time of faster growth and this would force up costs at an inflationary rate. But presumably, society would in time become accustomed to the lower growth rate and the inflationary consequences, if there had been any, would end.

This brings us to the question (which is important in itself whether or not it helps to explain inflation) of the effect of increased government spending on the rate of economic growth. There is a distinct difference between inflation and growth in that the increase of the inflation rate is obvious whereas a slowdown of the growth rate is not.

The argument that increased government spending, as a share of GNP, slows down the growth rate of real output runs along familiar lines. The higher taxes needed to finance the higher spending would weaken incentives to work and to invest, and would also absorb funds that otherwise would have been saved and invested. If the government borrows to finance its expenditures, that will crowd out private investment. A more recent version of this view is that the absorption of productive resources by the government cuts the supply of resources available to produce investment goods and marketable consumption goods, which will reduce private investment especially, since workers will resist reducing their consumption of marketable goods.[4] Another aspect to be considered is that increased government spending absorbs workers into public employment, where productivity is low and growing slowly if at all, and that this restrains the growth of total output.

None of these processes shows up clearly in the American experience. No "stagnation" of growth was evident during the period of high and rising government expenditures. From 1929 to 1956, real output in the United States grew at an annual rate of 2.8 percent. From 1956 to 1965, the real growth rate was 3.7 percent, and from 1965 to 1973, it was again 3.7 percent. Of course, real output declined in 1974 and 1975 and even the subsequent recovery in 1977 led to only a small increase in real growth between 1973 and 1977. But, as the paper by Geoffrey H. Moore in this volume shows, this was a cyclical phenomenon and it throws no light on the trend of output in the United States. For what they are worth, estimates of the future growth of potential output in the United States are close to the rate achieved in 1956 to 1973 and well above our previous trend.

One of the principal influences on the rate of economic growth is the expansion of the labor supply. The proportion of the population over sixteen years of age that was in the labor force was almost exactly the same in 1973 as in 1956. This does not suggest that taxes had a negative effect on the labor supply. There was some reduction

---

[4] This thesis is developed with respect to Great Britain in Robert Bacon and Walter Eltis, *Britain's Economic Problem* (London: The Macmillan Press, Ltd., 1976).

in the labor force participation of males, offset by a rise in the labor force participation of females. It might be argued that independent sociological and technological forces were causing the increases in the participation of females, whereas taxes, or taxes and transfers taken together, were discouraging the participation of males. But in actuality, the reduction in the participation of males was due to increased retirement among men over sixty-five, partly because of an increase in their relative numbers and partly because of earlier retirement. It is probably reasonable to expect this trend in an economy of rising affluence where more people can afford to retire at an earlier age. Most people provided for their retirement through the social security system but it should not be assumed that in the absence of social security, people would not have made other provisions. Probably the requirement of the social security system that limits the earnings of retirees receiving benefits encourages more retirement than might occur under a private system. This requirement is an effort to hold down costs, which suggests, in this case at least, that more government spending might increase the supply of labor.

A priori arguments about the effects of taxes on the labor supply have always been inconclusive. Income taxes, and most other kinds of taxes, reduce the taxpayer's total income and also reduce his net return from working. Reducing his total income would be expected to make him work more, whereas reducing the net return from working would tend to make him work less, and there is no way to tell theoretically which effect will dominate. Empirical studies in the United States at least have not solved this problem. Recent experiments to test the effects of a negative income tax have not found a significant deterrent to working, and this was also true of earlier studies of upper-income people. It should be recalled that we are talking about an increase in tax burdens on earned personal income which, aside from the social insurance contributions, was not dramatic —from 12.5 percent to 15.5 percent. The social insurance contributions have the special feature of yielding a benefit to many workers, which may moderate their adverse effects on work incentives. It used to be thought that the main disincentive effect of the income tax would be found among high-paid professionals and executives who faced in the earlier postwar years a marginal federal income tax rate of 70 percent. The maximum rate has since been reduced to 50 percent.

There is evidence that the "natural" rate of unemployment—the rate that would prevail in stable conditions—has increased during the past decade, and that would be a factor tending to reduce the labor supply. This development is discussed elsewhere in this volume by Phillip Cagan. Apparently, it has many causes, one of which may be the tax and transfer system, notably the unemployment compensation system. The size of this effect is uncertain and much disputed, but is hardly likely to exceed 1 percent of the labor force.

It would probably be an outside estimate to say that the effect of the increase of government taxes and expenditures between 1956 and 1973—mainly through its effects on retirement and unemployment—was to reduce the labor supply in the latter year 2 percent from what it would otherwise have been. If those lost workers had been of average productivity, that would have reduced the annual rate of GNP growth between the two years from 3.8 percent to 3.7 percent.

Effects of the growth of the budget on private savings are equally difficult to ascertain. The ratio of gross private saving to GNP in years of high employment has been very stable for a long time despite enormous changes in taxes, government expenditures, and other factors. This stability continued in the period reviewed here. Gross private saving was 16.3 percent of GNP in 1956, 16.7 percent in 1965, and 16.1 percent in 1973. It may be argued that what counts for growth is not gross private saving but net private saving. This is somewhat less stable, but does not reveal any adverse trend over the period as a whole. Net private saving as a fraction of net national product was 7.7 percent in 1956, 9.1 percent in 1965 and 8.3 percent in 1973.

The allocation of the national output among major categories of use, when the economy was at high employment, was also remarkably stable:

Table 3
PERCENT OF GNP IN CONSTANT (1972) DOLLARS

	1956	1965	1973
Personal consumption expenditures	60.8	60.3	62.2
Business fixed investment	9.7	10.3	10.6
Residential construction	4.8	4.7	4.8
Inventory change	0.9	1.2	1.3
Net exports	1.1	0.9	0.6
Total government purchases	22.8	22.6	20.4
Federal	(12.8)	(10.9)	7.8
State and local	(9.9)	(11.8)	12.6
Total	100.0	100.0	100.0

Source: Calculated from *National Income and Product Accounts of the United States, 1929-74*, Statistical Tables (U.S. Department of Commerce, Bureau of Economic Analysis), and *Survey of Current Business*, July 1976.

The stability in the share of business fixed investment is particularly important for assessing the effects of the budget on growth. It should be recalled, of course, that we are dealing with a period in which the effective rate of corporate profits taxation was stable.

The preceding discussion does not show that the growth of government spending and taxes had no adverse effects on economic growth during the period 1956 to 1973. Possibly there were such effects, offset by other developments, and the rate of growth of the economy might well have been larger if government spending and taxes had risen less rapidly. However, any proof of that thesis would require a much more elaborate investigation of the sources of economic growth in the United States than anyone has so far conducted. But in my opinion the evidence suggests that the effects are at least uncertain and probably small.

How Did the Budget Get so Big?

If it is correct that the increase of government spending retarded growth of output insignificantly, if at all, the effect of the increased spending was to take a larger share of income away from those who earned it and either give it to other people or return it to the earners in a form that the government, not the earners, chose. One could take the position that the national income is the common property of the society, which the government is entitled to dispose of as it considers best. I do not think this position has general support in this country. I think the generally accepted view is that income is the property of those who earn it and that there is a presumption in favor of the owner's right to use it as he wishes, a presumption that can be overridden only in case of extraordinary social need.

If that is the prevailing view, how do we explain the growth of government spending and taxing in the past twenty years? One explanation would be that there has been an increase in the extraordinary social needs that government can meet, and an increased recognition of such needs. Another explanation would be that the decision-making process has been biased in favor of a bigger increase of spending than the American people would have found necessary and desirable if the choices had been presented to them in a more open and balanced way.

We started in 1956 with defense expenditures equal to 9.7 percent of the gross national product, which would decline to 6 percent by 1973. We also had a tax system that was collecting 26 percent of the GNP in revenues, which would yield large increases of revenue as the economy expanded. There was a potential for large tax reductions, relative to the GNP, unless nondefense spending grew very rapidly. The question is why there was no tax reduction. Why did the claims of taxpayers for relief receive so little attention relative to the claims for increased spending?

A large part of the answer, in my opinion, is that increased spending always seemed to be a bargain, because it did not have to be matched by an equal decision to tax more. This may be seen by looking separately at the social insurance funds, the other federal funds, and the other state-local funds.

A commitment to higher social security benefits in the future always seemed a bargain because the present workers, who would be the future beneficiaries, would not be asked, either immediately or later, to pay the cost of the increased benefits. The present workers would pay the immediate costs, and even something more, which accounted for the build-up of some reserves in the funds until 1973, but they would not be asked to pay enough to accumulate a fund which, with interest, would cover the benefits being promised them. The difference would be paid by a later generation of workers not present when the decision was made.

Increasing nondefense expenditures, other than social insurance, at the federal level always seemed a bargain because there was a large flow of revenue available for that purpose, without requiring any overt action to raise taxes. This flow came partly from the reduction of defense spending relative to the GNP. It also came from the revenues yielded by growth and inflation. And, given the consolidation of the federal accounts, it came from the surplus in the social insurance funds.

The taxpayers did get some tax reduction out of this; federal taxes, other than social insurance contributions, fell from 16.0 percent of GNP to 13.7 percent. And it is also true that the increase of spending was at the expense of more tax reduction, and in that sense there was a choice between spending more and taxing less. But there is no doubt that forgoing tax reduction is less burdensome on the political decision makers (and therefore less of a restraint on spending) than a requirement to raise taxes would be. Surely federal expenditures would have been less if Congress had faced the need to legislate the whole tax code anew each year.

As previously noted, one of the things the federal government did with its inflow of revenues was to increase its grants-in-aid to the states and localities. Most of this took the form of matching grants. This made increased spending at the state-local level seem attractive, because a dollar of taxes raised at that level might attract another dollar—or another nine dollars, depending on the matching formula— from the federal government.

So the deck was stacked everywhere against the taxpayer and in favor of more spending. This disadvantage might have been offset in part if the taxpayer had been more forcefully represented in the political process. But it is a cliché of government, at the federal level at least, that there are more votes in thirty dams than in $10 billion of tax reduction spread evenly and thinly across the population.

There is no representative of the taxpayers' interest in the executive branch of the federal government, unless the President himself takes on that role. The Treasury deals with taxes, but its interests are in simplification, stability, and closing loopholes—meaning limiting the taxpayers' ability to pay less taxes. The Office of Management and Budget is arrayed on the side of resisting departmental claims for expenditure, but its ambition does not usually extend to cutting expenditures enough to permit tax reduction. In the Congress, the Senate Finance Committee and the House Ways and Means Committee have many functions other than tax legislation, and many of them are more rewarding. A tax reduction bill is likely to earn less gratitude than resentment from people who think they did not get their fair share. And if among the 100 most active lobbies in Washington there is one working on behalf of the average taxpayer, it has not come to my attention in thirty-nine years in that city.

Possibilities for Change

How much less the increase of government spending would have been in the past twenty years if the choice between lower taxes and higher spending had been more explicitly faced, and if the taxpayer interest had been more strongly represented, no one can say. But clearly, we should try to move in that direction. It is hard to argue that the consequence would be inferior budget decisions.

An important step would be to reduce the automatic growth of the revenues at the federal level, so that the government would have to make a more deliberate choice to tax more when it wanted to spend more. I have suggested elsewhere a system of "zero-based taxing," under which all federal tax rates would revert to zero periodically, perhaps every four years, and the government would decide anew the level of taxation.[5]

---

[5] *Wall Street Journal*, January 3, 1977 (editorial page).

That is perhaps too radical an idea to be taken seriously. A minimum move, on the other hand, would be to index the tax system against inflation, so that real revenues would not increase because of a rise of the price level. This idea has been spelled out, with proposals for doing it, in a study by William Fellner, et al.[6] If it had been in effect during the last ten years, it would not necessarily have resulted in less taxes than are in effect today, but the government would not be in the position of seeming to give substantial tax reductions while inflation was restoring all or most of the lost revenue to it. One can think of measures intermediate between this and zero-based taxing that would schedule automatic tax rate reductions unless the government took action to prevent them.

Restoring and accumulating surpluses in the social security trust funds so that more of the costs incurred for the current generation of workers would be paid by the current generation of taxpayers would be desirable. At the least, this would have the merit of correcting the impression that the current generation will get something for nothing, or much for little, and weaken the temptation to enlarge future commitments.

If this is done it would be desirable to separate the federal social security trust funds from the rest of the budget, so that surpluses generated in the trust funds would not automatically become available for expenditure in the other accounts. To make that meaningful, we would have to abandon the idea that the proper size of the combined surplus in the trust accounts and other federal accounts is whatever is needed to stabilize the economy. This is not a logical idea, in any case, as long as monetary policy is a variable. The budget should be managed on the principle that the larger the surplus in the trust accounts, the larger the combined surplus should be. This would not rule out variations in the size of the combined surplus as economic conditions varied.

Decisions would be more balanced if the federal government would slow down the expansion of its grants to the states and localities and transform existing ones to eliminate the matching requirement. The idea that the federal government always has a flow of revenue to share with the states and localities has proved illusory. In effect, the federal government is sharing its unlimited ability to borrow and shielding the lower levels of government from the discipline of the credit market. The matching provision makes expenditures seem worthwhile to the states and localities that might not seem worth-

---

[6] William Fellner, Kenneth W. Clarkson, and John H. Moore, *Correcting Taxes for Inflation* (Washington, D.C.: American Enterprise Institute, 1975).

while if they had to pay for them. Each party, the federal government and the state-local governments, thinks it is getting more than it is paying for.

An Office of Taxpayer Advocacy should be established in the executive branch of the federal government. This is needed much more than an Office of Consumer Advocacy. The consumer is protected mainly by the market and also by several government agencies and lobbies. But the average taxpayer is not protected by the market and has no agency or lobby to defend him. The Office of Taxpayer Advocacy should not be involved in the tax problems of individual taxpayers. Instead it should make the case within government for tax reduction.

The Senate Finance Committee and the House Ways and Means Committee should be relieved of all responsibilities other than that for internal revenue going into the general fund. They would be no longer concerned with social security, revenue sharing, or foreign trade, for example. There should be some important people in the Congress whose public reputation and approval depends only on what they have done for the taxpayer; this should be the role of the leadership of the Finance and Ways and Means Committees.

Claims upon the federal budget are going to be more intense in the next decade than they have been in the preceding two. We have probably come to the end, for a while, of the decline in defense spending as a share of the GNP. There is clear resistance to raising payroll taxes further, and unless there is some change of policy we cannot expect the continued surpluses in the social insurance funds that helped the general funds in the years before 1973. There will not be room for continued rapid growth of nondefense spending with the same cuts in federal taxes we have had in the past. It might seem that the easiest course would be to extract from the federal taxpayer not only the present share of his income but also the enlarged share resulting from a growth of real income and inflation. That should not be allowed to happen by default, simply because we failed to give due weight to the taxpayer's claim to his own income.

MONEY SUPPLY AND THE BUDGET: CURRENT AND FUTURE PROBLEMS OF DEMAND MANAGEMENT

William Fellner

Summary

In deciding on the course of demand-management policy, it is important to take account of observed past regularities linking the money supply—particularly the M_2 stock—to the money GNP. However, these regularities, recently explored in work undertaken at the American Enterprise Institute by the present writer jointly with Dan Larkins, must not be projected into the future mechanically. The regularities developed in an economic environment shaped by the behavior of various other factors, including policy variables. Presumably, the relation between M_2 and money GNP would not continue unmodified if the behavior of other variables changed significantly from that of periods for which the past regularities have been observed. While greater emphasis will be placed here on the qualification involving other variables than is the case in the writings of some authors conventionally regarded as monetarists, considerable significance will be attributed to observed relations that have linked the money stock to the money GNP—considerably more significance than the critics of the monetarist position have attributed to it. At present, it does not seem possible to avoid reliance on personal judgment in appraising the complex consequences of the behavior of the other variables. Their influence does not come through strongly in the usual regressions that make room for the effect of interest rates on the demand for money per unit of income.

I shall conclude that if the policy variables shaping the environment were made to develop appropriately, a monetary policy leading to about a 10 percent increase in M_2 from the last quarter of 1976 to the last quarter of 1977 would have a good chance of leading to a desirable rate of cyclical recovery, including a reduction of the measured unemployment rate by nearly 1 percentage point during the year. Subsequently, money growth should be reduced gradually but consistently to keep us on the way to practical stability of the price level. A good chance of achieving these results is, of course, a far cry from near-certainty of achieving them, but this is the line of policy that at present seems most promising.

As for the economic environment in which monetary policy operates, it seems particularly important to avoid the significant uncertainties and inefficiencies which would result from renewed experimentation with wage and price controls or with types of specific wage-price intervention differing from such controls only in name. Fiscal variables also contribute importantly to shaping the environment, since the relationship between money supply and the money GNP can be modified by these variables. But the new American policy makers made a premature diagnosis when suggesting during the 1976 presidential campaign, and concluding promptly afterwards, that additional fiscal demand stimulus should be applied in 1977 and 1978 in order to have the proper monetary policy produce the desired effects. The Carter administration acted right when, in April 1977, it withdrew the tax-rebate proposal representing a major part of its "stimulus package" for 1977. While this withdrawal did not affect the administration's 1978 package, which was in fact somewhat increased by Congress, it did reduce the 1977 package appreciably. The lesson to be learned from this and from other experiences is that a policy concerned with each successive short period inevitably must rest on very inadequate information and guesswork. The desirable policy line is one guided by longer-run considerations, and a consistent policy of this sort has a good chance of exerting a strong influence also on the short-run behavior of market participants.

Turning to long-run oriented adjustments that would have a desirable effect also on the presumed course of the economy in the near future, a strong case continues to exist for eliminating the automatic increase in the real tax burden that develops in an inflationary period. In such periods, all taxpayers experiencing a rise in the nominal incomes corresponding to given real incomes are moved into higher tax brackets, and this effect is added to the upward tax-push brought about by real growth with a graduated income tax structure. At the same time, in an inflationary period, profit taxes and capital gains taxes are levied on merely nominal, inflationary revaluations of stocks of physical capital and of securities, the real value of which has not risen. Tax adjustments expressing full correction for the pre-

sumptive inflation during 1978 might have cost the Treasury as much as the tax cuts and additional public-employment expenditures that have been adopted for that fiscal year, but the correction for inflation could have been phased in over a period longer than a single year by a rule that would have taken account of the preferences of the taxpayers. The same is true of some other needed tax adjustments. This would have been desirable particularly because at present it seems that the fiscal deficit will increase from 1977 to 1978, after a decline from 1976 to 1977. The case is strong for reducing and gradually eliminating the deficits of the near future while the economy is recovering to the neighborhood of its normal growth path.

Money and Monetarism, Other Variables, and the Objectives of Demand Management

There is no necessary link between (1) the distinctive analytical position which leads "monetarists" to stress the *instrumental role* of money aggregates in influencing aggregate demand, and (2) the convictions of most economists regarded as monetarists about the *objectives* which demand management should try to achieve. Monetarism should presumably be defined with respect to the *first* rather than the second of these criteria, but there nevertheless appears to be some degree of jointness of attitudes concerning (1) and (2). Most economists considered monetarists by the first of the two criteria have all along shown understanding for an essential proposition which relates to the *objectives* of demand-management policy, and which was stressed in the 1976 volume of *Contemporary Economic Problems.* The like-mindedness of monetarists with us in this regard may be considered a fairly well-established fact, though there is no reason to assume that all monetarists (properly defined by our first criterion) agree *or* that all their critics disagree with us on the objectives of demand management.

According to the proposition developed in our 1976 volume on this issue, demand-management policy should aim for objectives defined in terms of *aggregate nominal demand* (money GNP), and the policy should thereby *condition* market expectations to price-level targets which the authorities are determined to enforce by not accommodating lasting deviations from them. This should be done without reliance on administrative wage and price controls which in a Western-type political system are unsuitable for holding down inflationary pressures. The price-level targets must be pursued with consistency and they must be credible; I find it very difficult to imagine that any target other than that of the gradual return to practical price-level stability—illustrated by the period 1951–1965 with its less than 2 percent rate of price increase in the United States—would satisfy this condition. No sustainable gain in employment can be achieved by accommodating inflationary cost and price trends, because such accommodation leads to accelerating inflation, the aftermath of which is a very painful setback. As we suggested earlier, if the markets of a country cannot be made to adjust their cost and price-setting practices to a policy that limits current-dollar effective demand in view of the authorities' price-level objectives—if instead of an adjustment of cost and price trends, a state of chronic "stagflation" develops under such a policy—then that country is likely to be moving toward comprehensively and very uncomfortably controlled economic and political systems at the sacrifice of essential political and economic values. On the way there, such a country may become stranded for a long time in an area of inefficiency and low performance.

Our policy makers have disregarded these propositions for many years following the mid-1960s, and these propositions have been disregarded for even longer, and to an even greater extent, in some countries abroad. While, as was pointed out, many monetarists have shared the views expressed above and on earlier occasions, the label *monetarism* refers not to this question of objectives but to the role of money aggregates in the determination of income flows (the first of the two criteria described at the outset of this section). The label refers to the conviction that unwieldy and all-too-complex analytical frameworks can be conveniently simplified—and can be made useful without significant loss of accuracy—by adopting a monetary policy, the essential implication of which is a stable relation involving the supply of money and the money GNP. However, a stable relation in this sense does not necessarily imply constancy of any ratio of two variables, since a relation between variables may well be more complex than to suggest that specific conclusion.

Monetary policy is an exceedingly important tool of demand management, and its proper conduct clearly depends on how the relationship between the money stock and money GNP is viewed. I shall develop and explain here my suggestions concerning the merits and the limitations of approaches building on a stable relation between monetary aggregates and the money GNP. Basically, the view taken here is that in order to have a reasonable chance of avoiding major instability of the relation between the money supply and the money GNP, we do need to watch other factors, including fiscal variables, that "set the stage" for that relation. Weighing the role of the other factors will, at our present stage of knowledge, inevitably involve reliance on considerations requiring personal judgment, rather than merely using estimates of regression coefficients, and the monetary relations do provide a useful point of departure for the appraisal of prospective aggregate demand.

Shifting the Emphasis from M_1 to M_2

M_1 is the monetary aggregate defined as currency plus demand deposits; M_2 includes additionally the savings accounts and time deposits (other than large-denomination negotiable certificates of deposit, or CDs) held in commercial banks; M_3 includes, in addition to M_2, the deposits in the thrift institutions; and M_5 includes, in addition to M_3, the large-denomination negotiable CDs.[1] The ratio of any of these M aggregates to the GNP is the reciprocal of the "GNP velocity" of the aggregate in question.

The relation of M_1 to the money GNP has been explored in detail by numerous researchers. Reasonably good results have been obtained with analytical constructs (models) that postulated a lowering of the ratio of M_1 to money GNP with a rise in the real GNP and/or with rising short-term interest rates. These models have implied for a rising real GNP a rise in real (price-corrected) M_1 holdings, but they have implied a distinctly smaller than proportionate rise of the real M_1 holdings—hence a reduction of M_1 holdings per unit of GNP. They project, therefore, a tendency of the "GNP velocity" of M_1 to rise along the growth path of the economy. At the same time, the models incorporated constant regression coefficients indicating to what extent the M_1 holdings per unit of GNP would decline for any given real GNP, if, other things equal, interest rates should rise, and to what extent the M_1 holdings per unit of GNP would rise, if interest rates should decline.[2]

In fact, Table 1 and Figure 1 show that M_1 per unit of GNP has declined consistently during the period with which we shall be concerned—from the early 1950s through 1976. The rate of decline of this ratio has varied over this period: It was steep from 1953 to 1966; then for five years there occurred a considerable degree of flattening; and, since then we have experienced a renewed significant dip. At

---

[1] To give an idea of the orders of magnitude at the end of 1976: M_1 amounted to about $310 billion of which about $80 billion was currency; M_2 amounted to about $740 billion; M_3 to about $1,240 billion; and M_5 to about $1,300 billion.

[2] For well-known illustrations, see Stephen M. Goldfeld, "The Demand for Money Revisited," *Brookings Papers on Economic Activity*, 3, 1970, and Jared Enzler, Lewis Johnson, and John Paulus, "Some Problems of Money Demand," ibid., 3, 1973.

Table 1
RELATING M_1 TO SIMULTANEOUS GNP

Year	M_1 per Unit of GNP[a]	Year	M_1 per Unit of GNP[a]
1952	0.361	1965	0.243
1953	0.351	1966	0.232
1954	0.356	1967	0.228
1955	0.337	1968	0.224
1956	0.323	1969	0.221
1957	0.309	1970	0.218
1958	0.308	1971	0.215
1959	0.295	1972	0.209
1960	0.284	1973	0.202
1961	0.280	1974	0.196
1962	0.266	1975	0.191
1963	0.259	1976[b]	0.180
1964	0.252		

[a] Money stock is average for year. GNP is measured at annual rate for the same year.
[b] Preliminary.

some point of this development, M_1 models of the type discussed above, which had earlier shown a fairly good predictive performance, started accumulating an exceedingly poor and worsening record. Just at which stage they started to be misleading depends partly on which specific model we consider and partly on the degree of accuracy on which we insist. Some observers maintain that the models started malfunctioning seriously only during the past two or three years. But in their exploration of M_1 demand functions, Phillip Cagan and Anna Schwartz found indications of a significant change in the values of the parameters, including the coefficients of the income and the interest-rate variables, when longer periods were compared with subperiods following 1965.[3]

Common-sense considerations help to explain why M_1 models of this sort should have gone wrong at some stage of the development reviewed. With the passage of time, savings accounts and time deposits in the commercial banks—other than large-denomination certificates of deposit—have gradually become increasingly close sub-

[3] See Phillip Cagan and Anna J. Schwartz, "Has the Growth of Money Substitutes Hindered Monetary Policy?" *Journal of Money, Credit and Banking* (May 1973).

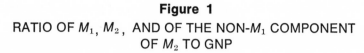

Figure 1

RATIO OF M_1, M_2, AND OF THE NON-M_1 COMPONENT
OF M_2 TO GNP

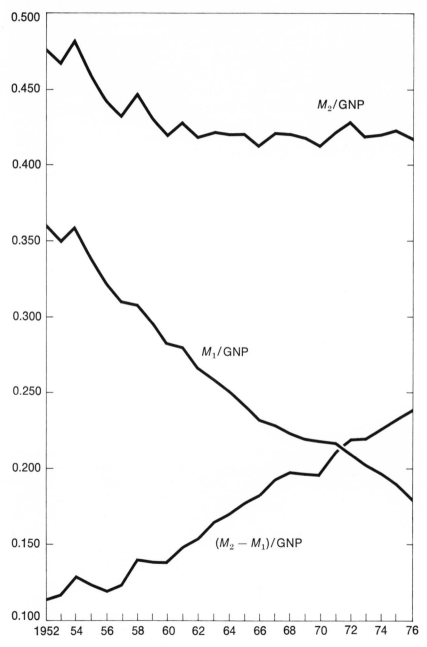

stitutes of the non-interest-bearing deposits (demand deposits) included in M_1. Time deposits and savings accounts in the commercial banks are included in the money aggregate defined as M_2, but not in M_1. Hence, regularities earlier observed for M_1 have become disturbed by the fact that, from the depositors' point of view, the difference between the "moneyness" of M_2 and that of M_1 has been significantly reduced. Depositors have gradually become more and more confident of not facing any serious risk of seeing their checks bounce if they own interest-bearing deposits in the same commercial bank as that in which they keep their demand deposits. The prompt transformation of savings accounts into demand deposits (checking accounts) has become costless and practically effortless. This is rather generally recognized and stressed in recent writings.

However, we feel that another change has also acquired considerable importance in providing incentives for increasing the ratio of interest-bearing deposits in commercial banks to interest-free deposits, hence in making it advisable that the economist should concentrate his research on the relation of M_2 to GNP rather than on the M_1 relationship. The public is usually willing to make a stronger effort to avoid or to reduce actual losses than to acquire additions to its real wealth. Expressed differently, the disutility of a reduction from 100 to 80 is greater than the disutility of being denied a 20 percent increase beyond 100. This follows from what in economics is called the principle of diminishing marginal utility. Up to about 1965, the owners of interest-free demand deposits came reasonably close to maintaining intact the real value of their M_1 holdings, though they were, of course, forgoing the addition to their wealth that could be earned on interest-bearing accounts. After 1965, with inflation accelerating, the conviction must have been spreading that, year after year, a continuous reduction of the real value of money holdings was involved in maintaining a stock of M_1. The hope of reducing or eliminating this loss by shifting to interest-bearing deposits must have become a more important objective than had been that of adding to real wealth the amount of the interest that could be earned. To be sure, there has also occurred a gradual increase in the regulated interest rates the commercial banks are allowed to pay on time deposits and savings accounts, and, as we have seen, there has occurred also a substantial increase in the smoothness of transferring money from interest-bearing to checking accounts in the same bank. Yet we should not overlook the fact that the continuous erosion of the real value of any given amount of M_1 must have strengthened the desire to hold M assets in a less costly form. This desire must have increased even if the relative shift to interest-bearing varieties meant that more of the M holdings had to be subjected to a transformation process—to one that has gradually become very smooth—before it could be used directly as means of payment.

It is thus understandable that the performance of models purporting to explain the behavior of M_1 (currency plus demand deposits) should have become increasingly disappointing and that the attention of the observer had to turn increasingly to the behavior of the broader M_2 aggregate, consisting of M_1 plus the interest-bearing deposits in the commercial banks (other than large-denomination CDs). The even broader monetary aggregate defined as M_3—including, in addition to M_2, the deposits in the thrift institutions—also has a legitimate place in monetary analysis. Yet, while institutional and technological developments are conceivable that would ensure a practically costless and effortless transfer of the thrift-institution deposits into checking accounts also, there has so far remained a greater difference in immediate "moneyness" between these deposits and checking accounts than between savings accounts and checking accounts in the same bank. Also, while interest rates paid on commercial-bank time deposits and savings accounts have been rising, the rate-differentials between thrift-institution deposits and interest-bearing commercial-bank deposits (in favor of the former) have been diminishing. As a result of these developments, it has become advisable to have the M_2 aggregate in mind when taking a look at the relationship of the money stock to money GNP.

Good Behavior of a Relation Involving M_2: Its Interpretation and Its Limitations

The "Trendlessness" of M_2 per Unit of GNP. Over the past decade and a half the trend in the M_2 to GNP ratio has been horizontal, that is, the ratio has been "trendless." It is easier to tie in the behavior of this ratio during the period in question with its earlier behavior if we date the period of trend-horizontality from 1962 than if we date it slightly further back. It could be dated alternatively from 1960, but in that case the transition from the preceding period of downward trend to trend-horizontality would be very abrupt. This can be seen from Table 2 and Figure 1 for yearly data and from Table 3 for the quarterly series. The ratio in question is the reciprocal of what is called the GNP velocity of M_2.

For the fourteen-year span 1962 through 1975, the mean value of the M_2 to GNP ratio was 0.421. The average deviation from this

Table 2

RELATING M_2 AND ITS NON-M_1 COMPONENT
TO SIMULTANEOUS GNP

Year	M_2 per Unit of GNP[a]	(M_2-M_1)[b] per Unit of GNP	Year	M_2 per Unit of GNP[a]	(M_2-M_1)[b] per Unit of GNP
1952	0.475	0.114	1965	0.420	0.177
1953	0.468	0.117	1966	0.414	0.182
1954	0.484	0.128	1967	0.422	0.193
1955	0.460	0.123	1968	0.421	0.197
1956	0.444	0.121	1969	0.417	0.196
1957	0.433	0.124	1970	0.413	0.195
1958	0.448	0.140	1971	0.426	0.211
1959	0.433	0.137	1972	0.428	0.219
1960	0.420	0.137	1973	0.420	0.219
1961	0.427	0.147	1974	0.421	0.225
1962	0.420	0.154	1975	0.423	0.232
1963	0.424	0.165	1976[c]	0.416	0.236
1964	0.421	0.169			

[a] All money stocks of the table are averages for year. GNP is measured at annual rate for the same year.

[b] This difference consists of savings accounts and time deposits (other than large CDs) in the commercial banks.

[c] Preliminary.

mean is 0.68 percent in the yearly series. The standard deviation is 0.97 percent of the mean in the same series, and it is 1.19 percent in the quarterly data. The maximum deviation from the mean is a shade less than 2 percent in the yearly and about 3 percent in the quarterly series. Even after the usual revisions of recent data, the 1976 figures are practically certain to remain consistent with the foregoing description.

The average deviation turns out to be larger if we compute it each time from the preceding period's observed value than if we compute it from the entire period's mean value, 0.421. In the former case the average deviation is 1.05 percent in yearly data, in contrast to the 0.68 percent average deviation relative to the 1962–1975 mean.

A value much closer to 0.68 percent is obtained if the average deviation is computed by comparing each year's M_2 per unit of GNP with the mean value of this ratio for the preceding years, starting with 1962. In that case 0.85 percent is obtained for the average deviation. This is worth noting because, during the period 1962–1975, the mean

Table 3

QUARTERLY DATA RELATING M_2 TO SIMULTANEOUS GNP

Year	Quarter	M_2 per Unit of GNP	Year	Quarter	M_2 per Unit of GNP
1952	1	0.475	1961	1	0.432
	2	0.480		2	0.429
	3	0.478		3	0.427
	4	0.467		4	0.422
1953	1	0.463	1962	1	0.419
	2	0.463		2	0.419
	3	0.467		3	0.419
	4	0.477		4	0.422
1954	1	0.481	1963	1	0.424
	2	0.486		2	0.425
	3	0.487		3	0.423
	4	0.480		4	0.423
1955	1	0.470	1964	1	0.419
	2	0.464		2	0.419
	3	0.456		3	0.421
	4	0.451		4	0.426
1956	1	0.450	1965	1	0.422
	2	0.447		2	0.421
	3	0.443		3	0.419
	4	0.437		4	0.419
1957	1	0.433	1966	1	0.416
	2	0.434		2	0.416
	3	0.430		3	0.414
	4	0.436		4	0.411
1958	1	0.448	1967	1	0.415
	2	0.455		2	0.422
	3	0.449		3	0.425
	4	0.441		4	0.425
1959	1	0.439	1968	1	0.423
	2	0.430		2	0.419
	3	0.435		3	0.420
	4	0.428		4	0.424
1960	1	0.415	1969	1	0.423
	2	0.415		2	0.420
	3	0.422		3	0.412
	4	0.429		4	0.411

Table 3 (continued)

Year	Quarter	M_2 per Unit of GNP	Year	Quarter	M_2 per Unit of GNP
1970	1	0.408	1974	1	0.423
	2	0.410		2	0.422
	3	0.413		3	0.419
	4	0.422		4	0.421
1971	1	0.420	1975	1	0.428
	2	0.426		2	0.428
	3	0.428		3	0.420
	4	0.429		4	0.416
1972	1	0.428	1976 [a]	1	0.414
	2	0.427		2	0.415
	3	0.429		3	0.416
	4	0.427		4	0.420
1973	1	0.421			
	2	0.422			
	3	0.421			
	4	0.418			

[a] Preliminary.

value of the entire span was, of course, unknown, while the mean values of the preceding spans were available.

Introducing a brief lag between the M_2 stock and the money GNP slightly lowers the standard deviation of the 1.19 percent for quarterly data, but this results almost entirely from the improvement achieved in specific subperiods in which money creation was significantly reduced or significantly accelerated. In most other subperiods the lagless relation works out better.

A further comment to be added here relates to the sectoral breakdown, which can be undertaken only by very crude methods. To the trendlessness of M_2 per unit of GNP in the economy as a whole there seems to have corresponded a very mildly upward-tilted trend of M_2 per unit of income in the household sector.

With reference to a policy suggestion in the summary introducing this paper, we note that, by preliminary estimates, the economy's overall ratio of M_2 to money GNP was 0.420 in the final quarter of 1976, this ratio being very nearly the same as the average ratio for the period 1962–1975. If the ratio of M_2 to money GNP should remain approximately at this level during 1977, an increase of M_2 by about 10 percent from the last quarter of 1976 to the last quarter of 1977 would be associated with an increase in money GNP of about the same magnitude. This would leave room for an increase in real GNP of close to 5.5 percent and a small reduction of the previous twelve-month period's inflation rate, on the way to a further gradual reduction of the rate of increase of M_2 and inflationary growth. Room would be left for this outcome, but the proportions in which the economy will use up the available effective demand for real growth and price increases in any one year are, of course, not firmly predictable. Even the most consistent anti-inflationary policy would have to be prepared to see oscillations of the inflation rate on the way down.

Regression Analysis of Offsetting Tendencies. One way of trying to explain the horizontality of the M_2 to GNP trend for the economy as a whole is to examine whether the effect of variables that have tended to raise the M_2 to GNP ratio have happened to offset—almost *precisely*—the effect of variables that have tended to lower the ratio. Such an exploration can be based on regression analysis. The regression results, on which we have reported elsewhere in detail,[4] are not entirely negative, but they leave us at best with mixed feelings about their worth. Regression analysis does suggest the possibility that rising interest rates have tended to reduce the M_2 to GNP ratio, and that this has been offset by the contrary effect of one or more of the basic variables that typically rise along the growth path of the economy *or*, conceivably, by the rising uncertainty concerning borrowing opportunities during an inflationary period.

However, the coefficients we have found in some of these regressions do not seem to have an acceptable degree of stability for the decade and a half in question, and other regressions have other undesirable properties (for instance, very low adjustment coefficients which lack plausibility in this context). It is worth noting also that if the trendlessness of the M_2 to GNP ratio over this period is to be explained along these lines—by mutually offsetting forces—the cessation of the forces working in one direction would result in merely a very slow change of this ratio in the other direction. This follows from the estimates of the parameters in the regressions to which we have referred. It is particularly noteworthy that the elasticity of the M_2 to GNP ratio with respect to money-market rates is small, even

---

[4] See William Fellner and Dan Larkins, "Interpretation of a Regularity in the Behavior of M_2," *Brookings Papers on Economic Activity*, 3, 1976.

if the coefficient in question turns out to be statistically significant in these regressions.

Broader Trends: The Shift toward Higher-Yielding M Assets. The post-1960 stabilization of the M_2 to GNP ratio within the ranges explained above may be interpreted more convincingly with reference to broader trends rather than in terms of regressions postulating offsetting effects of the explanatory variables. Soon after World War II, thrift-institution deposits increased their standing as substitutes for deposits in commercial banks, in large part because deposit insurance for thrift-institution deposits was spreading rapidly. Also, these institutions could afford to maintain a rate differential relative to the commercial banks because the demand for mortgage loans was running high and the thrift institutions specialized in the supply of such loans. These changes were stressed in the analysis presented in 1963 by Milton Friedman and Anna Schwartz.[5] In a later contribution, Friedman called attention to the fact that from the early 1960s on there had been a tendency for the ratio of M_2 to money income to remain unchanged.[6] This tendency continued through 1976.

A reasonable interpretation of this regularity suggests keeping in mind the following. After World War II, when thrift-institution deposits (components of M_3 but not of M_2) started increasing, there developed at first a rapid rate of substitution of these deposits for M_2. In the most rapid phase of this substitution process, not only did the public accumulate its entire addition to the M_3 to GNP ratio in the form of thrift-institution deposits, but at the same time it reduced its M_2 to GNP ratio. This phase of the postwar development lasted until the early 1960s. Such substitution processes usually weaken after a while, and the slowing of this process is apparent from the early 1960s on. While the entire addition to the M_3 to GNP ratio has continued to be accumulated in the form of thrift-institution deposits, the M_2 to GNP ratio has not become further reduced. The slowing of the substitution process expressed itself also in a reduced rate of increase in the M_3 to GNP ratio (in fact, even the aggregate defined as M_5, consisting of M_3 plus the large-denomination negotiable CDs, rose less rapidly relative to GNP than had earlier the M_3 aggregate alone). All this is relevant to an understanding of the behavior of the various M aggregates, which can be read from our tables and

---

[5] Milton Friedman and Anna J. Schwartz, *A Monetary History of the United States, 1867-1960* (Princeton: Princeton University Press, for the National Bureau of Economic Research, 1963).

[6] Milton Friedman, "How Much Monetary Growth?" *Morgan Guaranty Survey* (February 1973).

Figure 2
RATIO OF M_3 AND OF M_5 TO GNP

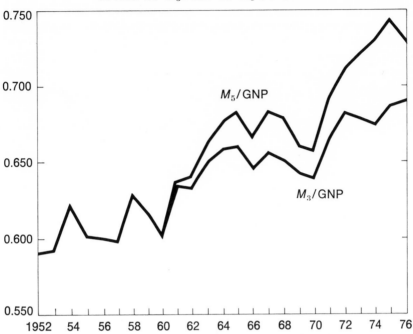

Note: These graphs, showing an upward trend, disclose a tendency of the ratios depicted to decline in cyclical expansions but to rise more in the weak phases of the cycle, so that any decline during an expansion starts from a higher level than on the previous occasion. Relative to their trend, some of the graphs in our other figures also show traces of this tendency.

figures, including Table 4 and Figures 2 and 3. Yet from our present point of view, the essential phenomenon here is that at some stage of the slowing substitution towards the higher-yielding M components, the M_2 to GNP ratio *ceased to decline further.*

This broad interpretation of the observed trends makes a good deal of sense. Such an interpretation does not contradict hypotheses suggesting a balancing of forces that may have worked in opposite directions and may have led to the result that since the early 1960s the M_2 to GNP ratio has remained fairly constant. But the broader interpretation does help us to understand why finer details, including the effects of changes in interest rates, are difficult to identify with much precision.

The Reliability of the M_2 to GNP Ratio as a Guide to Policy. The main question these developments raise for policy makers relates to

Figure 3

RATIO OF THRIFT-INSTITUTION DEPOSITS AND OF
LARGE NEGOTIABLE CERTIFICATES OF DEPOSIT TO GNP

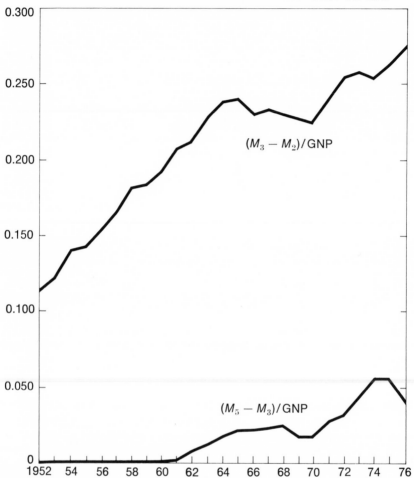

Note: Same as Figure 2.

the degree of confidence that may be placed in obtaining a specific rate of money GNP by letting a specific stock of M_2 come into existence. This is a particularly important question for authorities trying to condition market expectations and cost trends to a desirable behavior of the price level. Such a policy must aim for rates of nominal (current-dollar) GNP which, at the end of an adjustment period, leave no more room than is required for normal growth with practical price

98

Table 4

RELATING M_3, M_5, AND SOME OF THEIR COMPONENTS TO SIMULTANEOUS GNP

Year	M_3 per Unit of GNP[a]	M_5 per Unit of GNP	$(M_3 - M_2)$[b] per Unit of GNP	$(M_5 - M_3)$[c] per Unit of GNP
1952	0.589		0.114	0
1953	0.591		0.123	0
1954	0.623	Same	0.139	0
1955	0.602	as	0.142	0
1956	0.600	M_3/GNP	0.156	0
1957	0.598	through	0.165	0
1958	0.628	1960	0.180	0
1959	0.616		0.183	0
1960	0.613		0.193	0
1961	0.634	0.637	0.207	0.002
1962	0.633	0.640	0.213	0.008
1963	0.650	0.663	0.227	0.013
1964	0.657	0.676	0.236	0.019
1965	0.659	0.681	0.239	0.022
1966	0.645	0.668	0.231	0.023
1967	0.656	0.681	0.234	0.024
1968	0.652	0.677	0.231	0.025
1969	0.643	0.660	0.227	0.017
1970	0.639	0.656	0.225	0.017
1971	0.665	0.693	0.239	0.028
1972	0.682	0.714	0.254	0.032
1973	0.677	0.723	0.257	0.045
1974	0.675	0.731	0.254	0.056
1975	0.687	0.743	0.264	0.056
1976[d]	0.690	0.730	0.274	0.040

[a] All money stocks are averages for year. GNP is measured at annual rate for the same year.

[b] This difference consists of thrift institution deposits.

[c] This difference consists of large negotiable CDs. They were first introduced in 1961.

[d] Preliminary.

stability, such as existed in the United States, for example, in the fourteen-year period preceding the adoption of inflationary policies around 1965. Only by a policy aiming for appropriate constraints expressed in terms of nominal demand will it be possible in the future to avoid a repetition of the mistake of "accommodating" inflationary cost and price trends. "Accommodation," expressing itself in the creation of more nominal demand to make room for observed or projected inflationary trends, has always created an environment in which employers and workers come to anticipate increasingly the consequences of a lax demand policy and in which, therefore, the inflation rate tends to steepen from period to period. While a merely gradual return to noninflationary conditions may also be said to involve accommodation, it is involved at a consistently diminishing rate and merely during a transition period.

Even if a stable relation between M_2 and money GNP could safely be projected into the future, it would have to be remembered that the monetary authority creates reserves and currency—so-called high-powered money—rather than M_2. Yet, of late at least, the Federal Reserve seems to have been fairly successful in regulating reserves in a way that enabled it rather closely to approximate its M_2 targets.[7] The question remains as to the degree of confidence with which we may expect the trendlessness of the relationship between M_2 and money GNP to continue.

Mechanically projecting into the future a horizontal, or any other, trend in the M_2 to GNP ratio is, of course, anything but a safe operation. At the same time, we would be unjustified in disregarding an experience such as the trendlessness of the ratio in question for the past decade and a half. This is so even if basing predictions of money GNP on a relationship involving M_2 is not the only method that has proved reasonably successful over the past years.

Some forecasters using very different methods have, to be sure, also had a fairly good record of forecasting money GNP. For the period 1962 through 1975, the forecasts published in the Annual Reports of the Council of Economic Advisers (CEA) early each year show an average deviation of 1 percent from the money GNP of the calendar year that followed. While the corresponding figure for the deviations of the M_2 to GNP ratio from the mean value of 0.421 was only about 0.7 percent, the results of a simple GNP forecasting exercise based on the M_2 to GNP relationship would have been influenced *additionally* by errors in forecasting the coming year's M_2. Furthermore, for the subperiod following 1966, the CEA forecasts of

---

[7] For 1976, for example, this assumption is borne out by the data found in Table 19, p. 81, of the *Annual Report of the President's Council of Economic Advisers*, Washington, D.C., 1977, provided the Federal Reserve was aiming for the high region of its published M_2 target zone (as was rather generally believed).

money GNP had an average deviation of 0.7 percent, while the average deviation of the M_2 to GNP ratio from the 1965–1975 mean was about 0.8 percent. The M_2 to money GNP ratio has played no essential role in the forecasting exercises of the CEA, which have been heavily "judgmental," even if they have been preceded by an inspection of large econometric models as well as by a more informal evaluation of recent information.

Judgmental elements must enter into any reasonable appraisal of future prospects, regardless of what kind of formal exercise or analysis of regularities—monetary and/or other—precedes the appraisal. Yet the specific regularities in the behavior of the relationship of M_2 to GNP are "objectively" observable facts. They surely warrant enough interest to raise the question: What should one watch specifically before relying on the continuation of the regularities?

Not only must we remain aware of the limitations of analysis relating to broad aggregates, such as the "economy as a whole," and not only do we have to remember the influence of institutional developments in the financial markets on the demand for various M categories, but we must ask ourselves also the more general question whether other variables are not apt to change to such an extent as to interfere with the continuation of observed relations between M_2 and money GNP.

Variables Other than Money. Comments were made earlier on the weaknesses of regression results attributing the trendlessness of M_2 per unit of GNP to offsetting movements in real GNP on the one hand, and interest rates on the other. These shortcomings are likely to stem in large part from the role of unidentified ("left-out") variables. Some of these left-out variables are not even adequately measurable with reliance on available statistics, and others, while measurable, might exert a much more complicated influence than can be expressed in equations simple enough for regression analysis. At the present state of knowledge, one should not pretend to have very firm convictions about the potential role of all these further variables, including fiscal ones. There is little doubt that the economic environment could be shaped in such a way that the observed monetary regularities would not continue. The present study will call attention to merely two of the many circumstances that could bring about such a change. These two are particularly relevant to the ongoing debate over policies.

In the first place, it is clear that suppressing inflationary tendencies by wage and price controls tends to modify the relation of the money stock to total expenditures, and that this will express itself in the temporary accumulation of excess liquidity relative to money GNP as long as policy efforts of this kind are successful. Not only did this show very strongly during World War II, but even in the experience of the recent decade and a half the highest ratio of M_2 to money GNP is observed for the year 1972, when Phase 2 controls were in effect. As the controls are relaxed or eliminated, or as the public finds ways of getting around the controls and of responding to market forces, the temporary deviations from the normal money to GNP relations tend to become restored.

However, in the present circumstances an additional important consideration deserves to be stressed. In the event of renewed experimentation with presumably more durable administrative interferences of this sort, investors would find future returns increasingly unpredictable. This would make it very difficult to foresee the course of the future behavior of investors and of the public at large in respect to liquidity ratios, as well as in many other respects. At present there exists a good deal of uncertainty as to the intentions of the policy makers concerning controls, and in the appraisal of the future course of the economy this is an adverse factor. During the 1976 presidential election campaign the possibility was left open that the Carter administration would want to rely on "stand-by" controls of the comprehensive type, but more recently official statements were made and repeated to the effect that this was not the intention. On the other hand, the energy program outlined by the President in April 1977, and what may turn out to be informed rumors about a health program under consideration, will give many observers the impression of a substantial degree of control-mindedness in areas of great significance.

We now turn from interference with the operation of markets to fiscal variables. The role of these in shaping the economic environment for a successful monetary policy poses questions that have also given rise to lively controversies. Consider, for example, a situation in which, after a recession, an economy tends to become stuck at a distinctly subnormal rate of resource utilization and shows no signs of rising to higher rates in the near future. Is it then convincing to argue that the relation of M_2 to money GNP will nevertheless remain the same as in a past period, so that by promoting the creation of a specific quantity of M_2—a quantity read from past relations—it will be possible to achieve a money GNP falling in a rather narrow range? Or should credence be given to a claim of those oriented toward fiscal policy? The claim is that, given any money supply, tax reductions and/or increased government expenditures will speed up aggregate spending, at least temporarily, and that this is needed to raise capacity utilization rates to a level at which private investment will take over. Even if we place emphasis on the monetary regularities explained above, the possibility remains that, in such circumstances, raising the capacity utilization rates is needed to put the economy into the range of activity in which the past monetary relations have been observed. In this case, a temporary stimulus provided by fiscal policy may have lasting effects, and the automatic disappearance of the initial deficit when business activity rises may put an end to the stimulus approximately at the time when this is desirable. This would imply that, in such circumstances, the "crowding out" problem could also lose its importance. During the period in which the deficit raises interest rates to some extent, the additional investment induced by even lower rates would be small as compared with the investment that may be induced by the favorable effect of the fiscal stimulus on capacity utilization rates.

This is the problem deserving the most attention in the appraisal of the recent controversy between those who favored the adoption of a fiscal demand stimulus in 1977, and those who opposed it. In principle this *is* a legitimate problem for analysis. However, its practical significance in the present policy context depends on whether, prior to the new political leadership's commitment to a "fiscal stimulus" for the fiscal years 1977 and 1978, it was appropriate to conclude that the economy was showing clear signs of insufficient strength during a recovery that had started in the second quarter of 1975. We believe that the signs on which the policy of administering additional fiscal stimuli was based were far too unclear for arriving at firm conclusions late in 1976, when decisions were in fact reached concerning the need for a stimulus. As concerns fiscal 1977 this was realized subsequently, and in April a major part of the proposals for that year were withdrawn. On the other hand, the administration did not change its stimulus proposals for fiscal 1978, and Congress enlarged the 1978 package by additions made on the expenditures side of the budget.

The New Administration's Fragile Case for Fiscal "Demand Stimulus"

The Recent Record: 1976 over 1975. It can be seen from various sources—among these the 1976 Annual Report of the Council of Economic Advisers—that the initial conception of the policy makers of the Ford administration has been to attain for 1976 over 1975, "year over year," an increase of approximately 12 percent in money GNP. The expectation was expressed that this would result in a

6 percent (or slightly higher) increase in real GNP, combined with a reduction of the inflation rate to 6 percent, and accompanied by a decline of the measured unemployment rate by not much less than 1 percentage point.[8]

An appreciably faster rate of expansion was regarded as unsafe, for good reasons. While it is rarely possible to obtain genuine professional consensus on precise numerical appraisals, a very large part of the profession agreed that speed limits had to be observed carefully if the recovery was to last and if it was to lead subsequently to movements of the economy in the neighborhood of a sustainable growth path. This was widely—we may say, generally—recognized even if many critics of the Ford administration's policies favored higher speed limits than did the administration's advisers. But the criticism seemed unconvincing at that time and seems no more convincing in retrospect.

The composition of the labor force has changed significantly over the past two decades: the representation of adult women and of teenagers of both sexes has increased substantially, and thus there has occurred a rise in the proportion of persons entering or re-entering the labor force who become temporarily included among the unemployed before finding a job. Also, our unemployment compensation system has become significantly extended, both in coverage and in the duration of benefit payments. In spite of these changes, which raise our measured unemployment rates, no observer has doubted that the 8.5 percent average unemployment rate of 1976, or the nearly 8 percent rate of late 1976, resulted from the temporary difficulties encountered during an adjustment period after a steeply inflationary interlude of considerable duration. No observer doubted that those rates could be reduced significantly, and that this could be done gradually without reliance on inflationary stimuli that would backfire again, as they have in the past. But in the given circumstances, institutional factors limit the individual worker's ability to underbid the wages earned by others, and, quite aside from this, most workers are aware that transfer payments spare them any significant penalty for waiting until they can obtain a suitable job. Even the 8 percent or higher unemployment rates of the recent past, with a slightly more than fifteen-week average duration for those falling in that category, proved compatible not only with rising money wage rates but also with an upward tilted real-wage trend. As was pointed out in the guide to the volume, it is an essential characteristic of the situation in which

---

[8] See *Annual Report of the President's Council of Economic Advisers*, 1976, Government Printing Office, pp. 24 ff.

policy makers must reach their decisions that the rising wage trend *was not in fact underbid* by the more than 7 million unemployed shown at that time in our statistics.

Even with the moderate "1976 over 1975" speed limit of about 6 percent actually observed for real growth, the rise of adjusted [9] average hourly earnings in the private nonfarm sector amounted to 7.2 percent in nominal terms, of which only a 1.4 percent increase remained in "real" terms because the annual increase in the cost of living (CPI) still was running at 5.7 percent. From December 1975 to December 1976 the increase in the CPI was somewhat smaller, and all these numbers came out somewhat more favorably, with the slightly lower increase of 6.9 percent in nominal hourly earnings and the somewhat higher increase of 2.1 percent in real hourly earnings. It would clearly have been unconvincing to conclude that the high measured unemployment rate had removed the inflationary risk of trying to move faster. We shall soon see why it would have been equally unconvincing to conclude that low-capacity utilization rates made it harmless to set the speed limit higher.

The likelihood is great that a *rapid* move toward the appreciably lower measured unemployment rates that will be attained *after* the adjustment period would lead not only to various specific price pressures directly but also to an attempt to steepen the trend in real wages by tilting up the money-wage trend further. This would again result in a steepening of the price trend with no improvement of the trend in real wages—the prelude to accelerating inflation, soon to be followed by a recession. If, on the other hand, speed limits *are* observed, a gradual reduction of the unemployment rate should prove compatible with a gradual reduction of the steepness of the money-wage and price trends, as was the case in the recent past.

In fact, from 1975 to 1976, on a year-to-year basis, the projected 6 percent real growth rate *was* accomplished and the inflation rate decelerated to the neighborhood of 5 percent. For 1976 as a whole the unemployment rate was 0.8 percentage points lower than for 1975, down to 7.7 percent from 8.5 percent.

The Recent Record: The Second Half of 1976 and the Outlook. On the other hand, the specific sequence of events during 1976 aroused suspicions about the recovery. Few members of the economics profession felt that these suspicions should be brushed aside without being given careful thought. But careful thinking should have led to

---

[9] The adjustment is for the effects of interindustry shifts, and in manufacturing also for overtime.

the conclusion that the suspicions were not based on sufficient evidence for being guided by a pessimistic diagnosis in the weeks following the November elections, when policy makers who were about to take office declared the need to administer additional fiscal stimulus.

Since the upturn in 1975 the cyclical expansion rate had been very high in some quarters and very low in others. For example, it was very low in the last two quarters of 1976, creating the suspicions mentioned above about the continuation of the recovery at a reasonable rate. From the second to the fourth quarter of 1976 the real GNP expanded by no more than 3.3 percent at an annual rate, and the inflation rate was about the same as that observed "year-over-year." At the same time, the unemployment rate *rose* during those two quarters to almost 8 percent, from the 7.4 percent level to which it had temporarily declined (from the highest level of almost 9 percent, which had been observed for the second quarter of 1975). The sharp zigzagging of the real expansion rate with a significant slowdown in the second half of 1976 had not been predicted earlier.

Supporters of additional fiscal stimulus argued that when the earlier expansionary forces, generated by a change of inventory investment from strongly negative to positive, had come to an end, the 1976 rise in nonresidential fixed investment was insufficient for maintaining the expansion rate at the level initially projected. This argument was, in turn, usually based on expressions of the view that the capacity utilization rates had remained too low for inducing a sufficient volume of new investment. Further, while it was admitted that given the rate of change of a country's money supply the significance of the *long-run* effects of fiscal policy raises controversial questions, it was suggested that in the present context the emphasis should be placed on the immediate short-run demand-raising effect of tax cuts and of increased public spending because this effect would help improve capacity utilization rates. Yet this argument was far from conclusive. It was inconclusive even in the post-election weeks when its influence on the political authorities proved very weighty, and it certainly gained no validity in the light of the events that followed somewhat later.

Deficiencies of the Case for Additional Demand Stimulus. One reason why the argument was inconclusive from the outset is that in the relatively recent past—at the end of 1971—a very similar case could have been made for using additional fiscal stimuli to help the economy over a capacity utilization hump, and that case would have proved faulty. At that time any further stimulus would have added to the significant inflationary difficulties that had to be faced subsequently. The similarity to the present situation expresses itself in the fact that, after the recession of 1970, the 1971 rate of cyclical expansion was very weak. In real terms the annual rate of expansion was merely 3.1 percent in the second half of 1971. Moreover, in the beginning of 1972 the average capacity utilization rates were about the same as at the end of 1976, even if with more dispersion (they were higher in a number of specific industries but lower in others). Nevertheless, what followed in 1972 was a rapid upswing, with an expansion rate of 7.3 percent of the real GNP from the last quarter of 1971 to the last quarter of 1972, with a decrease of the unemployment rate from 6.0 percent to 5.3 percent during the same interval, and with an appreciable decrease of the budget deficit. The rate of increase of M_2 was the same during 1972 as during 1971—about 11 percent—and a strong case can be made for the proposition that the lagged effects of a monetary expansion rate, which had become too high, made a major unintended contribution to the severe inflationary pressures of the following period. It turned out that administering additional fiscal stimulus would have been a big mistake at that time.

Reasoning by such analogies is, of course, never conclusive. But in the given circumstances the uncertainties attaching to forecasts were disturbing enough—and the dangers of failing in the effort gradually to reduce inflation to insignificance great enough—to suggest that the decision to try to administer additional fiscal stimulus was premature. In fact, very soon after the new administration had committed itself to a fiscal-stimulus package, the data then becoming available strongly suggested a renewed acceleration of the expansion process. Furthermore, by February 1977 the revisions of the previous quarter's national income accounts data led to the conclusion that, while the rate of increase of real GNP had indeed been very small in that quarter (2.4 percent at an annual rate), real final sales had increased during the quarter at an annual rate of no less than 5.7 percent—a rate that had been rising continuously through the successive quarters of 1976. The low GNP growth rate for the final quarter of 1976 had resulted from the fact that the substantial inventory accumulation of the third quarter of 1976 was followed by very little inventory accumulation in the next quarter.

By the early part of 1977 it also became clear that the exceptional cold wave of the winter would have an adverse effect on developments during the first quarter of the year, but this was a matter of temporary supply limitations and not one calling for a demand stimulus. For the first quarter of 1977 the annual growth rate of real

GNP nevertheless was 6.9 percent, although the increase in real final sales was only 4.3 percent. By the time the administration withdrew the tax-rebate component of its 1977 fiscal-stimulus proposals, the then recent "real" statistics, including industrial production and retail sales, were showing substantial strength while, on the other hand, the recent price data contained the threat of renewed acceleration. By April 1977, with the stimulus packages still before Congress, the unemployment rate had declined to 7 percent.

During a cyclical recovery process, the fiscal variables normally assume values yielding diminishing budget deficits, and it is unclear why in the present circumstances a deviation from this pattern—an increase in the deficit from 1976 to 1977 as a result of fiscal stimulus —should have been required to set the stage for allowing the previous relation of M_2 to money GNP to be realized. This is why our analysis has led to the suggestion that, at present, a monetary policy aiming for about a 10 percent increase in M_2 from late 1976 to late 1977 describes the most reasonable course, with the fiscal deficit declining in the course of the cyclical recovery. Had the earlier proposed tax rebate been enacted, there would probably have occurred an increase in the deficit from fiscal 1976 to fiscal 1977, but at present it seems that there may well be some reduction (conceivably even by about to $10 billion).[10] However, the estimates are as yet quite tentative and they point to a renewed increase of the deficit for fiscal 1978. A brief survey of the 1977 and 1978 "stimulus package" will be found in the next section.

We shall return to the problem of tax reductions in more detail, particularly because the tax-raising effect of inflation has created a strong case for making a downward adjustment in tax rates defined for nominal incomes. The case rests on long-run considerations, rather than on doomed fine-tuning efforts, and the adjustments could have been reconciled with the objective of a gradual reduction of the deficit.

The 1975 Tax Rate Reductions and the Current Proposals Compared with Correcting Taxes for Inflation

The Fiscal Measures Enacted in 1975 and 1977. An earlier study has shown how a correction of the federal tax structure for inflation would

---

[10] In view of the discussion that will follow later, we should keep primarily the national income accounts budget in mind. Also, comparison of fiscal 1977 with the twelve-month period preceding it requires "redefining" fiscal 1976 as if it too had run from October 1st to September 30th, rather than from July 1 to June 30. A deficit of about $60 billion results for the adjusted fiscal year 1976. See also footnote 15.

have compared with the rebate and tax cut enacted in 1975.[11] The rebate was applied at that time to the 1974 tax liabilities, simultaneously with a reduction of the effective rates for 1975. The lowered rates have remained in effect since that time.

In the study referred to, it was shown that the resulting reduction of federal tax revenues *viewed in the aggregate* merely offset the tax-raising effect of inflation over a limited period. The tax-raising effect of inflation results only partly from the fact that when the nominal (current-dollar) income of individuals rises proportionately to the inflation rate, some proportion of their unchanged real incomes is taxed in a higher bracket than before. The effect of inflation results partly also from the fact that business enterprise, when replacing its equity-financed inventories and fixed capital, comes to be taxed on amounts representing merely the inflationary revaluation of a physically unchanging quantity of capital. Furthermore, the inflationary revaluations of securities and residential buildings are also taxed as capital gains at the time of sale.

It was shown in the 1975 study referred to above that, at that time, *10 percent* inflation (and an increase in nominal incomes by this same percentage) raised the individual income tax revenue of the federal government by about *16 percent* in nominal terms, and that, within wide limits, this *proportion* was fairly insensitive to the amount of inflation assumed. For the inflation-induced excess tax burden of business enterprise and of individuals paying capital-gains taxes, such proportions are much less stable and the computations are more complex. But for correcting the individual tax structure the principles are basically simple. Here the bulk of the distortion can be removed by stepping up in proportion to the inflation rate the exemption limits, the tax credits, the standard deduction, and the lower and upper limit of each bracket interval.

In the aggregate the tax reductions adopted in 1975 represented no more than the partial elimination of preceding inflationary excess taxation, and the distribution of the cuts differed substantially from what would have been indicated by the overtaxation itself. A detailed analysis of the problem discloses, for example, that the correction for inflation of individual income taxes would have given those with an adjusted gross income of $20,000 and over between 43 and 44 percent of the aggregate amount by which taxes were reduced, whereas in the actual cut they received only between 14 and 15 percent of the

---

[11] See William Fellner, in collaboration with Kenneth W. Clarkson and John Moore, *Correcting Taxes for Inflation* (Washington, D.C.: American Enterprise Institute, 1975).

total.[12] The argument that Congress is free to change the tax structure is, of course, valid, but the argument can hardly stand the stretching involved in the claim that undoing unlegislated overtaxation is an act of generosity not requiring any explanation by the legislators of who gets stuck to what extent with unintended overtaxation and who is spared this overtaxation.

The second line of defense of this arbitrariness was no sturdier. For example, the statement was made that wealthy taxpayers make use of loopholes which lighten their tax burden even without tax-rate adjustments. However, that is patently no excuse for hitting the "above $20,000" as a whole, and it is particularly no excuse for hitting those in the group who *have* paid high taxes. Note that to the extent that they have avoided taxes, they would not benefit from rate adjustments anyway. Further, the suggestion that tax allowances are particularly "stimulative" to the economy if given to taxpayers below some arbitrarily chosen income level lacks underpinnings in economic research. The suggestion misses the point, especially insofar as providing stimulus to investment is said to be a crucial objective.

The distribution of the tax cuts which will make up the 1977 and 1978 package will be similarly arbitrary. For the fiscal year 1977 the Carter administration's initially proposed "stimulus package" included:

(1) $11.4 billion of rebates ($50 per person) on earlier tax liabilities, with the proviso that payments of the same size per person are to be made to nontaxpayers as well;

(2) an increase in the standard deduction causing a current revenue loss of $1.5 billion; [13]

(3) a cut of business taxes amounting to $0.9 billion;

(4) an increase of fiscal expenditures, mainly of the public employment type, in the amount of $1.9 billion.

Altogether, the total revenue losses and additional expenditures were estimated at $15.7 billion for fiscal 1977. The first of these items —the proposal for the rebate—was withdrawn before it could have been enacted, and the business-tax proposal of the administration was modified for fiscal 1977 and also for 1978 in such a way as to be of noteworthy benefit only to small business. For fiscal 1977 the budgetary cut may thus have been reduced to roughly $5 billion. At the same time, Congress has made additions to the public-employment

---

[12] Ibid., pp. 18-19.

[13] The "current" revenue loss due to the higher standard deduction is small because the withholding schedules (in contrast to the ultimate tax liabilities) have been changed only as of July 1.

oriented component of the program, and it has further increased the standard deduction for married couples (even if reducing it somewhat for single individuals), but this will express itself mainly in the expenditures and revenues during fiscal 1978.

For fiscal 1978, with no rebate in that year, the revenue reduction caused by the initial Carter program due to the permanent increase in the standard deduction was estimated at $5.7 billion; the addition (as compared with previously contemplated levels) to expenditures, mainly of the public-employment type, at $7.7 billion; and the cut in business taxes at $2.4 billion. Thus, for fiscal 1978 the total would have amounted to $15.9 billion and with the additions made by Congress the amount is likely to come out at not much less than $20 billion.[14] All these revenue estimates are, of course, subject to revision.

The share of the adjusted gross income groups above $20,000 in the permanent increase of the standard deduction is negligible. From income levels falling in the $15,000 to $20,000 range and upward the excess taxation caused by inflation has not been fully removed. For single individuals the break-even point is located even lower.

A large part of the 1978 program is made up of its public-employment component. Expenditure programs involving public employment and/or subsidized employment in the private sector, if combined with training on the job, are among the promising means of reducing hardcore unemployment, which continues even during a process of sustainable normal growth. But if the intention is to provide employment to the temporarily unemployed during a cyclical recovery, public employment programs are of very doubtful value because it is unclear to what extent the state and local governments administering these programs with funds obtained through revenue sharing merely hire for the program workers whom they would have hired anyway. If there is additional employment, it is unclear to what extent such programs channel into less productive jobs workers who before long would have been hired for more productive ones. The enlargement of these programs will, of course, raise the deficit for 1978.

On the other hand, the case for tax-rate adjustments can be based on a much firmer argument than that provided by the alleged need

---

[14] See the statements of Secretary of the Treasury W. Michael Blumenthal, OMB Director Bert Lance, and CEA Chairman Charles L. Schultze, before the House Budget Committee on January 27, 1977; and the subsequent *Fiscal Year 1978 Budget Revisions*, Executive Office of the President, Office of Management and Budget, February 1977. Differences between the January and the February figures are very small. In the text the February ones are used.

for short-run fiscal stimulus. A clearly valid argument develops from the fact that, without such adjustments, inflation is continuously raising the real tax burden in a haphazard fashion. This fact, however, suggests that the excess taxation should be removed from *each* group of taxpayers. Such an operation would require distributing the tax cuts in the proportion in which the excess burden has risen, and any problem involving a revamping of the tax structure would then have to be faced candidly as a separate problem rather than by subterfuge. The marginal tax rates involved in the graduated taxation of individual incomes, and in the taxation of the profits (including capital-stock revaluations) of corporations owned by persons in various income classes, obviously give rise to problems of considerable complexity that need to be weighed consciously. In most Western countries these matters are decided by compromises, taking account of several somewhat contradictory considerations. Changing the tax burden in relation to real incomes again and again by allowing inflation to raise the effective rates to all taxpayers violates the rules of any orderly process. And, as concerns capital gains, how could the practice be defended of taxing an asset holder on a "gain" that reflects no more than the inflation that took place during the holding period? Indeed, taxes are often imposed on nominal gains reflecting less than the inflation that has occurred. Disregarding these problems has much in common with deliberately making computational errors in arriving at the effective tax rates.

How would the fiscal costs of correcting taxes for inflation compare with the costs of programs that have been adopted? For the full fiscal year 1978, the Carter proposals would have involved about $16 billion as the sum of tax cuts and additions to public-employment oriented expenditures, and, with the further additions made since that time, the cost is apt to rise to the neighborhood of $20 billion. In comparing this budgetary cost with that of eliminating the inflationary excess taxation, we shall start here with the individual income tax. On the assumption that a 10 percent inflation rate raises the federal individual income tax intake by 16 percent, an inflation rate of roughly 5 percent in 1978 would cause excessive income taxation of no more than about $6 billion in that single year (about 3 percent of about $180 billion). This estimate of the cost of undoing the distortion of individual income taxes is made for the present purpose on the assumption that the 1978 inflation rate will be about the same as the 1976 rates, that is, will still be quite a bit higher than would be the case in the event of continuous deceleration of inflation without any oscillations of the rate. Hence, for fiscal 1978, the budgetary loss caused by correcting *all* federal taxes for inflation could reach the actually adopted program's total of nearly $20 billion if the inflation-adjustment of corporate taxes, and the extra cost of the adjustment of the capital gains tax, took up about $13 billion in 1978. This is a generous estimate of what would be needed for inflation-adjustment in fiscal 1978 beyond the $6 billion considered above for individual income taxes. Correcting for inflation would have been no more expensive than will be the program which was in fact adopted.

However, at present it seems likely that the deficit will rise from 1977 to 1978, and it follows that in order to move gradually towards budgetary balance it would be preferable to *phase in* the correction of business taxation for inflation. This would in all probability happen automatically if enterprises making use of the provision enabling them to exclude inflationary revaluations from their tax base were also held to reporting correspondingly lower profits to their stockholders, and if they were given a limited option as to the date by which they will have completed the shift to the new method of reporting. Experience with problems of similar character suggests that the transition would then be gradual because many enterprises would want to avoid a sudden shift to reporting significantly reduced profits. Furthermore, we should presumably assume that the die is cast for most of the fiscal year 1978, and that any program considered in this discussion could start taking effect at best in the late part of that fiscal year.

Correcting the tax structure for inflation should be separated from structural changes falling in the category of tax reform proper. Some of the proposals relating to the latter category of problems suggest that the reforms in question would also have to be phased in gradually, but the present paper is not concerned with that complex of problems.

Reasons for Eliminating the Deficit during the Recovery. The large budget deficit which developed during and immediately after the recent recession should be gradually reduced as the economy recovers.[15] By the time we arrive in the neighborhood of a normal

---

[15] For the national income accounts deficit of fiscal 1976, see footnote 10. There, for the sake of comparability with fiscal 1977, the duration of fiscal 1976 was adjusted to the twelve-month period from October 1 to September 30, although officially the fiscal year had been defined as extending over the twelve-month period from July 1 to June 30, through fiscal 1976 and 1977. The first fiscal year extending from October 1 to September 30 is 1977. Without so adjusting the duration of fiscal 1976, the deficit of that fiscal year would have been only slightly higher than the figure found in footnote 10. The largest deficit had developed in

growth path at sustainable degrees of resource utilization—rather than at some arbitrarily defined "full employment level" which may never be attained—we should have eliminated the deficit, or, preferably, should be running a moderate surplus.

Why this is a desirable objective can be understood best by going through the following stages of reasoning.

(1) Over the American postwar period of practical price-level stability—1951–1965 viewed as a whole—we had a very close approximation to balance in the national income accounts budget of the federal government; hence, private capital formation was not reduced by a reduction of available savings through any noteworthy dissaving of the federal government.

(2) Compared with that period, more of our future private capital formation will serve "environmental" programs rather than promote productivity trends in the usual sense and thus trends in real wage rates.

(3) There are good reasons for trying not to allow productivity-raising investment to fall behind our past noninflationary experience along the growth path of the American economy. Investment resulting in per capita growth strongly overlaps with the development component of research and development, since the feasibility and worth of new technological methods is not truly established before these methods have become introduced on an industrial scale. The acquisition of new technological knowledge deserves to be promoted by policy makers, to some extent even at the expense of current consumption, because the economic advantages of knowledge acquisition spread, in part, freely over the economy. The advantages are not fully captured by those incurring the costs of innovating.

(4) Quite aside from these economic considerations, social friction would be likely to increase if, as a result of weak productivity trends, real-wage trends became significantly less favorable for workers.

(5) Hence it would be exceedingly undesirable to build into the economy elements that along the future normal growth path would affect capital formation adversely compared with the standards observed in a noninflationary period; and we need to remember that at that time we were running no noteworthy deficit over the years.

These considerations speak strongly for a gradual move toward the complete elimination of our budget deficit as the economy moves

---

fiscal 1975. It slightly exceeded $70 billion for the fiscal year extending from July 1, 1974, to June 30, 1975. This was about 5 percent of the same period's GNP.

back toward normality. As a result of the increased weight of investments not directly related to productivity trends (point 2 above), a case could be made for moving gradually into a state described not by balance but by surpluses. On the other hand, in contrast to earlier postwar periods, the state and local governments have for some years now been running an appreciable surplus, and, given the federal government's national income accounts budget, a surplus in the state and local budgets frees resources for private capital formation. On balance of these considerations, it is reasonable to aim for a sustainable normal growth path with no deficit or perhaps with a moderate surplus.

Given the uncertainties of economic forecasting, it would be useless to try to map anything like a precise course for the reduction of deficits as we approach sustainable levels of resource utilization. But it does seem an eminently reasonable rule to aim for consistent reductions of the deficit as the recovery process progresses. To achieve this, it would in any event be necessary to moderate the upward trend in fiscal expenditures. The need in the future to prevent a rise in the real tax burden of the sort that has recently developed mostly from inflation, makes it particularly important to observe the requirement for moderation.

Conclusions: The Long and the Short Run. Policy makers can choose one of two ways of reconciling an interest in the long run with that in the short run. For one, they can concern themselves primarily with the longer run, trusting that a steady and credible concern with promoting favorable market results for efficient producers will have a significant influence on short-run market behavior as well. Reliance on markets for making short-run behavior fall in line with presumed long-run results requires, of course, that market forces should be allowed to manifest themselves freely enough, but this leaves a good deal of room for policy objectives that the market mechanism does not automatically achieve. The course so described does not imply commitment to the specific numerical past relations observable for some chosen historical "long run." It does imply resisting the temptation to adjust policies in short intervals to what at any time appear to be the prospects for the immediate future. The alternative way of viewing the relationship between the short and the long run is to build up in one's mind the prospective long-run course of an economy by developing a policy concern with each successive short period, and to expect the long run to acquire the desirable properties with which one is trying to endow each of its short components.

115

Given the serious imperfections of foresight, the lags in making policy measures effective, and the uncertainties created by frequent changes of the policy course, the fine-tuning concern with the successive short runs has proved highly counterproductive. This to me seems to be the main lesson to be learned from the recent past, and the policy suggestions here presented attribute substantial importance to this lesson. However, these suggestions also take account of the desirability to build safeguards against "transitory" difficulties that are apt to develop in specific phases of dynamic development and that may become unduly drawn out.

The suggestions made in this paper relate to (1) the gradual reduction of inflation to insignificance, that is, to a rate similar to that which obtained in the 1951–1965 period in the United States; (2) the consistent use of monetary policy, for the cost-conditioning process needed for achieving this anti-inflationary objective without resort to wage and price controls; (3) correcting the tax structure for inflation, and separating this problem from those raised by basic tax reform proposals; and (4) the gradual elimination of the fiscal deficit during the current recovery and keeping the budget approximately balanced in periods in which the economy is moving close to a sustainable growth path.

Given such a policy, the measured unemployment rate that would establish itself in the United States after an adjustment period is the lowest rate sustainable over spans of reasonable duration in the given institutional setting. Any lower rate would soon shoot up. In particular, this sustainable rate *cannot* be reduced by administering inflationary stimuli because these will boomerang with a brief delay. The sustainable rate of measured unemployment *can* be reduced by the removal of institutional rigidities which limit competition, and an attempt should be made to remove many of these. But, as was said in the guide to the volume, we also need to recognize that some of these rigidities reflect widely shared value judgments, in which cases we should be looking not for ways of wholly removing the rigidities in question but for the arrangements that take account of the accepted value judgments with the least harmful effects on other desirable objectives. In no event should we favor or even tacitly accept rigidities that increase the sustainable rate of unemployment and then set for ourselves employment-policy goals that could be achieved only in the absence of these rigidities. That would be a very dangerous course in the future as it has been in the past, though it is a course that has often yielded a short-run political payoff to its advocates.

LESSONS OF THE 1973-1976 RECESSION AND RECOVERY

Geoffrey H. Moore

Summary

The 1973–1975 recession was the worst of the six recessions since 1948 in terms of the decline in real output, but not in terms of the decline in employment. Employment has become increasingly resistant to recession, and this trend is likely to continue, largely because of the growing importance of the service industries. Recession-prone industries, which employed 53 percent of the total work force in 1955, employed only 41 percent of the work force in 1972; and a further decline to 36 percent is expected by 1985.

The increase of 6 million jobs during the first two years of the present recovery has been accompanied by a reduction of only 1 million unemployed. In earlier recoveries the trade-off has been closer to two- or three-to-one. Employment figures now give a very different indication of the vigor of recovery than do unemployment figures. The influx of women and young people into the work force has made a major difference because they are more frequently unemployed as a result of starting new jobs or leaving them. Improved unemployment insurance coverage and the much larger number of families with more than one worker have also kept unemployment from declining as rapidly as new jobs are filled. These developments have raised the unemployment rate without necessarily signifying greater hardship.

In watching for another recession, the lagging indicators—unit labor costs, interest rates, and inventories—should not be neglected. During 1973 the rapid rise of these indicators was a warning of impending recession; and during 1974 and early 1975 their rapid decline signaled the 1975 recovery.

For every business cycle downturn since 1948 there has been a matching downturn in the inflation rate, and for every upturn in the business cycle there has been a matching upturn in the inflation rate. This rule held during the 1973–1976 recession and recovery, but with longer lags than usual. The latest upturn in the rate of inflation occurred in April 1976, about a year after the recovery began. In the past, as well as during the current recovery, inflation began to accelerate long before the economy reached low levels of unemployment or high levels of capacity utilization. Inflation of both wages and prices has been much more closely related to the percentage of the working age population that is employed. This percentage has increased to near record levels in recent months, and the rate of inflation has advanced from its low of 4.7 percent in April 1976 to 8.7 percent at the latest reading.

Just as leading indicators of the business cycle can be used to anticipate the next direction taken by the economy, leading indicators of the inflation rate can be used to anticipate the next direction to be taken by the rate of inflation. The rate of change in the wholesale prices of crude materials (excluding foods, feeds, and fibers) has systematically turned up or down before the corresponding turns in the rate of change in the consumer price index by intervals averaging about six months. The most recent upswing in the rate of increase in materials prices persisted for more than two years, and anticipated the recent acceleration in consumer prices by about a year.

The Business Cycle is Back!

What the recession of 1973–1975 taught, if it taught anything, was that the business cycle is still to be reckoned with. Like many previous recessions, this last recession was preceded by speculation in the securities markets, in the commodities markets, and in real estate markets; by rapid increases in prices; and by even more rapid increases in costs and hence by a squeeze on profits. Also, like many previous recessions, it became international in scope. The recession was worldwide, not "made in America."

Many of the familiar sequences among the reactions of different economic processes were repeated during 1973–1975 but with some differences. This was true in other industrial countries as well as in the United States. One important difference was the longer lag in the reaction of prices and costs to the reduction in demand. When the reaction finally came, the rate of inflation was substantially reduced, but the reduction did not begin until the recession was almost over. Another distinction shared by many industrial countries was a high and rising level of unemployment that persisted long after the recovery in output and employment began. The unemployment problem is not exclusively an American disease.

Table 1 shows some basic facts about the 1973–1975 recession in the United States, and compares its length and severity with eleven preceding recessions dating back to 1921. Clearly it was longer, deeper, and more widespread than its two immediate predecessors, 1960–1961 and 1969–1970, or the mild setback of 1926–1927. In some respects, though not all, it was worse than the three recessions of the 1950s and that of 1923–1924. But in severity it did not come close to the depressions of 1920–1921, 1929–1933, or 1937–1938.

Prior to the 1973–1975 recession there was a clear trend toward shorter and milder recessions. One of the important questions is whether this trend still persists. Before concluding, in view of the high unemployment rates of 1975–1976, that the trend has come to an end, consider Figure 1, which shows the duration and size of the declines in real GNP, industrial production, and nonfarm employment in successive recessions. For nonfarm employment, surely not the least important measure of the three, the trend toward shorter and milder recessions has persisted. Why this is so, and why it is not true of unemployment, and perhaps not of production, will be considered in the next section.

Short recessions, those which lasted a year or so, used to be called "inventory recessions." The term has gone out of fashion, but the phenomenon has not. As Table 2 shows, the $82 billion or 7 percent decline in real GNP from a peak in the fourth quarter of 1973 to a trough in the first quarter of 1975 was accounted for partly by a decline in final sales to consumers and private businesses (not to government) but even more by a decline in investment in inventories. The build-up in stocks of goods reached an annual rate of $25 billion at the peak; at the trough, stocks were being liquidated at the rate of $20 billion per year. The $45 billion turnaround accounted for more than half the total decline in output. Inventory adjustments are still a powerful factor in the business cycle.

It is important to know this because inventory swings have a short life span. Hence, when they are a dominant factor accounting for the change in output, a reversal can be expected fairly soon. In three of the five short recessions since 1948, none lasting much more than a year, the decline in investment in inventories exceeded the decline in output. That is, final demand in real terms continued to rise. Those were inventory recessions *par excellence*. During the other two recessions (1953-1954 and 1957-1958) the inventory factor accounted

119

Figure 1

THREE MEASURES OF THE DURATION AND DEPTH
OF RECESSIONS, 1920–1975

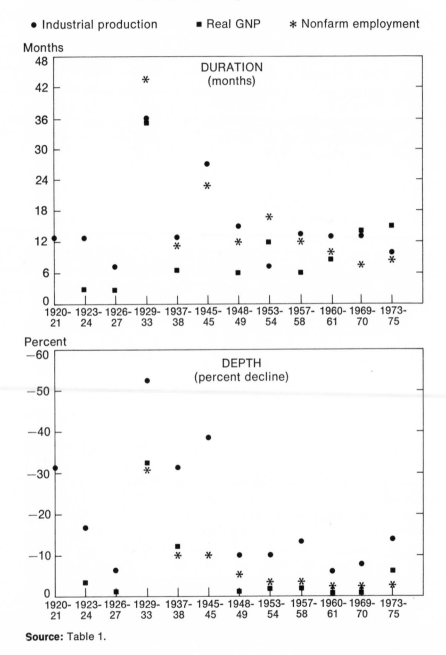

● Industrial production   ■ Real GNP   ✻ Nonfarm employment

Source: Table 1.

Table 1

SELECTED MEASURES OF DURATION, DEPTH, AND
DIFFUSION OF BUSINESS CYCLE CONTRACTIONS

Business Cycle Contraction, from Peak (topline) to Trough (next line)

	Jan. 1920 July 1921	May 1923 July 1924	Oct. 1926 Nov. 1927	Aug. 1929 Mar. 1933
Duration (in months) Business cycle				
chronology	18	14	13	43
GNP, current dollars	N.A.	6	12	42
GNP, constant dollars	N.A.	3	3	36
Industrial production	14	14	8	36
Nonfarm employment	N.A.	N.A.	N.A.	43
Depth (percent) [a]				
GNP, current dollars	N.A.	−4.9	−3.0	−49.6
GNP, constant dollars	N.A.	−4.1	−2.0	−32.6
Industrial production	−32.4	−17.9	−7.0	−53.4
Nonfarm employment	N.A.	N.A.	N.A.	−31.6
Unemployment rate				
Maximum	11.9[c]	5.5[c]	4.4[c]	24.9[c]
Increase	+10.3[c]	+2.6[c]	+2.4[c]	+21.7[c]
Diffusion (percent) Nonfarm industries, maximum percentage with declining				
employment [b]	97	95	71	100
	Sept. 1920	Apr. 1924	Nov. 1927	June 1933

N.A. = Not available.   (Table continues on following pages.)

[a] Percentage change from the peak month or quarter in the series to the trough month or quarter, over the intervals shown above. For the unemployment rate, the maximum figure is the highest for any month during the contraction and the increases are from the lowest month to the highest, in percentage points.

[b] Since 1948, based on changes in employment over six-month spans in 30 non-agricultural industries, centered on the fourth month of the span. Prior to 1948 based on cyclical changes in employment in 41 industries.

[c] The maximum figures for 1921, 1924, 1928, and 1933 are annual averages (monthly data not available). Increases, in percentage points, are for 1919–21, 1923–24, 1926–28, and 1929–33.

for about half the decline in output, just as it did in 1973–1975. Of course, any decline in output has repercussions, because of its effect on employment, earnings, profits, and so forth. However, because of the self-reversing character of inventory movements, it is much more encouraging to see final demand either continue to rise or decline only slightly in the face of an inventory decline than to see the

Table 1 Continued

	May 1937 June 1938	Feb. 1945 Oct. 1945	Nov. 1948 Oct. 1949	July 1953 May 1954
Duration (in months)				
Business cycle chronology	13	8	11	10
GNP, current dollars	9	6	12	12
GNP, constant dollars	6	N.A.	6	12
Industrial production	12	27	15	8
Nonfarm employment	11	22	13	16
Depth (percent)[a]				
GNP, current dollars	−16.2	−11.9	−3.4	−1.9
GNP, constant dollars	−13.2	N.A.	−1.4	−3.3
Industrial production	−32.4	−38.3	−9.9	−10.0
Nonfarm employment	−10.8	−10.1	−5.2	−3.4
Unemployment rate				
Maximum	20.0	4.3	7.9	6.1
Increase	+9.0	+3.4	+4.5	+3.6
Diffusion (percent)				
Nonfarm industries, maximum percentage with declining employment[b]	97	N.A.	90	87
	Dec. 1937		Feb. 1949	Mar. 1954

impetus for an economic downturn originate with or be dominated by a decline in final demand itself.

During the recession of 1973–1975, indeed, there was a serious drop in the demand for houses, hotels, factories, and other construction. More than a third of the $82 billion decline in real GNP during this period can be traced directly to this source. In addition, lagging construction demand affected also spending for furnishings and equipment and the accumulation of inventories of such items. Construction, it appears, fell victim to the high interest rates engendered by inflation, to the profit squeeze that blunted investment incentives, and to speculative overbuilding in some places.

The continued rise in the output of services, including government services, during the recession helped to offset the decline in output of goods and structures. Once again the economy was cushioned by the services sector, a phenomenon that has become increasingly significant because services now provide a much larger proportion of the total number of jobs than they did twenty or thirty years ago.[1]

Table 1 Continued

	Aug. 1957 Apr. 1958	Apr. 1960 Feb. 1961	Dec. 1969 Nov. 1970	Nov. 1973 Mar. 1975
Duration (in months)				
Business cycle				
chronology	8	10	11	16
GNP, current dollars	6	9	d	3
GNP, constant dollars	6	9	15	15
Industrial production	14	13	14	10
Nonfarm employment	14	10	8	9
Depth (percent)[a]				
GNP, current dollars	−2.8	−0.4	d	−0.2
GNP, constant dollars	−3.2	−1.2	−1.1	−6.6
Industrial production	−14.3	−7.2	−8.1	−14.6
Nonfarm employment	−4.3	−2.2	−1.6	−3.0
Unemployment rate				
Maximum	7.5	7.1	6.1	8.9
Increase	+3.8	+2.3	+2.7	+4.2
Diffusion (percent)				
Nonfarm industries,				
maximum				
percentage with				
declining				
employment[b]	88	82	83	90
	Sept. 1957	Aug. 1960	June 1970	Jan. 1975

[d] No decline.

Source: U.S. Department of Commerce, U.S. Department of Labor, Board of Governors of the Federal Reserve System, National Bureau of Economic Research. For a fuller version of this table, see Solomon Fabricant, "The Recession of 1969–70," in *The Business Cycle Today*, V. Zarnowitz, ed. (New York: National Bureau of Economic Research, Inc., 1972), pp. 100–10.

The recovery that began early in 1975 was sparked first by a slower liquidation of inventories, then by a modest accumulation. The output of services continued to rise, but at a slower rate than the output of goods and structures, so that services again played a stabilizing role by moderating the rate of expansion of GNP, just as they

---

[1] It could be argued that, if the magnitude of a decline in total demand is determined by other factors, such as a sharp decline in the money supply, the existence of recession-proof sectors merely shifts the burden of the decline to other sectors, without any cushioning effect on the total. No doubt there are shifts of this sort, but it also seems reasonable to suppose that the effects of a given external shock will be smaller when impacting a more resistant economy. The fact, as demonstrated in the next section, that total employment has become more recession-resistant than has output, and that this trend is associated with the greater importance of service industries in total employment than in output, supports this hypothesis.

Table 2

CHANGES IN REAL GNP DURING RECESSION AND RECOVERY (1973–76)

	Level (in billions of 1972 dollars)			Change (in billions of 1972 dollars)		Percentage Change[a]	
	At Business Cycle Peak (1973:4)	At Business Cycle Trough (1975:1)	24 Months After Trough (1977:1)	During Recession (1973:4 to 1975:1)	During 24 Months of Recovery (1975:1 to 1977:1)	During Recession (1973:4 to 1975:1)	During 24 Months of Recovery (1975:1 to 1977:1)
Gross national product	1,243	1,161	1,302	−82	+141	−7	+11
Final sales	1,217	1,182	1,293	−35	+111	−3	+9
Change in business inventories	25	−20	9	−45	+29	−4[c]	+2[c]
Output of							
Services	536	550	595	+14	+45	+3	+8
Nondurable goods	342	319	348	−23	+29	−7	+8
Durable goods	236	193	248	−43	+55	−18	+23
Structures	129	99	111	−30	+12	−23	+9
Purchases by[b]							
Consumers	820	790	895	−30	+105	−4	+13
Businesses	170	114	144	−56	+30	−33	+18
Government	252	257	262	+5	+5	+2	+2

a For both columns the level at peak (1973:4) = 100.

b Derived as follows: Consumers—personal consumption expenditures plus residential structures; businesses—nonresidential fixed investment plus change in business inventories plus net exports; government—purchases of goods, services, and structures.

c Expressed in terms of final sales at peak (1973:4) = 100.

Source: U.S. Department of Commerce, *Survey of Current Business.* Detail may not add to totals because of rounding.

had previously moderated the rate of contraction. By the first quarter of 1977, two years after the recovery began, total output was well above its level at the preceding (1973) peak, and final demand even more so. The rise in inventory investment had not contributed as much to the expansion as its previous decline had contributed to the contraction. The greatest weakness was still in the output of structures.

Figure 2, which traces the course of real GNP during the current and the five preceding recoveries, indicates that the rapid rise in output during the first year and the slower rise during the second year of recovery were not unusual. Indeed, the 1975–1976 recovery closely paralleled the median of the previous five recoveries. The variations among the recoveries are shown by the dots placed on the chart at the 12th, 24th, and 36th months of expansion. Yet the central tendency is obvious, and the 1975–1976 recovery hewed closely to it.

The median line indicates some acceleration in the growth of GNP in the third year of recovery, but the scatter of points representing the individual recoveries becomes wider. Nevertheless, the median forecast of economists participating in the Business Outlook Survey, conducted each quarter by the American Statistical Association and the National Bureau of Economic Research, corresponds closely to the path traced by the median line in Figure 2. The forecast made in May 1977 suggests an acceleration in the real GNP growth rate to about 6 percent between 1977:1 and 1978:1, which exceeds the preceding year's rate (about 4.5 percent) but is below the rate during the first year of recovery (about 7 percent). This pattern resembles that of previous recoveries, but is more optimistic. If the forecast proves correct the 5.7 percent annual growth rate in GNP during the first three years of recovery will exceed that achieved in four of the five previous recoveries, the exception being the recovery that was boosted by the Korean War in 1950–1951.

Further insight into the progress of the current recovery and the prospects for its continuance can be obtained by examining economic indicators that typically lead or lag the comprehensive measures of output, income, employment, and trade. Within many economic processes, such as the employment of people, the production of goods and services, and the building of houses or factories, are developments that indicate further developments. For example, changes in the length of the workweek indicate subsequent changes in the number of workers employed, largely because workweek changes can be made quickly and are often less costly. Similarly, an increase in new

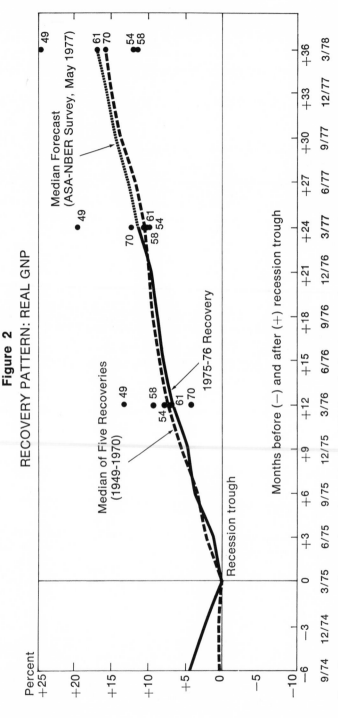

Figure 2

RECOVERY PATTERN: REAL GNP

Median Forecast
(ASA-NBER Survey, May 1977)

Median of Five Recoveries
(1949-1970)

1975-76 Recovery

Recession trough

Months before (−) and after (+) recession trough

Note: Data represent changes from the level of real GNP at the business cycle trough quarter, expressed as percentage of the level at the preceding business cycle peak quarter. For the current cycle, the peak level was $1,242.6 billion 1972 dollars (1973:4), and the trough was $1,161.1 billion (1975:1). The recoveries are identified by the years in which their trough dates occurred (1949, 1954, 1958, 1961, 1970, 1975).

Source: National Bureau of Economic Research, Inc.

orders for goods may precede increased output, and an increase in new building permits or in construction contracts may precede increased construction employment. When several such leading indicators are integrated into a composite index, the index assists forecasters in anticipating movements in the economy as a whole.

The U.S. Department of Commerce index of leading indicators reached its low point for the last recession in February 1975, and followed with a sharp recovery (see Figure 3). This index became widely known during the election campaign of 1976, though indexes of this type have been in existence since 1949. The reason for its new notoriety was that it dramatized the so-called pause in the economy in the summer and autumn of 1976, and raised a question whether the recovery was continuing. Since the index usually falls prior to a recession, its decline in August and September 1976 was widely noted.

Unfortunately, the concern that this engendered was not tempered by knowledge of two historical facts. First, most economic data are subject to revision. The decline to September, when first published, was 1.5 percent, and the October index showed no improvement. The revised figures now show the decline to September to be 0.2 percent, and the index not only rose in October but reached a new high. Although it could not have been known at the time what the revisions would indicate, the fact that there would be revisions as more information became available *was* known, and the approximate magnitude of the revisions to which the index is subject was also known. This should have inspired greater caution in the interpretations made.

Second, during previous recoveries, most of the gain in this index has occurred during the first year, after which there has been a slower rise, even though aggregate economic activity continues to expand for another year or two. The broken line in Figure 3 indicates the average or median for the recoveries prior to 1975–1976. The index makes a strong advance during the first nine months of the recovery, after which it usually remains relatively stable. The solid line, representing the current recovery in the index, reached the average line in July 1976 and has remained close to or slightly above it since that time. Consequently, the decline in the index from July to September, even before the revisions, was not an unusual development warranting great concern. One of the lessons of this recovery is that we should profit from the lessons of earlier recoveries.

History suggests that when the next recession begins, it will have been preceded by a decline in the leading index, lasting at least four

Figure 3

RECOVERY PATTERN: INDEX OF TWELVE LEADING INDICATORS

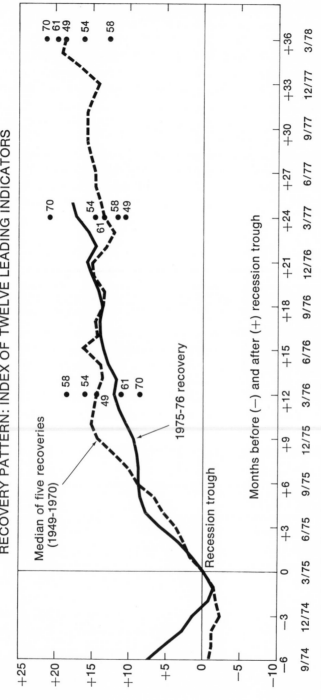

Note: Changes in the index from the business cycle trough to the current month are expressed as percentages of the preceding business cycle peak. The peak and trough levels are centered three-month averages. For the current cycle, the peak level was 130.1 (November 1973) and the trough was 107.6 (March 1975), with 1967 = 100. The five earlier recoveries are identified by the years in which their trough months occurred: October 1949, May 1954, April 1958, February 1961, and November 1970.

Source: National Bureau of Economic Research, Inc.

or five months, and big enough so that it is not likely to be wiped out by revisions. The smallest of these prerecession declines, 2.5 percent over a five-month period, appears large and long compared with the original 1.5 percent decline from July to September 1976, and enormous compared with the revised 0.2 percent decline. Other prerecession declines in the index have ranged from 3 to 6 percent.

In watching for signs of recession, or even of slowdown, the index of lagging indicators should not be neglected. Though this index receives little attention in the press, it does have real prognostic value. This fact has been observed repeatedly in business cycle studies, and its validity was reinforced during the 1973–1976 recession and recovery. This point is illustrated in Figure 4, in which the data are expressed as rates of change measured over six-month intervals.[2] Rates of change that are below the long-run average (roughly 3.7 percent per year for all series shown) are shaded. For real GNP, below average rates of change coincide approximately with the periods of recession, which are represented by the vertical cross-hatched columns.

In most instances, the rate of change in the leading index precedes the movements in real GNP by a few months. The rate of change in the lagging index, as plotted in the bottom line in the chart, lags behind both the leading index and real GNP. However, when the lagging index is plotted upside down, as in the top line of the chart, its movements lead both the leading index and real GNP.

This is not a mere reflection of the fact that when a lagging series reaches a peak, for example, shortly after a business cycle peak, the series peak will almost certainly precede the next business cycle trough. In that trivial sense every lagging indicator, or even every coincident indicator, is a leading indicator of the next opposite turn in the business cycle. But this mechanical relation cannot account for the fact that the turns in the lagging indicators are both closely associated with, and usually lead, the opposite turns in the leading indicators. However, this has indeed been the case according to nearly one hundred years of business cycle records in the United States and shorter records in other countries.[3] Furthermore, the economic rationale underlying this phenomenon becomes evident once

---

[2] A short interval, such as one month or three months, tends to highlight irregular variations in the data but also reflects recent trends. A longer interval, such as six months or a year, disposes of some of the irregularities, but is less current. For working purposes, use of several rates of change measured over both short and long intervals is desirable. See the *Chartbook on Wages, Prices and Productivity* published monthly by the Bureau of Labor Statistics, charts 2 and 4.

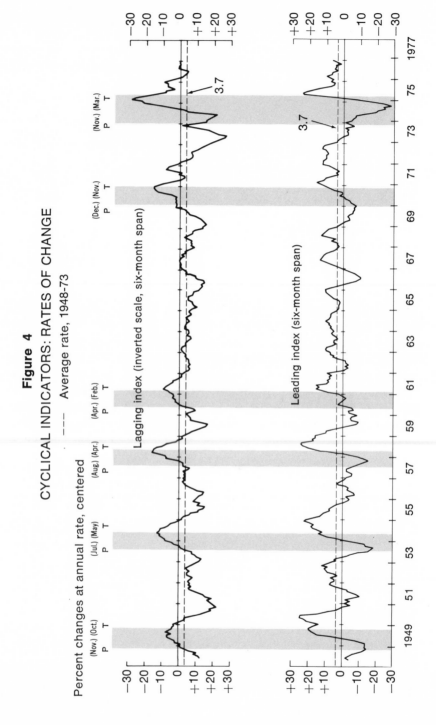

Figure 4

CYCLICAL INDICATORS: RATES OF CHANGE

Average rate, 1948–73

Percent changes at annual rate, centered

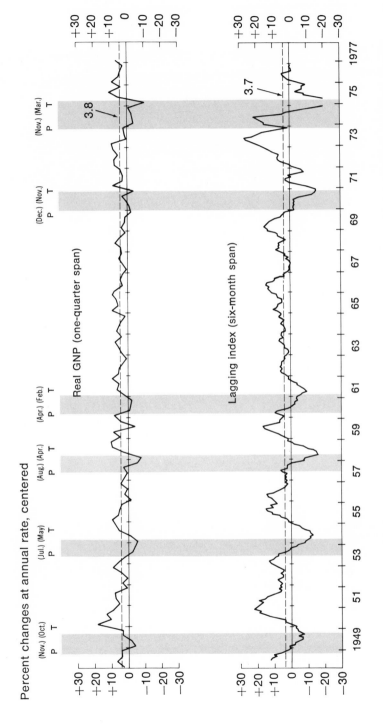

Source: U.S. Department of Commerce, *Business Conditions Digest.* Note, however, that the rates of change shown in the source are for three-month rather than six-month spans. Shaded areas are recessions.

the nature of the lagging and leading economic indicators is considered.

Several of the lagging indicators represent costs of production, for example, interest rates and unit labor costs. When they advance rapidly they may exert a depressing effect on profits, on new commitments to invest in capital goods, and on stock prices, all of which are leading indicators. A rapid increase in the level of inventories (a lagging indicator) sometimes reflects undesired accumulation and prompts a cutback in orders (a leading indicator). A large increase in bank loans outstanding (a lagging indicator) may be related to excessive inventory holdings or repayment problems and prompt a reduction in net credit extensions supplied by banks or requested by their customers (a leading indicator).[4] Consequently, it is reasonable to expect a high point in the rate of change in the lagging index to be closely followed by a low point in the rate of change in the leading index.

Figure 4 shows that this sequence of events took place in 1973, prior to the onset of the recession. It is also evident that a reversal occurred in 1974, prior to the start of the recovery. Even the slowdown of the recovery in 1976 was mirrored by the appropriate movements in the lagging index. Clearly, the lagging indicators and their implications should become better understood.

Employment, Good; Unemployment, Bad

Although total output began to decline late in 1973 and unemployment began to rise, the number of people with jobs kept on growing

---

[3] See Geoffrey H. Moore, ed., *Business Cycle Indicators* (New York: National Bureau of Economic Research, 1961), vol. 1, pp. 234-36; Geoffrey H. Moore, "Generating Leading Indicators from Lagging Indicators," *Western Economic Journal*, vol. 7, no. 2 (June 1969), pp. 137-44; Kathleen H. Moore, "The Comparative Performance of Economic Indicators in the United States, Canada, and Japan," *Western Economic Journal*, vol. 9, no. 4 (December 1971), pp. 419-28; Geoffrey H. Moore and Philip A. Klein, "Monitoring Business Cycles at Home and Abroad," *National Bureau of Economic Research*, manuscript.

[4] In order to detect large increases in the lagging indicators rates of change may be examined, as in Figure 4. Also, the ratio of the coincident index (which represents the general level of output, employment, income, and trade) to the lagging index may be computed. As does the inverted rate of change, this ratio shows a close relationship to the leading index, and often leads it. See *Business Conditions Digest*, November 1975, and later issues. Another way to detect increases in lagging indicators is to eliminate the long-run trends from the leading, coincident and lagging indexes, and to compare the resulting "growth cycle" turning points. See the forthcoming report by Victor Zarnowitz and Charlotte Boschan in the Fifty-Seventh Annual Report of the National Bureau of Economic Research, 1977.

until the autumn of 1974. This was an unusual occurrence during a recession, and was attributable to the continued growth of the services sector.

The service industries, public and private, are a more important provider of jobs than of output. In 1973 the service industries accounted for two-thirds of all jobs but for less than half of total output.[5] As a result, the rise in jobs in the service sector during 1973–1974 offset the decline in jobs in goods production (mining, manufacturing, and construction) more than the rise in services output offset the decline in goods output. Consequently, the decline in total employment in the economy was delayed, and when it came it was relatively mild and brief. Table 1 shows that the nine-month, 3 percent reduction in nonfarm employment was one of the smallest and shortest recession declines on record. A similar statement can be made in regard to total civilian employment, as indicated in Table 3. The decline in total employment in 1974–1975 was shorter than in four of the previous five recessions, and the percentage decline was smaller than in three of them. While the 1973–1975 recession was the worst recession since the 1930s in many respects, in terms of actual loss of jobs it was relatively mild.

This is an important finding because the reason for it is of long standing and promises to hold in future recessions. The point is that the proportion of employed persons who work in the service industries has been rising steadily for many years, and jobs in the service industries are for the most part more recession-proof than are jobs in the goods-producing industries. Employment in the goods-producing industries (not including farming) reached a peak in December 1973 at 25 million jobs and declined for eighteen months thereafter, reaching a low of 22.3 million jobs in June 1975. This represented an 11 percent decline and a loss of 2.7 million jobs. Meanwhile, during the same eighteen months, employment in the service industries rose from 53 million to 54.2 million jobs. Although this was a gain of only 2 percent it represented 1.2 million additional jobs, offsetting nearly half the loss of jobs in the goods industries.

In recent decades employment in the service industries has increasingly helped absorb the shock of recessions. In 1948, service industries provided 40 percent more nonfarm jobs than did the goods industries; and by 1973 they provided more than twice as many jobs as did the goods industries. The stabilizing effect of service industry

---

[5] This comparison overstates the difference, because industries like retailing and transportation, counted as service industries in the employment data, contribute services that are included in the output of goods in the GNP accounts.

Table 3
DECLINES IN TOTAL EMPLOYMENT

	Months	Percent
July 1974–March 1975	8	2.5
April 1970–March 1971	11	0.7
September 1960–April 1961	7	1.3
July 1957–April 1958	9	3.0
March 1953–July 1954	16	3.8
July 1948–June 1949	11	3.0

employment has correspondingly increased. The growing proportion of service industry employment promises to help alleviate the problems posed by future recessions. According to projections made by the Bureau of Labor Statistics, continued growth in the relative importance of the service sector through 1985 may be expected. By 1985 the service industries will be providing 2.7 jobs for every job provided by the goods industries, and will continue to cushion cyclical declines concentrated in the latter.

The trend is analyzed more precisely in Table 4, in which industries that experienced large declines in employment in past recessions are distinguished from those that did not. Most of the industries in the recession-prone group produce goods; all of the industries in the recession-proof group produce services. One service industry, transportation, communications and public utilities, would be in the recession-proof group except for the fact that it includes employment in the transportation of goods, which declines substantially in recessions. The other, more curious exception, is the federal government. Federal government employment declined substantially in each of the five recessions from 1948 to 1970, and rose during the intervening expansions.[6]

A comparison of the average changes in column one of Table 4, with the 1973–1975 changes in column two, shows that this last recession was fairly typical. All the employment declines were concentrated in the recession-prone industries. Federal employment rose, in contrast to past performance, as did employment in mining, in clear response to the energy problem. The employment declines in construction and in the production of nondurable goods were unusu-

[6] See Walter Ebanks, "The Stabilizing Effects of Government Employment," *Explorations in Economic Research*, vol. 3, no. 4 (Fall 1976), National Bureau of Economic Research.

ally sharp. In general, however, the averages for previous recessions were a fair guide to the differential impact of the 1973-1975 recession.

Columns three to six in Table 4 show how employment shifted between 1955 and 1972, and how it is expected to shift by 1980 and again by 1985. The shift away from the recession-prone industries has been dramatic. These industries supplied 53 percent of all jobs in 1955, but only 41 percent in 1972. By 1980 this group's share of employment is expected to fall to 38 percent, and to 36 percent by 1985. Every one of the recession-prone industries shows a declining trend in relative importance. Every one of the recession-proof industries shows a rising trend in relative importance.

The bottom section of Table 4 shows how these shifts have affected and will continue to affect recessionary declines in total employment. The assumption is that cyclical changes in various industries remain the same, but that their importance shifts depending upon growth trends. Between 1955 and 1985 the magnitude of the shift, past and future, is sufficient to cut the cyclical decline in total employment substantially. Had the relative importance of the different industries in 1973 been the same as in 1955, with each industry experiencing the percentage changes that they did during the 1973–1975 recession, total employment would have dropped 2.8 percent as compared with the 1.9 percent decline that actually occurred. With the projected 1985 distribution of employment, the decline in total employment during a similar recession would be less than 1 percent. That is, a recession with just as sharp an effect on individual industries would have half the total impact, because the industries most severely affected by the recession would be less important.

The effects of the continued vigorous growth in services may be noted in the recovery that has occurred since 1975. From its July 1975 low, employment in the goods industries rose by two million through May 1977. At the same time services employment rose by 3 million. The goods industries in May 1977 were still below their previous peak level of employment in December 1973 by 800,000 jobs, but the service industries had far more than compensated by creating nearly 5 million additional jobs since December 1973.

The extraordinary growth in jobs, however, has not solved the problem of unemployment. Indeed, in some respects it has made it bigger. One of the most difficult lessons to be learned from the recent recession and recovery is that the nature of the trade-off between employment and unemployment has changed enormously in the past quarter-century. The creation of one new job can no longer be counted upon to remove one person from the unemployment rolls.

Table 4

THE IMPACT OF RECESSION ON INDUSTRIAL EMPLOYMENT

	Percentage Change in Employment		Percentage Distribution of Total Employment in			
	Average, five recessions 1948–1970 (1)	November 1973 to March 1975 recession (2)	1955 (3)	1972 (4)	1980[a] (5)	1985[a] (6)
Industries declining most in recessions:						
Durable manufactures	−11.9	−10.9	14.9	13.0	12.9	12.4
Mining	−9.6	+10.8	1.3	0.8	0.8	0.7
Transportation, communication, and public utilities	−4.5	−3.3	6.6	5.5	5.1	5.0
Agriculture	−3.8	−7.3	9.8	4.0	2.7	2.1
Nondurable manufactures	−3.5	−8.7	11.5	9.5	8.6	8.2
Contract construction	−3.1	−13.5	5.4	5.4	5.1	5.3
Federal government	−3.0	+2.4	3.3	3.1	2.8	2.7
Industries declining least in recessions:						
Wholesale and retail trade	−0.8	+0.5	20.1	21.7	22.1	21.2
Personal and business services	+1.8	+4.5	15.9	19.8	20.9	22.0
Finance, insurance, and real estate	+2.4	+1.5	4.0	5.0	5.3	5.5
State and local government	+4.5	+6.0	7.2	12.2	13.7	14.9

Summary (total or average):

Industries declining most in recessions	−6.1	−8.0	52.8	41.3	38.0	36.4
Industries declining least in recessions	+1.6	+2.9	47.2	58.7	62.0	63.6
All industries						
Actual	−3.0	−1.9	100.0	100.0	100.0	100.0
Weighted by 1955 distribution	−2.7	−2.8				
Weighted by 1972 distribution	−1.7	−1.4				
Weighted by 1980 distribution	−1.5	−1.1				
Weighted by 1985 distribution	−1.4	−0.9				

[a] Projected.

Note: For an earlier version of this table see Geoffrey H. Moore, "Some Secular Changes in Business Cycles," *American Economic Review* (May 1974), p. 134. It is based upon data published by the Bureau of Labor Statistics. The data used to compute recession changes (columns one and two) are from the establishment survey (jobs) except for agriculture, where the household survey (persons) is used. The data used for the distribution of employment (columns three to six) are based on the jobs concept also, but differ from those used to measure recession changes largely because they include self-employed, unpaid family workers, and paid household employees. The total number of jobs represented in the distributions are: 1955, 65,745,000; 1972, 86,551,000; 1980, 101,856,000; 1985, 109,466,000. See Ronald E. Kutscher, "Revised BLS Projections to 1980 and 1985: An Overview," *Monthly Labor Review* (March 1976), p. 8, and "The United States Economy in 1985: Projections of GNP, Income, Output and Employment," *Monthly Labor Review* (December 1973), p. 39.

Source: U.S. Department of Labor, Bureau of Labor Statistics.

Few would have believed that, at the low point of the recession in March 1975, if the economy provided 6 million more jobs over the next two years unemployment would not be reduced by more than 1 million. Yet that is what happened: six additional jobs had to be created for every person taken off the unemployment count. During the four recoveries in the 1950s and early 1960s, the corresponding ratio (increase in jobs to reduction in unemployment) ranged from one-to-one to three-to-one. Only in the 1970–1972 recovery did the experience match the latest recovery.

The reasons for this development are not yet fully understood. The working-age population has been increasing more rapidly in recent years than before, causing unemployment to increase at a faster rate as younger men and women seek jobs. Another factor has been the growth of the service sector. Retail stores, hospitals, hotels, schools, and other service establishments employ large numbers of adult women and teenagers, often on a part-time or seasonal basis. Their growth has provided jobs for the rapidly increasing number of women and young people seeking work. But since these groups enter and exit the labor force and shift from job to job much more frequently than do adult men, they are more frequently unemployed. Even in the best of economic times they experience more unemployment than do adult men, because they are between jobs more often or seeking a job for the first time.

Consequently, service industry growth, which has gone hand in hand with the growth in the number of women and young persons in the job market, has increased both employment and unemployment. The result has been that a bigger increase in jobs is required to produce a given reduction in unemployment.

Other factors have served to alter the relationship between the creation of jobs and the reduction of unemployment. The duration of unemployment benefits has increased in recent years, which helps people get by without a job for longer periods. More families have two wage earners, which often means that one can seek work for a longer time while the other supports the household. This kind of "family unemployment insurance" has become much more important than it used to be. In the first quarter of 1976, about half of the eight million persons unemployed were members of families in which another member of the household had a full-time job. Comparable data for earlier periods do not exist, but there has clearly been a rising trend in the proportion of families with two or more workers.[7]

---

[7] See Howard Hayghe in the *Monthly Labor Review*, May 1976, p. 13, and December 1976, p. 47 for the relevant data.

Desirable as the change in family employment patterns and in unemployment benefits may be on other grounds, one effect has been to make it more difficult to reduce unemployment by stimulating employment.

It is vital that this situation be understood, for the creation of jobs has significant effects on human welfare and on the economy, whatever its effect on unemployment. Obviously, additional jobs usually increase earnings and output. The recovery since the spring of 1975, for example, has resulted in an increase in the percentage of the population with jobs, even though it hasn't reduced commensurately the percentage who are seeking work. In March 1975, 551 out of every 1000 persons of working age (sixteen and over) were employed. By May 1977, 571 per 1000 were employed, an increase of 20. Meanwhile the number unemployed in this group of 1000 fell from 51 to 43, a reduction of only 8. Even if the number unemployed had not declined at all, the increase in the number employed would have made it easier for them to support the rest, including the unemployed.

Often forgotten, in the emphasis that is placed on the unemployment rate, is the proportion of the population that is neither employed nor unemployed, that is, the proportion not counted as part of the labor force. It makes a difference whether this proportion is increasing or decreasing, partly for the reason just mentioned—how many there are to support—and partly because it has some bearing on how tight the labor market is. To bring this matter to light, there is much to be said for redefining the unemployment rate to make it a percentage of the working-age population rather than a percentage of the labor force (the sum of the employed and the unemployed). This would make the unemployment rate comparable with the employment percentage and also with the percentage of the working-age population not in the labor force. All three percentages are significant, and for ease of understanding it is desirable to compute them from the same base.

Consider, for example, Table 5, which compares the employment situation in May 1977, the twenty-sixth month of the current recovery, with the situation in the twenty-sixth month of the five preceding recoveries. All figures are computed as a percentage of the working-age population. That population rises quite steadily over time, and is not subject to the vagaries of economic fluctuations and policy initiatives that affect employment and unemployment, and hence the labor force. Table 5 shows that (1) the percentage employed was higher in May 1977 than in the corresponding month of any of the

Table 5
DISTRIBUTION OF THE WORKING-AGE POPULATION IN THE TWENTY-SIXTH MONTH OF SIX RECOVERY PERIODS

Twenty-sixth month of recovery	Percentage Distribution of the Population Sixteen and Older				
	Civilian employed	Armed forces	Unem- ployed	Not in labor force	Total
May 1977	57.1	1.3	4.3	37.3	100.0
January 1973	56.1	1.6	2.9	39.4	100.0
April 1963	54.2	2.2	3.3	40.3	100.0
June 1960	55.3	2.1	3.1	39.5	100.0
July 1956	56.0	2.5	2.6	38.9	100.0
December 1951	55.9	3.2	1.8	39.1	100.0

Source: U.S. Bureau of Labor Statistics.

previous recoveries, (2) the percentage in the armed forces was smaller than in any previous recovery, (3) the percentage unemployed was higher than in any previous recovery (having increased rather steadily from one recovery period to the next), and (4) the percentage not in the labor force was smaller than in any previous recovery.

Considering unemployment alone, the current recovery has been the least auspicious of the six. It is curious, however, that the unemployment figures suggest that recoveries have become steadily weaker ever since 1949. It is especially curious because the employment figures do not show this. According to them, the current recovery is the best ever by a full percentage point, which at present population levels means about a million and a half people. That is, if the recovery had merely turned out to be second best, a million and a half fewer people would be employed than were actually employed in May 1977.

The steady reduction in the percentage of the population engaged in the armed forces raises the question what effect this reduction has had upon employment and unemployment. The figures do not answer this question, of course, but they do show that if the armed forces are included with the civilian employed, the May 1977 employment percentage is no longer the best. It falls below those of the 1951 and 1956 recoveries, when the armed forces were much larger than today. No doubt this was one factor that kept unemployment low.

Finally, the current low percentage of the working-age population not in the labor force suggests that those previously outside the labor force have now entered it. This implies that those not in the labor force constitute a kind of reserve labor force. While many of those not in the labor force are unable to work for various reasons (family responsibilities, school attendance, or illness), others report that they both want and intend to seek work. The fact that the proportion of the working-age population not in the labor force has become smaller means that shifts do take place and that this group includes some potential employees. The reduction in this secondary labor reserve has offset to some extent the rise in the number unemployed, the primary labor reserve. Some of those who previously reported that they were not seeking work are now doing so, shifting from the secondary to the primary reserve. Other former secondary reserve members have found jobs and are counted as employed. Under these circumstances, the unemployment rate does not accurately measure the tightness or ease in the labor market. Changes in the secondary labor reserve must be considered also.

This is one of the factors that underlies the change in the employment-unemployment trade-off. A larger increase in employment relative to the reduction in unemployment during a recovery period means that the secondary labor reserve has become smaller. Moreover, this affects the economy's capacity to expand employment. Hence it is important to take into account the effect of the size of the secondary reserve when considering the subject of wage and price inflation.

Inflation on the Run

The question is, uphill or down? In trying to determine whether the inflation is worsening or improving, or how economic policies are affecting it, it is well to look carefully at the peaks and valleys of the past. When was the inflation rate highest? When did it start to climb? Under what circumstances did it descend or ascend? For this purpose, it is useful to have an historical chronology of the rate of inflation similar to the National Bureau of Economic Research's business cycle chronology. Indeed, it is useful to relate one to the other, for some of the most important lessons of the recent recession and recovery are to be found in that relationship.

Table 6 updates an inflation chronology published several years ago, and incorporates a few minor revisions. It is based upon the rate of change in the consumer price index (CPI) measured over a six-month interval, and adjusted to eliminate the regular seasonal fluctuations that affect many prices. The peaks are the dates when

Table 6

A CHRONOLOGY OF PEAKS AND TROUGHS IN THE RATE OF INFLATION

Date of		Inflation Rate at (percent)		Change in Rate during (percentage points)		Duration of (months)	
Peak (1)	Trough (2)	Peak (3)	Trough (4)	Downswing (5)	Upswing (6)	Downswing (7)	Upswing (8)
October 1947	November 1948	13.5	-4.2	-17.7	18.2	13	24
November 1950	November 1952	14.0	-0.6	-14.6	2.7	24	8
July 1953	September 1954 [a]	2.1	-1.4	-3.5	5.7	14	22
July 1956	July 1958	4.3	-0.2	-4.5	2.6	24	12
July 1959	March 1961	2.4	0.1	-2.3	3.9	20	58
January 1966	January 1967	4.0	1.3	-2.7	5.3	12	36
January 1970 [a]	October 1971	6.6	2.8	-3.8	9.8	21	33
July 1974	April 1976	12.6	4.7	-7.9		21	
Average: 1947–76		7.4	0.3	-7.1	6.9	19	28

[a] Revised, due to a change in seasonal adjustment. The corresponding dates given in *The Cyclical Behavior of Prices* were August 1954 and February 1970.

Note: The chronology is based on the rate of change in the consumer price index, seasonally adjusted, computed over six-month intervals and expressed at an annual rate. The rates are dated in the middle month of the six-month interval. For example, the rate for April 1976 (4.7 percent) is the change from January 1976 to July 1976, annualized. Except as noted, the dates through 1970 are from Geoffrey H. Moore. *The Cyclical Behavior of Prices*, Bureau of Labor Statistics, Report 384, 1971, p. 7. See pp. 4-5 for a discussion of the relative merits of different price indexes and alternative measures of their rates of change for this purpose.

the rate of increase in the CPI reached its highest point and began to recede, and the troughs are the dates when the rate reached its lowest point and began to rise. In the first four cycles, 1948–1958, the trough rates were negative—the price level declined. After that the trough rates were positive. Indeed, there has been an almost unbroken rise since 1948 in the level of the trough rates, from a negative 4.2 percent in November 1948 to a positive 4.7 percent in April 1976. This of course is symptomatic of the long upswing in the rate of inflation. It is noteworthy, however, that the trend does not show up as clearly in the peaks, which start out at a two-digit level (13.5 and 14.0 percent) and end up at a two-digit level (12.6 percent).

What Table 6 shows, then, is that there were seven upswings in the rate of inflation between 1948 and 1974, and eight downswings. The downswings lasted a year and a half, on the average, with a range of one to two years (column 7). The upswings were longer and more variable, ranging from less than a year to nearly five years, and averaging more than two years (column 8). If the final date in the table is correct, the eighth upswing has been under way since April 1976. At this writing the latest rate, covering the six-month span from November 1976 to May 1977, is 8.7 percent, a four percentage point rise since the trough.

Table 6 also shows that the upswings in the rate of inflation were rather small between 1952 and 1966. The smallest rise during this period of relative stability was about 2.5 percentage points. The Korean War generated the largest rise, 18 percentage points, while the second largest rise, 10 percentage points, occurred during 1971–1974. The latest downswing, 8 percentage points, between July 1974 and April 1976, was substantial but was surpassed in 1947–1948 and 1950–1952.

One of the most important relationships to understand is the one between the inflation rate and the business cycle. Table 7 matches the two chronologies. The match is not perfect, because in 1950–1952 and in 1966–1967 the inflation rate declined without a business cycle downturn. At both times, however, there was a marked slowdown in economic growth.[8] For every business cycle downturn that did occur, then, there was a matching downturn in

---

[8] These slowdowns, as well as an additional one in 1962-1964, have been identified in a "growth cycle" chronology developed by Ilse Mintz at the National Bureau of Economic Research. See her article, "Dating United States Growth Cycles," in *Explorations in Economic Research*, vol. 1, no. 1 (Summer 1974), pp. 1-113. For a revised and updated growth cycle chronology, see the forthcoming report by Victor Zarnowitz and Charlotte Boschan in the Fifty-Seventh Annual Report of the National Bureau of Economic Research.

the inflation rate. For every business cycle upturn, there was a matching upturn in the inflation rate. In other words, every recession was accompanied, sooner or later, by a decline in the rate of inflation. Conversely, every expansion in business activity was accompanied, sooner or later, by a rise in the rate of inflation.

The "sooner or later" phrases in the preceding sentences are given precision by the entries in columns five and six of Table 7. On three occasions the decline in the inflation rate began before the business cycle peak, twice the decline in inflation coincided with the cyclical peak, and once the decline in the inflation rate lagged eight months behind the business peak. This last case developed in the most recent downturn, but it may be recalled that the decline in business activity was relatively moderate until the autumn of 1974, which may explain the unusual lag. Only one of the upturns in the inflation rate preceded the business cycle upturn, three followed the business cycle upturn by just a few months, while the last two lagged by about a year. Hence it appears that there has been a tendency for downturns in the inflation rate to precede downturns in the business cycle, and upturns to follow the business cycle upturns. But "sooner or later" the turns do come, without exception.

Moreover, it is apparent that, except on the two occasions when the economy slowed down markedly but did not experience a contraction of business cycle proportions, downturns in the rate of inflation have occurred only when recessions occurred. In other words, a substantial slowdown or an absolute decline in real economic activity has been both necessary and sufficient to reduce the rate of inflation.[9] The 1973–1975 recession repeated that lesson, although it took longer than usual for this to become apparent.

If, as Table 7 demonstrates, the rate of inflation reaches its lowest point in the vicinity of a business cycle trough, inflation must begin to accelerate while economic activity is still at a fairly low ebb, well before it has fully recovered from recession. At that time unemployment is still relatively high. It is interesting to compare the dates when the unemployment rate reached its peak with the date when the inflation rate reached its trough, as in Table 8.

On four occasions the inflation rate began to rise within two months of the date when unemployment reached its highest level, that is, when the unemployment rate was in the range of 6 to 7.5

---

[9] The 1962-1964 slowdown in economic growth (footnote 8) is not matched by a clear-cut decline in the inflation rate. This is the only instance where a slowdown was not accompanied by a reduction in the inflation rate.

Table 7
RELATIONSHIP BETWEEN THE BUSINESS CYCLE AND INFLATION

Business Cycle		Inflation Rate (CPI)		Lead (−) or Lag (+) of Inflation Rate at Business Cycle (months)	
Peak (1)	Trough (2)	Peak (3)	Trough (4)	Peak (5)	Trough (6)
November 1948	October 1949	October 1947	November 1948	−13	−11
a	a	November 1950	November 1952	a	a
July 1953	May 1954	July 1953	September 1954	0	+4
August 1957	April 1958	July 1956	July 1958	−13	+3
April 1960	February 1961	July 1959	March 1961	−9	+1
a	a	January 1966	January 1967	a	a
December 1969	November 1970	January 1970	October 1971	+1	+11
November 1973	March 1975	July 1974	April 1976	+8	+13

a No corresponding business cycle turn.
Source: National Bureau of Economic Research, Inc.

Table 8
THE TIMING OF INFLATION RATE TROUGHS
AND UNEMPLOYMENT RATE PEAKS

Inflation Rate	Unemployment Rate	Lead (−) or Lag (+) of Inflation Rate
Trough (1)	Peak (2)	(months) (3)
November 1948	October 1949	−11
November 1952		
September 1954	September 1954	0
July 1958	July 1958	0
March 1961	May 1961	−2
January 1967		
October 1971	August 1971	+2
April 1976	May 1975	+11

Source: Column (1)—Table 6; Column (2)—U.S. Bureau of Labor Statistics.

percent.[10] A high level of unemployment has not prevented an increase in the rate of inflation, nor has a low level of unemployment been a prerequisite for inflation. As Arthur Burns said more than a quarter of a century ago, "Inflation does not wait for full employment." [11]

The beginning of a period of rising inflation is often a time when many plants have excess capacity. Underutilization does not seem to prevent increases in prices when demand is rising. Table 9 shows the capacity utilization rate in manufacturing at the time (to the nearest quarter) the inflation rate began to rise. In only two instances, 1952 and 1967, was the utilization rate relatively high when inflation began to accelerate. In all the other instances the upswing began when utilization rates were at 80 percent or lower. It is also apparent that the rising trend in the inflation rate at its cyclical troughs during the past twenty-five years cannot be accounted for by a trend toward higher utilization rates at these times, because the utilization rates show no such trend.

---

[10] On these four occasions when the inflation rate began to rise, the unemployment rate was: September 1954, 6.1 percent; July 1958, 7.5 percent; March 1961, 6.9 percent; October 1971, 5.9 percent. When the rate began to rise in April 1976 the unemployment rate was 7.5 percent. On the other three occasions when the inflation rate began to rise unemployment was much lower: November 1948, 3.8 percent; November 1952, 2.8 percent; January 1967, 3.9 percent.

[11] Introduction to Wesley C. Mitchell, *What Happens during Business Cycles: A Progress Report* (New York: National Bureau of Economic Research, 1951), p. xxi.

Table 9

CAPACITY UTILIZATION RATE AT THE TIME OF
AN INFLATION RATE TROUGH

Inflation Rate Trough		Capacity Utilization Rate Manufacturing	
Date (1)	Rate (percent) (2)	Date (3)	Rate (percent) (4)
November 1948	−4.2	1948:4	80.4
November 1952	−0.6	1952:4	89.8
September 1954	−1.4	1954:3	79.1
July 1958	−0.2	1958:3	75.4
March 1961	0.1	1961:1	73.8
January 1967	1.3	1967:1	88.2
October 1971	2.8	1971:4	79.0
April 1976	4.7	1976:2	80.2

Source: Columns (1) and (2)—Table 6; Columns (3) and (4)—Board of Governors of the Federal Reserve System.

A measure of utilization that shows a closer association with the rate of inflation than does either the unemployment rate or the capacity utilization rate is the percentage of the working-age population employed in civilian jobs, which we call the employment ratio. From a statistical point of view alone the employment ratio has much to recommend it. The denominator, the noninstitutional population sixteen years old and over, is of course an estimate, but it is not subject to the conceptual problems of defining who is in the labor force or how much capacity manufacturing plants have. The numerator, the number of persons sixteen years old and over employed in civilian jobs is a more objectively definable concept than is the number of the unemployed. Also, it is easier to adjust for seasonal variations. Compared with the capacity utilization rate, the employment ratio has the advantage of being based on a large sample survey conducted by the U.S. Census Bureau under controlled conditions with known errors of estimation, whereas the production figures are assembled from a variety of sources and are partly based upon measures of input (kilowatt hours of power utilized or of man-hours employed). In addition, the employment figures cover the entire economy; the capacity utilization rate is limited to manufacturing.[12]

---

[12] For further discussion of the employment ratio in relation to other measures of capacity utilization, see Geoffrey H. Moore, *How Full is Full Employment?* (Washington, D.C.: American Enterprise Institute, 1973).

The employment ratio measures directly how far the civilian economy has reached in order to extend employment opportunities to the entire population of working age. It implicitly takes into account, as noted in the preceding section, the utilization of the secondary labor reserve as well as the primary reserve. When the ratio falls below previously attained levels, it suggests that the nation still has some further capacity to expand employment though perhaps at the cost of short-run increases in the rate of inflation. Some empirical evidence on the relationship between the employment ratio and the rate of increase in wages and prices is contained in Figures 5A and 5B.

The right-hand panel in Figure 5A shows that when the employment ratio is high the rate of increase in hourly compensation is high, whereas when the employment ratio is low the rate of increase in compensation is low. The right-hand panel in Figure 5B shows that a similar relationship exists between the employment ratio and the rate of change in consumer prices. The left-hand panels in Figures 5A and 5B relate the wage and price information to the unemployment rate, and reveal no apparent correlation.[13] Experience in this regard during the recession and the recovery of 1973–1976 is fairly consistent with the historical record, although the rates of increase in wages and prices during 1975 were considerably higher than the levels previously associated with the employment ratio. This latter development was the result of the unusual lag in the adjustment of the inflation rate to the recession, as noted above.

It would appear, then, that the employment ratio has useful properties as a measure of inflationary pressures. In particular, the record suggests that maintenance of a stable employment ratio is one of the requirements to prevent upward pressure on the inflation rate. This does not mean that total employment should not grow. It means that to maintain a constant employment ratio employment growth should not exceed the growth of the working-age population. In recent years, that population has been growing at a rate of about 1.7 percent per year. Hence employment can grow at a similar rate without changing the employment ratio. This rate of growth is equivalent to an annual increase of about 1.5 million persons employed. Since the long-run rate of growth in worker productivity is about 2 percent per year, total output (real GNP) can grow at the rate of nearly 4

---

[13] For further analysis of this record see Geoffrey H. Moore, "Unemployment, and the Inflation-Recession Dilemma," in William Fellner, ed., *Contemporary Economic Problems, 1976* (Washington, D.C.: American Enterprise Institute, 1976), pp. 163-82. For a comparative study of U.S. and Canadian experience, see Christopher Green, "The Employment Ratio as an Indicator of Aggregate Demand Pressure," *Monthly Labor Review* (April, 1977), pp. 25-32.

percent per year with a stable employment ratio, and without upward pressure on the inflation rate from this source.

Just as the business cycle chronology has been helpful in the development of leading, coincident, and lagging indicators of recession and recovery, so the inflation chronology can be helpful in developing leading, coincident, and lagging indicators of inflation. Judging from the poor forecasting record for the rate of inflation, it would be useful to devote more attention to this subject. Forecasts of the inflation rate have shown a marked tendency to lag behind events, more so than forecasts of the level of output or income.[14] Yet leading indicators of the inflation rate do exist. The record for one of them is displayed in Table 10.

The idea of an index of sensitive prices is an old one. It has long been observed that prices in freely competitive markets are especially responsive to changes in supply and demand, while prices that are fixed by contract or custom, or are changed only after considerable negotiation, are sluggish. It is also known that prices of agricultural products are especially affected by erratic changes in supply conditions: crop failure, weather outlook, stocks on hand, and so forth. Prices that are affected primarily by demand conditions and respond quickly to changes in them—such as scrap steel, rubber and hides—are represented in the wholesale price index for crude materials (not including foods, feeds, and fibers). These prices are sensitive to the inventory change, which itself is a key leading indicator of the business cycle. Also, since materials prices represent one of the costs of production, they exert, no doubt with a lag, an influence on the price of the finished goods they enter into.

It is to be expected, therefore, that the rate of change of this price index would not only fluctuate more widely, but also more quickly in response to cyclical change than would indexes that represent a broad spectrum of many types of prices of goods and services, such as the consumer price index. Table 10 and Figure 6 bear out this expectation. With only one exception in thirty years, the index of crude materials has begun to accelerate or decelerate prior to the corresponding movements in the consumer price index. The lead times vary widely, but the average is about six months. It is, indeed, an early warning indicator of the rate of inflation.

In the recent recession, the materials price index reached its maximum rate of increase about six months before the consumer

---

[14] For a comparison see Geoffrey H. Moore, "The President's Economic Report: A Forecasting Record," *NBER Reporter*, April 1977, pp. 4-12 (National Bureau of Economic Research).

Figure 5A

HOURLY COMPENSATION, UNEMPLOYMENT RATE,
AND PERCENTAGE OF POPULATION EMPLOYED, 1948–1976

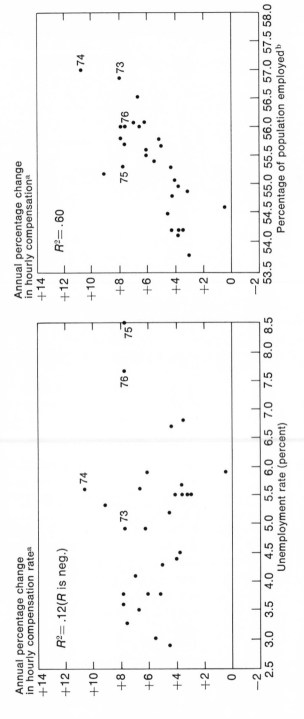

Note: The correlation (R^2) is based on data ending with 1974.
[a] Fourth quarter of preceding year to fourth quarter of current year, private nonfarm sector.
[b] Civilian employment as percent of noninstitutional population sixteen years of age and over.
Source: U.S. Department of Labor, Bureau of Labor Statistics.

Figure 5B

CONSUMER PRICE INDEX, UNEMPLOYMENT RATE,
AND PERCENTAGE OF POPULATION EMPLOYED, 1948–1976

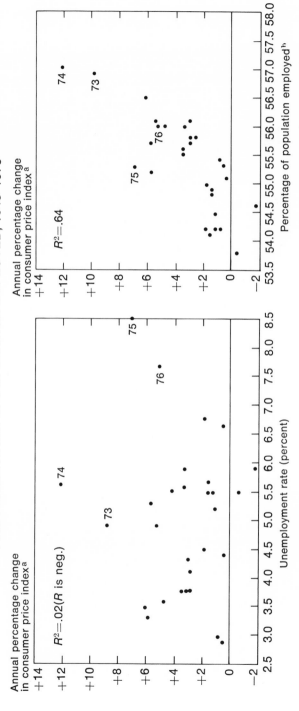

Note: The correlation (R^2) is based on data ending with 1974.
[a] December of preceding year to December of current year.
[b] Civilian employment as percent of noninstitutional population sixteen years of age and over.
Source: U.S. Department of Labor, Bureau of Labor Statistics.

151

Table 10
A LEADING INDICATOR OF INFLATION: CRUDE MATERIALS PRICES[a]

Inflation Rate (CPI)		Rate of Change in Crude Materials Prices[b]		Lead (−) or Lag (+) of Crude Materials Prices (months)	
Peak (1)	Trough (2)	Peak (3)	Trough (4)	Peak (5)	Trough (6)
October 1947	November 1948	August 1947	April 1949	−2	+5
November 1950	November 1952	July 1950	August 1951	−4	−15
July 1953	September 1954	April 1953	October 1953	−3	−11
July 1956	July 1958	September 1955	October 1957	−10	−9
July 1959	March 1961	July 1958	August 1960	−12	−7
January 1966	January 1967	December 1965	October 1966	−1	−3
January 1970	October 1971	May 1969	August 1970	−8	−14
July 1974	April 1976	January 1974	December 1974	−6	−16
Average lead (−) or lag (+)					
At peaks				−6	
At troughs					−9
At peaks and troughs					−7

[a] The crude materials price index is the wholesale price index for crude materials (not including foods, feeds, and fibers). Its rate of change is measured over a six-month interval, seasonally adjusted, centered in the middle month of the span.
[b] Between April 1961 and April 1962 there was a decline in the index that was not matched by a corresponding decline in the inflation rate (CPI).
Source: National Bureau of Economic Research.

Figure 6

INFLATION INDICATORS

(annual percentage rates)

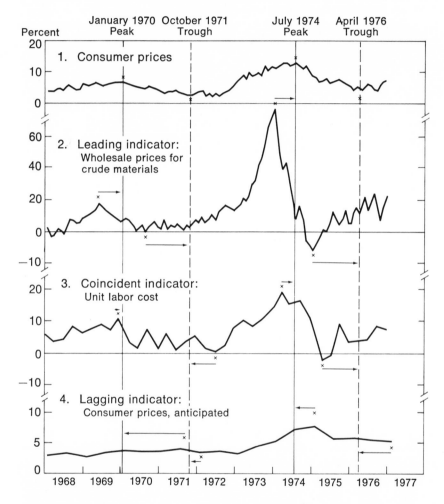

Note: The intervals covered by the rates are: Lines 1 and 2, six months; line 3, one quarter; line 4, eight months. The rates are entered within these intervals. The x's mark the peaks and troughs in the series and the arrows show the lead or lag with respect to the inflation rate (line 1).

Sources: Lines 1-3: U.S. Bureau of Labor Statistics. Crude materials prices exclude foods, feeds, and fibers. Unit labor cost is for nonfarm business sector. Line 4: John A. Carlson, "A Study of Price Forecasts," *Annals of Economic and Social Measurement,* National Bureau of Economic Research, vol. 6, no. 1 (Winter 1977), pp. 33-34.

price index did so, and declined dramatically during the next twelve months. Shortly before the recession ended the materials index reached its maximum rate of decline. Since then it has pursued an irregular upward course, reaching rates of increase between 15 and 20 percent per year in the second half of 1976. Recent rates have subsided from these levels, but the upswing which persisted for more than two years gave fair warning of the upswing in the CPI rate that began in April 1976.

Costs of materials are one important element of the cost of production, labor costs are another. The movements in the rate of change in labor costs per unit of output are roughly coincident with those in the rate of inflation (see Table 11). Between 1947 and 1976 the peaks and troughs of the rate of change in unit labor costs occurred before those in the inflation rate in seven instances, were coincident with those in the rate of inflation twice, and occurred later seven times. If cyclical turns that occurred within three months of each other are counted as roughly coincident, nine of the sixteen fall in this group. The average of the leads and lags is close to zero.

Since fluctuations in unit labor costs are closely associated with the inflation rate, and since, as noted in Table 7, the inflation rate has tended recently to lag behind the business cycle, it is of interest to see whether there has been a similar shift in labor costs (see Table 12).

The correlation between the leads or lags of the inflation rate and those of unit labor cost is $+.80$. The shift toward lags in recent cycles appears in both rates, and the tendency toward longer lags at troughs than at peaks also appears in both rates. Labor costs and prices are indeed closely related to one another, in roughly coincident fashion.[15] No doubt this is partly because costs affect prices, but also because prices affect costs and both are affected by other things.

The swings in the rate of change of unit labor costs are typically wider than swings in the rate of inflation, and the latest cycle was no exception. The labor cost rate rose from almost zero in mid-1972 to about 18 percent (annual rate) early in 1974. A year later the rate was negative, as costs declined briefly with the sharp recovery in output. The trend since then has been upward; the rate in the first quarter of 1977 was 6 percent. The upswing in this roughly coin-

---

[15] It may seem that the frequent leads in the unit labor cost rate at business cycle peaks are inconsistent with the National Bureau's classification of unit labor cost as a lagging indicator of business cycles. The difference is due to the fact that although costs often continue to rise after business activity has reached its peak, their rate of increase may begin to decline before the peak. In these instances costs lag, but their rate of increase leads.

Table 11
A ROUGHLY COINCIDENT INDICATOR OF INFLATION: UNIT LABOR COST

Inflation Rate (CPI)		Rate of Change in Unit Labor Cost		Lead (−) or Lag (+) of Unit Labor Cost at Inflation (months)	
Peak (1)	Trough (2)	Peak (3)	Trough (4)	Peak (5)	Trough (6)
October 1947	November 1948	July 1947	July 1949	−3	+8
November 1950	November 1952	January 1951	July 1951	+2	−16
July 1953	September 1954	October 1952	July 1954	−9	−2
July 1956	July 1958	January 1956	October 1958	−6	+3
July 1959	March 1961	July 1959	October 1961	0	+7
January 1966	January 1967	April 1966	April 1967	+3	+3
January 1970	October 1971	January 1970	July 1972	0	+9
July 1974	April 1976	April 1974	April 1975	−3	−12
Average lead (−) or lag (+)					
At peaks				−2	
At troughs					0
At peaks and troughs				−1	

Note: The unit labor cost index is for the nonfarm business sector. Its rate of change is measured from quarter to quarter, seasonally adjusted, centered in the first month of the later quarter, that is, the change from the first to the second quarter is centered in April, from the second to the third, in July, and so forth.
Source: Columns (1) and (2)—Table 6; columns (3) and (4)—U.S. Bureau of Labor Statistics.

Table 12

LEAD (−) OR LAG (+) OF THE INFLATION RATE AND THE UNIT LABOR COST RATE AT BUSINESS CYCLE PEAKS AND TROUGHS

(months)

Business Cycle Peak	Inflation Rate (CPI)	Unit Labor Cost Rate	Business Cycle Trough	Inflation Rate (CPI)	Unit Labor Cost Rate
November 1948	−13	−16	October 1949	−11	−3
July 1953	0	−9	May 1954	+4	+2
August 1957	−13	−19	April 1958	+3	+6
April 1960	−9	−9	February 1961	+1	+8
December 1969	+1	+1	November 1970	+11	+20
November 1973	+8	+5	March 1975	+13	+1

Source: Tables 7 and 11.

cident indicator is also consistent with the latest upswing in the rate of inflation.

An example of a lagging indicator of the inflation rate may be found in a series of economic forecasts of the consumer price index prepared each June and December by about fifty economists surveyed by Joseph Livingston of the *Philadelphia Inquirer*. We shall use the series recently compiled and analyzed by John A. Carlson.[16] The forecasts cover an eight-month interval, beginning two months before the date of the survey, which is when the latest price indexes would be available to most of the respondents. The June survey covers the interval from April to December, and we center that forecasted rate of change in August. Similarly, the rates obtained from the December survey are centered in the following February. On this basis the peaks and troughs in the forecasted rates can be identified and compared with the actual rates. Since the forecasts are obtained only every six months, the peak and trough dates are less precise than those from the actual rates, which are available every month. However, they show clearly that the forecasted rates lag behind the actual rates in most instances (see Table 13). The average lag is about six months.

Unlike the rates of change in unit labor costs, the forecasted rates of change in the consumer price index exhibit much smaller

---

[16] John A. Carlson, "A Study of Price Forecasts," *Annals of Economic and Social Measurement*, National Bureau of Economic Research, vol. 6, no. 1 (Winter 1977), pp. 27-56.

Table 13

A LAGGING INDICATOR OF INFLATION: CPI FORECASTS

Inflation Rate (CPI)		Eight-month Forecast Rate (CPI)				Lead (−) or Lag (+) of Forecast Rate at Inflation (months)	
		Peak		Trough			
Peak (1)	Trough (2)	Date (3)	Percent (4)	Date (5)	Percent (6)	Peak (7)	Trough (8)
October 1947	November 1948	February 1948	2.8	August 1949	−6.7	+4	+9
November 1950	November 1952	February 1951	3.6	a		+3	a
July 1953	September 1954	a		February 1954	−1.2	a	−7
July 1956	July 1958	February 1957	1.4	August 1959	0.1	+7	+13
July 1959	March 1961	February 1960	1.0	February 1961	0.2	+7	−1
January 1966	January 1967	a		a		a	a
January 1970	October 1971	August 1971	3.9	February 1972	3.0	+19	+4
July 1974	April 1976	February 1975	7.7	February 1977	5.1b	+7	+10b
Average lead (−) or lag (+), in months							
At peaks						+8	
At troughs							+5
At peaks and troughs						+6	

a No corresponding turn.
b Tentative. The latest survey figure, for February 1977, is the lowest to date.
Source: The forecast rates are from the Livingston survey as compiled by John A. Carlson, "A Study of Price Forecasts," and pertain to eight-month intervals centered on February or August of each year. The surveys are made in the preceding December or June.

swings than do the actual rates. In 1974–1975, for example, the highest rate forecast was 7.7 percent (the rate centered on February 1975). The actual peak, reached seven months earlier, was 12.6 percent. There were similar underestimates at all the preceding peaks. The trough levels, however, were not underestimated as much, and the forecasts clearly tracked the secular rise in each successive trough throughout the period (see Table 10, column 6).

The latest forecast in this series is for the period October 1976-June 1977, centered on February 1977. It shows a continuation of the down-trend in the forecasts that began in October 1974. Hence, if we have identified the latest inflation rate trough correctly (April 1976) the forecasted rate lags the actual rate by at least ten months. As of December 1976, when the latest survey was taken, there was no consensus among forecasters that an acceleration of inflation was under way.

It is, of course, unwise to depend upon a single leading indicator, a single coincident indicator, or even a single lagging indicator, since all are fallible. Our examples merely illustrate the idea that indicators of inflation with interesting properties can be found. Much more research must be done before we have a fully annotated and theoretically sound set of leading, coincident, and lagging indicators in this field.

WAGE AND PRICE BEHAVIOR: PROSPECTS AND POLICIES

Marvin H. Kosters

Summary

The recession of 1974–1975 was followed by a substantial reduction in inflation. The transition to lower inflation was rapid, but it was preceded by a period of slow growth and a steep recessionary decline in output. The decline in inflation was also large, although the rate remained high—dropping only temporarily below the 6 percent range in 1976. The decline from rates of increase of over 10 percent for both prices and wages in 1974, however, was a significant response to the sharp cyclical slump in demand and production.

The decline in inflation shown by measures of average wage and price increases was accompanied by important differences in behavior among sectors of the economy. Changes in relative prices and wages reflect shifts in demand or supply and differences in responsiveness to such shifts, and they are normally a major, pervasive part of the economic process. But their significance extends beyond the well known, though insufficiently recognized, point that relative price and wage changes are the response of the marketplace to change and give rise to the incentives that effect it.

Examining changes among sectors of the economy can provide insights into the sources of differences in sensitivity to market forces, the influence of pricing conditions and wage-setting arrangements on such differences, and the effects of changes that occur on structural balance. The responsiveness to market conditions of average rates of wage and price increase is, of course, the net result of the responsiveness shown in the various sectors of the economy. Examining sectors where there has been little response to general market slack *can provide clues as to possible sources of differential behavior. Changes in relationships between wages and between costs and prices establish the conditions from which subsequent changes occur, and imbalances in structural relationships as they develop set the stage for adjustments to restore balance. Thus, future developments are to a significant extent the outgrowth of conditions generated by developments in the immediate past.*

Differences in wage behavior among sectors of the economy in 1975 and 1976 can be traced to both institutional and market sources. In industries where the extent of unionism was high and coverage by long-term collective bargaining agreements was common, wage increases were large and relative wages rose sharply to unusually high levels. While wages under long-term collective bargaining agreements would normally be expected to respond less quickly to current market conditions than wages set by more frequent decisions, extensive coverage by cost-of-living escalator provisions in long-term agreements operated to reduce directly the size of wage increases when prices rose more slowly. Nevertheless, industries in which the extent of unionism was high showed large wage increases compared with less unionized sectors.

Economic factors, sometimes together with institutional features, also contributed to differential wage behavior among sectors. Average wage increases were very large, and increases in relative wages were particularly pronounced for sectors selected on the basis of three kinds of economic factors: (1) reduced direct competition from foreign sources associated with the transition through flexible exchange rates from an overvalued dollar and limited domestic labor market competition; (2) operation under cost-based, rate-of-return-oriented, economic regulation; and (3) energy products production, in which sharp price and demand increases occurred. On the other hand, wages in the construction sector, where the slump in demand was severe and labor market competition apparently increasing, showed smaller-than-average wage increases and a significantly reduced relative wage level.

The net result of the differential wage behavior that occurred during 1975 and 1976 was substantially wider wage differentials and increased dispersion in relative wages among industries. While the rise in relative wage dispersion is likely to be partly cyclical in character, the sharp rise that occurred brought relative wage dispersion to an unusually high level. This is in contrast to the rise that occurred in the recession of 1970, where the rise represented a recovery to more normal levels after the decline during the period of tight labor markets preceding the recession.

To the extent that the rise to very high relative wage dispersion is cyclical in origin, it is subject to at least partial reversal under pressures from tightening markets. The ways in which adjustments can occur, however, are influenced by the wage-setting arrangements that are prevalent in high-wage sectors. Coverage by collective bargaining agreements is concentrated disproportionately in the high-wage sectors, particularly coverage by long-term agreements with cost-of-living escalator provisions. Consequently, wage paths for an important share of workers in high-wage sectors are established for a considerable period, and their relative wage positions are extensively protected by cost-of-living escalator provisions that respond to more general price and cost trends.

The structure of relative wages that has resulted from wage behavior in recent years contributes an element of inflationary bias to labor market conditions. Wage paths established by long-term agreements with escalators limit the potential for restoring relative wage balance through smaller-than-average rates of wage increase in many high-wage sectors. These contractual wage-setting arrangements also place limitations on the range of government policies that could be introduced to foster restraint in these sectors. Pressures for larger-than-average wage increases in a wide range of relatively low-wage sectors with less formal wage-setting arrangements are likely to accompany tighter labor markets. Attempts to restrain wage increases in these sectors by direct government action would be administratively difficult and their implications for equity awkward to defend.

The variation in behavior of wages among sectors of the economy, however, emphasizes the significance for overall wage trends of competitive conditions that impinge on particular sectors as distinct from general labor market tightness. Government policies with microeconomic effects on particular industries, accordingly, can have an important influence on aggregate price and wage performance. Thus, while moderate demand growth is an essential element in restraining inflation, government policies to strengthen the force of competition in particular industries can contribute importantly to achieving inflation restraint and higher levels of resource utilization. The most significant way in which government policies would contribute to inflation restraint through microeconomic decision making may be through avoiding policies that support or push up prices or wages in particular industries or that have the effect of reducing the force of competition from domestic or foreign sources.

Introduction

By spring, 1977, two years had elapsed since the trough of the recession of 1974–1975. During this two-year period, real output rose by almost 12 percent, with about two-thirds of the increase coming in the first year. Despite the pace of the recovery, the unemployment rate remained high—over 7 percent. Both the high level of unemployment and the fact that the rate had declined so little after two years of normal cyclical recovery were exceptional compared with earlier postwar cycles.

Before the recession, consumer prices were rising at the extraordinary rate of 12.2 percent during 1974. After the recession, two developments concerning the rate of inflation are especially noteworthy. First, the rate of price increase declined sharply from rates experienced before the recession—from over 10 percent during 1974, to 7 percent during 1975, and to 4.8 percent during 1976. Second, despite this impressive decline, the inflation rate was still high by historical standards. The inflation rate even in 1976, for example, was three times the average rate that prevailed during the fifteen years between the Korean and Vietnam wars.

The slower rate of price increase that occurred during the two years after the recession was accompanied by a slower rate of increase in wage rates. The decline of average wage increases was less pronounced than for prices, but the preceding rise had also been less pronounced for wages than for prices. Wage increases were noticeably smaller in 1975 and 1976, however, than during the last three quarters of 1974.

The slowdown in wage increases was highly uneven, however, among the major sectors of the economy. Wage increases much larger than average have continued in several of the most highly unionized, high-wage industries covered by long-term wage agreements. Moreover, in most of these industries, cost-of-living escalator provisions link the behavior of wages in the future so closely to price performance that further moderation of wage increases is virtually precluded in the absence of slower consumer price increases. These conditions contribute an inflationary bias to wage and price prospects and pose difficult problems for policy makers trying to achieve a gradual reduction in inflation.

Labor Costs and Prices

The slack in product and labor markets that came with the recession was accompanied by the pronounced decline in inflation since 1974.

The slowdown in inflation for both prices and wages, of course, was a reflection of this sharp overall reduction in demand and the considerable market slack that has persisted through 1975 and 1976. The magnitude of changes in demand varied among sectors of the economy, of course, and the sensitivity of wages to demand changes among sectors also varied with differences in the effects of competition in each sector. The timing and magnitude of the wage-price response was also conditioned by a network of linkages between wages and prices. These linkages include relationships between prices and costs, specifically labor costs. Other linkages include relationships between prices and wages (through escalator provisions, for example) and among wages in various sectors of the economy.

General Wage Trends. The slowdown in hourly labor cost increases became evident in the first part of 1975, near the low point of the recession. The rate of increase in private nonfarm average hourly earnings declined from over 10 percent in mid-1974 to 7.4 percent in the second quarter of 1975, and rates of increase varied within a range of about 6.5 to 8.6 percent during the following two years (see Table 1). While the behavior of the hourly earnings index was quite similar during this period, the rate of increase in hourly compensation declined more abruptly (see Table 2). After four successive quarters during which hourly compensation increases exceeded 10 percent, the rate of increase declined to 7.1 percent in the second quarter of 1975. The large hourly labor cost increases that had occurred in the preceding year were temporary in character, paralleling, with some lag, the burst of inflation that began in 1973. During the year preceding this temporary surge, both average hourly earnings and the hourly earnings index were increasing at rates of about 7 percent.

While the slowdown in hourly labor cost increases that occurred between late 1974 and the second quarter of 1975 were unusually large for such a short period, there was apparently very little further reduction in rates of wage increase in the following two years. Because quarterly changes in wages expressed as annual rates show a great deal of variability over time and between hourly earnings and compensation, measures of quarterly changes should be interpreted cautiously. Annual increases in hourly earnings and compensation (measured over four-quarter spans), however, varied between about 7 and 8 percent for the two years ending with the first quarter of 1977 (see Tables 1 and 3).

The major sources of differences between changes in the hourly earnings index and hourly compensation (which correspond roughly

Table 1

AVERAGE HOURLY EARNINGS INCREASES, 1974-1977

(annual percentage change)

| | 1974 | | | 1975 | | | | 1976 | | | | 1977 |
	II	III	IV	I	II	III	IV	I	II	III	IV	I
Percentage change from preceding quarter (by sector)												
Private nonfarm	7.1	10.0	10.6	9.3	9.1	7.4	8.5	8.0	6.9	6.6	7.2	6.4	8.3
Manufacturing	7.3	11.4	11.9	10.8	10.0	8.7	8.5	8.1	7.4	6.4	9.0	6.6	7.8
Construction	3.9	8.4	12.7	6.4	6.6	7.7	6.8	4.1	5.7	7.5	5.3	3.5	5.6
Percentage change from preceding year (by sector)												
Private nonfarm	7.0	7.8	8.7	9.3	9.8	9.1	8.5	8.2	7.7	7.5	7.2	6.8	7.1
Manufacturing	6.8	8.2	9.4	10.3	11.0	10.3	9.5	8.8	8.2	7.6	7.7	7.4	7.4
Construction	3.8	5.2	7.0	7.8	8.5	8.3	6.9	6.3	6.1	6.0	5.6	5.5	5.5

Source: U.S. Department of Labor, Bureau of Labor Statistics.

to measures of wage rates and hourly labor costs, respectively) are shown in Tables 2 and 3. These sources include changes in overtime and employment patterns, differences in coverage and changes in supplementary benefits, and they result in significant discrepancies between quarterly changes in the hourly earnings index and hourly compensation (see Table 2). Manufacturing overtime changes, inter-industry employment shifts, and changes in the share of nonproduction workers are primarily cyclical, with reversals in their effects shown for annual changes (see Table 3). However, increases in supplementary benefits have generally exceeded increases for wages alone, contributing about one-half of one percentage point annually to hourly labor cost increases during the period from 1974 to 1977. The ratio of supplementary benefits to wages has been rising, with much of the rise attributable to higher employer contributions for social security.

Labor Costs, Productivity, and Prices. The tendency for relatively slow or even negative productivity growth during the late stages of a cyclical recovery and the early stages of a downturn has frequently been noted. This tendency was exacerbated prior to the 1974–1975 recession by the oil embargo of late 1973 and the period of virtually no increase in aggregate output that followed. Output per hour declined in each quarter of 1974, and failed to rise above the level of the previous year until the second quarter of 1975 (see Tables 2 and 3).

The persistent decline in output per hour that occurred before the trough of the recession was reached in the spring of 1975 came at a time when hourly labor costs were rising at rates averaging over 10 percent. This condition resulted in increases in labor costs per unit of output of about 15 percent throughout 1974. This trend was not really reversed until the second quarter of 1975. When large increases in output per hour occurred, they were promptly translated into slower price increases. The price deflator for the nonfarm business sector dropped from a 13.5 to a 2.6 percent rate of increase in the second quarter of 1975. This rapid transition to slower price increases was apparently a reflection of the severity of the recession, although price swings from quarter to quarter during this period were less pronounced than were changes in unit labor costs.

The initial sharp recovery in productivity when the trough of the recession was passed was followed by changes in output per hour that varied significantly from quarter to quarter, but averaged out to a rate of about 3 percent by 1976. Increases in hourly compensation

Table 2

WAGES, LABOR COSTS, PRODUCTIVITY AND PRICES IN THE NONFARM SECTOR OF THE ECONOMY, 1974–1977

(percentage change from preceding quarter at annual rate)

	1974				1975				1976				1977
	I	II	III	IV	I	II	III	IV	I	II	III	IV	I
Hourly earnings index[a]	7.2	10.3	10.4	9.4	9.0	7.3	8.4	8.0	6.9	6.7	7.1	6.4	8.2
Effect on hourly labor costs of:													
Manufacturing overtime[b]	−0.3	−0.5	0.2	−0.6	−1.1	0.0	−0.7	0.1	0.5	−0.3	0.1	0.1	0.4
Interindustry shifts[c]	−0.4	−0.7	−0.3	−0.1	−1.6	−1.5	−0.1	−0.3	−0.1	0.5	−0.7	0.8	−0.1
Nonproduction workers[d]	2.1	1.2	1.0	2.6	4.4	0.6	−1.6	−1.1	0.6	0.5	0.7	0.1	3.5
Self-employed[e]	0.2	0.2	0.2	−0.2	−0.3	0.3	0.3	−0.7	0.2	0.4	0.3	−0.1	−0.4
Supplementary benefits[f]	0.8	0.2	0.3	0.6	1.2	0.4	0.1	−0.2	0.9	−0.1	−0.4	−0.3	−1.3
Hourly compensation[g,h]	9.6	10.7	11.8	11.7	11.6	7.1	6.4	5.8	9.0	7.7	7.1	7.0	10.3
Output per hour[h]	−4.1	−6.5	−3.0	−3.4	1.1	11.8	8.9	−2.8	5.4	4.4	2.6	−1.2	4.1
Unit labor cost[h]	14.3	18.4	15.2	15.6	10.4	−4.2	−2.3	8.9	3.4	3.2	4.3	8.3	6.0
Price[h]	9.4	17.0	13.4	13.5	13.5	2.6	5.3	6.2	4.3	3.6	5.8	5.9	3.5

a The hourly earnings index is based on average hourly earnings of production and nonsupervisory workers in the private nonfarm sector, adjusted for overtime (in manufacturing only) and interindustry employment shifts. Changes in the index differ from actual average hourly compensation changes for the nonfarm business sector because of differences in employee coverage, shifts in relative employment among industries and between production and nonproduction workers, and inclusion of overtime (in manufacturing) and supplementary benefits.

b The effect of adjustment for manufacturing overtime in the index is computed from the difference between straight-time and gross average hourly earnings in manufacturing, with manufacturing assumed to account for one-third of the index.

c The effect of interindustry shifts is computed from the difference between actual changes in average hourly earnings and average hourly earnings changes based on fixed employment shares.

d This adjustment is computed as the difference between changes in gross average earnings for production and nonsupervisory workers in the private nonfarm sector and changes in hourly wages and salaries for all employees in the nonfarm business sector. Thus, it includes the effect of small differences in employee coverage by type of enterprise (government enterprises are included in the nonfarm business sector and nonprofit institution production workers are included in the private nonfarm sector, but not vice versa), in addition to the inclusion of nonproduction workers in hourly wages and salaries for the nonfarm business sector.

e This adjustment reflects the inclusion of estimates of compensation for self-employed workers in the private business sector. (It is computed as the difference between changes in hourly compensation for "all employees" and "all persons.")

f Supplementary benefits include such items as contributions to social security, private pensions, and health and welfare plans. Their effect is computed as the difference between changes in hourly compensation and hourly wages and salaries for all employees.

g Hourly compensation is a measure of average hourly compensation for all wage and salary workers and the self-employed in the nonfarm business sector.

h Hourly compensation, output per hour, unit labor costs, and prices are for the nonfarm business sector of the economy.

Source: U.S. Department of Labor, Bureau of Labor Statistics.

167

Table 3
WAGES, LABOR COSTS, PRODUCTIVITY AND PRICES IN THE NONFARM SECTOR OF THE ECONOMY, 1974–1977
(percentage change from same quarter a year earlier)

	1974				1975				1976				1977
	I	II	III	IV	I	II	III	IV	I	II	III	IV	I
Hourly earnings index[a]	7.0	7.4	8.1	8.6	8.6	7.6	7.1	6.9	7.1	7.4	7.1	7.0	7.3
Effect on hourly labor costs of:													
Manufacturing overtime[b]	−0.1	−0.2	−0.1	−0.3	−0.5	−0.4	−0.2	0	0.3	0.3	0.1	0.1	0.1
Interindustry shifts[c]	0.1	0.6	0.7	1.0	1.6	1.9	1.6	1.3	0.3	−0.2	0	−0.3	−0.3
Nonproduction workers[d]	0.2	0.6	0.7	1.0	1.2	0.8	0.1	−0.8	−1.0	−0.6	−0.2	0.2	0.3
Self-employed[e]	0	0.1	0.2	0	−0.1	0	0	−0.1	0.1	0.1	0.1	0.2	0
Supplementary benefits[f]	0.5	0.5	0.5	0.6	0.6	0.6	0.5	0.4	0.3	0.2	0.3	0.5	0.6
Hourly compensation[g,h]	7.7	9.0	10.1	10.9	11.4	10.5	9.1	7.7	7.1	7.2	7.4	7.7	8.0
Output per hour[h]	−2.6	−3.3	−3.8	−4.3	−3.0	1.4	4.4	4.5	5.7	3.9	2.4	2.8	2.4
Unit labor cost[h]	10.6	12.7	14.5	15.9	14.9	8.9	4.5	3.0	1.3	3.2	4.9	4.8	5.4
Price[h]	7.6	10.6	12.5	13.3	14.3	10.6	8.6	6.8	4.6	4.9	5.0	4.9	4.7

Notes: See notes to Table 2.
Source: U.S. Department of Labor, Bureau of Labor Statistics.

were slightly less than 8 percent, so that concomitant price increases at a rate of about 5 percent were roughly in line with the average rate of increase in unit labor costs.

Collective Bargaining Developments

Wage increases under collective bargaining agreements followed a pattern somewhat similar to that for general wage increases. This pattern is evidenced by the data for effective wage changes under major collective bargaining agreements. These data show wage increases of 7.0 percent in 1973 and 9.4 percent in 1974, with the increases tapering off to 8.7 percent in 1975 and 8.1 percent in 1976 (see Table 4).

The largest new wage settlements were negotiated in 1975, both for first-year wage changes and for average wage increases over the life of the contracts. Wage increases under prior settlements and escalator provisions were also larger in 1975 than in 1974. However, because the fraction of workers under major collective bargaining agreements who received increases under current settlements in 1975 was relatively small (28 percent), effective wage changes were smaller in 1975 than in 1974 despite the larger wage increases under each type of adjustment. The large contributions to effective wage increases that came from prior settlements and escalator provisions in 1975 were the legacy of contracts negotiated previously. Moreover, settlements negotiated during 1975 were larger than in 1974 even though price increases were smaller and unemployment was higher.

The reduction in the average size of new wage settlements in 1976 and the trend toward smaller effective wage increases under major collective bargaining agreements in both 1975 and 1976 contributed to slower hourly labor cost increases after 1974. Wage developments under collective bargaining agreements show a lagged response to changing conditions compared with general wage increases during this period, however. The fact that a large share of the workers under major collective bargaining agreements are under multi-year contracts contributed to the lag.[1] At the same time, widespread coverage by cost-of-living escalator provisions in long-term contracts contributed to shortening the lag in response to market

---

[1] Major collective bargaining agreements are situations covering 1,000 or more workers. About 10 million workers are covered by major agreements, accounting for about 12 percent of private nonfarm wage and salary workers, and about 80 percent of the workers under major agreements are covered by three-year contracts.

Table 4

WAGE CHANGES UNDER MAJOR COLLECTIVE BARGAINING SETTLEMENTS, 1970–1976

(percentage)

	1970	1971	1972	1973	1974	1975	1976
Wage settlements							
First-year wage changes	11.9	11.6	7.3	5.8	9.8	10.2	8.4
Average over life of contract[a]	8.9	8.1	6.4	5.1	7.3	7.8	6.4
Percentage of workers affected by new settlements[b]	43	38	23	52	50	28	45
Effective wage rate changes[c]							
Total	8.8	9.2	6.6	7.0	9.4	8.7	8.1
Adjustment resulting from:							
current settlement	5.1	4.3	1.7	3.0	4.8	2.8	3.2
prior settlement	3.1	4.2	4.2	2.7	2.6	3.7	3.2
escalator provisions	0.6	0.7	0.7	1.3	1.9	2.2	1.6
Escalator coverage							
Percentage of workers covered by escalators[d]	26	28	41	39	39	50	58

Note: Data relate to collective bargaining situations covering 1,000 or more workers in private nonfarm industries.

[a] Averages over life of contracts do not include wage increases under cost-of-living escalator provisions.

[b] Percent of estimated workers covered in major collective bargaining situations for which new wage settlements were negotiated during the year.

[c] Effective wage rate changes are wage rate changes actually put into effect during the year. They include wage increases under new settlements, deferred increases under previously negotiated contracts, and increments under cost-of-living escalator provisions.

[d] Estimated percentage of workers under major collective bargaining agreements as of the beginning of the year. By January 1977 coverage had risen to 61 percent.

Source: U.S. Department of Labor, Bureau of Labor Statistics.

conditions, both when the rate of inflation rose in 1973 and 1974 and when it declined in 1975 and 1976.

Prospective wage increases under collective bargaining agreements can be assessed by examining wage increases built into long-term contracts negotiated during 1976. Wage increases over the life of contracts negotiated in 1976 averaged 6.4 percent, with little variation according to contract duration. Two- and three-year contracts, however, show smaller increases in the latter years. For two-year contracts, average first-year increases were 7.8 percent compared to 5.8 percent second-year increases; for three-year contracts, first-year increases averaged 8.7 percent compared to 5.6 percent second-year and 4.8 percent third-year increases. These increases do not include payments under escalator provisions, however, and while only 17 percent of the workers under two-year contracts are covered by escalators, 73 percent of workers under three-year agreements are covered by escalator provisions. These data suggest the possibility of a continuing trend toward slower wage increases, but they also indicate that such a trend will be contingent upon price behavior.

The potential significance of payments under cost-of-living escalator provisions is illustrated by the data shown in Table 5. During 1976, payments under escalator provisions averaged between 3 and 4 percent, while consumer prices rose by 4.8 percent. Deferred wage increases scheduled to be placed into effect during 1977 average 5.6 percent—slightly higher than in 1976 (see Table 6). The higher deferred increases scheduled for 1977 assume particular significance because, first, a slightly larger share of workers covered by major agreements will be affected by escalator provisions; second, few of the escalator provisions contain "caps" or limits; and, third, wage increases resulting from deferred increases and escalator payments combined may be larger than would be suggested on the basis of comparisons with data for earlier years. The reason for this third point is that some contracts provide for wage increases that are structured as escalator payments even though they are not contingent on price increases up to a given rate. Wage increases under these provisions are included in estimates of deferred increases, but only a small fraction of the workers scheduled to receive deferred increases in 1977 are affected by this type of provision.[2]

In the collective bargaining sector, the complex pattern of differences in contract duration, expiration dates, and contract provisions prevents the identification of any clearly defined breaks in the collective bargaining cycle. However, some semblance of a three-year cycle has emerged, with two years in which new negotiations are scheduled for large numbers of workers followed by a relatively light year. The years 1976 and 1977 are marked by relatively heavy negotiations, while 1978 can be expected to be a relatively light year for negotiations, as was 1975. Consequently, future wage increases

---

[2] Only about 400,000 workers were covered by agreements containing these "guaranteed" payments under cost-of-living escalator provisions in 1976, compared to over 1 million workers in 1974 and 1975.

Table 5

CONSUMER PRICE INCREASES AND WAGE INCREASES UNDER COST-OF-LIVING ESCALATOR PROVISIONS OF MAJOR COLLECTIVE BARGAINING AGREEMENTS, 1969–1976

(percentage)

	1969	1970	1971	1972	1973	1974	1975	1976
Increase in consumer price index	6.1	5.5	3.4	3.4	8.8	12.2	7.9	4.8
Wage increases under cost-of-living escalator provisions								
All industries	1.6	3.7	3.1	2.0	4.1	5.8	4.8	3.5
Manufacturing	1.7	3.8	3.7	1.8	4.0	7.2	5.2	3.2
Nonmanufacturing	1.4	2.6	1.8	2.2	4.7	2.0	4.1	4.0

Note: Data on wage increases under cost-of-living escalator provisions relate to all workers covered by escalator provisions under collective bargaining agreements covering 1,000 workers or more in private nonfarm industries. Consumer price increases are from December to December and wage increases are mean percentage increases during the year.

Source: U.S. Department of Labor, Bureau of Labor Statistics.

for a large share of the workers under major agreements are set under the terms of agreements negotiated in 1976 and 1977. That is, under these agreements the wage paths for many workers are already established for periods of up to three years, including their linkage to price behavior, with little potential for modification of these wage paths until the new round of contract expirations begins during 1979.

In part because large numbers of workers in several basic industries are affected, some of the major settlements that are reached during the two heavy bargaining years are highly visible and receive a great deal of public attention. For example, major settlements reached in 1976 that are often viewed as having considerable pattern-setting significance include those covering workers in the automobile, rubber, electrical equipment, and trucking industries. Major negotiations in 1977 include the steel industry settlement and bargaining in the telephone communications, railroad, and bituminous coal mining industries. Attention is frequently focused on these major settlements not only because of their direct effect on hourly labor costs but because of their possible pattern-setting significance for wages elsewhere in the economy. For example, the terms of settlements in the farm equipment manufacturing industry have historically been similar to those in the automobile manufacturing industry that are

Table 6

INCREASE IN HOURLY EARNINGS AND NEGOTIATED WAGE INCREASES UNDER MAJOR COLLECTIVE BARGAINING SETTLEMENTS, 1968–1977

(percentage change)

	1968	1969	1970	1971	1972	1973	1974	1975	1976	1977[a]
Average hourly earnings, private nonfarm	6.3	6.6	6.6	7.1	6.5	6.4	8.2	8.9	7.2	
Wage increases under major collective bargaining agreements[b]										
All industries										
First year	7.4	9.2	11.9	11.6	7.3	5.8	9.8	10.2	8.4	
Deferred	4.6	5.4	5.8	7.7	6.0	4.8	5.1	5.2	5.4	5.6
Construction										
First year	8.7	13.1	17.6	12.6	6.9	5.0	11.0	8.0	6.1	
Deferred	n.a.	n.a.	10.1	13.1	11.6	7.3	5.3	8.0	8.1	6.4
Manufacturing										
First year	7.0	7.9	8.1	10.9	6.6	5.9	8.7	9.8	8.9	
Deferred	3.9	4.0	4.6	4.8	4.5	4.4	4.6	4.4	4.9	5.0
Nonmanufacturing (excluding construction)										
First year	7.6	9.6	14.2	12.2	8.2	6.0	10.2	11.9	8.6	
Deferred	n.a.	n.a.	5.2	7.6	7.3	5.0	5.6	5.1	4.9	6.0

[a] Deferred wage increases for 1977 are estimates of wage increases scheduled to be put in effect during the year, excluding increases that may occur under cost-of-living provisions.

[b] Data on wage increases are mean percentage changes for collective bargaining agreements covering 1,000 workers or more in private nonfarm industries. First-year wage changes include all changes negotiated during the year and going into effect during the first twelve months of the agreement. Deferred wage increases are increases provided for in agreements after the first twelve months and put into effect during the year, excluding cost-of-living escalator increases.

Source: U.S. Department of Labor, Bureau of Labor Statistics.

negotiated by the same union. Similar observations may be made about the relationship between settlements reached in the basic steel industry and collective bargaining in other primary metals industries, such as copper and aluminum, as well as in metal fabricating industries, such as metal cans.

The extent to which major collective bargaining settlements exert a pattern-setting influence on other wages in more indirect and subtle ways is a controversial question. Certainly, the dispersion in the size of wage settlements and differences in other terms of contracts negotiated in the same year demonstrate that strict yearly pattern following is not the rule. Evidence of dispersion is not conclusive evidence, however, that spillover effects operating through the magnitude of wage increases, or through relative wage relationships, are unimportant and can therefore be disregarded.

Dispersion in wage increases and differences in other contract terms are the results of many contributing factors, including differences in market conditions among sectors of the economy and differences in the responsiveness of wages to market conditions. While all of the contributing factors are not easily identified, part of the dispersion is systematically related to differences in the terms of expiring contracts and differences in the provisions of newly negotiated contracts. Information from contracts negotiated during 1976 provides evidence in support of these points.

Contracts extending over a period of time are made with a view toward the future, with interrelationships among the various provisions in the contracts and the uncertainty of future developments in mind. One of the most significant of these interrelationships is the one between escalator provisions and the size of fixed wage increases. There is a tendency for larger fixed negotiated wage increases in contracts without escalator provisions, and this tendency is naturally more evident in measures of wage increases over the life of contracts than for first-year wage increases. It is also more evident in the manufacturing sector, in which long-term agreements are more prevalent, than in other sectors (see Table 7). Restricting the comparison to the manufacturing sector also avoids the tendency for larger fixed wage increases under contracts without escalators to be obscured by the inclusion of construction, in which short-term contracts are common and recent wage increases have been relatively small.

The difference of about 3 percent in annual wage increases for manufacturing between contracts with escalators and those without escalators (see Table 7) should not, however, be viewed as a measure

Table 7
WAGE SETTLEMENTS AND COST OF LIVING ESCALATORS
(annual percentage changes)

Wage Settlements in 1976

	All contracts	Contracts with escalators	Contracts without escalators
First-year wage changes			
All industries	8.4	8.4	8.3
Manufacturing	8.9	8.6	9.8
Nonmanufacturing	7.7	8.1	7.4
Construction	6.1	—	—
Changes over life of contracts			
All industries	6.4	5.7	7.3
Manufacturing	6.0	5.2	8.0
Nonmanufacturing	6.8	6.6	7.0
Construction	6.2	—	—

Changes Under Previous Agreements and 1976 Settlements

	1976 settlement	Previous settlement excluding adjustments under escalators	Previous settlement including adjustments under escalators
Changes over life of contracts			
All industries	6.4	6.1	8.0
Contracts with escalators	5.7	5.2	8.6
Contracts without escalators	7.3	7.2	7.2

Source: U.S. Department of Labor, Bureau of Labor Statistics.

of expected price behavior as it affects collective bargaining settlements. In addition to possible differences in contract duration, other terms of the contracts, differences in market conditions, and differences in bargaining strength may significantly influence this difference. Moreover, measures of average increases over the life of contracts also include first-year wage increases, which may reflect circumstances other than those relating to the future.

In addition to the forward-looking element reflected in the size of wage settlements, there is also a backward-looking element that is likely to be reflected predominantly in the size of first-year wage increases. In some instances this backward-looking element is explicitly an issue in particular negotiations, as, for example, in the auto workers' negotiations in 1970 and the rubber workers' negotiations in 1976. It is also reflected, however, in data on settlements reached during 1976 that show wage increases under previous settlements by the presence or absence of escalator provisions. Although no industry stratification is available for these data shown in the lower part of Table 7, the data show larger-than-average new settlements for contracts without escalators, following smaller-than-average total wage increases received under the expiring agreements. The larger-than-average wage increases received under expiring agreements with escalators were attributable to the significant contribution to annual rates of wage increase—from 5.2 to 8.6 percent—from escalator payments.

Wage Relationships

The systematic relationship between differences in the size of current wage increases and wage increases realized in the past or provided for in the future reflects the tendency for relative wage relationships in the economy to remain relatively stable. While this general tendency can be viewed as the result of an absence of sharp or abrupt changes in the main forces that give rise to observed wage differentials, significant changes in relative wages have occurred over time, and short-term changes have frequently occurred that were subsequently reversed. Consequently, a description of recent changes in relative wage relationships can by itself give little insight into likely wage behavior in the future. Since relationships that have prevailed in the past will not necessarily be maintained, the implications of wage trends resulting from long-term contracts may be limited to the wages of only those workers covered.

The implications of relative wage patterns for future wage prospects depend on the main forces that gave rise to these patterns and on the influence these forces can be expected to exert in the future. However, the sources of wage differentials are diverse, the data available for analysis are limited, and possible sources of change are not easily foreseen. The contribution that an examination of relative wage patterns can make to insights into wage prospects, therefore, depends on the extent to which judgments can be made about the main sources of pressures for adjustments.

Differences in wage behavior among industries are not necessarily associated with high or rising overall rates of wage increase. Indeed, the marked changes in relative wage relationships that have occurred since 1974 were associated with a reduction in the average rate of wage increase.[3] As in the case of price behavior, changes in relative wages must be distinguished from average changes in overall wage levels. However, information on developments in particular industries and markets can contribute useful insights into the prospective behavior of the aggregate wage level. Price or wage trends in individual sectors of the economy often reflect policies and institutional or market developments more or less specific to a particular sector, but the resulting impetus to prices or wages can contribute directly to change in the aggregate. Of course, in the short run, pressures for offsetting adjustments in other sectors may counterbalance specific wage or price movements, leaving the aggregate level unaffected. Such short-run adjustments, however, also create conditions such that forces for subsequent reversal of these adjustments may assert themselves when market conditions change.

Analysis of Relative Wages. The implications of changes in relationships among wages can be approached from a number of different perspectives. The main focus of this analysis is on short-term changes in wage relationships among industries. While such an analysis could be conducted as an effort to trace wage differentials and changes in relative wages to their sources, the purpose here is to examine short-term changes with a view toward exploring why such changes have occurred and toward judging their significance for overall wage prospects. The rationale for this approach is that it can provide useful insights into wage prospects without a detailed treatment of all of the factors that influence wage differentials. A brief discussion of some of the most important features of wage differentials and their sources is warranted, however, to place this analysis in perspective.[4]

At a broad level of generality, the major economic sources of wage differentials are differences in training, work experience, and

---

[3] The influence of departures from normal relationships among wages has apparently depended on cyclical factors and other circumstances surrounding the nature of the distortions. In some discussions of factors influencing rates of wage increase, however, distortions in historical relationships are viewed as major contributors to large average rates of increase. See D. Q. Mills, *Government, Labor, and Inflation* (Chicago: University of Chicago Press, 1975), chapter 5.

[4] Several references to the literature on wage differentials are contained in Marvin Kosters, "Wages, Inflation, and the Labor Market," in William Fellner, ed., *AEI Studies on Contemporary Economic Problems, 1976* (Washington, D.C.: American Enterprise Institute, 1976).

ability among workers. Empirical measures that are the closest counterpart of this concept are skill levels, usually described in terms of job classifications. Levels of schooling, special training, age, and type and duration of work experience are also viewed as measures of skill levels. Economic measures of skill levels are to a large degree empirical constructs derived from relationships between compensation levels and the personal and demographic variables characterizing workers. Distributions of skill levels differ among industry sectors and are subject to change over time.

Although economically relevant measures of skills are generally derived on the basis of compensation measures, wages compose only one component of overall compensation. Supplementary benefits account for an increasingly important share of total compensation, with the range of benefits including contributions to pension plans, health insurance, paid holidays and vacations, supplementary unemployment benefits, sick leave, and disability insurance. Average hourly earnings do not reflect differences in the costs of supplementary benefits or the value of these benefits to workers. Moreover, compensation measures that include estimates of the costs of supplementary benefits would still leave out important factors, such as differences in workers' perceptions of the status or risks associated with a job, the potential contribution to higher earnings that results from work experience, and other aspects of working conditions. As in the case of skill levels, these elements of overall compensation vary among industries and over time and pose severe measurement difficulties.

Wage differentials and changes in relative wages can also be the result of changes in market power, with either labor or product markets possible sources of such a change. For example, unionization or strengthening of a union's bargaining position could lead to a rise in relative wages. Conversely, erosion of union bargaining power, as, for example, through growth of nonunion construction activity, could lead to a reduction in relative wages. Changes in labor legislation could alter bargaining power through its influence on labor markets, just as government policies or legislation could shift market power through their influence on product markets. For example, regulation of prices and market entry may tend to insulate prices and wages in the regulated industry from the pressures of demand changes; and imposition of import quotas or tariffs would mitigate the influence of competition from foreign sources. Conversely, government policies that foster more market flexibility and introduce more competition would strengthen the influence of market conditions on price and wage trends.

The possible influence of unionization on wage differentials through changes in market power and possible spillover effects from pattern-setting settlements has already been noted. In addition, wage contracts can also result in at least temporary insulation from current market forces. Long-term contracts establish a wage path that normally prevails until expiration, with the wage path under contracts with escalators contingent upon price behavior during the contract period. As a result, long-term wage contracts can, at least temporarily, introduce a degree of rigidity that gives rise to relative wage relationships that depart from normal patterns.

Relative wage positions for workers at particular skill levels may also reflect changes in relative supply or demand. For example, a rise in the supply of younger, less experienced workers could depress their relative wages. Similarly, a decline in demand in a major industrial sector, such as construction, could lead to reduced relative wages in that industry. An increase in labor force participation of women could, unless offset by compensating demand changes, depress their relative wages. In addition, of course, if women are paid differentially lower wages because of the occupational or skill categories in which they seek employment, more intermittent work experience, or weaker labor force attachment, a disproportionate increase in the fraction of women employed in a particular industry would reduce average wages in that industry relative to other industries.

There are also several channels through which general or cyclical changes in demand could influence relative wages. Though cyclical patterns vary, changes in overall demand levels are usually translated into disproportionate changes in demand for cyclically sensitive industries. In addition, differences among industries in the responsiveness of wages to changes in demand can temporarily alter wage differentials. More generally, differences in hiring and training investments for workers at different skill levels tend to produce disproportionate cyclical swings in demand and in employment for workers with lower skills. This channel through which wage differentials are influenced by cyclical demand changes may be the main source of the pattern reflected in historical data that show a relatively wide dispersion of relative wages among industries during periods of cyclical slack and reduced dispersion during periods of high demand.[5]

It is important at this point to distinguish between secular and cyclical changes in wage relationships. Since the main focus of this analysis of labor market developments and wage prospects is on

---

[5] Ibid., pp. 142-47.

short-term adjustment issues, many of the demographic and other factors that influence long-term wage relationships can be regarded as less significant because they are not generally subject to abrupt short-term changes. Second, since changes in relative wage relationships among industries are the subject of the analysis, the fact that wages represent an incomplete measure of compensation should have limited effects on the analysis, because other elements of compensation can be viewed as changing only gradually among industries. Finally, although historical wage data show evidence of a secular tendency toward smaller wage differentials among skill levels, with much of the narrowing associated with cyclical periods of unusual labor market tightness, this tendency is not necessarily reflected by wage differentials among industries. Dispersion of relative wages among industries has shown a cyclical tendency toward wider dispersion during periods of persistently high unemployment and narrower dispersion during periods of persistently low unemployment. The significance of this historical tendency for this analysis is that cyclical changes in wage relationships among industries are subject to reversal through cyclical change.

Dispersion of Relative Wages. The relationship between dispersion of relative wages among industries and unemployment has been noted in econometric studies.[6] Relative wage dispersion changes gradually compared with unemployment, so that sharp cyclical peaks in unemployment are not accompanied by abrupt changes in dispersion. Instead, persistent differences in average levels of unemployment have been accompanied by sustained movements in dispersion. Measures of relative wage dispersion among industries are not generally sensitive to differences in the industries covered, except in the case of construction. Dispersion measures are sensitive to the inclusion of construction wages because the level of wages in construction is above wage levels in most other high-wage sectors and relative to other high-wage sectors, construction wages have behaved differently. A brief discussion of construction wage behavior follows the discussion of wages in other industries in the private nonfarm sector.

Changes in the dispersion of relative wages since World War II are shown in Figure I. The path of change can be characterized as generally rising after the wartime years, when relative wage dispersion was compressed, until the beginning of the 1960s. During the 1960s dispersion declined during a period of tightening markets.

---

[6] See, for example, M. L. Wachter, "The Wage Process: An Analysis of the Early 1970s," *Brookings Papers on Economic Activity*, 1974 (2), pp. 507-24.

Figure 1

CHANGES IN RELATIVE EARNINGS AND UNEMPLOYMENT

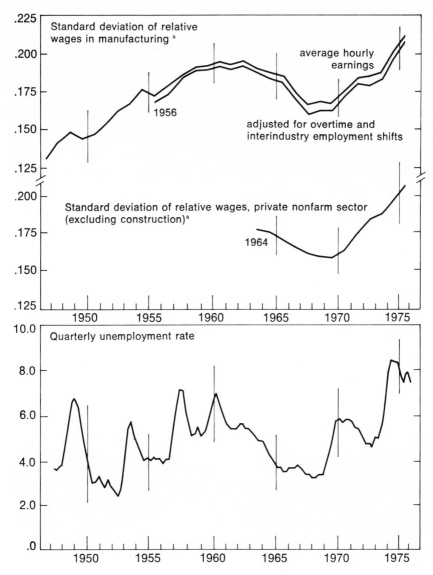

a Standard deviation of natural logarithms of average hourly earnings for the industry sectors included.

Source: U.S. Department of Labor, Bureau of Labor Statistics.

After stabilizing in the late 1960s, dispersion increased with the rise in demand toward a cyclical peak in 1972–1973.

Each of the measures of dispersion shown in Figure 1 again rose sharply in 1975 and 1976. Moreover, by 1976 they had risen to levels higher than the highest levels they had reached earlier in the postwar period. On the basis of historical patterns, high and increasing dispersion could be expected in view of the period of high unemployment and extensive market slack that followed the 1974–1975 recession. While wages on the average rose much less rapidly after 1974, the sharp increase in the dispersion of relative wages in 1975 and 1976 indicates that the deceleration in wage increases was concentrated in the relatively low-wage industries of the economy.

The marked unevenness in the slowdown of wage increases after 1974 was apparently not generally a result of unusually large "catch-up" wage increases for industries in which wages had fallen behind during the period of high inflation. This is suggested by the fact that the unevenness in wage increases was accompanied by a large increase in dispersion to an unusually high level. Examination of the individual industries also shows that industries in which large wage increases occurred were not, in general, industries for which relative wage positions were low by historical standards. In this respect, the uneven pattern of wage increases occurring in 1975 and 1976 was in sharp contrast with the pattern of wage increases in 1970–1972 that followed the preceding recession. At that time, there was a noticeable tendency for large wage increases to occur in industries in which relative wages had previously declined, with the result that dispersion rose from the trough it had reached in the late 1960s.

The pattern of uneven wage increases during 1975 and 1976, under the relative wage conditions that prevailed then, raises questions about the possible sources of unresponsiveness of wages in the high-wage industries to slack labor market demand. Since the high-wage industries tend to be more highly unionized, the extent of unionism, types of bargaining arrangements, and other factors should be examined. The relationship between unionization and wage developments during 1975 and 1976 may be examined by dividing industries in the private nonfarm sector for which relevant information on extent of unionism and earnings is available into three categories (see Table 8), which form the principal basis for comparisons in this analysis.

Data on wage developments by extent of unionism (see Tables 9 and 10) show that the largest wage increases since 1974 occurred in heavily unionized industries (Table 9), even though relative wage

Table 8
EXTENT OF UNIONISM: PRIVATE NONFARM SECTOR

High Union

Metal mining (10)
Bituminous coal (12)
Contract construction (15-17)
Ordnance and accessories (19)
Paper and allied products (26)
Primary metal industries (33)

Electrical equipment and supplies (36)
Transportation equipment (37)
Railroad transportation (4011)
Local and suburban transit (411)
Motor freight (42)
Communications (48)

Medium Union

Food and kindred products (20)
Tobacco manufactures (21)
Apparel and other textile products (23)
Lumber and wood products (24)
Chemicals and allied products (28)
Petroleum refining (291)
Rubber and plastics products (30)

Leather and leather products (31)
Stone, clay, and glass products (32)
Fabricated metal products (34)
Machinery, except electrical (35)
Electric, gas, and sanitation services (49)
Retail trade—food stores (54)

Low Union

Textile mill products (22)
Furniture and fixtures (25)
Printing and publishing (27)
Instruments and related products (38)
Misc. manufacturing industries (39)
Wholesale trade (50)
Retail trade: other (52, 55, 59)

Retail general merchandise (53)
Apparel and accessory stores (56)
Furniture and home furnishings stores (57)
Eating and drinking places (58)
Finance, insurance, and real estate (60-67)
Services (70-89)

Note: Numbers in parentheses are Standard Industrial Classification (SIC) codes. Industries were placed into categories according to the following criteria: *High Union:* All industries that are at least 75 percent unionized according to Bureau of Labor Statistics estimates, or are 50 to 75 percent unionized and at least 60 percent covered by major collective bargaining agreements (as indicated by the ratio of workers covered by major agreements to production worker employment). *Medium Union:* Industries that are 25-75 percent unionized and 10 to 60 percent covered by major collective bargaining agreements. *Low Union:* All industries that are 25 percent or less unionized or are 25 to 50 percent unionized and less than 10 percent covered by major collective bargaining agreements.

Source: Information on unionization and coverage by major agreements is contained in Bureau of Labor Statistics, *Directory of National Unions and Employee Associations of 1973*, p. 81, and Douglas LeRoy, "Scheduled Wage Increases and Escalator Provisions in 1977," *Monthly Labor Review*, January 1977, p. 24.

Table 9

CHANGES IN AVERAGE HOURLY EARNINGS BY EXTENT OF UNIONISM

(annual percentage rate of change in annual averages)

	1973-1976	1974-1976	1975-1976
Private nonfarm sector			
Private nonfarm index	8.1	8.0	7.3
High union (including construction)	9.4	9.9	9.0
High union (excluding construction)	9.8	10.1	9.2
Medium union	8.8	9.1	8.3
Low union	7.4	7.1	6.1
Manufacturing sector			
Adjusted average hourly earnings	8.8	8.7	7.3
High union	9.5	9.6	8.1
Medium union	8.8	9.1	8.2
Low union	7.4	7.2	6.2

Note: Percentages are computed as arithmetic averages of the changes for sectors within each of the extent-of-unionism categories. Manufacturing data are adjusted for overtime.

Source: U.S. Department of Labor, Bureau of Labor Statistics.

positions in these industries were already high compared with earlier experience (Table 10). This pattern is evident for both the entire private nonfarm sector and the manufacturing sector, although average hourly earnings outside manufacturing have shown a secular rise compared to average hourly earnings within manufacturing. The size of wage increases and the rise in relative wage positions for the high-union category of the private nonfarm sector are also larger when construction data are excluded.

The ratios reported in Table 10 also show that the rise in average hourly earnings ratios for high-union sectors in 1975 and 1976 was large relative to average differences in these ratios during the two preceding decades when overall levels of dispersion were significantly different. The average ratios for these two decades, of course, tend to obscure differences that may have existed during these periods. The annual data in Figure 2 show changes that occurred in these ratios during these two decades. These data show that average wage differentials for the high-union industries rose when overall

Table 10

AVERAGE HOURLY EARNINGS RATIOS BY EXTENT OF UNIONISM

(based on annual averages of hourly earnings)

	1955-1964	1965-1974	1974	1975	1976
Private nonfarm sector					
High union (including construction)	1.25	1.25	1.28	1.32	1.33
High union (excluding construction)	1.20	1.17	1.21	1.25	1.27
Medium union	1.02	0.99	0.99	1.02	1.03
Low union	0.87	0.86	0.84	0.84	0.83
Manufacturing sector					
High union	1.17	1.11	1.11	1.15	1.16
Medium union	1.02	0.98	0.98	1.00	1.01
Low union	0.96	0.91	0.89	0.90	0.98

Note: Ratios are averages of ratios for average hourly earnings in each industry relative to private nonfarm hourly earnings. The ratios for manufacturing are based on industry data adjusted for overtime.

Source: U.S. Department of Labor, Bureau of Labor Statistics.

dispersion increased, and that the rise in these ratios was unusually sharp in 1975 and 1976.[7]

It should be noted that these ratios and rates of increase are based on unweighted averages for the industries included in each of the extent-of-unionism categories. Employment shares in each of the extent-of-unionism categories are shown in Table 11. Within each of the extent-of-unionism categories, employment shares were also very different among industries, but unweighted averages seem most appropriate for tracing relationships among wages in specific industries.

Since factors such as the structure of bargaining arrangements and contract characteristics may have contributed to recent uneven wage behavior, and may possibly be reflected in measures based on the extent of unionism, wage behavior in several sectors was exam-

[7] These average hourly earnings ratios reflect differences in skill levels, demographic characteristics of workers, and all other factors that influence wage levels in particular industries in addition to whatever independent contribution to wages may be attributable to differences in the extent of unionism alone. The source for a detailed and comprehensive analysis of measurement of union-nonunion wage differentials is H. Gregg Lewis, *Unionism and Relative Wages in the United States* (Chicago: University of Chicago Press, 1963).

Figure 2

AVERAGE HOURLY EARNINGS RATIOS
BY EXTENT OF UNIONISM, 1955-1976

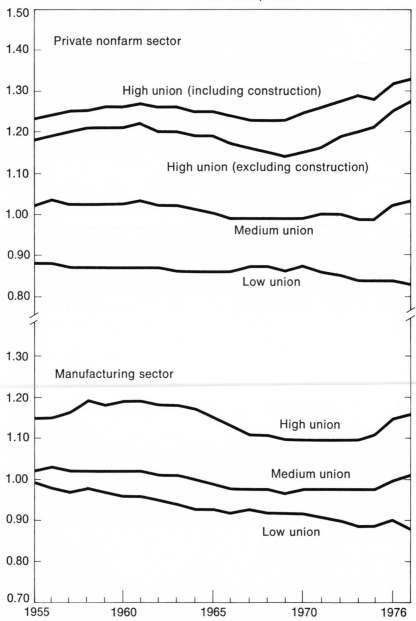

Source: U.S. Department of Labor, Bureau of Labor Statistics.

Table 11
EMPLOYMENT SHARES BY EXTENT OF UNIONISM
(percentage)

Sector	Private Nonfarm (including construction)	Private Nonfarm (excluding construction)	Manufacturing
High union	19	14	29
Medium union	20	21	52
Low union	59	62	18

Note: Employment shares are based on 1976 average total payroll employment data for sectors noted. Shares may not add up to 100 percent due to rounding and exclusion of some small industries for which relevant data were not available.

Source: U.S. Department of Labor, Bureau of Labor Statistics.

ined more closely. First, broadly defined industries with high coverage by major collective bargaining agreements with built-in cost-of-living escalator provisions were selected. Second, more narrowly defined industries were selected for which coverage by major agreements corresponded closely to industry definitions for which wage data are available. Also, all of these industries were covered at the beginning of 1977 by long-term collective bargaining agreements that included cost-of-living escalator provisions.

Changes in average wage ratios for these two groups of industries are shown in Table 12, and wage increases since 1974 are shown in Table 13. The general pattern for both groups of industries selected on the basis of high coverage by major agreements is similar to that for the high-union category, although changes in relative wage positions are somewhat more pronounced, particularly in the case of more narrowly defined industries. Annual ratios for these groups relative to private nonfarm average hourly earnings are shown in Figure 3, along with ratios for the construction industry. These ratios also show wider swings than the high-union category.

Changing relationships between the size of wage increases among industries classified by extent of unionism are also reflected by data on wage increases for workers in union and nonunion manufacturing establishments (see Table 14). These data show periods with very large wage increases for workers in union establishments relative to those in nonunion establishments. Large differences in wage increases occurred in 1970 and 1971 and again in 1975, the most recent year for which information on effective wage increases

Table 12
AVERAGE HOURLY EARNINGS RATIOS FOR SELECTED INDUSTRY GROUPS WITH HIGH COVERAGE BY MAJOR AGREEMENTS WITH ESCALATORS
(based on annual average of hourly earnings)

	1955-1964	1965-1974	1974	1975	1976
Broadly defined industries[a]	1.24	1.22	1.28	1.32	1.35
Narrowly defined industries[b]	1.29	1.26	1.31	1.36	1.37

Note: Ratios for selected groups of sectors are averages of ratios for the industry sectors in each group relative to the private nonfarm hourly earnings.

[a] Broadly defined industries include the following: metal mining (10); railroad transportation (4011); bituminous coal (12); local and suburban transportation (411); primary metals (33); motor freight (42); transportation equipment (37); and communications (48).

[b] Narrowly defined industries include: steel (331); tires and inner tubes (301); metal cans (341); bituminous coal (12); farm machinery (352); trucking (421); motor vehicles (371); and telephone communications (481).

Source: U.S. Department of Labor, Bureau of Labor Statistics.

in these categories is available. Classification of industries by extent of unionism shows apparent differences in responsiveness. Classification by other, more detailed characteristics shows wage behavior that stands out even more sharply from average wage behavior than that shown by classifications based on unionism alone. Thus, factors such as industry structure, bargaining structure, and contract char-

Table 13
CHANGES IN AVERAGE HOURLY EARNINGS FOR SELECTED INDUSTRY GROUPS WITH HIGH COVERAGE BY MAJOR AGREEMENTS WITH ESCALATORS
(annual percentage rates of change in annual average)

	1973-1976	1974-1976	1975-1976
Private nonfarm index	8.1	8.0	7.3
Broadly defined industries	10.0	10.3	9.7
Narrowly defined industries	9.9	9.8	8.2

Note: Percentages are computed as arithmetic averages of the changes for industries within each of the selected groups of industries.

Source: U.S. Department of Labor, Bureau of Labor Statistics.

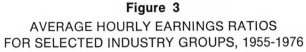

Figure 3

AVERAGE HOURLY EARNINGS RATIOS
FOR SELECTED INDUSTRY GROUPS, 1955-1976

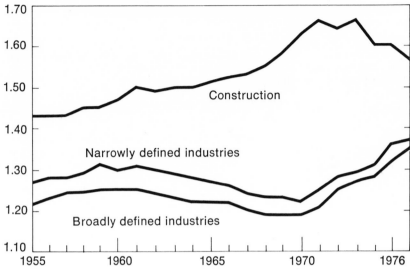

Source: U.S. Department of Labor, Bureau of Labor Statistics.

acteristics, possibly in combination with specific industry demand conditions or other factors, may influence wage behavior more strongly than the presence of unionism alone.

The selected narrowly defined industries have a number of characteristics in common: high coverage by major agreements, three-year wage contracts, coverage by cost-of-living escalator provisions included in the contracts (by the end of 1976), close correspondence between the coverage of major agreements and the industries for which average hourly earnings data are available, and relatively complete coverage by major union contracts of the type of industrial activity concerned. At the same time, the kinds of activities in these various industries are quite different, and production levels and product demand differed among them. Moreover, contract expiration dates and the terms of expiring contracts, such as the presence of cost-of-living escalators and whether there were limits on payments under escalator provisions, differed among them. Despite these differences, however, rates of increase in average hourly earnings in these disparate industries were quite similar over the past two contract periods. This similarity indicates a tendency for tandem wage

Table 14
WAGE CHANGES FOR MANUFACTURING PRODUCTION WORKERS IN UNION AND NONUNION ESTABLISHMENTS, 1969–1975

(percentage change)

	1969	1970	1971	1972	1973	1974	1975
Mean general wage change put into effect							
Union	5.3	6.4	7.1	5.4	6.4	8.7	8.1
Nonunion	4.6	4.7	4.0	4.4	6.0	7.7	5.9
Mean first-year wage change under new general wage decisions							
Union	7.3	7.6	9.2	5.7	6.0	8.1	8.7
Nonunion	4.6	4.6	3.9	4.4	5.9	7.5	5.7

Note: Wage changes put into effect during the year include those resulting from current decisions, prior decisions, cost-of-living adjustments, or any combination thereof. First-year wage changes for union workers include all changes negotiated during the period and scheduled to go into effect during the first twelve months of the agreement. For nonunion workers, they include all changes made under decisions during the period.

Source: U.S. Department of Labor, Bureau of Labor Statistics.

paths to emerge for these various industries even though, according to some measures, such as first-year wage increases, their wage behavior differed widely.

Analyses of the terms of several of the largest and most visible contract settlements that were negotiated in 1976 and the first part of 1977 point toward a continuation of relatively large wage increases under these three-year contracts. Nearly one-fifth of all workers covered by major collective bargaining agreements are included in the five settlements for which data are shown in Table 15. Differences in fixed wage increases (not including escalators) among these contracts are to a large extent accounted for by differences in first-year increases, which are in turn related to differences in the terms of expiring contracts.[8] The agreements also include escalator provisions that, allowing for 6 percent inflation, raise estimates of total

---

[8] The collective bargaining settlements for these industries were analyzed in detail by the Council on Wage and Price Stability. The results of the analyses are summarized in Executive Office of the President, Council on Wage and Price Stability, *Collective Bargaining*, February 1977, and *An Analysis of the Steel Settlement*, June 1, 1977. In the rubber industry the large fixed wage increase in

annual wage and benefits over the life of contracts to between 9 and 10 percent for the contracts with the smallest fixed wage increases.

The large settlements that have been negotiated in many major bargaining situations and the effects of these settlements on relative wages raise questions about why wage behavior in these industries has shown so little responsiveness to the recession of 1974–1975. While the slower price increases in 1975 and 1976—combined with smaller payments under cost-of-living escalator provisions—made a contribution toward slower economy-wide wage increases, larger-than-average wage increases still occurred in these industries. In order to obtain additional insight into possible sources of the apparent lack of wage responsiveness in some high-wage sectors, wage behavior for industries characterized by three types of economic circumstances are examined in more detail. These economic factors are: the influence of strong, direct competition in world markets, the influence of extensive economic regulation, and the influence of being engaged in the production of energy products.

Industries for which competition in world markets is particularly strong and direct include motor vehicles, metal mining, and primary metals, of which steel is a major component. The most noteworthy development pertinent to changes in competitive conditions in world markets in recent years was the shift from an overvalued dollar to flexible exchange rates. The devaluations of the dollar in 1971 and 1973 can be viewed as steps in this transition. During 1975 and 1976 the average level of an index of currencies for sixteen major trading partners was about 12 percent higher relative to the dollar compared to its average level in 1970 and 1971 prior to the devaluation. In the cases of automobiles and, especially, steel, two of those trading partners, Japan and Germany, are of particular importance. The values of the Japanese and German currencies were higher by amounts averaging about 20 percent and 45 percent respectively for the same period—shifts that were sufficiently large to significantly reduce competitive pressures from abroad in these industries.[9]

Among the industries subject to significant competition in world markets, those selected for examination of its influence on wage be-

---

the 1976 settlement followed an expiring contract without cost-of-living escalator provisions, and expiring contracts in the trucking and electrical equipment industries included escalator provisions with "caps." Expiring contracts in the automobile and steel industries, on the other hand, included cost-of-living escalator provisions without "caps."

[9] The data on relative currency values were taken from Executive Office of the President, Council on International Economic Policy, *International Economic Report of the President*, January 1977.

Table 15

WAGE AND BENEFIT INCREASES UNDER COLLECTIVE BARGAINING: 1976 AND SELECTED SETTLEMENTS

(annual percentage increases over life of contracts)

	Average Annual Increase
Industry aggregates, 1976	
Wages (agreements covering 1,000 workers or more)	
All industries	6.4
Manufacturing	6.0
Construction	6.2
Wages and benefits (agreements covering 5,000 workers or more)	
All industries	6.6
Manufacturing	6.1
Construction	6.7
Selected settlements, 1976 and 1977	
Wages (not including escalator payments)	
Trucking (1976)	7.2
Electrical equipment (1976)	7.2
Rubber (1976)	8.7
Automobiles (1976)	4.2
Steel (1977)	4.1
Wages (including allowance for escalator payments)[a]	
Trucking	9.7
Electrical equipment	9.9
Rubber	11.7
Automobiles	8.4
Steel	9.1
Wages and benefits (including allowance for escalator payments)[a]	
Trucking	10.4
Automobiles	9.8
Steel	9.3

[a] The allowance for escalator payments is computed on the basis of an assumed 6 percent annual rate of increase in the consumer price index during the duration of the contract.

Source: Executive Office of the President, Council on Wage and Price Stability, *Collective Bargaining,* February 1977, and *An Analysis of the Steel Settlement,* June 1, 1977.

havior were highly unionized industries with wages or wage patterns established under major collective bargaining agreements. While competition in world markets is an important factor in many other industries, such as textiles and apparel manufacturing, domestic competition, particularly competition in the labor market, is stronger in most of these industries than in industries such as automobiles and steel. In the industries selected for examination, wage increases from 1974 to 1976 exceeded the average for other sectors by about two percentage points, and relative wages rose to a historic high (see Tables 16 and 17). The reduction in competitive pressures from

Table 16
AVERAGE HOURLY EARNINGS RATIOS FOR SELECTED INDUSTRIES

	1955-1964	1965-1974	1974	1975	1976
Average for selected:	1.31	1.29	1.34	1.40	1.44
Industries affected by world market competition	1.32	1.28	1.35	1.41	1.43
Industries affected by extensive economic regulation	1.17	1.19	1.25	1.27	1.30
Industries engaged in energy production	1.45	1.40	1.42	1.53	1.58
Average for all other industries	0.98	0.97	0.96	0.97	0.97

Note: The three groups of selected industries include the following:

World market competition:
  motor vehicles (371)
  metal mining (10)
  steel (331)

Extensive economic regulation:
  railroad (4011)
  local and suburban transit (411)
  motor freight (42)
  telephone communications (481)
  electric, gas and sanitation services (49)

Energy production:
  bituminous coal (12)
  petroleum refining (291)

All other industries:
  The remaining sectors enumerated in Table 8.

Source: U.S. Department of Labor, Bureau of Labor Statistics.

Table 17

CHANGES IN AVERAGE HOURLY EARNINGS FOR
SELECTED INDUSTRIES

(annual percentage change)

	1973-1976	1974-1976	1975-1976
Private nonfarm index	8.1	8.0	7.3
Average for selected industries	10.7	11.3	10.0
Industries affected by world market competition	11.4	10.5	8.8
Industries affected by extensive economic regulation	9.0	9.9	10.4
Industries engaged in energy production	11.6	13.5	10.9
Average for all other industries	8.0	8.0	7.0

Note: For industries included in these selected groups, see the note to Table 16.
Source: U.S. Department of Labor, Bureau of Labor Statistics.

abroad resulting from the decline in the value of the dollar may have contributed to the wage behavior observed in these industries. Wage behavior in these industries in 1975 and 1976 suggests that, given the industrial structure and the bargaining structure in these industries, alleviation of competitive pressures from abroad may have been translated primarily into larger wage increases instead of into more jobs and improved competitive conditions.

Industries operating under extensive economic regulation include transportation, telephone communications, and electrical, gas, and sanitation services. Since these industries are generally characterized by cost-based, rate-of-return regulation, wages are subject to relatively weak competitive pressures. So long as wage trends in these industries do not appear to be significantly out of line with trends in other industries with which they might be compared, the costs that they represent are unlikely to be challenged in regulatory proceedings. Wages in these sectors are consequently insulated from competitive pressures even during periods of extensive general market slack.[10]

---

[10] A lack of cyclical sensitivity of wages in regulated industries is noted in Robert E. Hall, "The Rigidity of Wages and the Persistence of Unemployment," *Brookings Papers on Economic Activity*, 1975 (2), pp. 301-35.

The industries that are engaged in energy production are bituminous coal and petroleum refining. The petroleum refining industry is both an energy producing industry and one that has been subject to pervasive economic regulation since 1973. Special conditions have been present in the bituminous coal mining industry that do not exist in the other sectors discussed. In addition to sharply higher product prices, subsequent pressures for increased production rates and requirements for experienced workers to implement government mine safety programs may have contributed to rising relative wages as an essential element in attracting workers to the coal industry.

Relative wages rose to unusually high levels by 1976, and larger-than-average wage increases occurred in the immediately preceding years in industries affected by extensive economic regulation and those engaged in energy production, as in the case of industries affected by world market competition (see Tables 16 and 17). The behavior of average hourly earnings ratios for these industries during the period from 1955 to 1976 is shown in Figure 4. The rise in relative wage ratios after 1973 and 1974 was particularly pronounced in the energy producing industries and those affected by world market competition.

Figure 4

AVERAGE HOURLY EARNINGS RATIOS
FOR SELECTED INDUSTRIES, 1955-1976

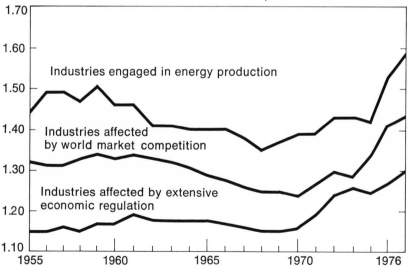

Source: U.S. Department of Labor, Bureau of Labor Statistics.

Construction

The construction labor market differs in several important ways from other labor markets. There is a great deal of flux in construction employment, with workers moving frequently between employers, job sites, areas, and union and nonunion work. The construction product is usually to some degree custom built, and work that must be done "on site" cannot be imported, which limits the channels through which competition can occur. For the unionized component of construction activity, wage scales are established for geographic areas. For public construction projects, wage levels are bolstered by the Davis-Bacon Act and similar state and local laws which require payment of "prevailing wages" in the area in which the construction takes place. These special characteristics differentiate construction labor markets from other labor markets and may have contributed to the divergent behavior of construction wages.

Construction wages rose more rapidly than other wages in the economy throughout the 1960s. By 1970 extremely large union wage settlements in construction gave rise to serious concern not only on the part of purchasers of new construction but also on the part of employers in other industries who feared the threat of spillovers from construction wage patterns. These conditions contributed to the introduction of a system of wage controls in construction in early 1971. The rising divergence between construction wages and other wages was stabilized after the introduction of these controls, although stabilization may also have been facilitated by other factors.[11]

Two developments that are particularly relevant in analyzing the stabilization and subsequent decline of relative wages in construction are the growth of nonunion or "open shop" construction activity and the major slump in construction demand after 1973 (see Figure 5). The disproportionately large union wage settlements in construction during the late 1960s were accompanied by, first, a widening differential between union and nonunion construction wages and, second, by an increase in open shop construction activity. Erosion of the union share of construction occurred through the growth of open shop contractors, "double breasted" operations with union and non-

---

[11] See Marvin Kosters and J. Dawson Ahalt, *Controls and Inflation: The Economic Stabilization Program in Retrospect* (Washington, D.C.: American Enterprise Institute, 1975), for a discussion of the role and influence of wage and price controls in the construction industry.

Figure 5

CONSTRUCTION ACTIVITY, EMPLOYMENT, AND
RELATIVE WAGES, 1960-1976

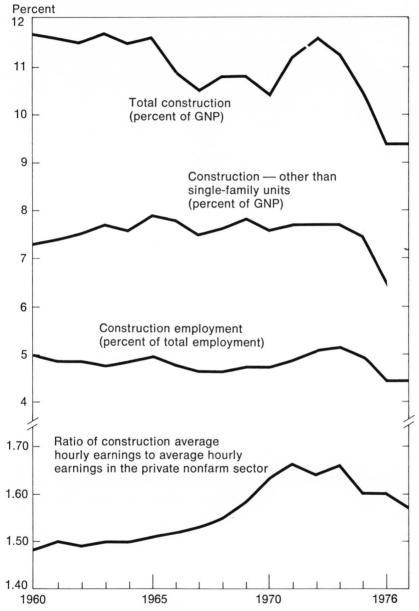

Source: U.S. Department of Commerce, Bureau of Economic Analysis and U.S. Department of Labor, Bureau of Labor Statistics.

197

union activity controlled by the same owner, and mixed construction crews.[12]

After more than a decade of generally strong construction demand, the slump in construction activity after 1973 was so pronounced that, had wages failed to respond, an extraordinary lack of sensitivity to market conditions would have been demonstrated. The fact that the slump was concentrated in components of the construction industry where union activity was strongest—industrial, public, and multi-unit housing construction—increased competitive pressures from open shop contractors and nonunion workers. Some of the decline in the rate of increase of construction wages and in relative wages as measured by construction average hourly earnings may be attributable to the consequent change in the mix of union and nonunion workers included in the average. However, collective bargaining settlements negotiated in the construction industry also brought lower rates of wage increase than those negotiated in most other sectors.

Concluding Discussion

The experience of more than a decade of inflation has had far-reaching effects. It has resulted in widespread revision of inflation expectations, as reflected, for example, in long-term interest rate levels. It has contributed to the development of ways to make it easier to live with inflation, as represented, for example, by cost-of-living escalator provisions in wage contracts. It has led to government policies designed to compensate for the effects of inflation, as represented, for example, by indexation of social security payments. Because inflation has been accompanied by difficulties in maintaining high employment, it has also stimulated interest in the process by which inflation is generated and transmitted through wage and price behavior and in policies that could contribute to reducing inflationary tendencies.

The resistance that inflation has shown during periods of market slack has sometimes been interpreted as evidence of pervasive rigidity in price and wage trends or lack of competitiveness in the economy. Yet there has been considerable variability in price and wage behavior among sectors of the economy. This variability re-

---

[12] See Herbert R. Northrup and Howard G. Foster, *Open Shop Construction* (Philadelphia: University of Pennsylvania, Industrial Research Unit, The Wharton School, 1975), for an extensive analysis of the growth of open shop construction activity.

flects shifts in relative prices and wages that have occurred in the context of a generally rising price level. These relative price and wage shifts demonstrate an important degree of flexibility in response to changing market forces, though these adjustments are not usually achieved without transitional costs.

The capacity for adjustment in the economy shown by relative wage and price shifts has been apparent in spite of many forces that tend to inhibit flexibility. Government policies, ranging from legislation that provides for minimum or prevailing wages to regulatory agencies that establish procedures for setting prices and rates, are major sources of rigidity. Moreover, the impact on markets and jobs of large adjustments often brings support for government action to mitigate or delay such adjustments, and thereby reduce transitional adjustment costs. The force of customary or traditional relationships, particularly for wages, also often places limits on the speed or size of adjustments. And when short-term market forces have brought about adjustments, if such adjustments represent temporary departures from structural balance, pressures for restoration of conditions for a sustainable equilibrium usually assert themselves.

While past changes in relative prices or wages provide no certain guide to developments that can be expected to occur in the future, insights into the sources of change can often be found by examining the history of the immediate past. Wage developments in the labor market illustrate this point. If differences in the size of wage increases among industries were essentially random, little insight could be gained from tracing changes that occurred in the past. If they were a result of historically accidental contract expiration dates, insights would be limited mainly to wages under the contracts involved. However, if larger-than-average wage increases occurred in industries where wages had fallen behind wages in other industries, these could be regarded as "catch-up" wage increases representing movements toward structural balance. To the extent that such wage increases represented movements toward a sustainable equilibrium—bringing relative wages into balance with other wages in the economy—there might be little pressure for further adjustment.

The large union wage increases (relative to average wage increases and except for construction) that occurred in 1970 and 1971 appear to be consistent with the "catch-up" interpretation. Relative wages had previously declined in these industries. For wage behavior in 1975 and 1976, however, this does not seem to be a satisfactory interpretation. In 1975 and 1976, larger-than-average wage increases in many high-wage industries brought relative wages in these industries to unusually high levels. Factors that seem to have contributed to this result include economic regulation, competitive conditions in world markets, and energy developments.

From the perspective of labor market developments in the immediate past that are likely to influence future wage and price performance, two aspects of labor market conditions are particularly significant. First, wages for a disproportionate share of the high-wage industries are established under long-term wage contracts that include cost-of-living escalator provisions. These wage-setting arrangements tend to support the high relative wage positions achieved in these industries. Second, to the extent that the wide relative wage dispersion that had developed by 1976 is attributable to cyclical market slack, persistent tightening of labor and product markets is likely to be accompanied by pressures that would lead to reduced dispersion in relative wages. However, since long-term contracts with cost-of-living escalator provisions limit the extent to which pressures for reduced dispersion can be accommodated by slower wage increases in high-wage industries, strengthening labor market demand is likely to bring about adjustment toward reduced dispersion through larger-than-average increases in low-wage industries. These wage structural relationships contribute an element of inflationary bias to labor market conditions.

In the formulation of policies designed to moderate inflation, current labor market conditions should be taken into account because they form the context in which such policies would be pursued. The wage paths established under long-term contracts, directly influencing wages for the workers covered and raising standards for the comparisons that normally serve as a basis for wage increases of other workers, form one important aspect of the labor market context. The prospect of pressures for larger wage increases at the lower end of the wage distribution to reestablish more normal relative wage relationships forms another aspect. Wages at the lower end of the wage distribution are usually set under less formal arrangements than in many of the high-wage industries, and wage decisions in the low-wage industries are distributed more widely over a large number of small firms and units. These circumstances pose severe practical and administrative problems, in addition to issues of equity or fairness that would arise, in formulating an incomes policy approach to moderating inflation.

Other policy approaches are available, however, with more potential for sustained effectiveness than incomes policies. The other government policy approaches that could contribute to moderating inflation essentially involve taking into account the inflationary consequences of decision making over the entire range of government activities, regulations, and decisions. Government programs and policies affect virtually every industry and area of activity in the economy, and actions by government in most cases influence price and wage behavior. Production costs are often raised by the imposition of standards or requirements, not only through the direct costs of meeting the conditions imposed but also through the litigation and delays that frequently are a part of regulatory processes. Price supports, minimum or prevailing wage requirements, and rate-setting procedures tend to insulate parts of the economy from market forces as well as often contributing directly to higher costs and prices. The extent of competition is influenced by policies that limit entry of firms or that reduce foreign competition. The significance of policies influencing particular markets and industries for wage and price behavior is suggested by recent wage behavior in the selected industry groups discussed earlier. The heavy flow of decision making in all of these areas presents a continuing stream of opportunities for taking the inflationary implications of government action into account. While decision making in these areas that gives priority to moderating inflation involves difficult political choices, this general policy approach would be far less disruptive of labor-management relationships and other voluntary and private mechanisms for developing solutions to economic problems than an incomes policy approach. This microeconomic approach to inflation policy could make an effective and sustainable contribution to inflation control, in part because it would also contribute to more efficient resource usage and higher production and employment levels.

RESOURCE ADJUSTMENT IN AMERICAN AGRICULTURE AND AGRICULTURE POLICY

D. Gale Johnson

Summary

The current debate on agricultural policy is very similar to the one that took place after World War II. In the earlier debate there was a contest between those who favored high price supports and those who favored primary reliance upon market forces with price supports set at levels that would normally have little effect upon market prices. In the end those favoring the high price supports won the day.

High price supports resulted in output of many farm commodities substantially greater than could be sold. The government accumulated, and very quickly, large supplies of cotton, wheat, and the feed grains. Efforts were made to dispose of the excess production through food aid and export subsidies. When these efforts proved unsuccessful, programs were undertaken to restrict production. In 1961 it became clear that high prices and ineffective efforts to limit output were politically unacceptable because of accumulations of stocks and the high costs of maintaining those stocks. At this time efforts were made to facilitate agricultural adjustment and to permit the prices of most farm products to move gradually to market clearing levels, using direct payments to maintain farm income.

It required another decade to achieve an approximate balance between the demand for and supply of agricultural products. While there was substantial diversion of land from production during the early 1970s, later events indicated the effects of the land diversion in restricting farm output were quite small, perhaps no more than 2 percent.

There have been major changes in American agriculture during the past three decades. These changes mean that price policies and acreage diversion will have even less effect on farm incomes in the future than during the past. The changes also mean that the governmental costs of establishing price guarantees above market clearing level are likely to exceed our past experience significantly.

The incomes of farm people have increased significantly during the past two decades. Relatively little of the increased income can be attributed to the government programs. Increasingly, farm people have been relying upon nonfarm sources of income as a major component of their total incomes. In 1960 nonfarm income accounted for 39 percent of the income of the farm population; in 1975, more than half. In 1960 the per capita disposable income of the farm population was 54 percent of the same income measure for the nonfarm population; in 1975 the percentage was 90 percent. The increase in the relative income position of farm people was achieved while farm output prices were either stable or declining.

One of the dramatic changes has been the integration of the farm labor market and the general labor market. In 1975 almost half of the employed farm population had nonfarm jobs; in 1960 approximately a third had nonfarm jobs. Of equal significance in indicating the integration of the labor markets is the fact that the proportion of farm workers who have nonfarm residences (that is, do not live on farms) has increased from a quarter in 1960 to more than two-fifths in 1975. The potential for adjustment through the labor market has improved radically since the end of World War II.

Another important change in American agriculture has been the increase in the share of output exported. The output of one out of three acres of cropland is sold in the international markets. The prosperity of agriculture depends upon a large and growing international market.

Given the changes that have occurred in American agriculture, there are significant limits on what can be accomplished by farm price policy. Price supports or direct payments can have very little influence on the returns to farm labor and management, except in the very short run. The farm labor supply can adjust quite promptly to either favorable or unfavorable incentives in agriculture. Even the short-run benefits would go primarily to families that have incomes above the national average.

If target prices and/or loan rates are set above market clearing levels the primary effect will be to increase the price of farm land. This means that the beneficiaries of high support or target prices will be the current owners of land, many of whom do not live on farms.

Because of the importance of exports, it is essential that price supports or loan rates be kept sufficiently low to permit products to move freely into international trade. If this is not done, the United States will become the residual supplier and be able to export only after the other exporters have disposed of their supplies. Once the United States loses its competitive advantage in international markets, as a result of the price supports, stocks will accumulate and the pressure will be great to use export subsidies to retain export markets. The use of export subsidies will make it extremely difficult for us to achieve any liberalization of trade through modification of the policies of the importers, such as the European Economic Community.

The final section of the paper considers the methods of reducing price and income variability. Three measures are considered: Trade liberalization; target prices at levels approximating market prices under average conditions; and a reserve program. Trade liberalization would contribute significantly to a reduction of price and income variability, but relatively little can be expected from this alternative in the next few years. Target prices—if set at appropriate levels—could reduce income variability without a major effect upon the use of agricultural resources. However, if target prices are set too high, the prices will either induce too many resources to be engaged in agriculture or require acreage diversion and other methods for controlling output in order to keep the cost of the deficiency payments within politically acceptable levels.

If reserves are properly managed, they could contribute to price stability. However, it is difficult to obtain appropriate management in a political setting. The reserves that we have had in the past have been the unwanted consequences of price supports that were set too high. Another difficulty with a governmental reserve program is that once there are stocks in governmental hands, the reserves held by the private market decline.

The primary objective of the paper has been to show that great care must be taken in the formulation of farm price policy if the errors that were made in the past are not to be repeated. In fact, the changes that have occurred in American agriculture since the end of World War II will mean that what appear to be relatively small departures of target prices and loan rates from market clearing levels will soon result in significant misallocation of resources and unacceptably large governmental costs.

Introduction

In the closing years of the 1940s policy decisions were made that had a major impact upon agricultural resource use and adjustment for the next two decades. During World War II and in the immediate postwar years there was a lively debate about the future course of agricultural policy generally and of farm price policy particularly. There was considerable professional, academic, and political support for a policy of full production and moderate price supports. While the Agricultural Act of 1948 embodied this view, in the end Congress and the administration opted for price supports at levels that quickly resulted in the accumulation of large stocks of the major farm crops.[1]

The relatively moderate provisions of the Agricultural Act of 1948 were not scheduled to take effect until 1950. The outcome of the national election of 1948 led to new farm legislation that repealed the provisions of the 1948 act before they became effective. The 1949 act represented a victory for the proponents of high price supports. The election of a Republican as President in 1952 changed nothing since the Congress remained in Democratic hands. The inability of a divided government to agree on price policy meant that throughout most of the 1950s price supports were at high levels and significant efforts to limit agricultural output were not made.

The primary policy response to the rapid accumulation of stocks held by the Commodity Credit Corporation in the early 1950s was the Agricultural Trade and Development Act of 1954 and the payment of substantial export subsidies on several farm products.[2] While some efforts were made through acreage allotments and acreage diversions to limit the production of the major farm crops, the measures were ineffective.

It was not until 1961, when it became obvious that high prices and ineffective efforts to limit output were politically unacceptable due to accumulations of stocks and the high costs of maintaining those

---

[1] Two excellent books provide discussions of the farm policy debate following World War II. One is Murray R. Benedict, *Farm Policies of the United States, 1790-1950* (New York: The Twentieth Century Fund, 1953), chapter 18. This book also provides a detailed description of the development of agricultural policy up through 1950. The other is Willard W. Cochrane and Mary E. Ryan, *American Farm Policy, 1948-1973* (Minneapolis: University of Minnesota Press, 1976), chapter 5. Cochrane and Ryan have produced an exceedingly valuable reference work covering the farm commodity programs since World War II.

[2] On June 30, 1952 loans outstanding and commodities owned by the Commodity Credit Corporation had a value of $1.5 billion; a year later the value was $3.4 billion; and on June 30, 1954, it was $6.0 billion. *(Statistical Abstract of the United States, 1961, p. 632.)* During the 1950s export subsidies paid on wheat averaged approximately a third of the export price. Export subsidies were also paid on cotton and, to a lesser degree, on the feed grains. In addition to the explicit export subsidies, approximately 30 percent of agricultural exports in fiscal years 1956 and 1957 were exported through P.L. 480 (the Agricultural Trade and Development Act of 1954).

stocks, that efforts were made to facilitate agricultural adjustment and to permit the prices of most farm products to gradually move to market clearing levels, using direct payments to maintain farm incomes.[3]

It required tens of billions of dollars of taxpayer funds and more than two decades of time to adjust agricultural resources so that American agriculture could be fully competitive in world markets and provide a satisfactory return for farm resources. It was not until the early 1970s that the consequences of decisions made in the late 1940s to avoid or postpone the resource adjustments required by the circumstances of the postwar period were largely eliminated. Obviously it is not now possible to prove that if there had been a better understanding in the late 1940s of the agricultural adjustment process and that if there had been programs to facilitate adjustment rather than to impede it, the adjustment period could have been substantially shortened and the governmental costs greatly reduced.[4] But it is important that past mistakes not now be repeated in the formulation of farm commodity programs.

There have been major changes in American agriculture since 1950. These changes are described and emphasized in this essay. An important implication of these changes is that a return to the commodity and price policies of the 1950s and, to some degree, those of the early 1960s would result in even greater costs to taxpayers than in the past and even more modest income benefits to farm people. Policies and programs that attempt to increase the net incomes of resources engaged in an activity through demand or price are based on the assumption of a low elasticity of supply of output and of the various resources engaged in that activity. The farm policy of the United States, as well as of other industrial countries, has long rested on the assumption that the supply of farm products in the aggregate was little affected by prices received. If this were true in the past, it is much less so currently. The short-run elasticity of supply, say for up to two or three years, undoubtedly is very low, and thus there can be substantial short-run variation in farm prices and incomes. But for

---

[3] For a description of the farm commodity programs and their evolution during the 1950s and 1960s, see Cochrane and Ryan, *American Farm Policy, 1948-1973*, chapter 3.

[4] The resource adjustments required after World War II differed only in degree and not in kind from the adjustments continuously required of agriculture in an economy in which economic growth occurs. The low income elasticity of demand for farm products and the increasing productivity that occurs in modern agriculture mean that the share of the nation's resources devoted to agriculture must decline over time. For discussion of the process see D. Gale Johnson, *World Agriculture in Disarray* (New York: Franklin Watts, 1973), chapters 4 and 5.

longer periods of time, farm output now has much greater responsiveness to prices than was true a quarter-century ago.[5]

Nor can it be expected that efforts to control or limit output of crops by the traditional method, namely diversion of land, will be as effective in offsetting the output effects of above market equilibrium prices or returns as in the past. There are two primary reasons for this change—land now constitutes a much smaller fraction of total farm inputs than it did three decades ago and the possibilities of substituting other inputs, such as fertilizers, seeds, herbicides, and insecticides, for land have increased significantly.

Thus, compared with the past, the potential effectiveness of price measures to increase farm incomes over a period of time and of land diversion as a means of minimizing governmental costs of the price measures have been seriously eroded. The effectiveness of these measures was never very great, but at least during the 1950s it required almost a decade before the governmental costs became politically intolerable. If similar measures were adopted today, it is almost certain that the governmental costs would become unacceptable in a much shorter period of time.

Farm Prices and Incomes

As a prelude to the main topic of this paper—agricultural adjustment—it is useful to review recent farm price and income developments. The changes that have occurred during the last decade have been striking, to put it mildly. In order to minimize the distortions or changes that reflected general price level changes, the income and price data in the following tables have been expressed in terms of 1967 dollars or in price ratios with 1967 as a base.

---

[5] It is exceedingly difficult to obtain an empirical estimate of the long-run elasticity of supply of total farm output. When there has been a significant change in the real price of farm output, other than the long-run trends, there have been major disruptions in the rest of the economy such as war or the depression of the 1930s. The sharp increase in farm prices after mid-1972 lasted a relatively brief period of time and was almost certainly not expected to be permanent. The presumption that the long-run elasticity of supply has increased is based on the increased importance of purchased inputs that have a very high elasticity of supply and the major changes in the farm labor market that have occurred in the past quarter-century. The changes in the labor market are discussed in detail below. Luther Tweeten has estimated that the long-run elasticity of supply of farm output is approximately unity. See his paper, "Agricultural Policy: A Review of Legislation, Programs and Policy" presented at a conference on Food and Agricultural Policy, sponsored by the American Enterprise Institute for Public Policy Research in Washington, March 10 and 11, 1977. Other papers presented at this conference are relevant to an understanding of the current agricultural policy debate.

Table 1

AGRICULTURAL INCOME AND INCOME OF THE FARM
POPULATION, 1960–1975, IN 1967 DOLLARS

Year	Farm National Income (billion dollars)	Operators' Net Farm Income (billion dollars)	Operators' Net Farm Income Per Farm (dollars)	Per Capita Personal Income, Farm Population (dollars)	Disposable Per Capita Income, Farm Percent of Nonfarm (percent)
1960	18.3	12.8	3,230	1,304	53.9
1961	19.0	13.3	3,473	1,430	57.9
1962	19.1	13.3	3,590	1,515	59.4
1963	18.7	12.8	3,582	1,624	62.4
1964	17.4	11.3	3,263	1,640	59.5
1965	19.8	13.6	4,045	1,924	68.2
1966	20.6	14.2	4,373	2,096	71.7
1967	18.9	12.3	3,903	2,102	69.0
1968	18.6	11.8	3,859	2,216	70.5
1969	20.1	13.1	4,372	2,391	74.0
1970	19.5	12.4	4,202	2,473	74.0
1971	19.6	12.4	4,263	2,582	74.7
1972	22.7	15.2	5,288	2,911	83.4
1973	33.0	25.1	8,817	3,856	100.3
1974	25.6	17.5	6,206	3,223	92.7
1975	24.5	15.4	5,482	3,089	89.6

Source: U.S. Department of Agriculture, Economic Research Service, *Farm Income Statistics,* Statistical Bulletin no. 557 (July 1976). The price deflator used was prices paid for family living items.

Table 1 presents certain data on income from farming and the income of the farm population for 1960 through 1976. There is no strong reason for starting the period with 1960 except that in so doing one includes a substantial part of the period when there were large government direct payments to agriculture, substantial acreage diversion, and export subsidies on major crops.

The data in Table 1 indicate a significant increase in all measures of deflated farm income and the income of the farm population between 1960 and 1975. National income produced in agriculture increased by approximately 34 percent and operators' net income per farm by 70 percent. Perhaps the most accurate indicator of the income of farm people was the deflated per capita income from all sources, which increased somewhat more than 135 percent. The last column of Table 1 shows the relationship between the per capita disposable income of the farm and nonfarm population. The data indicate a sub-

Table 2

FARM OUTPUT PRICES RELATIVE TO PRICES
PAID BY FARMERS, 1960 TO 1976

(1910–1914 = 100)

Year	Parity Ratio	Parity Ratio, Adjusted[a]
1960	80	82
1961	79	83
1962	80	83
1963	78	81
1964	76	80
1965	76	81
1966	79	85
1967	73	79
1968	73	79
1969	73	79
1970	72	77
1971	69	73
1972	74	79
1973	91	94
1974	86	87
1975	76	76
1976	71	71

[a] Includes direct government payments to farmers as though such payments represented part of the prices received.

Source: U.S. Department of Agriculture, Crop Reporting Board, Statistical Reporting Service, *Index Numbers of Prices Received and Prices Paid by Farmers, January 1965–April 1976, Revised,* Pr 1–5(76) (May 28, 1976), and *Agricultural Prices* (February 28, 1977).

stantial improvement in the relative income position of the farm families—from about 54 percent in 1960, to 69 percent in 1967, and 90 percent in 1975. Between 1967 and 1975 real per capita income of the farm population increased by 47 percent.

What lies behind the substantial increase in deflated farm income indicated in Table 1? One possible answer might be that real farm prices were significantly higher in 1975 than in the 1960s. Table 2 presents data on the parity ratio—the ratio of prices received to prices paid for commodities, services, taxes, interest, and wages.

Two measures of the parity ratio are presented. The first is the traditional ratio; the second is defined as the adjusted ratio which includes government payments to farmers. If the traditional parity ratio is used (column 1), one finds that in 1975 real farm prices were approximately 4 percent greater than in 1967, while in 1976 real farm prices were about 3 percent below 1967. If the adjusted parity ratio is used, real farm prices in 1975 were approximately 4 percent below 1967 and 10 percent below in 1976. Thus the increase in real farm income between the late 1960s and 1975 and 1976 cannot be attributed to an improvement in real farm prices if some recognition is given to direct government payments which were to a significant degree related to farm output.

Was the reason for the increase in deflated real national income from agriculture a significant increase in the resources used in agriculture? Table 3 presents information relevant to the answer to this question. The first five columns give data on production inputs as measured by the U.S. Department of Agriculture. The first of the columns measures total inputs, including current purchased inputs as well as labor, land, and capital items. The second column is a

Table 3

MEASURES OF INPUTS USED IN AGRICULTURE,
1960 TO 1976

(1967 = 100)

Year	Total Inputs	Non-purchased Inputs	Labor	Real Estate	Mechanical Power and Machinery	Real Value of Farm Assets (January 1)
1960	99	120	145	100	98	84
1961	98	117	139	100	95	84
1962	98	114	133	101	95	86
1963	98	111	128	100	94	89
1964	98	108	122	101	94	92
1965	99	104	109	100	95	93
1966	98	101	103	100	97	98
1967	100	100	100	100	100	100
1968	101	100	97	99	101	102
1969	100	99	93	98	101	103
1970	100	96	90	97	100	102
1971	101	96	89	96	100	102
1972	101	94	85	96	99	106
1973	101	95	85	96	103	114
1974	101	95	83	94	102	126
1975	99	92	81	94	104	120
1976						126

Source: U.S. Department of Agriculture, Economic Research Service, *Changes in Farm Production and Efficiency*, Statistical Bulletin no. 561 (September 1976) and Board of Governors of the Federal Reserve System, Division of Research and Statistics, *Agricultural Finance Databook*, Annual Series (September 1976).

measure of nonpurchased inputs—the inputs provided by farm operators.[6] The next three columns measure most of the inputs included in the national income of agriculture—labor, farm real estate, and mechanical power and machinery. The measure of total inputs indicates that there was no significant change between 1960 and 1976. Nonpurchased inputs declined by 23 percent while labor declined by approximately two-fifths, farm real estate declined by 6 percent, and mechanical power and machinery increased slightly.

The sixth column of the table provides another measure of capital assets used in agriculture—the total value of farm assets deflated by the prices paid by farmers for items used for living. The deflated value of these assets increased by 50 percent between 1960 and 1976. It should be noted that much of this increase in the real value of such assets was due to the change in the real price of farm real estate and not to an increase in the quantity of farm real estate. The actual quantity of farm real estate (farm land and buildings) changed little, if at all. The real value of non- real-estate assets, both physical and financial, increased by 16 percent over the period while the real value of farm real estate increased by two-thirds. The increase in the real value of farm real estate primarily reflected the shift in demand for land since, as noted, the quantity of farm real estate was unchanged.

The picture that emerges is that income from agriculture has increased in real terms even though real farm prices have declined or remained unchanged. The total quantities of resources used in agriculture changed little, if at all. The real net income of farm operators from farming has increased by less than the net income from agriculture, but it has increased, nevertheless, in spite of the decline in real farm prices since 1960. The increase in the per capita real personal income of the farm population has been substantial, in part because of the decline in the number of farm families dependent upon agriculture and in part because of the substantial increase in real income from nonfarm sources. The changing importance of nonfarm incomes of farm people is discussed in some detail below.

The increase in real national income of agriculture and in real operators' net farm income reflects an increase in productivity in agriculture, a substantial improvement in the quality of inputs used in agriculture, or both. Concern has been expressed that productivity growth in agriculture has been slowing down, but the increase in real national income from agriculture that has occurred since 1960 while deflated output prices have declined indicates that productivity growth

---

[6] The inputs include operator and family labor and operator-owned real estate and other capital inputs.

has been at a substantial rate. The inputs whose returns are included in farm national income are approximately the same inputs included in nonpurchased inputs in Table 3. The only important difference is that mechanical power and machinery is excluded from the nonpurchased inputs, but there has been little increase in this input category since 1960.

Obviously real farm prices may decline further and perhaps substantially during the next few years. Presumably such an expectation underlies the discussions of the farm price and income policy that is now under way. However, the income data presented here indicate that if current real farm prices are maintained or even decline somewhat, the real income from agriculture will remain above the levels of a decade ago.

Economic Growth and Agriculture

The most fundamental and pervasive development affecting American agriculture during the past quarter-century has been economic growth. Because of the characteristics of income elasticities of demand and resource substitutions and augmentations, agriculture declines in terms of its share of the nation's employment of labor and capital and of gross national product as per capita incomes increase.[7] There is no escape for agriculture from this consequence of economic growth, no matter how one defines agriculture or food—the traditional land, labor and capital employed on farms, all resources used on farms, or all activities involved in the production, processing, transportation, and marketing of food and fiber products.[8]

---

[7] For further discussion, see Johnson, *World Agriculture in Disarray*, chapter 5.

[8] Data are available on the total value of food and fiber output of the United States for 1958-1974 in 1967 dollars. The total value includes consumer expenditures on food, agricultural exports, and manufactured products utilizing agricultural products, such as cotton, as input. If these values are divided by the gross national product in 1958 dollars, the percentages are as follows:

1958	20.1
1970	16.7
1974	15.6

Consumer expenditures on food accounted for 72 to 78 percent of the total value of food and fiber output. In current dollars, the percentage of disposable income spent on food has been:

1960	20.0
1970	16.2
1974	16.8

(Donald D. Durost and James E. Kirkley, "Productivity Changes in the Food and Fiber System, 1958-74," *Agricultural Economics Research*, vol. 28, no. 4 [October 1976], p. 131, and U.S. Department of Agriculture, Economic Research Service, *Food Consumption, Prices and Expenditures*, Supplement for 1974 to Agricultural Economic Report no. 138 [1976], p. 77.)

If the activities of food and fiber production were not space related and so widely dispersed, the relative decline of agriculture and its slow absolute growth would present moderate adjustment problems. Fortunately, the degree to which agricultural resources are specifically bound by space changes as economic growth occurs. When non- farm-produced inputs account for an increasing share of farm output, the importance of land as a factor of production declines. Similarly the relative importance of labor that must perform its services in a particular location has declined. Thus one would expect that as agriculture becomes a smaller and smaller component of national income, the difficulties of adjustment to changing conditions are lessened.

Other features of economic growth may be of equal importance in reducing the difficulties that confront agriculture in adjusting to changing conditions. The enormous expansion of the communication network available to farm people has had an importance that cannot be overestimated. Starting with rural free delivery of mail, and then radio and now television, farm people have come to have essentially the same access to ideas and knowledge as do urban people. The access of farm people to education has improved with economic growth. The reduction in the time and money cost of transportation has also had a major role in integrating rural and urban communities. Many of these trends were well under way prior to World War II, but if one contrasts the costs of personal transportation today with what it was in the late 1930s, the change has been a substantial one.

A major implication of the changes in the sources of farm inputs, improvements in communication, increased education, and the reduction of the cost of transportation is that farm people now have available many more new margins at which they can make adjustments than was true even a quarter-century ago. These margins affect all of the inputs used in farming, obviously some more than others. Land is affected the least, but even in the case of land we now know that investment can be carried out that will significantly affect its productivity and that some land can be utilized in ways to reduce the amounts of other inputs required to produce a given output. The most flexible margins are probably for the annual purchased inputs, but relatively long lived assets, such as tractors and combines, can be effectively depreciated at different rates. Perhaps most important in terms of welfare, the labor of farm families now has a wide variety of alternatives of gainful employment other than performing farm labor or management functions.

Economic growth impinges upon farm people in numerous ways.

One of the consequences of economic growth is to require significant adjustments from farm people. Numerous other consequences of economic growth have increased the capacity of farm people to adjust to the effects of economic growth and lowered the costs of making the required adjustments. Put another way, it is now less difficult and painful for farm people to share in rising real per capita incomes than it was twenty-five years ago.

It is imperative that in the design of farm policies it be recognized that the economic welfare of farm people is dependent primarily upon the level and growth of incomes in the economy generally and to only a minor and temporary degree upon commodity price and payments programs. Farm programs that attempt to delay the adjustments required by economic growth will confer no long-run benefits upon farm people.[9] This is not to imply that there is no role for government in assisting agriculture and farm people. In an economy such as ours, where there are numerous governmental interventions that restrict competition and market adjustments, it does not follow that all governmental intervention in agriculture is undesirable. Some types of governmental intervention, such as the support of agricultural research, price reporting for farm products, and outlook information and analysis, are required to ensure that these activities are carried on at socially optimal levels. The large number of firms in agriculture means that in the absence of governmental efforts too little would be invested in these activities because marginal social returns would greatly exceed marginal social costs.

Further, given other accepted policies and programs, such as unemployment insurance and minimum wages and the failure of national policies to maintain a continuous high level of employment, measures that limit or reduce the extreme short-run variability of farm prices and income due to domestic economic instability or the destabilizing effects of the agricultural and trade policies of other countries can be justified on grounds of both equity and efficiency. While the long-run interests of American farm people will be best served by a market-oriented farm policy, it does not follow that all governmental intervention is undesirable. What does follow is that it is extremely difficult to devise and manage the proper forms of intervention with respect to prices and incomes. It is no easy task to do just enough to offset the most serious consequences of economic instability and governmental interventions in the rest of the economy while retaining most of the advantages of the price system in allocating resources and

---

[9] See Johnson, *World Agriculture in Disarray*, chapter 9.

in providing for the flow of farm products into the available markets. The importance of recognizing the current and prospective economic structure of agriculture and how agriculture relates to the rest of the economy in devising the appropriate forms of governmental intervention cannot be overemphasized. Major errors that will harm both farm and nonfarm people will result if such interventions rest on outmoded preconceptions of American agriculture as one that has little ability to adjust to its economic setting.

Elimination of Excess Resources in Agriculture

The income improvements described above, especially after the mid-1960s, were accompanied by a significant reduction in the amount of excess resources in agriculture.[10] I believe that by 1972 most, if not all, of what were considered to be excess resources in agriculture had been eliminated. The improved real income from agriculture was due not to higher farm prices and increased government payments but to major resource adjustments. As indicated in Table 2 the adjusted parity ratio, which includes direct government payments as equivalent to an increase in market prices, either remained quite stable or actually declined after the mid-1960s. The real income per unit of labor, management, and land increased and substantially so.

Some may disagree with the conclusion that most of the excess resources in agriculture had been eliminated by 1972. It is true that land was diverted from current crop production in 1972 as well as in many prior years. In fact, the diverted area in 1972 of almost 62 million acres was nearly the largest area diverted under the farm commodity programs. However, a large part of the diversion was illusory, and the overvaluation of the dollar resulted in an implicit tax upon agriculture roughly equal to the substantial direct government payments made in 1972 and the years immediately before.

In early 1973 I estimated that the acreage diversion programs had reduced the area devoted to the major crops by less than 25 million acres and perhaps by not more than 20 million acres. The return of this amount of land to production, accompanied by the other necessary inputs, would have increased gross farm production by about 2 percent as of the early 1970s.[11] This estimate assumed that

---

[10] The term *excess resources* is defined to mean resources that are not fully employed because at politically acceptable levels of prices output would exceed the quantity demanded at those prices. A similar term is *excess productive capacity*, which could be defined as the difference between the potential supply and the amount demanded at the politically determined prices and incomes.

[11] D. Gale Johnson, *Farm Commodity Programs: An Opportunity for Change* (Washington: American Enterprise Institute, 1973), pp. 33-42.

real prices for crops remained essentially unchanged. Obviously with the significant increase in real crop prices in 1973, 1974, and 1975, it was expected that the actual increase in acreage would exceed 20 to 25 million acres. And it did, but not by anything approaching the 62 million acres of land diverted in 1972. The increase in cropland harvested between 1972 and 1975 was 41 million acres.[12] Crop failure was essentially the same in the two years—in 1975 it was a million acres less than in 1972. Thus in response to a significant increase in expected prices in 1975 compared with expected prices in 1972, there was a positive acreage response. If I was correct in my estimate of the effect of the acreage diversion programs on acreage used for crops, the increase due to the positive price response was approximately 20 million acres or about 7 percent of the cropland that I estimated would have been harvested in 1972 without the acreage diversion programs at the real crop prices of the early 1970s.

Whether my estimate of the effects of acreage diversion programs on the value of crop output is somewhat high or low, I know that it is much closer to the mark than estimates of the effect of acreage diversion on farm output of nearly 7 percent in the late 1960s.[13]

Even with the higher expected real crop prices, total crop production increased by only 8 percent between 1972 and 1975. Obviously weather influences could affect these comparisons, but it may be noted that crop production per acre of cropland (including crop failure and summer fallow) were essentially the same in 1972 and 1975.[14]

There were aspects of governmental farm policy in addition to land diversion that could legitimately be said to have absorbed excess production capacity. The principal programs were price support activities of the Commodity Credit Corporation that resulted in inventory accumulations and export programs that resulted in subsidies of varying magnitudes. However, during 1970 and 1971, as well as in

---

[12] U.S. Department of Agriculture, Economic Research Service, *Changes in Farm Production and Efficiency,* Statistical Bulletin no. 561 (September 1976), p. 17.

[13] Leroy Quance and Luther Tweeten, "Excess Capacity and Adjustment Potentials in U.S. Agriculture," *Agricultural Economics Research,* vol. 24, no. 3 (July 1972), p. 60. In testimony before the Senate Committee on Agriculture and Forestry in July 1976 they said, "In short, 1972 acreage diversion reduced total farm output between 2 percent and 10 percent. The best estimate is perhaps 5 percent."

[14] If the change in acreage between 1972 and 1975 is measured by cropland used for crops (cropland harvested, crop failure, and cultivated summer fallow) rather than for harvested cropland alone, the increase in cropland was only 33 million acres. The area of summer fallow declined by 7 million acres. A substantial part of the land classified as diverted in 1972 was cultivated summer fallow which farmers had no intention of seeding in that year. For change in cropland used for crops, see USDA, *Changes in Farm Production and Efficiency,* p. 17.

1972, changes in inventories held by the CCC were negative and thus added supplies to the market rather than withdrawing them.[15] Experience since 1972 indicates that not all of P.L. 480 transactions (food aid) should be thought of solely as an outlet for unwanted agricultural products. In recent years the quantities of agricultural products shipped under P.L. 480 have been approximately half of the level of the early 1970s. It is reasonable to argue that for 1970 and 1971 the reduction of CCC inventories was an approximate offset to the increased demand due to the component of food aid that represented demand expansion. There were some export subsidies paid in 1970 and 1971, but by June 1972 these had been reduced to low levels.[16]

Direct governmental payments to farmers were in excess of $3 billion in 1970, 1971, and 1972. If there were few excess resources in agriculture, why were payments equal to 25 to 30 percent of net farm operator income required? Three comments are relevant. First, the payments did not represent an equal addition to net farm operator incomes. In other words, farmers did incur a loss of income because of acreage diversion, which was required for receipt of most of the payments. I have estimated that the increase in net farm income due to the payments was approximately $1.5 billion annually during the early 1970s or something less than half of the payments made.[17] This is, admittedly, a crude estimate and subject to error. But some real diversion occurred. And farmers who participated in the voluntary programs were induced to increase yields on the land actually cropped. Some amount went directly to landlords and was not retained by farm operators.[18]

Second, a large part of the increase in net income represented added income to land and not to mobile factors such as labor, current inputs, and capital equipment. Thus the payments did not go primarily to hold resources in agriculture but to enhance the returns to those who held land.

---

[15] For data on government farm program operations, see F. J. Nelson and Willard W. Cochrane, "Economic Consequences of Federal Farm Commodity Programs, 1953-72," *Agricultural Economics Research*, vol. 28, no. 2 (April 1976), pp. 54-55.

[16] In 1971-1972 total agricultural exports were $8.0 billion; export subsidies cost $237 million, primarily for wheat, rice, peanuts, and tobacco. U.S. Department of Agriculture, Economic Research Service, *Foreign Agricultural Trade of the United States (FATUS)* (May 1975), p. 74.

[17] Johnson, *Farm Commodity Programs*, pp. 45-49.

[18] Out of total government payments to farmers in 1972 of $3,961 million, $507 million went directly to landlords. See U.S. Department of Agriculture, Economic Research Service, *Farm Income Statistics*, Statistical Bulletin no. 557 (July 1976), pp. 63 and 50.

Third, it can be argued that the magnitude of the payments was roughly equal to the tax paid by American crop producers because of the overvaluation of the dollar during the first part of the 1970s. Crop products account for approximately 90 percent of U.S. agricultural exports. In 1970 and 1971 the value of production of crops for which exports were an important factor in the price of output was approximately $20 billion. Assuming the U.S. dollar was overvalued by 12 to 15 percent during those years, the dollar price of crops may have been depressed by approximately 10 percent compared with the prices that would have prevailed if the exchange rate had been an equilibrium one.[19] Thus it is not altogether unreasonable to argue that the government payments, after taking into account the real costs imposed upon farmers, were of approximately the same order as the tax imposed on crop producers by the overvaluation of the dollar. This tax may have been of the order of $2 billion, which is approximately the same as the increase in net farm operator income plus the increased income of nonfarm landlords resulting from the payments. Such rough equality, if it did exist, implies that if the dollar had not been overvalued in the early 1970s, and there had been no farm programs or payments, net farm income might have been approximately what it was. The one factor that has not been taken into account in this approximation is the effect on farm prices of the increase in farm output due to the return of the diverted acreage to use. As I have argued above, the increase in farm ouput due to the return of the diverted acreage was probably about 2 percent.

Increased Importance of Nonfarm Incomes

In most recent years approximately half of the income of farm families has originated from nonfarm sources.[20] Agriculture, as a business, in 1975 generated a gross income of $100 billion, yet in that year the nonfarm income of the farm population equaled the income of the farm population from farm sources.

Since 1967 half or more of the income of the farm population has

---

[19] To my knowledge, G. Edward Schuh was the first to point out the implications of the overvaluation of the dollar to American agriculture during the 1960s and early 1970s ("The Exchange Rate and U.S. Agriculture," *American Journal of Agricultural Economics*, vol. 56, no. 1 [February 1974], pp. 1-13). Obviously both supply and demand effects need to be considered.

[20] All of the data in this section may be found in USDA, *Farm Income Statistics*.

come from nonfarm sources.[21] The only exception was 1973 when net farm operator income was nearly 80 percent above the prior year. In 1950 only 31 percent of the income of the farm population was from nonfarm sources; in 1960, 39 percent.

Data are available, in a continuous series, on the off-farm income of farm operators only since 1960. In 1960 off-farm income accounted for 43 percent of the total income of farm operators; in 1970 to 57 percent and in 1975 to 56 percent.[22]

The estimates of the income of farm operators from farm operations and off-farm sources are available by value of sales classes. In 1975 only the farms with sales in excess of $20,000 had more income from their farming operations than from other sources. The number of such farms was 1,014,000 or 36 percent of all farms. For farm operator families with farm sales of $40,000 to $99,999, off-farm income accounted for 27 percent of total family income. It is true that 89 percent of total cash receipts from farming is on farms with sales in excess of $20,000. For all farm families with cash receipts of $20,000 or more, off-farm income accounted for 26.5 percent of net family income. In 1960 the 38 percent of the farms with 87 percent of the sales obtained 20 percent of their incomes from off-farm sources. Thus the increasing importance of off-farm income occurred for all farm sales classes, not solely for the families that operated the smaller farms.

The implication of the data on incomes by source is that even the farm families with the largest farm operations obtain a significant part of their income from off-farm sources. Consequently their welfare is not determined solely by their incomes from the farms they operate.

But perhaps the most striking income development for farm families from 1960 to date has been the remarkable increase in the relative and real income of the farm families operating small farms. In 1960 farm families with farm sales of less than $5,000 had family

---

[21] The Economic Research Service (USDA) provides two different estimates of farm and nonfarm income of farm people. The one referred to above refers to the income, by sources, of all persons living on farms. It thus includes hired farm workers who live on farms as well as farm operators who live on the farms they operate, but excludes a substantial number of farm operators who do not live on their farms and live in nonfarm areas. The series on incomes of farm operator families estimates incomes by source for all farm operators, excluding hired farm workers and their family members, and including those farm operators who do not live on the farms operated.

[22] Off-farm income includes income from all sources other than the farm operated and thus includes some income from farm sources, such as rent or wages from work on other farms.

incomes of less than two-fifths of the income of farm families with sales of $20,000 to $39,999. In 1975 the farm families with sales of less than $10,000 had three-fifths as large incomes as the families with farm sales of $40,000 to $99,999.[23] This reduction in the income inequality associated with the value of farm sales was due primarily to the ability of farm families on the smaller farms to find alternative uses for their labor.[24]

During the 1960s the per capita disposable income of the farm population relative to the nonfarm population increased from less than 54 percent (the average for 1959–1961) to more than 74 percent (the average for 1969–1971). In 1975 the percentage was almost 90. Of the total increase in the incomes of the farm population from 1960 to 1970, 62 percent was derived from nonfarm sources.[25] Much of the improvement in the relative income of farm families during the 1960s resulted from increased nonfarm earnings and not from increased agricultural earnings. In addition, some significant part of the increased marginal productivity of labor in agriculture resulted from changing factor proportions due to the migration of persons away from farms and to the increased use of the labor of farm families in nonfarm activities. This aspect of the resource adjustment process will be considered in greater detail below.

In the development of farm commodity policies, it should be remembered that only 36 percent of the farms are operated by families that receive more than half of their income from the farm they operate. And it is primarily these farms that would realize any significant benefit from various subsidies that might be involved.

The Labor Market

There has been a striking change in the integration of the farm and nonfarm labor markets during the past quarter-century. This integration has taken two forms. One is that an increasing percentage of the farm population that is in the labor force has nonfarm jobs. The other is that an increasing percentage of those who work at farm jobs resides elsewhere than on farms. These two changes occurred simultaneously with a high migration rate from farm to nonfarm residences during the 1950s and the 1960s. During each of the four five-year periods in

[23] In deflated dollars $10,000 in 1975 was approximately the same as $5,000 in 1960.

[24] It should be noted that we do not know how many of the 1,468,000 families on farms with less than $10,000 sales were the survivors of the 2,465,000 families that were on farms with less than $5,000 in sales in 1960.

[25] USDA, *Farm Income Statistics* (July 1976), p. 42.

those decades the annual migration rate off the farms exceeded 5 percent. And the migration rates were actually slightly higher during the 1960s than in the 1950s, even though the relative income position of farm people improved during the 1960s.

In 1960 the percentage of the employed farm population working in nonagricultural industries was 33; in 1970 it was 44; and in 1975 it was 47. Thus by 1975 almost half of all employed farm residents worked at other than farm occupations.[26]

Not only are increasing proportions of the farm population holding nonfarm jobs, but more of the farm jobs are being held by nonfarm residents. In 1960 a quarter of those employed in agriculture were nonfarm residents; in 1970, 38 percent and in 1975, 42 percent.[27] Nearly one out of six farm operators have nonfarm residences, and in 1975 they earned approximately a sixth of net farm income.[28]

If we consider jointly the distribution of employment of farm residents by farm and nonfarm occupations and the distribution of the residences of those who do farm work, it is obvious that the labor markets for farm people and for farm workers can no longer be described accurately as separated from the rest of the economy. Approximately half of the labor force members living on farms have nonfarm jobs; more than two-fifths of the farm workers are nonfarm residents. It seems obvious that the elasticity of supply of labor to agriculture has increased since the end of World War II and that the economic fate of persons living on farms is no longer so closely tied to events that affect agriculture.

The Farm Land Market

Since 1950 the value of land and buildings per acre has increased in every year except one, and in that year (1954) the decline was approximately 1 percent. From 1967 through 1976 farm land prices increased by 169 percent; deflated by prices paid for production and living items the increase was 44 percent. Over the same period the absolute value of Standard and Poors index of 500 common stocks increased only 14 percent and the real value declined by more than a fourth.

---

[26] U.S. Bureau of the Census and U.S. Department of Agriculture *Farm Population*, Series Census-ERS, P-27, no. 41 (June 1971) and no. 47 (September 1976). Comparable data are not available for 1950 due to the change in the census definition of a farm in 1960. On the basis of a comparable definition of a farm in 1950 and 1960, the percentage of the employed workers living on farms in nonagricultural jobs increased from 30 in 1950 to 42.5 in 1960 (P-27, no. 24 and no. 28).

[27] *Farm Population*, P-27, no. 21 and no. 47.

[28] USDA, *Farm Income Statistics* (July 1976), p. 40.

The deflated value of farm land and buildings per acre has increased consistently for three decades. During the 1950s the annual rate of increase was 3.2 percent; during the 1960s, it was 4.3 percent and from 1970 to 1976, it was 2.8 percent.[29] Thus the rising real price of farm real estate has not been a recent phenomenon.

From 1910–1914 to 1956 the average land price (excluding the value of buildings) decreased significantly relative to prices received by farmers, to net agricultural income, and to all input prices except fertilizer (see Table 4). However, since 1956 there has been a significant shift in the relative price of land. Compared to 1910–1914 the land price in 1974 had increased by 63 percent compared to prices

Table 4

FARM OUTPUT AND INPUT PRICE INDEXES,
1910–1914, 1956 AND 1974

	Price Index (1910–1914 = 100)			
	1956	1956 (Deflated by prices received)	1974	1974 (Deflated by prices received)
Prices received	235	100	467	100
Prices of inputs				
Farm wages	543	231	1,506	322
Building and fencing	374	149	778	167
Farm machinery	329	140	769	165
Farm supplies	279	119	409	88
Fertilizer	150	64	299	64
Motor vehicles	367	156	758	162
Land price per acre[a]	181[b]	77	762[b]	163
Net agricultural income[c]	288	122	759	163

[a] Excludes value of buildings.

[b] Average of land prices at beginning and end of calendar year.

[c] Includes net operator income, wages, interest on mortgage debt and rent to non-operator landlords.

Note: 1974 data used since prices paid indexes were revised for 1975 and later years, and categories for 1975 were not comparable to those used by Schultz.

Source: Theodore W. Schultz, *Economic Growth and Agriculture* (New York: McGraw-Hill, 1968), for first two columns, except net farm income, and U.S. Department of Agriculture sources.

[29] The deflator was the index of prices paid for family living and production. Over the period, the relative importance of buildings in the value of farm real estate declined from 28 percent to approximately 15 percent.

received and had increased relative to all input prices except farm wages. The increase in land prices from 1910–1914 was nearly identical to the increase in net agricultural income, which meant that between 1956 and 1974 land prices increased significantly more than did net agricultural income—320 percent compared to 163 percent.

There is no particular importance attached to the comparisons for 1956; all of the data in the first two columns of Table 4 were taken from an article by my colleague, Theodore W. Schultz, in which it was pointed out that there had been a secular decline in the relative price of land and of land rent. If somewhat earlier years had been chosen, the decline in the land price relative to prices received would have been even greater. What Table 4 indicates is that there has been a substantial change in land prices relative to both output and input prices since the mid-1950s. If the comparisons are carried through until the end of 1976, the changes appear to be even more dramatic.[30]

Why have land prices increased so significantly since 1950? Numerous explanations have been given. One popular explanation is that more of the land is now owned by nonfarm individuals and corporations than was true a quarter-century ago. This explanation is totally without merit; the percentage of land owned by nonoperator landlords was the same in 1974 as in 1960 or perhaps even a little less.[31] Another explanation is that there has been a substantial transfer of land from agricultural to nonagricultural purposes. It is true that since 1950 land in farms has decreased by more than 10 percent. However, most of this reduction was due to abandonment rather than absorption by urban areas or transportation use. Of the more than 100 million-acre reduction in land in farms between 1950 and 1969, less than 20 million acres were transferred to urban areas and transportation use.[32] It is further estimated that between 1950 and 1970

---

[30] Farm land prices (including buildings) increased by 37 percent from the average of 1974 to November 1976. Farm product prices declined by 3 percent between 1974 and 1976, and prices paid increased by 16 percent. From U.S. Department of Agriculture, Economic Research Service, *Agricultural Outlook*, AO-18 (January-February 1977), pp. 10 and 15.

[31] Carson D. Evans and Richard W. Simunek, *Balance Sheet of the Farming Sector, 1975: Supplement 1 to AIB 389*, U.S. Department of Agriculture, Economic Research Service (April 1976), pp. 19-20. The published series indicates that 65 percent of the farm real estate was owned by farm operators in 1960 and 71 percent in 1974. However, there appears to be a discontinuity in the series between 1969 and 1970 which may explain at least half of the increase in the percentage of farm real estate owned by the operator.

[32] Orville Krause and Dwight Hair, "Trends in Land Use and Competition for Land to Produce Food and Fiber," in *Perspectives on Prime Lands: Background Papers for Seminar on Retention of Price Lands* (Washington: U.S. Department of Agriculture, 1975), p. 2.

less than 5 million acres of cropland (out of approximately 480 million acres in 1950) was urbanized.[33] And this estimate includes some cropland that would have been abandoned for agricultural purposes even if it had not been incorporated into urban areas.[34]

Another explanation is that land prices have been bid up by farmers who wish to expand the size of their farms. In other words, if a farm is sold, the highest bidder may well be a farmer who wishes to add the land to an existing farm rather than a farmer who wishes to operate the farm as a complete unit. It is true that when an existing farm is put up for sale it is as likely to be bought for farm enlargement as it is to create a new operating unit.[35] But the effects of farm enlargement on land values must have been small. Farm operations can be enlarged by renting additional land as well as by buying land. In fact, the most significant change in land tenure patterns since World War II has been the growth of part-owner-operated farms—some land is owned and some is rented. In 1969 over half of all cropland was operated under this arrangement, and the average size of such farms was approximately twice that of farms operated by full owners.[36]

It is almost certainly more correct to explain the purchase of much of the farm land sold as due to the underlying economic factors that have resulted in the enlargement of the average size of farms than by the willingness or ability of existing farm operators to pay more for land for farm enlargement than farm operators who wish to establish a new operating unit. At any given time, the area of many of the farm units up for sale is too small to be the basis of an efficient farm unit. Thus the purchaser of such a unit, if the purchaser is to farm the land, must be one that can combine the land with other land in order to have an efficient farm unit.

Why have land prices increased so significantly since 1950? I do not have a wholly satisfactory explanation, but I believe that the following considerations have been relevant:

---

[33] Ibid., p. 9.

[34] Ibid.

[35] In 1975 the farm land sold was distributed as follows: Complete farm, 45 percent; part of another farm, 45 percent and part-time farm, 10 percent. After the sales, the distributions were: complete farm, 28 percent; part of a farm, 59 percent; and part time, 13 percent. Of complete farms sold in 1975, approximately half remained as complete farms. In 1960 about two-thirds of complete farms sold remained complete farms after the sale. USDA, *Agricultural Finance Databook* (September 1976), pp. 74-75.

[36] Bruce H. Johnson, *Farmland Tenure Patterns in the United States*, U.S. Department of Agriculture, Economic Research Service, Agriculture Economic Report no. 249 (February 1974), p. 40. The percentage of all land in farms operated by part owners was 57.5 percent compared with 51.8 percent of cropland.

1. Farm land prices were below long-run equilibrium levels in 1950 because of expectation of a severe downturn in farm prices and incomes.
2. The large increase in land prices during the 1950s represented a return to more usual or normal expectations concerning the appropriate rate for the capitalization of return to land.
3. During the 1960s two factors were at work—net agricultural income increased significantly, and the share of that income attributed to land or rent increased significantly.
4. The increase in the value of farm real estate since 1970 is consistent with the increase in net agricultural income, an increase in the share of income going to rent and an increase in the capitalization rate due, probably, to uncertainty about the future of net agricultural income.

Admittedly these considerations depend somewhat on what one might call casual empiricism. But not entirely.

The first observation is not new; I made essentially the same point in an article that I wrote in the late 1940s.[37] At that time there was concern that the land price increases through the early postwar period were resulting in an untenable situation. Based on the high rates of return on rented land through 1947 (10 percent or more) it seemed that agricultural income could decline significantly, and land prices could still be maintained or increased.

The second point is more tenuous. The current return on land was approximately 4.8 percent in 1950; it appears to have fallen to as low as 2.5 percent in 1960. The share of net rent in net agricultural income was approximately the same in 1950 and 1960 with net agricultural income in absolute dollars in 1960 being some 6 percent below the 1950 level.[38]

---

[37] D. Gale Johnson, "Allocation of Agricultural Income," *Journal of Farm Economics*, vol. 30, no. 4 (November 1948), pp. 733-34.

[38] The estimates of the current rate of return on land and the share of net agricultural income attributed to land presented in this section have been derived by relating net rent paid to nonoperator landlords to the current market value of land owned by the landlords and by estimating the total rent on all farm land by assuming that the rate of return on all land was the same as on rented land. This approach is described in my article "Allocation of Agricultural Income" referred to above.

The data on which these estimates are based have numerous limitations, and the estimates of the current rate of return could well be in error to a significant extent.

The sources of data are *Farm Income Statistics* (July 1976), and two other publications of the Economic Research Service, *Balance Sheet of the Farming Sector, 1976*, Agriculture Information Bulletin, no. 403 (September 1976) and *Balance Sheet of the Farming Sector, Supplement No. 1*, Agriculture Information Bulletin no. 389 (April 1976).

The third point reflects, in my opinion, the speeding up of the process of reducing the amount of excess resources in agriculture which resulted in an increase in net agricultural income during the 1960s and in the ratio of the per capita disposable income of the farm population relative to the nonfarm population. In addition, the early 1960s saw the sharp increase in government payments to farmers—from $700 million in 1960 to over $3 billion by 1966. As I have argued above, a large fraction of the payments accrued to land. In fact, the estimated share of land rent in net agricultural income increased from about 20 percent in 1960 to 30 percent by 1965 and 29 percent in 1969. The current rate of return on land increased from about 2.5 percent in 1960 to approximately 3.5 percent in the latter half of the 1960s.

Why has the share of rent in net agricultural income increased between 1970 and 1975 by 5 percentage points? [39] The increase could be due to a change in the agricultural production function, but I think the more likely explanation has been the shift in the relative importance of land intensive output (the crops) relative to more labor intensive output (livestock products) and a shift in relative prices favoring crops. Between 1970 and 1975 the output of livestock products decreased by 7 percent while crop output increased by more than 20 percent. The increase in livestock prices was 45 percent; the increase in crop prices was 100 percent.

Are current land prices too high? The context of this question is really whether farm land prices will decline in the years ahead. While instinctively I feel that the answer to the question should be in the affirmative, the discussion of the factors affecting land prices during the past three decades leads to the conclusion that the current prices will be sustained and, in fact, may well increase further.

If net farm operator income remains at approximately $24 billion and net agricultural income at approximately $40 billion (the levels of 1975 and 1976 and the projection for 1977), land prices are likely to

[39] A critical variable in the estimate of the share of net agricultural income attributed to rent is the percentage of the value of farm real estate owned by nonoperator landlords. The most recent series, contained in Supplement no. 1 to Agriculture Information Bulletin no. 389, appears to have a significant discontinuity between 1969 and 1970 (see Table 14). For 1969 it is estimated that 33.1 percent of all farm real estate was owned by nonoperator landlords; for 1970 the percentage given is 28.4. Such a large change could not have occurred in a single year. The series seems to be consistent from 1960 to 1969 and from 1970 to 1975, though one must remain somewhat suspicious about the data when such a large change occurs in one year. The increase in the percentage of net agricultural income attributed to rent between 1970 and 1975 is based on the assumption that there was no change in the importance of rented land in the total.

increase in the years ahead. If net rents paid in 1976 were at the 1975 level of $4.8 billion, the net current return on the farm real estate value of $422 billion at the beginning of 1976 was 3.6 to 3.9 percent. For 1960 through 1974 the average current return was 3.8 percent; however, for 1960 through 1971 (prior to the major increase in farm product prices) the current return averaged 3.3 percent. If farm and agricultural incomes remain at recent levels and if the current rate of return required to induce the ownership of land returns to the rate of the 1960s, further increases in land values are probable. Obviously other factors, such as the anticipated rate of inflation, will affect land prices, and I am not predicting that within the next three or four years the value of farm real estate might approach $500 billion. All I am saying is that it could do so if the above assumptions turn out to be correct. The most critical assumption is the future level of net income of agriculture. I would not rule out a decline in net agricultural income of 10 percent and of farm operator income of somewhat more in the years ahead. If this should occur there would probably be some downward pressure on farm real estate values, though if the income decline were assumed to be temporary the effects would be modest—perhaps nothing more than stability in the absolute value of farm real estate for a year or two before continuing its lengthy uptrend.

Increased Importance of International Trade

From 1925 through 1943 the United States was a net importer of agricultural products in most years. During the latter part of the 1930s, in part because of climatic factors and in part because of governmental programs, the value of agricultural imports was almost twice as great as that of exports. During most of the 1950s agricultural imports exceeded agricultural exports; it was not until 1960 that our agricultural exports consistently exceeded our agricultural imports. In 1974, 1975, and 1976 the value of agricultural exports was roughly double the value of agricultural imports.[40]

The value of U.S. agricultural exports has increased substantially in recent years. The share of agricultural exports in total U.S. exports has increased since the late 1960s—from a low of 16 percent in 1969 to 21 percent in 1975. But agriculture's share of total U.S. exports during 1971–1975 was below any five-year period since 1950, except for 1966–1970, though the differences have been small.[41]

---

[40] Historical data on agricultural trade from U.S. Department of Agriculture, *Agricultural Statistics*, 1972, p. 698. Recent years from *FATUS*.
[41] *FATUS* (December 1976), p. 12.

What is remarkable is that the share of agricultural exports in total exports has remained so great and has not declined significantly since World War II. The share of agricultural exports in total exports in the United States, at more than 20 percent, is almost double the comparable share for Canada. What might also be described as quite remarkable is that the U.S. share in world agricultural trade has increased since 1950—from 12.3 percent during 1951–1955 to 16.3 percent in 1971–1975. While the share of agricultural exports in total U.S. exports has not increased since 1950 but has remained approximately constant, the U.S. share in total world exports has declined since 1950 while, as noted above, the U.S. share in world agricultural exports has risen. The U.S. share of world nonagricultural exports was 20.5 percent in 1951–1955; in 1971–1975 it was 11.2 percent.[42] Thus, given the changes in the world market in terms of the opportunities for exporting agricultural and nonagricultural products, it appears that the comparative advantage of U.S. agriculture has improved significantly since World War II.

There has been a major change in the composition of U.S. agricultural exports since 1950. In 1950 cotton and tobacco together accounted for 44 percent of the value of agricultural exports, the grains for 29 percent, and oilseeds (including products) 6 percent. By 1960 cotton and tobacco accounted for only 18 percent of agricultural exports and in 1975 only 8 percent. By 1975 grains accounted for 53 percent and oilseeds 20 percent of agricultural exports.[43] Livestock products, including dairy and poultry, have accounted for slightly less than a tenth of agricultural exports for the past two decades. Grains and oilseeds—really soybeans—are the critical factors in the export performance of U.S. agriculture.

While there is no simple and accurate measure of the importance of agricultural exports to U.S. agriculture, some rough indicators may be appropriate. In 1975 exports provided an outlet for 100 million acres or 30 percent of all cropland harvested in the United States.[44] The percentage of crop output exported has been increasing rather steadily, except for a dip in the late 1960s, since 1950 when the percentage was about 15. If the value of agricultural exports is compared with cash receipts from marketings less farm purchases of feed and livestock, the percentage has increased from 12 percent in 1950 to

---

[42] Ibid.

[43] U.S. Department of Agriculture, Economic Research Service, *U.S. Foreign Agricultural Trade Statistical Report*, annual supplement to *FATUS*, fiscal years 1974 and 1975.

[44] USDA, *Changes in Farm Production and Efficiency*, p. 16.

30 percent in 1975.[45] Another rough measure of the importance of agricultural exports is the percentage of the output of various crops that were exported from the 1975 crop—feed grains, 25; wheat and flour, 55; soybeans, 50; tobacco, 30; and cotton, 40.[46]

This rather detailed depiction of the importance of agricultural exports has been presented for a purpose. U.S. agriculture, especially that part located in the Corn Belt and the Great Plains, has now become very much dependent upon international trade for its economic well-being. This has significant implications for the future of agricultural policy, and one can only hope that this strong dependence is recognized as farm commodity policies evolve in the years ahead.

There is a further question related to the importance of international trade to U.S. agriculture: Has the increased role of international trade contributed to price stability? The conventional answer to this question would be in the affirmative. Unfortunately, the agricultural and trade policies followed by the majority of the exporters and importers of agricultural products create substantial instability in international prices, especially for grains. More than half of the world's grain is produced and consumed under regimes that stabilize domestic prices for both producers and consumers by managing net trade to equalize supply and demand at the predetermined prices.[47] This result can be achieved by the use of variable levies and import subsidies or by state control of imports and exports; the former are used by the European Community and the latter by the Soviet Union and Japan.

The effects of such policies are to force the part of the world where domestic and international prices move in unison, or nearly so, to absorb the effects of variations in world demand and/or supply. The United States is currently one of the few countries that does not have differentials, either fixed or variable, between domestic and international prices. Consequently it accepts the price variability that is imposed by policies of other countries. The final section of this paper considers how greater price stability might be achieved.

The Limits of Farm Commodity Policy

The limits to farm commodity policy are of two kinds. One is that in the United States, if support prices are established significantly above market clearing levels, both the supply and the demand re-

---

[45] USDA, *Farm Income Statistics*, pp. 44 and 48 for net cash receipts.

[46] *FATUS* (October 1976), pp. 5-6.

[47] See my "World Agriculture, Commodity Policy and Price Variability," *American Journal of Agricultural Economics*, vol. 56, no. 5 (December 1975), pp. 823-28.

sponses would be large enough to result quickly in governmental costs that are politically unacceptable. The other is that policies that seek to increase farm incomes either through higher support prices or by direct payments related to output levels will not have a measurable sustained impact upon the returns to labor, management, and capital but only upon the rent and price of land.

Price supports or direct payments can have a modest short-run effect upon the return to farm labor and management, but because of the characteristics of the farm labor supply described earlier, the effect would persist only briefly. Furthermore, the short-run benefits would go primarily to families who have incomes much larger than the national average.[48]

The only significant effect of price-increasing measures in the long run is upon the rent and price of land. The agreement on this point among agricultural economists is now universal,[49] yet it does not seem to be fully recognized in political discussions.

If price supports are established above market clearing levels for the major farm crops, the output and demand responses would soon result in substantial accumulations of stocks by the Commodity Credit Corporation. Past experience has indicated that the government's ability to reduce production or prevent demand losses due to the higher prices is a limited one. The primary method that is politically acceptable for reducing production is to limit the use of land. But land now constitutes no more than 20 percent of the total inputs used in agriculture and, given existing farming technology, other inputs can be substituted for land with reasonable ease.[50]

The dependence of U.S. agriculture, particularly crop production, upon export markets greatly circumscribes the effectiveness of price

---

[48] For a discussion of the distribution of benefits resulting from U.S. farm commodity programs during the early 1970s, see Johnson, *Farm Commodity Programs*, chapter 5. In 1971 three-fifths of the direct government payments went to 21.5 percent of the farms; the average income of the families operating these farms was $19,552 and thus much above the national average for all families.

[49] For example, Cochrane and Ryan, *American Farm Policy, 1948-1973*, p. 371, state the following: ". . . it should be recognized that the alert, aggressive, expanding farmers were able to hold the income gains accruing to them from the farm programs and technological advance in the competitive context in which they operated in the long run *only insofar as they were land owners*. The income gains accruing to them from the farm programs and technological advance were through the competitive process capitalized into land values, and their unit costs of production increased through this land capitalization process." (Italics in the original.)

[50] For a succinct statement of the limits of acreage reduction as a production control measure, see Cochrane and Ryan, *American Farm Policy, 1948-1973*, p. 387.

increasing measures. The establishment of price supports during the 1950s occurred without adequate recognition of our export markets. Even with the payment of substantial export subsidies and the operation of large-scale foreign food aid programs, our agricultural exports suffered. It was not until the early 1960s when most price supports were set at or below world market levels that we began to realize our export potential.[51]

The United States could establish price supports above market clearing levels for the major crops and aggressively use export subsidies and foreign food aid in an effort to maintain or expand exports. This was the policy followed during the 1950s for certain major crops, especially wheat and cotton. But given our dependence on exports and our need to negotiate for reductions to barriers to trade in farm products, this would be a short-sighted and counterproductive effort. Further, the costs to the government of export subsidies could become so large as to create political problems.

The Agriculture and Consumer Protection Act of 1973 introduced the concept of target prices. The rationale of the target price was that it permitted setting price support or loan rates at relatively low levels—levels that would permit the available product to move freely into domestic and foreign markets. The target price was set at somewhat higher levels than the loan rates. If the price received by farmers was below the target price during a specified period of time, payments were made to farmers to make up the difference between the target price and the average price received. The quantity of product on which payment was to be made was not the total output, but the farmer's allotment. Each farmer's allotment represented his share of the na-

---

[51] Cochrane and Ryan clearly describe the conflicts that arose between the domestic programs of price support and international trade: "By their very nature, domestic programs of price and income support conflict with international trade, hence impede trade in agricultural commodities. . . . Undue concern with the objective of domestic farm price and income support in the period 1948-65 caused international trade in agricultural products involving the United States to suffer. A compromise between the objectives of domestic price and income support and international trade following 1965 has led to expanded trade and possibly real income benefits to consumers" (*American Farm Policy, 1948-1973*, p. 390). The adjustment of corn price supports occurred much earlier than 1965, with a major downward adjustment occurring in 1959. Unfortunately price supports were again increased in 1961 and 1962, though not back to the level of 1958. In 1963 there was a substantial reduction in corn price supports and corn moved freely into international markets. From 1954 through 1958 all feed grain exports averaged 6 million metric tons annually; during 1959-1962 exports averaged more than 11 million tons; and during 1963-1965, they were more than 16 million tons. Not all of the increase was due to the changes in price support policy, but a large part of the increase would not have occurred if price supports had remained at the 1956 level.

tional acreage required to meet domestic and export needs, as defined by the secretary of agriculture. The legislation also included a limit of $20,000 on the amount of such deficiency payments that could be paid to each farmer annually under the wheat, cotton, and feed grain programs.

The target price concept has clear advantages over the use of price supports to assure farmers a minimum level of returns. However, target prices can have some effects on output, though less than would a market price equal to the target price. When the target price is applicable, it is unlikely that it will cover total production of the crop; thus at the margin production decisions will be made primarily in terms of the expected market prices. Further, the limit on total payments will have an effect on production decisions for large farms that produce a significant percentage of the output of wheat and cotton, though the effect on feed grain producers would be rather small since relatively few feed grain producers would be affected by the payment limitations.

If target prices are set substantially above price support levels, the governmental costs can become large. John Schnittker recently estimated that if the target prices for wheat, cotton, feed grains, rice, and peanuts were set 10 percent above relatively low price supports for these commodities, the annual maximum budgetary costs of the deficiency payments "would be slightly under $2 billion." [52]

The federal government has significant limits on its ability to influence the market prices of farm products. The limits are less restrictive in the short run of one or two years than in the longer run of four years or more. Given time to respond to increased incentives, the supply response from farmers can lead to governmental costs of accumulated stocks, of deficiency payments, and of surplus disposal operations, both domestic and foreign, that can lead to public rejection of farm commodity programs. Since it is very difficult to correct errors of judgment with respect to future demand and supply developments affecting farm prices, it is essential that in the replacement or extension of the current farm legislation full consideration is given to the long run rather than giving undue weight to the next year or two. To do

---

[52] John A. Schnittker, "Policy and Programs for Agriculture," paper presented at Conference on Food and Agricultural Policy at the American Enterprise Institute for Public Policy Research, Washington, D.C., March 10-11, 1977. The price support levels suggested by Schnittker were below the actual prices received by farmers during February 1977 by the following percentages: wheat, 8; corn, 20; cotton, 40; rice, 11. No specific support or loan level was suggested for peanuts. Schnittker argues for low levels of price supports and modest differences between target prices and price supports because: "Federal payments which provide a large part of net farm income to farmers are no longer acceptable to the public."

otherwise will impose unnecessary adjustment costs upon farm people, because many of the resources invested in agriculture are not easily withdrawn without substantial cost.

Reducing Price and Income Variability

Recent experience shows clearly that agriculture is subject to significant price and income variability. Net farm operator income increased by almost 79 percent between 1972 and 1973 and then decreased by more than 20 percent in the following year. Prices received for all farm products increased by 43 percent between 1972 and 1973; for crops the increase was 53 percent followed by a further increase of 28 percent between 1973 and 1974. The prices of individual commodities varied even more. Between 1972 and 1974 food grain prices increased 176 percent; between 1974 and early 1977 food grain prices received by farmers had declined by more than 45 percent.

Food prices, at least rising food prices, are a matter of considerable public and political concern. Protests by consumers over rising food prices in 1973 through 1975 indicate that consumers also have an interest in reducing price instability for farm products. It might be noted that compared with 1967, the base year for the consumer price index, consumer prices of food for a full year relative to all other items in the index were never more than 12.5 percent above the base year except in 1974. By January 1977 food prices had risen only 6 percent faster than nonfood prices relative to the base year.

There are three policy measures that could be used to minimize price and income variability: (1) a significant liberalization of international trade in agricultural products; (2) establishment of target prices at levels approximating expected market prices under average conditions; and (3) a reserve program for the major storable food crops.

A large part of the price variability for the grains is due to governmental policies and not to fluctuations in production or final consumer demand. Governments of countries that consume significantly more than half of the world's grain have domestic agricultural policies of price stabilization with variations in net trade being the major means of achieving that objective. To the degree that such governments are successful in achieving domestic price stability at the consumer and producer levels, the effects of variability of production and of consumer demand fluctuations due to cyclical factors affecting incomes and employment are imposed upon that part of the world which permits domestic prices to vary with international prices.

World grain production varies little from year to year. A departure in any year of 4 percent from the trend level of world production is an extreme departure. Such a departure, if grain moved freely across national borders, could not result in price fluctuations of the magnitudes witnessed in recent years. Demand variability for grains, especially for grains fed to livestock, also occurs, but such variability is soon dissipated if market prices are permitted to function with little or no interference.

Trade liberalization would contribute significantly to price stability in international markets and in those countries that permit domestic prices to vary with international prices. However, it is exceedingly unlikely that the Communist countries will modify their domestic policies in any significant way. It is not much more likely that the European Community and Japan, which together consume a tenth of the world's grain, will soon abandon their policies of domestic price stability for the grains. One country—the Soviet Union—is responsible for a large portion of the annual variability in world grain trade. This is due to substantial annual variability in grain production and the policy of domestic price and supply stability. It may well be that the major exporters have no viable alternative but to monitor and control Soviet grain imports in order to minimize the destabilizing effects of the production variability and internal policies of the Soviet Union.[53]

I should note that I have used trade liberalization in a broad and somewhat unusual sense. Normally we think of trade liberalization in terms of reducing the average degree of protection. We have generally ignored the effects of specific types of protection upon price instability in the rest of the world. Two types of trade liberalization have been assumed. One is to reduce the average degree of protection; the other is to make domestic prices responsive to changes in world demand and supply conditions. In the short run it is primarily the latter form of liberalization that would contribute to greater price stability in international markets. Policies of domestic price stability, such as the Common Agricultural Policy, result in variable rates of protection as international prices change. From 1972 through 1974, for some important commodities, the nominal protection provided by the Common Agricultural Policy ranged from nearly 100 percent to a negative 40 percent or more. If the same average degree of protection had been provided by ad valorem tariffs, prices within the European Community

---

[53] See D. Gale Johnson, *International Grain Trade and the Centrally Planned Economies* (Washington: British North American Committee, 1977).

would have reflected the changing world market conditions, and its net trade in agricultural products would have reflected to some degree the effects of the price variability in international markets.

Target prices can be used to provide some degree of stability of returns and income for farmers with only modest effects on the allocation of resources. But if target prices are not to result in holding in or bringing in excess resources in agriculture, the levels established must be modest ones. The target prices cannot be related to parity or to some measure of costs of production but must reflect a reasonable estimate of expected prices under "normal" or "average" circumstances. If the target prices are set significantly above the expected prices and payments are made in most years rather than occasionally, resource and output decisions will be affected.

Some of the effects of target prices higher than those indicated in the previous paragraph could be reduced if the deficiency payments did not apply to the actual output but to some predetermined output level. In other words, reasonable effort should be made to minimize the effects of the target prices on production decisions; as far as possible the decisions on how many resources to commit to production should be based on expected market prices and not on the target prices. Any method of dispensing the deficiency payments has some effect on output; at a minimum the expectation of receiving the payments if market prices should fall below the target prices would influence production decisions to some degree. The objective should be to minimize the effects of the target prices on output.

Historically the political system in the United States has been unwilling to divorce direct payments from production entirely. Under the 1973 Agricultural Act farmers had to seed or plant crops on their bases or allotments or suffer loss of the base or allotment in future years if they collected the deficiency payments. While certain substitutions have been permitted, to maintain an allotment or base each farmer had to cultivate a very large part of his cropland. While the output effects of this provision, or similar provisions in prior legislation, have probably been small, there seems no rationale for such a requirement. If market prices are below the target prices, the presumption is that output is larger than the market will absorb at politically acceptable prices. If some farmers were to find it in their interest to let their land lie idle, this would reduce the amount of production and resource adjustments required of other farmers.

The third approach to reducing agriculture's price and income variability is through a storage or reserve program. However, a reserve program that does not involve a substantial subsidy of its costs will not provide a degree of price stability such as that achieved in the United States for wheat and the feed grains during the 1960s. Storage involves substantial costs. If a ton of grain is held in storage for seven years, the price on release must be double (in real terms) the purchase price to cover annual storage costs of $7.50 per ton and a real interest rate of 5 percent. In this example it is assumed that the value of the grain put in storage is $100 per ton.

Is it necessary for government to be involved in the holding of reserves? Experience has indicated that the private market is capable of holding reserves. But there are those who argue that the private market will not hold enough stocks, though "enough" is seldom defined. There are perhaps two main reasons why the private market will hold reserves only of limited size. One is that the risks are substantial. Two or three years of large crops and thus low prices may occur in a row, and holding stocks is a costly operation. The other reason is that there are only a few countries in the world in which governmental policy permits any incentive to private firms to hold stocks. The pricing of grains in the European Community, for example, does not provide an incentive for private firms to hold stocks in excess of working stocks. The prices of the various grains are effectively regulated by the control of imports and exports and at prices established in a political framework. In most recent years the differences in prices from one year to the next have been less than the cost of holding grain.

The United States is virtually the only country in which private stockholding has had any significant role. Even in the United States, throughout most of the 1950s and the 1960s, most stocks either were owned by the Commodity Credit Corporation or were held under a price support loan. One consequence of a U.S. governmental grain reserve policy is that it would not serve as a complement to private stockholding, but the former would replace the latter. It is true that the actual stockholding could be undertaken by private firms, but only through subsidies and by the government establishing the rules that would govern the accumulation and disposition of the stocks.

I have not included price supports or commodity loan rates as one of the measures for reducing price and income variability. This was deliberate. This does not mean that price supports are necessarily an inappropriate policy instrument. But if price supports are used, the levels established must be below actual market prices most of the time. If price supports are set at levels that have a significant influence on market prices there are two adverse effects. One is that the ability of American farm products to compete in international markets is seriously impaired. Other exporters can take away a substantial fraction of our export market by selling at prices a little below our support levels. When this would happen, either the United States would once again use export subsidies or stocks would accumulate in the hands of the government as farmers deliver their products to the Commodity Credit Corporation. The other adverse effect is that it would be impossible to operate a reserve program that did not involve substantial excess of costs over income.

Price supports set at low levels can assist farmers in the orderly marketing of their crops. The price supports or commodity loan programs provide a readily available source of credit that permits farmers to spread their marketings throughout the year and also reduces the risk from doing so. If price support levels were set low enough so that they were effective only very infrequently (say one year in five), the effects on the reserve program would be small enough to be ignored. In those years it would probably be profitable to add to the reserves.

A primary difficulty with price supports that are effective in many, if not most, years is the interference with exports. If exports are adversely affected by the price support levels, the temptation to resort to export subsidies or expanded food aid will be difficult to resist. If there are target prices, most farmers gain relatively little even in the short run from price supports. And it is not obvious that the taxpayers gain either. Presumably one of the arguments for having both target prices and price supports is to limit the cost of the deficiency payments. But our past experience shows very clearly that governmental costs begin to mount as soon as stocks owned by the Commodity Credit Corporation reach significant levels.

Concluding Comments

The primary objective of this essay was to document important changes that have occurred in American agriculture over the past quarter-century that are relevant to the formulation of agricultural policy. I hope that I have been successful in showing that governmental policy, if the costs of programs are to be held to politically acceptable levels, can have only minimal impacts upon farm prices and incomes. The increased importance of purchased inputs, the substantial integration of the farm and nonfarm labor markets, and the greatly expanded role of international trade in agricultural products mean that governmental intervention can influence events within only a very narrow range.

THE INTERNATIONAL MONETARY SYSTEM AFTER JAMAICA AND MANILA

Gottfried Haberler

Summary

The Second Amendment to the Articles of Agreement of the International Monetary Fund is now in the process of ratification. Its most important provision is that it legalizes the status quo of widespread floating of exchange rates.

The Bretton Woods system of fixed but adjustable exchange rates served the world well during its first twenty years, 1946–1966; it broke down in the early 1970s. Because of a basic defect in the mechanism of adjustment, the par value system could not cope with the severe stresses and strains of the period: Two-digit inflation, the oil shock, and severe recession. The evolution of the international monetary system from rigidly fixed exchange rates under the gold standard, via fixed but adjustable rates under Bretton Woods, to managed floating is briefly sketched in the second section of the paper, "The Present International Monetary System in Historical Perspective."

Few would envisage or recommend an early return to the par value system. But there is by no means universal satisfaction with the actual operation of the system of floating exchange rates. The view has become popular in some quarters that floating is at least to some extent responsible for world inflation, that weak countries are trapped in a vicious circle while strong currency countries enjoy a virtuous circle, the Western world thus being subjected to a process of polarization. It is shown in the third section ("Some Problems of Floating Exchange Rates") that these theories are not valid. Worldwide infla-

---

For many helpful suggestions I am very gateful to Alexandre Kafka, Thomas D. Willett, and William H. White.

tion made floating unavoidable and not the other way around. What is true is that, under floating, each country has to swallow the inflation it generates. It cannot alleviate inflation by running a trade deficit and thereby "exporting" the inflation to other countries as was possible under fixed exchanges, so long as reserves were sufficient and borrowing potential remained unimpaired. What cannot be excluded is that on some occasions the exchange rate may overshoot the equilibrium mark. This is the tiny kernel of truth in the vicious-circle polarization theory. But such overshooting cannot start a cumulative spiral unless accommodated by a permissive monetary policy, and a cumulative spiral once started can be stopped by tight monetary policy, although no serious inflation can be subdued without some transitional unemployment. Moreover, overshooting can be prevented by intervention in the exchange market.

Problems in managing the float are discussed in some detail. The amended charter states that the International Monetary Fund should exercise "firm surveillance" over exchange rate policies of its members to make sure that no country "manipulates exchange rates . . . to prevent effective balance of payments adjustment or to gain an unfair competitive advantage over the other members [of the Fund]" (Article IV, Section 1 of the amended charter). The Fund has already tried its hand at surveillance of exchange rate policies by formulating "Guidelines for the Management of Floating Exchange Rates" (1974). These guidelines are discussed, and in the Postscript to the present paper the recently adopted "Principles and Procedures for Surveillance over Exchange Rate Policies" (April 1977) are briefly considered and compared with the former guidelines. Also, the privately proposed and widely discussed system of "reference rate" is described and analyzed.

In the fourth section of the paper, the problem of international liquidity in a world of floating exchange rates is analyzed in some detail. In the prefloating period the problem of international liquidity or adequacy of international money reserves (gold, foreign exchange, SDRs, et cetera) played a very large role in the discussion of monetary reform, an excessively large role compared with the adjustment problem, in the opinion of many experts. Since the advent of widespread floating the liquidity problem has definitely taken the back seat behind the problem of adjustment. It is argued in the present paper that under fixed exchange rates there was a clear connection between global liquidity (international monetary reserves) and world inflation. However, international reserves and world inflation have become highly fragmented magnitudes under widespread floating. Although the Fund *dutifully publishes every month figures of global reserves and of "Per Cent Changes of Consumer Prices" for the world as a whole (a weighted average of consumer price changes in member countries), to correlate the two jumbles of figures and to attribute causal or policy importance to such correlations is no longer a meaningful exercise. The primary task of the Fund is to grapple with the adjustment problem by surveillance of exchange rate policies and not control of global liquidity. Inflation remains a major world problem but it has its roots in national policies of the major countries over which the Fund has almost no control.*

In the last section of the paper, the American policy of urging West Germany and Japan to speed up economic recovery and growth by more expansionary monetary and fiscal policies is discussed in some detail. The basic goal, that a sustainable rapid growth of the leading industrial countries would be highly beneficial for the whole world, is unobjectionable. But since both the West German and Japanese economies are expanding anyhow and both still suffer from what they regard as unacceptably high rates of inflation, the resistance of the West German and Japanese governments to the pressure to apply additional stimulative monetary and fiscal measures seems to be quite reasonable. The Keynesian argument that additional stimulus is safe, because there is still much unemployment and slack, is examined, as is the rival monetarist position that inflationary expectations have become so sensitive that any additional monetary stimulus merely results in higher prices and not in any increase in output and employment. Both views are found exaggerated, but it is concluded that a long drawn-out inflation has eroded money illusions so that we are now closer to the extreme monetarist than to the Keynesian position.

The objective of the more rapid expansion of the West German and Japanese economies, namely to stimulate imports into West Germany and Japan and to slow down their exports, can be achieved by letting the mark and yen appreciate in the exchange market. The West German and Japanese governments have declared that they will not resist if market forces tend to push their currencies up. Both currencies have, in fact, appreciated substantially recently, the mark by 15 percent on a trade-weighted basis in 1976. It is argued that the problem should be approached in terms of exchange rate policy and not, as it is so often done, in terms of setting more or less arbitrary current-account targets which are then to be achieved by inflationary policies of expansion.

In the Postscript it is reported that the U.S. government has dropped its pressure on West Germany and Japan to expand faster. At the London Economic Summit (May 1977) that policy was replaced by a commitment of the participating governments to carry out their stated growth targets. It was declared that "the most urgent task is to create more jobs," but that "inflation does not reduce unemployment, on the contrary it is one of its major causes." However, how to accomplish the twin objectives of reducing unemployment and winding down inflation at the same time was not indicated.

Introduction

At the conference in Kingston, Jamaica, on January 7–8, 1976, the Interim Committee of the Board of Governors of the International Monetary Fund hammered out the Second Amendment to the Articles of Agreement of the International Monetary Fund (IMF). The amended charter has been approved by the Board of Governors of the Fund; it is now in the process of ratification by the governments of the member countries; and, presumably, it will go into effect later this year. Thus came to an end the long drawn-out attempt at reform of the international monetary system which had formally started in September 1972.[1]

As the somewhat apologetic titles of the papers by Tom de Vries and Alexandre Kafka suggest, the substantive changes of the status quo wrought by the Second Amendment are not great; they can be summarized in a few sentences. The widespread floating which replaced the Bretton Woods par value system in 1973 has been legalized; the official gold price has been given up; and the demonetization of gold has been advanced a few steps. Independently of the amendment of the charter, the quotas of the Fund members have been increased by

---

[1] Two authoritative inside evaluations of the Jamaica agreement have appeared: Alexandre Kafka, *The International Monetary Fund: Reform without Reconstruction?* Essays in International Finance, no. 108 (Princeton, N.J.: Princeton University, International Finance Section, 1976), and Tom de Vries, "Jamaica or the Non-Reform of the International Monetary System," *Foreign Affairs*, vol. 54 (April 1976), pp. 577-605. The text of the amended charter along with the previous text has been published in *Proposed Second Amendment to the Articles of Agreement*, a report by the Executive Directors to the Board of Governors (Washington, D.C.: International Monetary Fund, 1976), 356 pages. See also Thomas D. Willett, *Floating Exchange Rates and International Monetary Reform* (Washington, D.C., AEI, 1977 forthcoming). After this paper was finished the imposing history and analysis of the international monetary system and the reform effort by Robert Solomon has appeared. *The International Monetary System, 1945-1976: An Insider's View* (New York: Harper and Row, 1977).

33 percent from about SDR 29 billion to SDR 39 billion, implying an equal increase in the total resources of the Fund. This is not a very large increase in view of the rapid growth (partly inflationary) of world trade since the last quota increase in 1971, the world recession notwithstanding. Apart from legalizing floating, the Second Amendment brings a large number of procedural and structural changes, of which only one may be mentioned: the Board of Governors is authorized to set up (by a vote of 85 percent) a new organ, the *Council* which, if it ever is created, would in fact be the continuation of the Interim Committee, a sort of executive committee of the Board of Governors with large decision-making power.[2]

The annual meeting of the Fund and its Bretton Woods twin, the World Bank, in Manila (October 4–8, 1976) was, as usual, a huge gathering of many thousand high-priced experts, ministers of finance, central bankers, and other high officials from all 130-odd member countries; international officials from the innumerable international agencies; and the usual army of hangers-on—bankers, economists, journalists, et cetera. There were no important decisions made in Manila. But some of the many speeches were interesting in revealing the current thinking of the leading financial officials about some of the current economic problems, for example about world inflation and recession and about the way in which the now legalized system of widespread floating operates.

The working of the present system of widespread managed floating is probably best understood by putting it into historical perspective. In the next section of this paper, I try to sketch very briefly why and how floating replaced the Bretton Woods par value system, the system of the adjustable peg. The following section takes up some features of the *modus operandi* of the floating system, especially some alleged shortcomings and cases of malfunctioning which have been discussed by professional economists and in official speeches in Manila. Next, I discuss the problem of control of global liquidity or the volume of international monetary reserves in a system of widespread floating. The final section briefly discusses the American advice to West Germany and Japan for a joint monetary expansion to promote economic expansion of the world economy.

---

[2] See Article XII, Section 1 of the amended charter. The composition and functions of the Council are set out in the new Schedule D to the Articles of Agreement.

The Present International Monetary System in Historical Perspective

From the Gold Standard to Bretton Woods. It is important to recognize the present system as the last stage of a continuous, or perhaps discontinuous, evolution from the gold standard to widespread managed floating via the Bretton Woods par value system. Under the gold standard, exchange rates were fixed and could be changed only in extreme circumstances—a rigidity which had disastrous consequences in the 1930s.[3] The major functional innovation of Bretton Woods was that the par value system provided for orderly changes of exchange rates in case of a "fundamental disequilibrium." The new system worked well during the first twenty years or so. During this period there were many exchange rate changes, almost all of them depreciations vis-à-vis gold and the dollar. The world recovered rapidly from the ravages of the war, trade barriers and payment restrictions were gradually reduced, and more and more currencies became convertible into each other. As a consequence, world trade grew by leaps and bounds, and the whole world, developed as well as developing countries, enjoyed a period of almost unprecedented growth and prosperity.

From Bretton Woods to Widespread Floating. In the mid-1960s the par value system developed troubles. Currency crises became more numerous and violent and followed each other at shorter intervals. The British pound was the first major currency that was involved. Later the dollar came under suspicion and unwanted dollar balances piled up abroad. Convertibility of the dollar into gold was "suspended" on August 15, 1971. The dollar floated down until it was devalued in terms of most currencies in the Smithsonian Agreement in December 1971. After another devaluation of the dollar early in 1973, widespread though managed floating of all major currencies began in March 1973.

The main reason for the breakdown of the Bretton Woods par value system was a basic defect in the IMF charter which made the system unfit to cope with the exceptional strains and stresses that

---

[3] See Gottfried Haberler, *The World Economy, Money, and the Great Depression 1919-1939* (Washington, D.C.: American Enterprise Institute, 1976). Saying that the gold standard had disastrous consequences in a worldwide depression does not imply that the gold standard would be bad in another environment. The structural changes which made the gold standard increasingly unworkable in the twentieth century have been described many times. I have discussed them in my book *Economic Growth and Stability: An Analysis of Economic Change and Policies* (Plainview, N.Y.: Nash Publishing Corp., 1974), chapter 8.

developed in the late 1960s and early 1970s.[4] This defect was that the method of occasional, discontinuous, and therefore large changes in exchange rates, the adjustable or jumping peg, opened the floodgate for disruptive speculation. Under this system, the speculators speculated against the central banks whose hands were tied because they had to support the par value of the currency. This makes speculation easy and almost riskless. Under the system of continuous floating, on the other hand, speculators speculate against each other and against the market which is a much more risky business.[5]

But why did this basic defect not show up earlier? In retrospect the explanation is not difficult. During the early years after the war, when the economies of Europe and Japan were prostrate from war destruction and exhaustion, U.S. industries enjoyed a quasi-monopoly position, and, later, foreign countries eagerly accumulated dollar balances to rebuild their international reserves. Generous U.S. foreign aid financed large deficits, and tight controls in many countries sup-

---

[4] One critic of the Bretton Woods system insists that it broke down not in 1971 or 1973 but in 1947 after the premature attempt to make the pound convertible (without any correction of the exchange rate!) had collapsed and the Marshall Plan was launched. (Lord Balogh, "Keynes and the International Monetary Fund," in *Keynes and International Monetary Relations: The Second Keynes Seminar held at University of Kent at Canterbury, 1974,* ed. A. P. Tirlwall [New York: St. Martin's Press, 1976], pp. 66-87.) This is a grossly misleading statement to put it mildly. The fact is that the Bretton Woods system did not become fully operational right after the formal establishment of the Fund in 1946. The Fund was never intended, and its resources were not large enough, to cope with the enormous capital requirements of the immediate postwar reconstruction. But the effectiveness and benefits of the system cannot be gauged *solely* by the size of its lending operations. Equally important are the underlying principles of, and the machinery provided for, continuous cooperation and consultations, especially with respect to exchange rate changes. This represents a major advance, and the benefits for the world economy have been very large right from the Fund's inception. These benefits endure even after the demise of the par value system.

[5] Probably the first to recognize the defect of a fixed rate system once the confidence in the fixity of the peg is gone was Frank D. Graham "Achilles Heels in Monetary Standards," *American Economic Review* (March 1940), pp. 16-32. Graham argued that when a serious disequilibrium has developed, the direction of any change of the exchange rate is clear, and "bear speculators are then presented with that rare and desired phenomenon a 'sure thing'" (p. 19). Thomas D. Willett has pointed out that Graham's important paper was completely ignored at the time in academic as well as in official policy discussions (*Floating Exchange Rates and International Monetary Reform*). Ten years later the sure thing criticism of the adjustable peg system was frequently made in the academic literature. See for example Milton Friedman's famous paper "The Case for Flexible Exchange Rates" written in 1950 and first published in *Essays in Positive Economics* (Chicago: University of Chicago Press, 1953) and James Meade's standard work, *The Balance of Payments* (London: Oxford University Press, 1951), chapter 17, "The Role of Speculation," pp. 218-31. It took two more decades for this insight to gain official recognition.

pressed remaining imbalances. Domestic supply shortages and extensive rationing in many countries made exchange rate adjustments appear of little use.

In the 1960s the dollar got into trouble, for several reasons. Because of the rapid recovery of Europe and Japan, U.S. industries lost their quasi-monopoly position. Numerous currency depreciations strengthened the competitive position of rival industrial countries. The strength of the dollar was finally undermined by the inflation in the United States that followed the period of price stability from 1958–1964, which the Eisenhower administration had bequeathed to its successors. When the Johnson administration delayed raising taxes sufficiently to finance the escalating war in Vietnam as well as the equally expensive "great society" programs and engaged in inflationary deficit financing, the dollar became hopelessly overvalued.

There is an alternative, though not necessarily contradictory, explanation of the decline of the dollar. For years, Jacques Rueff and Robert Triffin had predicted that, for reasons so well known that they need not be repeated, the gold dollar exchange standard could not have lasted even if the United States had succeeded in keeping its inflation to a tolerable level. It is a moot question what would have happened if the United States had kept the price level substantially stable after 1965. The fact that the role of the dollar as reserve and intervention currency and its function as *numéraire* have been well preserved in recent years of *comparative* price stability in the United States, despite floating and suspension of gold convertibility, suggests that the alleged instability of the dollar standard may have been exaggerated.[6]

Be that as it may, the worldwide wave of inflation after 1965 culminating in the price explosion of 1973–1974 made widespread floating inevitable. It is inconceivable that the industrial countries could agree on a common inflation rate, if the average rate of inflation is in the neighborhood of 10 percent, because tolerance for inflation and unemployment differs greatly from country to country. Differential inflation, the differential impact of the oil price rise, and differential recession experience finally convinced most advocates of

---

[6] See Lawrence Officer and Thomas D. Willett, "Reserve Assets Preference and the Confidence Problem in the Crisis Zone," *Quarterly Journal of Economics* (November 1969), pp. 688-95, and "The Interaction of Adjustment and Gold Conversion Policies in a Reserve Currency System," *Western Economic Journal* (March 1970), pp. 47-60. The authors argue that the case for the inherent instability of the reserve currency system has been greatly overdone. I find the Officer-Willett theory convincing if the reserve currency country keeps inflation sufficiently in check.

fixed exchange rates that floating is here to stay for the foreseeable future. The oil shock, which intensified the inflation although it did not start it, had the effect of moving the IMF Committee on Reform of the International Monetary System (Committee of Twenty) off dead center. Even after floating had become widespread, the committee had said again and again that "the reformed" system would be one of "stable but adjustable exchange rates" and that floating would be permitted only in "particular situations." According to Tom de Vries, "this made the work of the Committee look increasingly unreal. . . . The Committee was saved . . . by the quadrupling of the price of oil in the fourth quarter of 1973." [7]

It is interesting to reflect that the very success of the first twenty years of the Bretton Woods era has helped to expose the defect of the IMF Charter. The enormous growth of world trade, not only in nominal but also in real terms and in proportion to GNP, has increased the magnitude (if not the volatility) of cyclical and other swings in the trade and current-account balances. Similarly, increased capital mobility, a necessary ingredient of the rapid growth of the world economy, which was made possible by the gradual dismantling of exchange control, produced larger swings in the capital balance. Most important perhaps, frequent exchange rate changes have alerted more and more people, not only professional speculators, to watch for danger signals and to take quick actions to protect themselves from losses or to profit from anticipating parity changes.

There is another defect, in fact an internal contradiction, in the Articles of Agreement, which has become increasingly troublesome and will remain so in the future. What I have in mind is the fact that the charter looks favorably at capital controls; it not only permits

---

[7] De Vries, "Jamaica or the Non-Reform," p. 587. Similarly, Robert Solomon says "The fatal flaw in the Committee's endeavor was the unwillingness of its members to focus on the exchange rate regime." (*The International Monetary System*, p. 323.) In 1973 Professor Xenophon Zolotas, president of the Bank of Greece, warned that the committee's terms of reference to the effect that the future international monetary system "will be based on stable but adjustable parities with the possibility of floating in particular circumstances," are no longer "appropriate"; much greater flexibility was needed, he said. (Xenophon Zolotas, "Fixed Rates or Managed Float," paper published in the *Times* [London], November 28, 1973, reprinted in Xenophon Zolotas, *International Monetary Issues and Development Policies: Selected Essays* [Athens: Bank of Greece, 1977], pp. 236-41.) J. Marcus Fleming once remarked in rueful self-criticism: "At every stage in the discussion [of the reform of the international monetary system] reform proposals have lagged behind events and have been quickly outmoded by new events." (*Reflections on the International Monetary Reform*, Essays in International Finance, no. 107 [Princeton, N.J.: Princeton University, International Finance Section, 1974], p. 17.)

them, but in certain circumstances requires their imposition.[8] It is still not recognized widely enough that capital controls and the absence of restrictions on current transactions are incompatible. It is often possible to suppress imbalances temporarily and to prop up overvalued currencies by means of capital controls, but only at the high cost of increasingly severe distortions and restrictions of trade and other current transactions.[9] "Avoidance of restrictions on current payments" is perhaps the most basic objective of the Fund.[10] The reason for the incompatibility of capital controls and freedom of current payments is that it is very easy to camouflage capital transactions as current-account transactions. There exist legal and illegal methods of dis-

---

[8] These provisions were probably inspired by Keynes who, impressed by the weakening economic position of Britain, had become deeply distrustful of international capital movements. In his famous "Proposals for an International Clearing Union," he said: "There is no country which can, in the future allow the flight of funds for political reasons or to evade domestic taxation or in anticipation of the owner turning refugee." (Dictators and revolutionaries will heartily agree.) Keynes was, however, aware that capital controls "to be effective probably require machinery of exchange control for *all* transactions" and that controls would require "postal censorship" unless capital movements are controlled "at both ends." He therefore tried to persuade the United States to adopt the British system of tight controls. (Keynes's proposals are reprinted in *World Monetary Reform Plans and Issues*, ed. Herbert G. Grubel [Stanford, California: Stanford University Press, 1963], pp. 72-73.) Harry D. White, too, was skeptical about the desirability of free international capital flows. See his book *The French International Accounts 1880-1913* (Cambridge, Mass.: Harvard University Press, 1933), pp. 311-12. As early as 1943, Friedrich Lutz warned of the far-reaching deleterious implications of capital controls and concluded that "the only sound method of preventing short term capital movements of the speculative and political kind is to remove their causes." (*The Keynes and White Proposals*, Essays in International Finance, no. 1 [Princeton, N.J.: Princeton University, International Finance Section, 1943], p. 19.) For further discussions and references to the literature see my paper "The Case Against Capital Controls for Balance of Payments Reasons," in *Capital Movements and Their Control (Proceedings of the Second Conference of the International Center for Monetary and Banking Studies)*, ed. Alexander K. Swoboda (Leiden, Netherlands: A. W. Sijthoff, 1976). Available also as Reprint No. 62 (Washington, D. C.: American Enterprise Institute, 1976).

[9] A dual exchange rate, a pegged one for current transactions and a freely floating rate for capital transactions, is a method of controlling capital movements which has been used by a number of countries, notably France, Italy, and Belgium. The Belgian dual rate system is still in operation. So long as the discount of the capital transactions rate is small and not persistent (not higher than, say, 5 percent), the method works tolerably well. But whether it is efficient is another question. See my paper "The Case Against Capital Controls for Balance of Payments Reasons," cited in the preceding footnote. The Belgian case has been analyzed by Paul D. Grauwe, "The Belgian Dual Exchange Market System: An Inequitable and Ineffective System" in *Bank Credit, Money and Inflation in Open Economies*, ed. Michele Fratianni and Karl Tavernier (Berlin: Duncker & Humblot, 1976), pp. 389-402.

[10] The words in quotes are the title of Section 2 of Article VIII which bears the title "General Obligations of Members" (see footnote 1).

guising capital movements. An illegal method is, for example, over- or under-invoicing of exports and imports. A perfectly legal bypass of capital controls results from the fact that trade flows can become a substitute for capital flows: Suppose it is illegal to acquire claims abroad (securities of any kind) in anticipation of an expected depreciation of the home currency. The next best method of anticipating a substantial depreciation of the currency is to accumulate export and import commodities. Only very tight controls of current transactions could prevent this sort of disguised capital flow. Given the large volume of international trade, such speculative transactions and the well-known "leads and lags" can and often do move many billions of dollars in a short time across national boundaries. The international commodity boom of 1972–1973 may have been significantly intensified by such transactions—one way in which the par value system has contributed to worldwide inflation.

The conclusion is that widespread floating is here to stay. If in the future the world economy or at least its core, the industrial countries, are spared the great turbulences of the last few years, exchange rate fluctuations would become milder. But even in that case a return to the par value system is most unlikely. True, theoretically a system of fixed rates would be the ideal arrangement for most countries— provided it could be achieved without severe restrictions on international trade and payments and without imposing too much unemployment or inflation on any country. A necessary though not sufficient condition would be that inflation be substantially eliminated in all countries with fixed rates.

Unfortunately these conditions are rarely fulfilled in our modern world of sovereign states. Experience has shown again and again that a very high degree of harmonization of basic policy objectives (full employment, price stability, et cetera) and tight coordination of national policies are required to forestall the frequent emergence of large balance of payments disequilibria that cannot be handled by the par value system without disruptive speculation and currency crises. Such coordination or rather centralization of policy exists inside each country. But even the closely knit countries of the European Common Market have so far been unable to achieve the required degree of coordination of their national policies.

To avoid misunderstanding, a further remark is in order. Widespread floating does not mean that the currencies of all 130-odd members of the Fund fluctuate independently. There are many countries, especially small ones, that attach their currencies to that of some large country and are willing to accept the inflation that the policy of pegging may imply. According to Fund statistics, 81 currencies of the 122 currencies listed on June 30, 1975, were pegged to a single currency, 54 of them to the dollar. Only 11 currencies floated independently, but among the floaters were—and still are—most of the leading currencies of the world, the U.S. and Canadian dollars, the yen, the British pound, the French franc, the West German mark with its retinue of currencies ("snake" currencies and the Austrian schilling), and others. These countries accounted for 46.4 percent of the trade of Fund members, and the 81 currencies pegged to a single currency accounted for only 14.4 percent.[11]

If I say things which should be obvious and have been said many times before, my excuse is that they are so often forgotten, as many speeches in Manila have demonstrated once again.

Some Problems of Floating Exchange Rates

Recent Criticism of Floating. At Manila many complaints were voiced about the working of the floating system. Floating was defended by Canada, West Germany, and the United States, but most other comments were in a critical or plaintive mood.

A frequent charge was that floating has had inflationary effects. The governor for Italy said: "The high rate of inflation [in Italy] is due in no small part to the sharp depreciation of the lira in the first months of the year. The high degree of indexation of the Italian economy has blunted the usefulness of exchange rate depreciation since it leads rapidly to higher domestic inflation."[12] Similarly the governor of the Banque de France declared:

> Speculative anticipations by economic agents amplify the size of exchange rate movements. . . . A fall in the exchange rate in the market is reflected, even before the slightest impact is felt on export volume, in an immediate rise in the

---

[11] IMF *Annual Report for 1975* (Washington, D.C., 1975), Table 9, p. 24. The classification of currencies as floaters and peggers may be a little arbitrary in some cases, and since June 1976 the figures have changed somewhat. But the basic contours of the picture are clear and have remained the same.

[12] A high degree of indexation of wages and other incomes is a major roadblock for a stabilization policy whenever real wages have gotten out of line. For example, when an external deficit has to be eliminated because reserves are running out, the level of real wages ("absorption") has to be reduced if unemployment is to be avoided. In such a case indexation becomes a serious hurdle for adjustment, irrespective of whether the adjustment is attempted by internal deflation, depreciation, or downward float. If real wage rates cannot be reduced, unemployment becomes the only method to bring about the unavoidable reduction of absorption and the adjustment of the balance of payments.

> cost of imports. Thus, in the first phase, the external depre-
> ciation of the currency aggravates the internal inflation
> rate, . . . setting in motion a cumulative process at the end
> of which the currency's exchange value continues to fall.

Such remarks have been amplified and sensationalized by financial journalists. There has been talk of vicious and virtuous circles: Weak currency countries with high inflation rates such as Britain and Italy are said to be "trapped in a vicious circle," while strong currency countries with little or no inflation such as West Germany, Switzerland, and the United States (and also the Netherlands, despite an almost 10 percent inflation rate) are said to enjoy a "virtuous circle." Thus floating is said to "drive a wedge between industrial nations." [13]

A large part of the serious economic literature on floating and inflation has been carefully reviewed by Andrew D. Crockett and Morris Goldstein of the IMF. Their "overall conclusion [is] that the type of exchange rate system has little influence . . . on world infla-tion." But they find "a certain intuitive appeal" in the notion that in a world in which prices have become "rather inflexible, especially in the downward direction . . . devaluations will produce . . . a larger . . . effect on domestic prices than appreciations." [14]

What is true is that, under floating, an inflationary country will feel the consequences of inflation more quickly than under fixed exchange rates, because under the latter regime countries have the possibility of alleviating their inflation by running a deficit—*provided* they have an ample reserve or credit line to finance their deficit. In other words, under fixed exchanges a country can export some of its inflation, while under floating it has to swallow the inflation which it generates.[15] In that sense it can be said that floating has an infla-

---

[13] Paul Lewis, *New York Times* (October 10, 1976).

[14] Andrew D. Crockett and Morris Goldstein, "Inflation Under Fixed and Flexible Exchange Rates," International Monetary Fund *Staff Papers*, vol. 23, no. 3 (Washington, D.C., November 1976), pp. 509-44. This paper has been incorrectly quoted in the above-mentioned article in the *New York Times* as supporting the vicious-circle theory. In their letter to the *Times* of October 13, 1976, the authors called attention to the mistake.

[15] In modern economic jargon this simple proposition has been expressed by saying that there is a feedback from a depreciating currency on domestic prices and costs which in turn worsens the short-run trade-off between inflation and unemployment, that is, steepens the short-run Phillips curve. See for example Rudiger Dornbusch and Paul Krugman, "Flexible Exchange Rates in the Short Run," *Brookings Papers on Economic Activity*, 1976 (3), as quoted by Richard N. Cooper, "Five Years Since Smithsonian," *Economist* (December 18, 1976), p. 34. As D. H. Robertson once said: "Well, that is just fine. We all have our funny little ways of putting things." (*Utility and All That and Other Essays* [London: Allen and Unwin, 1952], p. 40.)

tionary effect on deficit countries. But by the same token it protects surplus countries from imported inflation. This is sometimes denied or played down on the ground that in the modern world, prices and wages are rigid downward. It is true that wage rigidity gives rise to the well-known Hayek-Schultze ratchet effect: every shift in demand raises the price where demand has increased, and these price increases are not offset by price declines where demand has decreased.[16] (Needless to add, this kind of ratchet inflation, too, requires a permissive monetary policy to occur.) It follows that wage rigidity *reduces* the anti-inflationary effect of an appreciation of the currency, but it does not *eliminate* it for two reasons: First, wage or price rigidity obviously will not prevent the decline of prices of noncompetitive imports (that is, of commodities that are not produced domestically) in terms of the *appreciated currency*. Second, as far as competitive imports (imports of commodities that are produced in the appreciating country) are concerned, additional supplies from abroad will at least slow down the ongoing inflation, although under a regime of rigid wages to a lesser extent and at a higher cost of unemployment than would be the case, if wages and prices were more flexible. West Germany and Switzerland provide dramatic proof, if proof is needed. Switzerland has been able to reduce the inflation rate practically to zero, and West Germany has reduced it to below 4 percent by letting their currencies sharply float up.

The fact that under floating the consequences of inflationary policies are felt immediately, because they cannot be alleviated by "exporting" part of the inflation to other countries, constitutes a strong incentive for financial discipline. Academic advocates of floating have often made that point. It has been recently supported in official statements. For example, Arthur Burns, not an ardent supporter of floating, told a congressional committee that "under the

---

[16] It has been objected that the ratchet mechanism—which explains inflation as the result of demand shifts raising prices where demand has increased, while failing to reduce prices where demand has decreased—does not operate in an inflationary environment for the following reason: In such an environment, industries where demand has decreased can make their contributions to keeping down the overall rate of inflation by reducing the rate of price and money wage rise without making the change negative. (See, for example, W. M. Corden, *Inflation, Exchange Rates, and the World Economy: Lectures on International Monetary Economics* [Oxford: Clarendon Press, 1977], p. 70.) This would be true if it were not a fact that in an inflationary environment *real* wages, too, tend to become rigid downward. Why do workers and their unions resist money wage restrictions in a stable price environment? Because they wish to protect their living standard. It follows that in an inflationary environment they resist a reduction in their real wage. Indexation is the collective expression of real wage resistance. Actually unions often go beyond real wage maintenance and insist on the customary real wage increase.

present regime of floating it is more necessary than ever to proceed cautiously in executing our expansionary policy. For faster inflation in the United States than abroad would tend to induce a depreciation of the dollar, which in turn would exacerbate our inflation problem." [17] Emile van Lennep, secretary general of OECD, said in his speech at the Manila meeting:

> It is, I think, now evident that the fears that more flexibility would ease the external discipline of deficit countries have proved unfounded. After a transitional period, governments have learned that because of the close interaction between domestic policies, exchange rates and inflation rates, a continuing tendency for their currencies to depreciate can be even more dangerous than a continuing loss of reserves.

It should be noted that van Lennep speaks of a "transitional period." Some countries may, indeed, have mistaken floating as a license to let down their guard against inflation. If so, they have been quickly taught a lesson.

It should perhaps be added that the fact that floating provides its own inducement to curb inflation does not guarantee that inflation will in fact be curbed. A strong inducement to disinflate can be overwhelmed by an even stronger propensity to inflate.

It is true that every long drawn-out inflation develops vicious circle properties and is apt to set "in motion a cumulative process" as the governor of the Banque de France said at Manila.[18] Inflation

---

[17] Statement before the Subcommittee on International Finance of the Committee on Banking and Currency, House of Representatives, April 4, 1974. Burns also noted that "no such intensification [of inflation] can take place under a regime of fixed exchange rates as long as international reserves remain sufficient to obviate the need for devaluation." This is often regarded as an advantage of the system of fixed rates. But the other side of the coin should not be forgotten. If country A alleviates its inflation by "exporting" some of it, inflation is intensified abroad. True, situations are thinkable in which deficit *and* surplus countries both would profit from the reserve flow under fixed exchanges. This would be the case if the surplus countries suffered from unemployment (recession) while the deficit countries are under inflationary pressure. But these are exceptional circumstances which, if they happen to exist at any moment, are not likely to last for any length of time. (For details and references to the literature see my *Money in the International Market*, 2nd ed. [Cambridge, Mass.: Harvard University Press, 1969], pp. 16-17, and my contribution "The International Monetary System: Some Recent Developments and Discussions" in *Approaches to Greater Flexibility of Exchange Rates: The Bürgenstock Papers*, ed. George N. Halm [Princeton, N.J.: Princeton University Press, 1970], pp. 113-23.) See also my "Comments" to Arthur B. Laffer's paper "Two Arguments for Fixed Exchange Rates," *The Economics of Common Currencies*, ed. H. G. Johnson and Alexander Swoboda (London: Allen and Unwin, 1973), pp. 35-39.

[18] Bernard Clappier, "Statement by the Governor of the Bank for France," *Summary Proceedings Annual Meeting 1976* (Washington, D.C.: International Monetary Fund), November 16, 1976, p. 74.

"feeds on itself," because people will try to reduce their cash balances by spending money faster on commodities and foreign money, and it cannot be excluded that on some occasions the exchange rate in the market may overshoot the long-run equilibrium. But the "cumulative" process could not go on without a permissive monetary policy, and the vicious circle can be broken by tight money, although not without causing temporary unemployment. Both Italy and Britain had plenty of opportunity to get out of the vicious circle, and they could have softened the transition to less inflation with the help of their huge foreign borrowing. Unfortunately, they did not utilize the breathing spell. This was not the fault of floating but was due to a failure to curb inflation by appropriate monetary policies.

It should be observed that import restrictions, whether in the form of tariffs, quotas, import deposit schemes, or a tax on the purchase of foreign exchange, do *not* alleviate the inflation. Financing a deficit by drawing down reserves or by borrowing abroad does reduce inflationary pressure because this policy permits an increase of the supply of goods in the home market. Import restrictions, in contrast, do not reduce inflationary pressures. On the contrary, they are counterproductive because of their protectionist effects which imply a misallocation of resources and thus reduce aggregate supply.[19] While devaluation and floating stimulate exports and discourage imports, import restrictions operate only on imports.

It could be argued that an import deposit scheme, unlike tariffs and quotas, may have a slight deflationary (anti-inflationary) side effect if the deposits are effectively sterilized for some time. But the same anti-inflationary effect can be achieved by monetary policy without the distortions caused by import restrictions. In summary, import restrictions cannot do anything that devaluation or floating plus an appropriate monetary policy can do more cheaply and efficiently.[20]

The main advantage that has been claimed for flexible exchange

---

[19] Here the usual marginal qualifications to the proposition that import restrictions reduce GNP should be mentioned: The terms of trade could conceivably be improved or, if there is a lot of unemployment in particular industries in the short run, a tariff can increase employment and production. Obviously, some of these qualifications do not apply to general import restrictions on balance of payments grounds imposed by any single country.

[20] The case against import controls for balance of payments reasons has been stated convincingly by W. M. Corden, I. M. D. Little, and M. FG. Scott, *Import Controls versus Devaluation and Britain's Economic Prospects*, Trade Policy Research Center Guest Paper, no. 2 (London, 1975). This paper presents a devastating criticism of the protectionist proposals for Britain that have been put forward in *The Economic Policy Review*, no. 1. (Cambridge: University of Cambridge, Department of Applied Economics, 1975). The *Review* is the organ of the so-called new school of the split group of Keynesian economists.

rates since Keynes is that it enables each country to pursue independently the demand-management policy which it prefers. Floating can protect a country from inflation or deflation, which under fixed exchanges is imposed on it by a balance of payments surplus or deficit. Keynes stressed the threat of having to submit to deflationary pressures from abroad; today inflationary pressures from abroad are the danger uppermost in one's mind. Doubts have been raised again recently about these claims for floating. For floating has not prevented a worldwide inflationary explosion, nor an equally worldwide stagflation and recession in 1973 and 1974, succeeded by an almost worldwide rapid recovery in 1975, which in turn was followed by a "pause" in 1976. A fairly large literature has sprung up under the heading of international transmission of economic disturbances, which investigates whether, under floating, there really was a greater divergence among different countries with respect to business cycles, price stability, monetary growth, et cetera, than there was under the par value system.[21]

As often happens, intensive econometric-statistical investigations have tended to obscure or lose sight of broad, basic facts and insights. One such fact is that, broadly speaking, in the intermediate and long run, exchange rate changes reflect divergent inflation trends.[22] But in the era of stagflation *divergent* inflation rates between countries do not necessarily preclude *convergence* of real business cycles, that is, of cyclical fluctuations in output and employment. Thus, it is not surprising that floating did not immediately change the worldwide nature of inflation, although some countries managed to reduce their inflation rate drastically (West Germany, Switzerland). The inflation explosion of 1973 had, after all, originated during the fixed rate system and was intensified in all countries by the oil price rise and the policy reactions

---

[21] This literature has been well reviewed by Marina v. N. Whitman in her contribution "International Interdependence and the U.S. Economy" in William Fellner, ed., *Contemporary Economic Problems, 1976* (Washington, D.C.: American Enterprise Institute, 1976). See especially pp. 194-208.

[22] See for example IMF *Annual Reports*, especially the one for 1975. There are, of course, short-run deviations between inflation rates and exchange rate changes. It is, furthermore, well known from the theory of the purchasing parity that occasionally fairly large, long-run deviations of exchange rates from the purchasing-power parity occur, if the latter is defined in terms of consumer price levels. These deviations are due to differences in productivity growth between countries. For details and references to the literature see Gottfried Haberler, "International Aspects of U.S. Inflation" in *A New Look at Inflation* (Washington, D.C.: American Enterprise Institute, 1973), especially pp. 91-93 and "Inflation As a Worldwide Phenomenon—An Overview" in *The Phenomenon of Worldwide Inflation*, ed. D. Meiselman and A. Laffer (Washington, D. C.: American Enterprise Institute, 1975), pp. 24-25.

to it. Nor is it surprising that attempts in all industrial countries to curb inflation produced, despite floating, a worldwide recession. It is practically impossible to reverse an inflationary trend without a transitional recession. Floating shields a country from *monetary* influences from abroad, in the sense that, under floating, countries cannot be forced (as they are under fixed rates) by inflationary neighbors to expand their money supply, or by deflationary neighbors to contract their money supply. But floating does not protect against *real* influences from abroad. Among such real influences, including those caused by monetary factors (by inflation or deflation), are changes in the terms of trade, the oil price rise, protectionist measures taken by foreign countries, recession abroad which reduces real demand for imports and implies a deterioration of the terms of trade, and foreign competition for particular industries.[23] All this follows from generally accepted economic principles which do not require any further econometric confirmation.

The upshot of this discussion is to confirm our conclusion that floating is here to stay for the foreseeable future. As Edward Bernstein put it, "the system of fluctuating exchange rates has worked reasonably well, much better than would have been possible if attempts had been made to perpetuate the Bretton Woods system of fixed parities by patchwork here and there." [24] We can take it for granted, however, that in most countries the float will be a managed one, although much can be said in favor of free, unmanaged floating. The question remains how floating should be managed.

Managed Floating. The amended Articles of Agreement permit each country to adopt the exchange rate system it prefers but enjoins them to "avoid manipulating exchange rates or the international monetary system in order to prevent effective balance of payments adjustment or to gain an unfair competitive advantage over other members" (Article IV, Section 1). The Fund is directed to "oversee the compliance of each member with its obligations," to "exercise firm surveillance of the exchange rate policies of members," and to "adopt specific principles for the guidance of all members with respect to these policies" (Article IV. Section 3).

---

[23] The literature on the problem of transmission of, and insulation from, different types of external disturbances under a regime of floating exchange rates has been well reviewed by Edward Tower and Thomas D. Willett in *Theory of Optimum Currency Areas and Exchange-Rate Flexibility*, Special Paper in International Economics, no. 11 (Princeton, N.J.: Princeton University Press, 1976).

[24] Edward M. Bernstein, "The Monetary Authorities and the Free Exchange Market," Speech at Foreign Exchange Conference of American Bankers Association, New York, November 4, 1976 (mimeo).

The Fund has already tried its hand at surveillance of floating. Based on the work of the Committee of Twenty, the executive directors adopted in June 1974 "Guidelines for the Management of Floating Exchange Rates." [25] These guidelines are supposed to form the basis of the Fund's annual "consultations with members with floating currencies," and observance of the guidelines will presumably be required when such countries borrow from the Fund.

The guidelines deal with the mode of interventions in the exchange market, in order to prevent "competitive alterations of exchange rates." The difference between "competitive alteration" and what formerly was called "competitive depreciation" is, presumably, that alteration is the wider concept which covers also the case of "competitive appreciation" (as it is sometimes called)—a policy of keeping the exchange rate higher than the market-clearing level and financing the resulting deficit by running down reserves or by official borrowing abroad.[26] Such a policy can also be described as deliberate exportation of inflation to keep down the country's own rate of inflation.

The new Article IV in the amended charter uses an even more comprehensive term than competitive alteration of exchange rates. It speaks of "manipulating exchange rates or the international monetary system" and enjoins countries to avoid such manipulations for the purpose of gaining "an unfair competitive advantage over other members."

It is important to adhere to the wider concept, "manipulation of the international monetary system," because it covers abuses of managed floating as well as those of par value changes. The 1974 guidelines deal only with manipulations by interventions in the exchange market under floating. But actually there seems to have been very little competitive depressing of floating exchange rates by interventions in the exchange market. True, Japan has been accused of depressing the yen by buying dollars and managing capital flows. But the case is not at all clear. (See Section 5 below for further discussion.)

Probably more important than interventions for the purpose of gaining "an unfair competitive advantage" is "dirty floating." It is important in my opinion to distinguish between dirty floating and merely managed floating. By dirty floating I mean such policies as

---

[25] See IMF *Annual Report for 1974* (Washington, D.C., 1974), pp. 112-16.

[26] Official borrowing surely should include part of the foreign borrowing by state enterprises and in some cases even officially induced borrowing by large private firms. It stands to reason that the line between genuinely private and official borrowing (and lending) tends to become more and more blurred in modern, highly planned, and manipulated economies, such as the British and Italian ones.

split exchange markets, multiple exchange rates, import deposit schemes, "taxes" on the purchase of foreign currencies differentiated according to the prospective use of the foreign currency, and the like. These policies shade off into a policy of comprehensive exchange control and thus violate one of the basic objectives of the Fund, to avoid "restrictions for balance of payments purposes on current account transactions," to use the language of the guidelines for floating.[27] As was shown earlier, the policy of having a separate exchange market for capital transactions unavoidably leads to restrictions and distortions of current transactions.

By merely managed floating, I mean a policy that confines itself to influencing the exchange rates by buying and selling of foreign exchange in a free exchange market in order to "prevent or moderate sharp and disruptive fluctuations from day to day and from week to week," [28] as well as to moderate, though not suppress or reverse, longer-run movements.

The 1974 guidelines, although they reiterate, as just mentioned, the basic objective of unrestricted current transactions, do not rule out dirty floating. On the contrary, the system of "separate capital exchange markets," in other words the system of dual exchange rates, one for current the other for capital transactions, is expressly mentioned in the official commentary on the guidelines, along with exchange market interventions and other policies, as an acceptable "action to influence an exchange rate." [29] This is unfortunate because the system of split exchange markets and dual exchange rates is the most widely used form of dirty floating.

There have been, in recent years, many cases of dirty floating of varying degrees of "dirtyness." Furthermore, there were last year two conspicuous cases of grossly mismanaged alterations (depreciations) of exchange rates—the Mexican peso and the Australian dollar. On November 28, 1976, the Australian dollar was devalued by 17.5 percent. It was probably the first case of outright competitive depreciation since floating has become widespread, as the *Economist* of London of December 4, 1976, pointed out. This judgment was reinforced by the fact that shortly after the devaluation, the Australian dollar was again revalued by a few percent in small steps. Clearly, a clean unmanaged or managed float would have been much better. Guidance by the Fund was either absent or was not heeded.

While the depreciation of the Australian dollar was not a float,

---

[27] IMF *Annual Report for 1974*, Guideline (5), p. 114.
[28] Ibid., Guideline (1), p. 115.
[29] Ibid., p. 115.

but an old fashioned par value change preceded and accompanied by the usual disrupting concomitants—speculative capital flows and over-shooting—the long overdue and equally mismanaged depreciation of the Mexican peso was first officially described as a float. Actually it, too, was a case of bungled depreciation combined with export taxes and other measures which violate basic objectives of the Fund, a case of dirty fixing rather than dirty floating. Guidance by the Fund has been either lacking or was spurned.

Now, let us consider the rules of exchange market interventions for managed, but not dirty, floating.[30] There is fairly general agreement that there are no objections to interventions to iron out short-term fluctuations.[31] Guideline (1) says that "members with a floating exchange rate should intervene on the foreign exchange market as necessary to prevent or moderate sharp fluctuations from day to day and from week to week." The guidelines draw the line separating short from medium run between the week and the month.[32]

In regard to fluctuations in the intermediate run, say from one to twelve months,[33] the situation is not so clear. Many experts who are,

---

[30] Clean floating and dirty floating are not always clearly differentiated. Many authors use the term *clean floating* synonymously with *free, unmanaged floating*. Others deny that there is such a thing as clean floating on the ground that "the authorities affect the exchange rate through their macropolicies whether they want it or not." (June Flanders, "Some Problems of Stabilization Policy Under Floating Exchange Rates," in *Trade, Stability and Macroeconomics: Essays in Honor of Lloyd Metzler*, ed. George Horwich and Paul A. Samuelson [New York: Academic Press, 1974], p. 123.) Of course, everything depends on everything else, and everybody is free to define his terms as he wants. But it would be rather awkward and misleading to speak of a managed, "unclean" float, if, instead of intervening in the exchange market, the monetary authorities of a country took steps to slow down an ongoing inflation by reducing the rate of monetary growth to stop a decline in external value of the currency.

[31] For a thorough discussion of the problems of official interventions which raises some doubts about the wisdom of trying to smooth short-run fluctuations in exchange rates, see Leland B. Yeager, *International Monetary Relations: Theory, History and Policy* (New York: Harper and Row, 1966), chapter 13, "Stabilizing Official Interventions," pp. 232-47.

[32] Guideline (1) has been criticized by Ethier and Bloomfield, because it seems to make interventions for the purpose of ironing out short-run fluctuations mandatory. (Wilfred Ethier and Arthur L. Bloomfield, *Managing the Managed Float*, Essays in International Finance, no. 112 [Princeton, N.J.: Princeton University, International Finance Section, 1975], p. 22.) The authors recommend that such interventions should be merely permitted. It could indeed be argued that mandatory interventions are incompatible with the amended charter, which gives every country the right to choose the exchange rate regime it prefers. (Ethier and Bloomfield wrote before the text of the amended articles became available.) But it could also be argued that the phrase *as necessary* in the text of Guideline (1) makes the guidelines immune to that criticism.

[33] The IMF guidelines define *medium-term* as a period of about four years (IMF *Annual Report for 1974*, Guideline (3)(b), p. 115).

in principle, in favor of floating (for example, E. M. Bernstein) feel strongly that since 1973, in many important cases, the fluctuations have been much larger than can be justified and that such excessive fluctuations should be moderated, though not suppressed, by official interventions in the exchange market. What the advocates of intervention have in mind primarily is fluctuations of the dollar exchange rate, in particular the dollar-deutsche mark (DM) rate.

The dollar-DM rate has indeed fluctuated sharply. For example from May 7, 1973, to July 6, 1973, the dollar fell vis-à-vis the DM by 21 percent; from July 6, 1973, to January 7, 1974, it rose by 28 percent; and it had fallen again by 16 percent by May 10, 1974. The currencies in the European snake and the Swiss franc exhibited similar fluctuations vis-à-vis the dollar. Later the fluctuations became much milder, and it should be pointed out that fluctuations of the trade-weighted effective exchange rate of the dollar were much smaller than those of the dollar-DM rate. For example from May 15, 1973, to July 16, 1973, the trade-weighted depreciation of the dollar was 1.7 percent, and from July 16, 1973, to January 15, 1974, the trade-weighted appreciation was 5.1 percent.[34]

It should be kept in mind, furthermore, that the years of 1973 to 1975 were a period of extreme turbulence and uncertainty in the world economy as well as in the U.S. economy. It was the period of the two-digit inflation followed by worldwide recession and stagflation, the period of the oil shock. Inflation rates in different countries diverged sharply and so did the impact of the oil shock and of the recession. There were special disturbing factors shaking the confidence in the dollar: the Watergate affair and the forced resignation of President Nixon had a debilitating effect on the U.S. administration's ability to pursue a consistently vigorous anti-inflation policy. There were erratic shifts in U.S. policies with respect to price and wage control and, at times, strong congressional pressure for a freeze or even a rollback of prices, wages, profits, and rents. The uncertainty associated with these events undermined the confidence in the dollar at home and abroad. Still another factor causing large fluctuations was that private operators in the marketplace had to adjust to the floating system. Speculators had become used to the easy task of speculating against the central banks whose hands were tied under the par value system (stable but adjustable exchange rates). Thus private firms—and pub-

---

[34] Export-weighted foreign currency cost, average of sixty-seven countries. Computed by Office of International Trade, U.S. Department of Commerce. The periods of the dollar-DM rate and the trade-weighted figures are not exactly the same because the latter figures are only available for mid-months.

lic agencies—had to learn how to live with the much greater risks of speculating against the market under flexible exchange rates. The failures of the Herstatt Bank in West Germany and the Franklin-National Bank in the United States, and large losses of other banks from foreign exchange dealings taught their lessons, but not without considerable cost.

With this in mind, it is not at all surprising that there were sharp fluctuations in exchange rates. Ex post it is deceptively easy to conclude that some of the fluctuations turned out to be unnecessary and that a lot of money could have been made by private or official counterspeculation. However, ex ante, most of the exchange movements looked quite reasonable. Given the high degree of turmoil and uncertainty of the period, there is no reason whatever to assume that the judgment of public officials (national or international) about the "appropriate exchange rate" (to use a phrase favored by the advocates of interventions), would have been better than that of the market. The record of official judgments about exchange rates and balances of payments prospects during the Bretton Woods period was anything but encouraging.[35] Time and again exchange rates were defended stubbornly and hundreds of millions of dollars were lost by central banks in what turned out to be wrong speculations.[36] The record of official interventions in the post-Bretton Woods area has not been any better in a number of cases. In Britain, Italy, Australia, and Mexico interventions have been highly destabilizing, over-valued currencies have been propped up for a while, and the subsequent inevitable plunge was then all the more abrupt and disrupting.

---

[35] It may be recalled that the Smithsonian realignment of exchange rates was based on what was supposed to be the best expert advice available anywhere in the world, an IMF econometric world model. Actually, the new pattern of exchange rates was proved to be hopelessly wrong within a few months. (It should be mentioned, however, that the American delegation had tried to get a larger devaluation of the dollar which they thought would be necessary to restore equilibrium and confidence.) But the Smithsonian agreement was hailed at the time as a tremendous achievement (and not only by politicians). Even now, hindsight notwithstanding, it is mentioned as an example that it is not utopian to assume that countries will be "able to agree regularly on a consistent structure of spot reference rates." (John Williamson, "The Future Exchange Rate Regime," *Quarterly Review, Banca Nazionale del Lavoro*, June 1975, p. 140.) Consistent perhaps, but totally wrong nonetheless.

[36] It should, however, not be overlooked that under the adjustable peg, central bankers and ministers of finance who contemplate a change in the exchange rate—up or down—have to pretend solemnly to the last moment that they would never, never do such a thing—an obnoxious feature of the par value system. Many examples of that painful behavior could be cited, even from the very recent experience in the European snake when the West German mark was appreciated by a few percent.

Since there is no evidence that the fluctuations of the dollar-DM rate did significant damage and since the fluctuations have become milder as the turbulence in the world economy and in the American economy subsided, the case for extensive official interventions in the market, except to iron out erratic very short-run fluctuations, is not very strong.

Reference Rates and Target Zones. Ethier and Bloomfield have argued that the working of the floating system would be greatly improved if countries could be persuaded by the Fund to set what they call reference rates or reference zones for their currencies. This proposal has been endorsed by John Williamson and is widely regarded as an imaginative, novel idea. In the 1974 Fund guidelines, too, there is mention that countries may set medium-term norms or target rates (or zones), and the official commentary to the guidelines explains that the "medium-term" might be considered to refer to a period of about four years.[37]

The difference between a par value and a reference rate (or reference zone) is that unlike the par value the reference rate need not be defended by interventions. Interventions would be permitted, but they would not be mandatory, and the interventions are subject to only one rule: If the exchange rate in the market is *below* the reference rate the central bank is allowed (not obligated) to intervene by selling foreign currencies in order to push the currency up to the reference rate; if the exchange rate is *above* the reference rate the central bank is allowed (not obligated) to intervene by buying foreign currencies in order to push the currency down to the reference rate. In other words, interventions must never push the exchange rate *away* from the reference rate, but interventions are permitted to move the exchange rate *towards* the reference rates. The reference rates should be "revised at periodic prespecified intervals, by some defined international procedure."[38]

The main advantage that is claimed for the reference rate proposal is that it would deal effectively with the problem of destabilizing speculation. Since there is no obligation for the central bank to intervene in order to keep the exchange rate at (or near) the reference

---

[37] Ethier and Bloomfield, *Managing the Managed Float*; Williamson, "The Future Exchange Rate Regime," pp. 127-44; and IMF *Annual Report for 1974*, Guideline (3)(b) and Commentary, p. 115. See also the interesting pamphlet by Raymond F. Mikesell and Henry N. Goldstein, *Rules for a Floating Rate Regime*, Essays in International Finance, no. 109 (Princeton, N.J.: Princeton University, International Finance Section, April 1975).

[38] Ethier and Bloomfield, *Managing the Managed Float*, p. 10.

rate, speculators would face greater risks than they face under the par value system. I agree with this argument. The reference rate system would be less prone to engender destabilizing speculation than the par value system.

But I am not convinced by the claim that, compared with a floating system without reference rates, the reference rate system would have the advantage of eliminating or sharply reducing the alleged danger of destabilizing speculation. Williamson says that the reference rates would provide "a focus for stabilizing speculation. [If] the rate moved away from the reference rate, the market would know that future interventions could only be in the direction of pushing the rate back towards the official reference rate, thus adding to the risk [of] further destabilizing behavior." [39]

I find this unconvincing. If destabilizing speculation is not discouraged under the par value system by the *obligation* of the central bank to defend the par value, why should it be discouraged under the reference rate system by the mere *permission* to defend the reference rates? All depends on whether the market finds the reference rates credible or not. Why should reference rates be more credible than par values? Reference rates that give the impression of being out of line and are therefore liable to be changed at the next "prespecified" revision are very likely to cause heavy speculation, unless the revisions are small and are made at short intervals. But changing the reference rates at short intervals would be tantamount to replacing the reference rate system by a crawling peg system or a trotting peg system à la Brazil. The fear that changes in the reference rate may trigger speculative capital flows may well induce central banks increasingly to treat reference rates as par values.

John Williamson says that the value of having a focus for stabilizing speculation is best demonstrated by the Canadian experience, where the U.S. $1 = Can $1 parity has long played this role of inducing stabilizing speculation. [40] Some defenders of fixed rates, for example Robert Mundell, have tried to explain away the undeniable success and stability of the Canadian float by the fact that the Canadian monetary unit is called a dollar and has historically been on a par (or nearly so) with the U.S. dollar, thus serving as "a focus for stabilizing speculation." I find that explanation of the stability of the Canadian dollar unconvincing. The stability of the Canadian dollar (until now) and the absence of volatile capital flows are due to a long

---

[39] Williamson, "The Future Exchange Rate Regime," pp. 134-36.
[40] Ibid., pp. 135-36.

tradition of political stability and responsible financial and monetary policies (which probably were, in part, motivated by the wish to preserve the near-parity of the Canadian and the U.S. dollar).[41] Destroy this tradition, and the picture will change overnight. Should we assume that Mexico—not to mention Argentina or Chile—could give its currency the stability of the Canadian dollar by renaming the peso a Mexican dollar? Could the stability of the lira be promoted by calling it the "Italian mark"? A reputation of political stability and responsible economic policies once lost may take a very long time to be regained.[42]

The assumptions made in the IMF Guidelines (3) (b) that "reasonable estimates of the medium-term norm" for a country's exchange rate can be made for "a period of about four years" ahead, as the official commentary to the IMF guidelines assumes, seems to me unrealistic to the point of suggesting a typographical error. Should it be four months or four quarters? [43]

Ethier and Bloomfield stress repeatedly that their "rule is defined in terms of explicit, central-bank *behavior* rather than in terms of presumed central-bank motivations." [44] The difficulty of implementing that prescription is highlighted by the following remarks of the authors: "[The] Rule should be applied only to official interventions [of] the central bank. . . . [It] would [not] apply to purchases of foreign exchange by a central bank directly from state enterprises that had been encouraged [by] the government [or the central bank?] to borrow abroad as has happened in Great Britain and Italy." [45] Since it is generally agreed that the huge British and Italian borrowings were made largely for balance of payments reasons, ignoring such transactions and restricting the rule to formal interventions by the central bank in the foreign exchange market would deprive the reference scheme of much of its relevance in the present day world.

Concluding Remarks. Our discussion of some problems concerning international surveillance of exchange rate policies has shown that it

---

[41] If this is the case, it confirms what was said above that floating carries with it a certain self-disciplinary, anti-inflationary incentive.

[42] The French franc was not saved by the fact that for many years (1865 to 1914) it was rigidly joined in a one-to-one relationship with the Swiss franc in the so-called Latin Union, which was organized in 1865 by France, Belgium, Italy, and Switzerland, and was joined by Greece in 1868.

[43] Balance of payments and exchange rate projections, even for only a year ahead, have been notoriously unreliable. For example see Willett, *Floating Exchange Rates* (forthcoming).

[44] Ethier and Bloomfield, *Managing the Managed Float*, p. 11. Italics in original.

[45] Ibid., p. 101.

is not at all easy to formulate meaningful guidelines for floating. It would probably be best to forget about reference rates, not to mention medium-term norms or target-zones for exchange rates for several years ahead. The simpler rule contained in the IMF Guideline (2) that no country should "normally act aggressively with respect to the exchange value of its currency (i.e., should not so act [intervene in the market] as to depress that value when it is falling, or to enhance that value when it is rising)," is probably all that is needed and can reasonably be justified.

Of course, the questions remain what "normally" means, what the exceptions might be, and how one can tell whether a country has in fact observed the rule not to intervene "aggressively." Obviously it is not sufficient to look at the formal interventions of the central bank in the exchange market and to ignore completely borrowing by other public agencies abroad.[46] It is hardly possible to spell out beforehand all possible exceptions to the rule. One has to rely on continuing multilateral surveillance among major countries and on the good judgment of the Fund. It is perhaps not unreasonable to hope the Fund will be able, in its regular annual consultation with members and in negotiations about member borrowing, to reach agreement on responsible policies without condoning every violation of the letter or the spirit of the Articles of Agreement.

This is after all not a new problem. It will be recalled that the original Articles of Agreement enjoined the Fund "not [to] object to a proposed change [in an exchange rate] because of the domestic social or political policies of the member proposing the change."[47] This injunction has not prevented the Fund from exercising, more or less discreetly, strong influence on members' economic and financial policies in annual consultations or by attaching strings to borrowing agreements.

Finally, let me repeat that guiding interventions under a managed float would be less important (and conceptually though not politically more difficult) than trying to dissuade countries from engaging in dirty floating in the sense defined above, that is, in the sense of split exchange markets, dual exchange rates, import-deposit schemes, and the like.

---

[46] For that reason the well-known American proposal of earlier years to use monetary reserve indicators for changes in exchange rates would require modification.

[47] Article IV, Section 3(f). The amended charter substantially repeats this injunction: "These principles [of surveillance over exchange arrangements] shall respect the domestic social and political policies of members." (Article IV, Section 3 [b]).

International Liquidity in a World of Floating Exchange Rates [48]

Adjustment, Confidence, Liquidity. In the 1950s and 1960s it became customary to discuss the problems of international monetary reform under the three headings of adjustment, liquidity, and confidence.[49] The adjustment problem is the problem of how to maintain or restore equilibrium in the balance of payments by some suitable automatic mechanism and/or policy measures under fixed, stable but adjustable, or floating exchange rates. To this point, the present paper has been concerned with adjustment problems, with special emphasis on floating.

Confidence and liquidity problems arise primarily under fixed or stable but adjustable exchange rates. Whether these problems arise also under floating, and if they do in what form, will be discussed presently. In the international monetary area, the confidence problem relates to reserve currencies, notably, the most important one, the dollar. The possibility that lack of confidence could lead to large, sudden switches between different reserve media, specifically from dollars into gold, was regarded as a major weakness of the international monetary system in the 1950s and 1960s. The theory of Rueff and Triffin that the dollar-gold standard and the pure dollar standard are inherently unstable because they would sooner or later lead to violent and disruptive confidence crises has already been mentioned.

Since the suspension of gold convertibility and the advent of widespread floating, little has been said or heard of the confidence problem. Does that mean that under floating there is no confidence problem? If the confidence problem is defined as it usually was in the 1950s and 1960s (for example by the Machlup study group mentioned in footnote 49) as the possibility of "sudden switches between dif-

---

[48] This section draws heavily on the author's paper "How Important Is Control Over International Reserves?" presented at the Marcus Fleming Memorial Conference on the International Monetary System, November 11-12, 1976, sponsored by the International Monetary Fund. The papers presented at that conference are to be published in 1977 by Columbia University Press, New York. In that paper I sketch the earlier history of the problems of international liquidity.

[49] The problems were set out in these terms in *International Monetary Arrangements: The Problem of Choice*, Report on the Deliberations of an International Study Group of Thirty-two Economists. (Princeton, N.J.: Princeton University, International Finance Section, 1964.) The initiator and organizer of the study group was Fritz Machlup. In later years the work was continued in numerous meetings of the so-called Bellagio group under the direction of William Fellner, Fritz Machlup, and Robert Triffin. See also the excellent comprehensive discussion of the adjustment, liquidity, and confidence problem in Leland B. Yeager's impressive treatise *International Monetary Relations, Theory, History and Policy*, 2nd ed. (New York: Harper and Row, 1976), esp. pp. 611-55.

ferent reserve media," there is no confidence problem any more under the present system of floating because the convertibility of currencies including the dollar into a "primary" reserve asset such as gold has been abolished. [50] In a wider sense confidence in a currency, a reserve currency or any other currency, is still and always will be a problem. Confidence in the dollar could conceivably be impaired. For example if the United States again experienced high inflation, the very large foreign dollar holdings—a legacy of the fixed rate system but now held voluntarily—could become a problem, threatening a depreciation of the dollar in terms of some other currencies.

I shall not, however, pursue that subject any further. Let me simply say that the conventional confidence problem as it was discussed in the 1950s and 1960s does not exist any more. But confidence in the stability of individual currencies is still important and if the currency in question is a widely held reserve currency, as the dollar, confidence in it becomes a matter of world concern. In Britain the problem of foreign sterling balances has been acute when confidence in the future of the pound waned.

International Liquidity. The problem of international liquidity, or better, of the adequacy or inadequacy of international monetary reserves, has received a lot of attention in the discussions on international monetary reform before the advent of widespread floating—in fact too much attention compared with the adjustment problem in the opinion of many observers, including the present writer. Innumerable plans for monetary reform aimed at assuring an adequate but not excessive supply of reserves have been put forward.[51] In the whole postwar period until the late 1960s the emphasis was on the alleged dangers of a *shortage* of international liquidity. British economists almost unanimously (with the notable exception of Sir Ralph Hawtrey) predicted dire consequences, deflation and depression, unless the perceived growing inadequacy of international reserves was counteracted by the adoption of one of the numerous plans for reserve creation ranging from doubling the gold price to setting up the IMF

---

[50] It should be recalled that convertibility has two distinct meanings—asset convertibility (convertibility into some "primary" reserve asset) and market convertibility (convertibility into other currencies in a free, unrestricted foreign exchange market). The dollar still is and always was fully convertible in the important market sense, except that for Americans (not foreigners) capital transfers were restricted for several years. These restrictions were lifted in 1974.

[51] See Fritz Machlup, *Plans for Reform of the International Monetary System*, Special Papers in International Economics, no. 3 (Princeton, N.J.: Princeton University, International Finance Section, 1964).

as a real world central bank, a lender of last resort, with broad money-creating powers. When the predicted deflation failed to materialize, and it became clear in the late 1960s and early 1970s that inflation and not deflation was the threat, the emphasis shifted from the danger of inadequacy of reserves to that of excessive reserve growth. In the closing years of the Bretton Woods era international reserves grew, indeed, by leaps and bounds, from SDR 93 billion in 1970 to SDR 180 billion in 1974, according to IMF statistics.[52] Through the mechanism of fixed exchanges, the U.S. inflation which got under way in 1965 spread swiftly through the whole world.[53] After the advent of widespread floating, the growth of reserves slowed sharply, and the largest part accrued to the oil-exporting countries. The OPEC countries are, however, a very special case, because as is fairly generally agreed, additional reserves of the oil countries should be regarded as part of their long-term foreign investments and not as the basis of increased money supply.

In view of all this, it is not surprising that the excitement and worry about international liquidity, which previously had dominated the discussions about monetary reform, have greatly abated. Does that mean that international liquidity is no problem any more? Almost but not quite. Indeed, under a free, unmanaged float there would be no liquidity problem. Under managed floating, on the other hand, countries need reserves to intervene in the market. But there are several reasons why the need for reserves is much less urgent under floating, even if it is managed, than under the adjustable peg.

The liquidity problem is intertwined with the adjustment and confidence problems. If the adjustment mechanism does not work well and stubborn balance of payments disequilibria occur frequently, large reserves are required; and if there is a confidence problem in the sense that large sudden switches between different reserve media cannot be ruled out, countries, especially reserve currency countries, need large reserves. On both grounds reserve need is sharply reduced under managed floating. On the one hand, the adjustment mechanism becomes much more efficient when exchange rates are allowed to float and, on the other hand, the confidence problem has all but vanished when currencies are no longer convertible at a fixed rate into some

---

[52] Total reserves of all IMF members, end of period in SDRs. See *International Financial Statistics*, any recent issue.

[53] This does not mean, however, that the United States was the only culprit. Many countries inflated even faster than the United States, and the majority of countries followed the U.S. lead without resistance, if not with pleasure—in some cases with the added satisfaction of being able to put all the blame on Uncle Sam.

ultimate reserve medium such as gold.[54] As we have seen, disruptive speculation is greatly encouraged and facilitated by the adjustable peg ("stable but adjustable rates") and is discouraged and made hazardous by floating.

The present international monetary system of widespread floating as legalized by the amended charter of the Fund—or nonsystem as those whose blueprints were not followed like to call it—has been criticized on the ground that it failed to put any limit or control on global monetary reserves or liquidity. To come to grips with this criticism let us consider how, under floating, global reserves should be defined and measured and how important the control of global reserves, however defined, still is.

Under fixed and even semifixed exchange rates these questions permit a fairly unambiguous and straightforward answer. Under the gold standard, global reserves were defined as the world stock of monetary gold. Later, under the gold exchange standard, balances of reserve currencies held by central banks of nonreserve countries should be added. Under the Bretton Woods system, reserve positions in the Fund and SDRs were further additions. Large changes in these world aggregates undoubtedly had something to do with fluctuations in the world price level, with waves of world inflation and deflation. I say "large changes," because one would surely not expect a close parallelism between minor fluctuations in these two very broad and even then (under the gold standard) somewhat hazy aggregates.[55]

Under widespread floating, the two aggregates, global reserves on the one hand and the world price level and its changes on the other hand, have become highly fragmented magnitudes. Moreover, close substitutes for monetary reserves, namely official and semiofficial borrowing, have grown by leaps and bounds in many countries. To be sure, the Fund dutifully publishes every month the percentage change in consumer prices for the whole world. This is some sort of an average of changes of consumer prices in all member countries. For example, in August 1976, the change in consumer prices for the world

---

[54] Let me repeat that the much more important market convertibility of currencies is fully preserved under floating, unless convertibility is restricted or abolished by exchange control. The danger of controls being imposed is much greater under the adjustable peg than under floating.

[55] On the so-called "international quantity theory" which postulates a *close* relationship between international liquidity and the world price level, and on the criticism that the international quantity theory has received from Marcus Fleming, Jacques Polak, Egon Sohmen, and Thomas Willett, see my paper, "How Important Is Control over International Reserves?" The criticism of the authors largely antedates the period of widespread floating. Floating has all but obliterated any correlation that may have existed between the two magnitudes.

as a whole over the previous twelve months was 10.5 percent. This figure is a weighted average of 5.6 percent for the United States, 1.5 percent for Switzerland, 396 percent for Argentina, 200 percent for Chile (down from 400 percent a year ago), et cetera. The Fund also publishes global reserves, of which foreign exchange is by far the largest component. These figures do not make allowance for the growth of reserve substitutes, that is, official and semiofficial borrowing. It is possible to correlate the two series, or rather, jumbles of figures. But who would be bold enough to attribute any causal significance to such an operation and derive policy conclusions concerning the adequacy of world reserves?

How would the Fund exercise control over global reserves? SDR creation and utilization of Fund quotas are under international control. But as mentioned, by far the largest component of world reserves consists of foreign exchange, mostly dollar balances. One can, of course, dream of a monetary reform that would concentrate all reserves including gold and foreign exchange in the Fund in exchange for SDRs.[56] That such a reform would be politically utterly impossible is perhaps not the main objection. It may not even be a nice dream. Given the present-day drift in international politics and power struggle, such a concentration of power in the hands of an international organization could become very dangerous. It would be bound to become an issue in the international class struggle that is now going on under the slogan of a "New International Economic Order."

My conclusion is that, in the present world of widespread floating, it is impossible to give a meaningful definition of global reserves, let alone to define an optimal or desirable level of global reserves or of reserve growth. It is the adjustment and not the liquidity problem that is of paramount importance, now more than ever. The Fund's main task should be "surveillance" of exchange rate policies, especially prevention of dirty floating and dirty fixing of exchange rates.

However, to say that control of global reserves is not an important or meaningful task for the Fund any more does not mean that for individual countries the size of their reserves and their external borrowing potential are unimportant, nor that the use countries make of their reserves and borrowing power cannot become a matter of international concern. It is possible that in the last few years there has been much international overborrowing and excessive lending by

---

[56] Before the advent of widespread floating, plans for the concentration and consolidation of world monetary reserves in the Fund have in fact been put forward by the dozen. (See Machlup, *Plans for Reform of the International Monetary System*, for an early selection.) The Committee of Twenty wrestled with this problem for years.

banks to shore up shaky balance of payments positions. Another development that may cause legitimate worries is the rapidly growing volume of lending by Western banks to Communist countries. All this may, indeed, cause serious troubles in the future. But if so, it has nothing to do with a lack of international control over the volume of *global* reserves in the conventional sense, and it could not have been prevented by such controls unless Fund control over global reserves were unconventionally interpreted to include control over money supply as well as over monetary policy in at least the major countries and perhaps Fund supervision over the lending policies of large banks.

Furthermore, discounting the importance of global reserves and their control does not mean that inflation is no problem. On the contrary, inflation is a major world problem. But it no longer has anything to do with a lack of control over *global* reserves. It has its roots in the *national* monetary, fiscal, and exchange rate policies of the major countries. The primary responsibility for curbing world inflation obviously falls on the leading industrial countries, especially the United States. This is so because, as noted above, the majority of smaller countries peg their currencies either to the currency of one of the leading industrial countries, most of them to the dollar, or to a basket of important currencies or SDRs. It is true that national monetary policies, inflation or deflation, in the many countries that peg their currencies to the dollar are profoundly influenced, if not fully determined, by the inflation, or absence of inflation, in the United States. If there is inflation in the United States, dollar balances are likely to pile up in countries that peg to the dollar, and inflation will spread. It follows that if the Fund could control inflation in the United States and in a few other key countries, it would substantially control world inflation. If control of *global* monetary reserves is unconventionally interpreted to include control of money supply, monetary policy, and inflation in the major countries then, and only then, could it be said that control of global reserves is necessary to prevent world inflation.

Actually the Fund can do nothing about inflation in the United States and only in exceptional cases about inflation in other major countries. (The British and Italian borrowing from the Fund may be such exceptional cases.) If the United States again lapsed into high inflation, the only effective measure to prevent the piling up of dollar reserves in countries that peg to the dollar and the spread of the U.S. inflation, would be to stop pegging to the dollar. In other words, if there is inflation in the United States, floating is the only effective policy to avoid both an excessive growth of international liquidity in the form of dollar balances and the spread of inflation.

The upshot is that the Fund can do very little about world inflation. It is easier, in fact, to think of Fund policies that would add, marginally though under realistic assumptions, to world inflation, than to identify measures that would help to curb inflation. Steps that would add to inflationary pressures are a general increase in the Fund's quotas and additional distribution of SDRs, especially if linked to foreign aid. Similarly adding to inflation would be a further proliferation and expansion of special lending facilities—such as the Oil Facility, the Buffer Stock Facility, the Extended Fund Facility, and the Compensatory Financing of Export Fluctuations.[57]

But by no means does this imply that such measures should not be taken under any circumstances. On the contrary, emergencies must be expected to occur from time to time which justify even large-scale credit operations by the Fund to forestall some major or minor disturbances of the world economy, including inflationary and protectionist reactions in some countries. What it does mean is that the inflationary implications of such lending should not be overlooked, just as a fire brigade when throwing water on an attic fire should not be oblivious to the damage that flooding can do to the rest of the house. The two dangers—the threatening disturbance and the inflationary side effect of the monetary measures taken—should be weighed against each other. Overreactions should be avoided, and the operations should be of the proper size and pinpointed[58] so as to minimize the danger of intensifying inflation.

To pursue this highly important problem any further would burst the frame of the present study. However, one more observation may be permitted: *Conditional* lending by the Fund—"provision of conditional liquidity" to use official language—can be used as an induce-

---

[57] Lord Robbins believes that it was a "fundamental flaw" in the Bretton Woods charter that "it contained no instruments which were capable of dealing with general inflation. . . . The plain fact is that the IMF was conceived as an institution providing safeguards against general deflation. . . . Moreover, what innovations have taken place since those days, the SDRs for instance . . . were conceived to be a safeguard against an alleged insufficient world liquidity." ("Domestic Goals and Financial Interdependence," Speech at International Monetary Conference, Frankfurt, April 28, 1977, published in *Auszüge aus Presseartikeln*, Deutsche Bundesbank, no. 28, Frankfurt am Main, May 6, 1977, p. 5.)

[58] To illustrate: An across-the-board distribution of additional SDRs or a general increase of country quotas in the Fund would clearly be an inflationary move. But the use of international liquidity, even of ad hoc-created additional liquidity, for a loan to an inflationary country as part of a comprehensive agreement on a change in policy that enables the country to get out of the inflationary rut can be defended as an anti-inflationary move.

ment for countries to put their financial house in order and to curb inflation. *Unconditional* lending is likely to be counterproductive because it is likely to tempt countries to delay needed structural reform and anti-inflationary measures and to postpone changes in exchange rates or floating that may be required.

World Inflation, World Recession, and the International Monetary System: Some Recent Policy Issues

Introduction. We have seen that the task of curbing world inflation falls squarely on the leading industrial countries because most smaller countries peg their currencies, formally or de facto, to the currencies of the leading industrial countries.

The same is true of world recession. If the leading industrial countries are in recession, the rest of the world suffers too, and when the leading countries recover from the recession, they pull the others along. We have seen that floating does not provide complete protection from recession abroad, because it shields a country only from purely monetary disturbances from abroad, which can be defined as foreign-induced changes in the money supply. But floating does not protect a country from *real* disturbances. And the effects of recessions are not purely monetary in nature. Nonmonetary (real) aspects of recessions are their differential impact on different commodities and industries (for example, on raw materials versus manufactured goods and, often overlapping, export versus import goods) and protectionist reactions. Against these real concomitants of recessions, which entail changes in the terms of trade,[59] floating provides no protection. But whatever the real disturbance, floating fully protects a country from purely monetary effects of recessions abroad, in the sense that no country can be forced, as it would be under fixed exchanges, to make things worse (possibly much worse) by actively bringing about or passively permitting a contraction in the money supply. In other words, what has been called a "secondary deflation" can be avoided under floating.[60] It is true that today no country would allow a monetary deflation to proceed very far, but under fixed or semifixed

---

[59] To visualize clearly the crucial importance of the terms of trade, consider the following hypothetical situation: country A has a recession, but its impact on all industries is uniform in the sense that *relative* prices remain unchanged and there are no protectionist reactions. In this unlikely, but not unthinkable, event country B would be able to protect itself from being infected by the recession abroad by letting its currency float down.

[60] In severe depressions of the past, for example, in the Great Depression of the 1930s, the secondary *monetary* deflation was a far greater calamity than the *real* maladjustments and distortions which may have started the depression in the first place. (On this issue see my study, *The World Economy, Money, and the Great Depression*, especially pp. 21-27.)

exchange rates sooner or later, after reserves have been exhausted, stringent controls would become necessary to stay out of a world recession. Floating obviates the necessity of imposing import restrictions on balance of payments grounds. (Restrictions on particular imports on protectionist grounds are of course a different matter.)

In the light of these general considerations I now discuss some recent policy issues.

The American Advice to West Germany and Japan. The first initiative of the Carter administration in the international economic area was to urge West Germany and Japan to join the United States in stimulating a more rapid expansion of their own economies in order to promote expansion of the world economy. The basic goal is unobjectionable: If the leading industrial countries are able to achieve sustainable rapid economic expansion and growth, they do a great service not only to themselves but also to the rest of the world.

But what is sustainable expansion and growth? This raises the question of inflation which may result from a too rapid expansion. Is it possible to accelerate the expansion that is going on anyway without intensifying the inflation? This question is rarely faced squarely. For example, the eighth report of the so-called Tripartite Committee of Private Economists from the European Community, Japan, and North America, a report that seems to reflect the official American position fairly accurately, confines itself to stating that "stronger expansion in the three countries . . . need not intensify inflation." [61] This may be true, but how it can be done is not explained, except for a hint at incomes policy and wage and price rigidity. At any rate, the usual Keynesian argument for this optimism to the effect that more rapid monetary expansion does not intensify inflation so long as there is still slack and unemployment in the economy is definitely insufficient. The spectacle of several years of severe stagflation should be enough to dispel complacency in that respect.

The problem of how to accelerate the expansion without intensifying inflation, which is in effect the dilemma of stagflation, cannot be discussed further at this point. It is more fully treated in other contributions to this volume and was discussed in the initial volume of *Contemporary Economic Problems.*[62] It suffices to say that, quite naturally, the administration assumes that its own stimulative package stays well within the bounds of prudence. Time will tell whether this

---

[61] *Economic Prospects and Policies in the Industrial Countries*, a tripartite report by sixteen economists from the European Community, Japan, and North America (Washington, D.C.: The Brookings Institution, 1977), p. 10.

[62] See especially the contributions by Fellner and Cagan in this volume. I expressed my views in an article, "The Problem of Stagflation," in the initial volume.

complacency is justified. Be that as it may, other governments may feel that they are expanding fast enough and that an additional stimulus would dangerously intensify the inflation which has nowhere been fully subdued (except in Switzerland). Thus, there were angry reactions in West Germany to the American suggestion of a more expansionary policy, and Chancellor Helmut Schmidt was reported to have said that West Germany does not need American advice, because the recovery was well under way, and West Germany has done better than the United States, with respect to both unemployment and inflation. Otmar Emminger, president of the German Bundesbank, in a closely reasoned speech, "The Role of the Strong Currency Countries in International Balance of Payments Adjustment," [63] stated that West Germany fully accepts the advice of IMF managing director, H. Johannes Witteveen, that strong currency countries should follow an expansionary policy as far as it is compatible with reasonable price stability and should not resist an appreciation of their currencies. Dr. Emminger noted that the West German public sector deficit was larger in terms of GNP than the American (including the administration's new stimulation package), and he pointed out that in 1976 the trade-weighted appreciation of the mark was 15 percent. The position of the Japanese government seems to be similar. Looking at the price picture one finds that inflation is still rampant in Japan. The consumer price index for December 1976 showed a rise of 10.5 percent since December 1975, and wholesale prices rose correspondingly.[64]

The upshot is that, with regard to inflation, both countries have good reasons to be concerned. It would therefore be unwise for the United States simply to urge them, as it is often done, to expand faster.[65] This would be tantamount to asking them to have more inflation, and the result would be, at best, an unsustainable burst of growth.

The intended contribution to the health of the world economy of an expansionary policy in West Germany and Japan is to stimulate imports of the two countries and put a brake on their exports, in short, to turn their current-account surplus into a deficit and so make life easier for their weak neighbors, Britain and Italy, and for less-developed countries.

[63] Speech before the Overseas Bankers Club, London, January 31, 1977. German text in Deutsche Bundesbank, *Auszüge aus Presseartikeln*, no. 9 (February 11, 1977), pp. 1-3.
[64] See IMF, *International Financial Statistics*, February 1977.
[65] For example: "American officials say that they again plan to urge Germany, Japan and other countries . . . to follow the Carter administration's example and give their economies an additional expansionary boost" (*New York Times*, February 28, 1977, p. 39).

The advice to the two countries is, in fact, often couched in precisely these terms: Get a current-account deficit.[66] Two questions arise. First, is a current-account deficit really of overwhelming or exclusive importance, and second, if and when a deficit is desirable, can it not be brought about by less objectionable means than an inflationary and therefore unsustainable expansion?

The answer to the first question is, I believe, that a current-account deficit is not in all cases desirable. It depends on circumstances, especially on what is on the other side of the balance. We should keep in mind that a current-account surplus reflects capital exports of some kind, and a current-account deficit implies capital imports. Not so long ago the United States was criticized for running a current-account deficit, on the ground that it was unbecoming for a rich country to import capital from poorer neighbors. Suppose the West German current-account surplus reflects capital exports to Britain and Italy, and loans or grants to less-developed countries— why is that objectionable?

The answer to this question will be: Times have changed. The new factor is that the non-oil-producing countries have to cope with an "incompressible" deficit vis-à-vis the OPEC countries. "The developing countries and the smaller OECD countries have already been carrying too large a share of the aggregate oil deficit. Clearly one has to expect Germany, Japan, . . . to accept a larger share of the aggregate deficit." [67]

It is true that the OPEC surplus is, in the short or even medium or long run, incompressible, but one should not give the impression that the OPEC surplus is a burden on the rest of the world which ought to be shared equitably. On the contrary, the fact that the OPEC countries invest a large part of their new riches abroad instead of spending them all on imports lightens the burden imposed by the high price of oil, at least temporarily. Many countries would experience a painful necessity of tightening their belts if West Germany and Japan "relieved" them of their oil deficit. To eliminate a deficit or to shift from a deficit to a surplus is a real burden because it requires a reduction of consumption and/or investment. Only in a Keynesian world of general high unemployment would the opposite be true; only in such a world can we have our cake and eat it too.

---

[66] See for example Robert Solomon, "Coping with Balance of Payments Surpluses and Deficits," statement before the Joint Economic Committee, February 8, 1977. The *Washington Post* reported about an interview with Fred Bergsten and Richard N. Cooper in which they urged West Germany and Japan to get a current-account deficit.

[67] Solomon, "Coping with Balance of Payments Surpluses and Deficits."

Keynesians surely will ask: With many million unemployed in the OECD area—are we not in a Keynesian world? The monetarist reply will be that since money illusion is all but gone, any additional expansionary move will merely heighten inflationary expectations and thus result in rising prices rather than in larger output and employment. I personally would not take this extreme monetarist position, which surprisingly has been taken by the Prime Minister of Great Britain, James Callaghan.[68] It is enough for my purpose to assume that we have reached the stage where inflationary expectations have become very sensitive to expansionary moves. In the short run, additional expansionary measures will cause some increase in output and employment but at the high cost of accelerating inflation, so that in the not too distant future, when inflation has to be stopped, the contraction of output and employment will be all the greater. In short, we have reached a point where we are much closer to the extreme monetarist position than to the Keynesian position.

Now I will turn to the second question raised above. Suppose a change in the West German and Japanese current balance from surplus to deficit is deemed desirable to provide a stimulus to the rest of the world—can it not be achieved by less objectionable measures than by an inflationary expansion? It surely can, either by an upward float or by removal of import restrictions.[69]

This, of course, raises again the question (which we touched earlier) whether the two countries have engaged in aggressive interventions (competitive depreciation) to prevent their currencies from

---

[68] In a speech to a Labour Party Conference on September 28, 1976 he said:

> We used to think that you could just spend your way out of a recession and increase employment by cutting taxes and boosting Government spending. I tell you, in all candour, that that option no longer exists, and that insofar as it ever did exist, it only worked by injecting bigger doses of inflation into the economy followed by higher levels of unemployment as the next step. That is the history of the past 20 years.

Professor F. A. Hayek, too, believes that the extreme monetarist position "unfortunately needs qualification. In many situations, inflation does reduce unemployment *in the short run*, but only at the cost of creating much greater unemployment later on." (Letter to the *New York Times*, May 15, 1977.)

[69] Lawrence Klein has clearly understood that. But his proposal (as reported in the press), that West Germany, Japan, and the United States should jointly appreciate their currencies by 10 percent is not a suitable method. It would constitute a backsliding into the defunct, inefficient adjustable-peg system (apart from the fact that the U.S. balance is already in deficit). It is true that in recent years, on several occasions, the mark has been appreciated vis-à-vis the other snake currencies. But this was an inner-European affair which does not affect the conclusion that the Klein proposal is out of date in the era of widespread though managed floating.

floating up. Japan has, in fact, been accused of having done just that. Looking at the relevant figures we find that Japanese reserves have indeed risen sharply from $12.8 billion at the end of 1975 to $16.6 billion at the end of 1976. (They were, however, much higher in 1973.) But the yen, too, has gone up sharply over the same period.[70] Hence, the increase in reserves does not, on the face of it, qualify as aggressive intervention in the meaning of the IMF guidelines for floating. West German reserves, too, have risen sharply from $31 billion at the end of 1975 to $34.8 billion at the end of 1976. But the West German figures of reserve changes are difficult to interpret because of intra-snake interventions. According to information supplied by the West German Bundesbank, intrasnake interventions accounted for more than the total increase in reserves. At any rate, as mentioned above, the mark has sharply appreciated in 1976, also vis-à-vis some snake currencies.

The upshot of this discussion is that, prima facie, there is no indication that the two countries have pursued a policy of aggressive intervention to reverse market trends in contravention of the IMF rules. Be that as it may, complaints, if any, should focus on exchange rate policy and not on the attainment of some crude current-account targets to be achieved by an inflationary expansion. If any country feels aggrieved by the exchange rate policy of another country, the proper forum for raising complaints is the IMF, whose duty is to "oversee the compliance of each member with its obligations." One of these obligations is to avoid "manipulating exchange rates . . . to gain an unfair competitive advantage." [71]

There remains the question of removing import restrictions. Strong currency countries have always been urged by their weak neighbors to liberalize their import policies and to abstain from subsidizing exports. Preaching freer trade is a good thing at any time, and when there exists a payments imbalance, reduction of import restrictions serves two purposes at the same time. It helps to restore short-run equilibrium and promotes long-run efficiency. I conclude that urging freer trade on others is fine. But it would be a mistake to expect spectacular results,[72] and we should practice what we preach.

---

[70] There was a moderate drop in the last quarter of 1976 which was, however, more than made up by February 1977.

[71] Amended Articles of Agreement of IMF, Article IV, Sections 1 and 3 (see footnote 1).

[72] In the case of West Germany, the appeal to liberalize imports is directed to the wrong address. Import policy is made by the European Community (EC) in Brussels. It can be argued that the EC import policy should be liberalized, but the short-run balance of payments impact of such liberalization on the strong and weak currency members of the EC would be quite uncertain.

Postscript

After this paper was written, several important developments occurred in the international monetary area. On some of them I would like to comment briefly in this postscript.

(1) The United States quietly shelved its policy of bringing pressure on West Germany and Japan to adopt more expansionary policies than the governments of these countries thought advisable in view of the danger of intensifying inflation. The reasons for this shift are not difficult to divine. The West German and Japanese governments resisted being pushed into higher inflation, and then when the U.S. administration suddenly quashed the $50 tax rebate, largely on the ground that it would be too inflationary, the administration could not well ask other governments to assume risks of inflation which it had refused to take itself.

But the call for more rapid monetary expansion at home and abroad, which is in fact a call for higher inflation rates, can still be heard in many quarters. This is especially pronounced in Britain where some economists speak of deflation when the inflation rate declines from 25 to 15 percent. They in effect have adopted Latin American standards according to which there is deflation when prices rise by 20 percent or less, stability reigns when prices rise by 20 to 35 percent, and inflation begins at a 35 or 40 percent rise. Lord Robbins was moved to exclaim: "I confess that, as a Britisher, I am filled with shame when I hear reports that public personalities in my country are urging others to rates of expansion designed to help us out of our self-created difficulties."[1] Lord Robbins indicated that the criticized British invitations to inflate faster are addressed not only to West Germany and Japan but also to the United States.

(2) At the Economic Summit in London (May 1977), the pressure on low-inflation, strong-currency countries to accommodate their weaker neighbors by stepping up their expansionary policies was dropped. It was replaced by a pledge of strong economy countries to see to it that their stated growth targets are realized by adoption, "if needed," of "additional measures within prudent limits." What these additional measures are is not stated. But the Official Communiqué of the Economic Summit states flatly that "our most urgent task is to create more jobs while continuing to reduce inflation. Inflation does not reduce unemployment. On the contrary, it is

[1] Lord Lionel Robbins, "Domestic Goals and Financial Interdependence," opening address at the Frankfurt Monetary Conference, April 28, 1977. Reproduced in *Deutsche Bundesbank: Auszüge aus Presseartikeln*, no. 28, Frankfurt (May 8, 1977), p. 3.

one of its major causes."[2] The emphatic restatement, at the highest level, of the proposition that inflation does not provide a long-run solution to the unemployment problem is very welcome. But what happens if the actual growth rate falls below the stated target, as is so often the case? What "additional" measures are then to be applied? Those questions have not been answered. Suppose the pursuit of the stated growth target would lead to a more rapid rise in prices, as may well be the case. Inflation has been ruled out as a measure to stimulate growth and employment. What is to take its place?

In brief, how the twin objectives of reducing unemployment and inflation are to be achieved at the same time—in other words, how to tackle the dilemma of stagflation—is not indicated in the communiqué or in the official commentary. These problems cannot further be discussed here.[3]

(3) Unfortunately, the excessive stress of the previous policy on current-account deficits of the industrial countries which are to be achieved by rapid expansion—noninflationary expansion in the new version—continues to mar even the latest statements of the U.S. policy. Thus Michael Blumenthal in an otherwise excellent speech[4] at the International Monetary Conference in Tokyo (May 25, 1977) had this to say:

> The current account position of the U.S. has already shifted dramatically, from a surplus of $11 billion in the recession year 1975 to a deficit this year of perhaps $10 to $12 billion. [Since then the estimate of the expected deficit has been sharply raised.] That shift is making a major contribution to the stability of the international monetary system. . . . What is now required is a similar shift in the position of surplus countries such as Japan, Germany, Switzerland, and the Netherlands.[5]

---

[2] For text of Communiqué of Economic Summit and official Appendix to Communiqué see *IMF Survey* (May 16, 1977), pp. 152-55.

[3] They were discussed at some length in the 1976 edition of *Contemporary Economic Problems*.

[4] The secretary of the treasury stressed that "flexibility of exchange rates is essential for both surplus and deficit countries"; neither of the two groups should "resist market pressures" for change in their exchange rates; weak currency countries "should pursue stabilization policies which will provide a basis for sustained growth while reducing inflation"; the IMF should supervise exchange-rate policies of its members, and IMF assistance should be appropriately conditional, et cetera. All that is sound and reasonable and is in complete accord with the policy pursued by the previous administration.

[5] Official press release of Department of the Treasury, "Remarks by W. Michael Blumenthal, Secretary of the Treasury. International Monetary Conference, Tokyo, Japan, May 25, 1977."

The secretary realizes that the U.S. current-account deficit reflects U.S. capital imports: "We receive substantial inflows of capital from OPEC and elsewhere." But he did not say where all the capital should come from if the other rich countries followed the U.S. example and shifted into a heavy current-account deficit financed by capital flows "from OPEC and elsewhere." Is it desirable, one may ask, that the rich countries as a group import substantial amounts of capital not only from OPEC but also from poorer and less-developed countries?

There is, however, another interpretation possible. The quoted speech did not say what countries the speaker had in mind when he said the United States receives capital from OPEC *and elsewhere*. "Elsewhere" may refer to other industrial countries.[6] There have, in fact, been reports that capital is fleeing from European countries to the United States in substantial volume. This would explain the strength of the dollar, despite the large U.S. current-account deficit.

While Secretary Blumenthal took a relaxed view with respect to the large U.S. current-account deficit (rightly in my opinion), concern has been expressed in some quarters. The annual report of the Bank for International Settlements[7] warned that the large U.S. deficit may weaken the dollar and could cause troubles. Others see in the deficit a drag on output and employment. I would suggest that under floating these worries are exaggerated. The deficit is partly due to the fact that the U.S. economy has been recovering from the last recession faster than other industrial countries. This situation may well reverse itself when the cyclical expansion of the other industrial countries accelerates. Of course, nobody can precisely foresee the future pattern of these cyclical developments. And there are in addition the equally unpredictable capital flights from some foreign countries. Some of these influences can be expected to cancel out, and floating will take care of the rest.

As far as the drag on output and employment are concerned, it is true that if the current-account deficit disappeared—say, because of inflationary developments abroad giving U.S. industries an improved competitive position—it would constitute an expansionary stimulus for the U.S. economy. But the evaluation of such developments should be considered in the broader context of the overall monetary

---

[6] However, the interpretation of "elsewhere" as including less-developed countries is suggested by the fact that (as noted on p. 236 above) less-developed countries have been mentioned, along with Italy and Britain, as weak-currency countries that should be relieved of the "burden" of having to shoulder a disproportionately large share of the OPEC deficit.

[7] *Bank for International Settlements*, 47th Annual Report, Basle, June 1977, p. 4.

and other macroeconomic policies. The United States is engaged at present in the delicate policy of slowing down inflation without interrupting the ongoing cyclical expansion. In this picture the current-account deficit is just one item—not a negligible one to be sure, but one among many and not one of the large items. Inflation is still uncomfortably high and we should therefore be grateful for the contribution of the current-account deficit to the fight against inflation, although it may be a small one.

There is also the question of how to reduce the deficit. Nobody has proposed U.S. interventions in the exchange market to depress the dollar, probably because that would have inflationary effects. Pressure on other countries to expand and inflate faster has been officially abandoned. If inflation or expansion abroad reduced the U.S. current-account deficit, the inflationary impact on the United States is the same as an equivalent depreciation of the dollar. Other countries should observe the rules of the game of the floating system and refrain from manipulating exchange rates to "gain an unfair competitive advantage" and the Fund "shall exercise firm surveillance over the exchange rate policies of its member" (Article IV of the amended charter of the IMF). But nobody has suggested that the U.S. deficit is due, except perhaps marginally, to such misbehavior of foreign countries, and to the extent that a change in the exchange-rate policy of some foreign countries has an effect on the U.S. deficit, the inflationary consequences for the United States are the same as those of a general, equivalent depreciation of the dollar brought about by U.S. intervention in the exchange market.

Should the stance of monetary-fiscal policy be changed because of the current-account deficit? The orthodox reaction would be to tighten monetary-fiscal policy. But this would be an inappropriate application of a fixed-parity rule to the floating system. Under floating, unlike a fixed rate system, the short-run effect of tighter money would be uncertain, because higher interest rates might attract still more capital and thus drive up the exchange value of the dollar. But there is a more fundamental objection to that policy. At the present time the stance of monetary-fiscal policy is a delicate balancing act: it tries to keep inflation down without endangering the ongoing expansion. (The current-account deficit permits the pursuit of a slightly easier monetary-fiscal policy than otherwise would be advisable.) That delicate balance would be upset if monetary-fiscal policy were used to reduce the deficit.

This adds up to the recommendation of a policy of benign neglect for the balance of payments. Since it has been so often misunderstood, I hasten to add that benign neglect does not mean neglect of the danger of inflation or insensitivity to the evils of unemployment. What it does mean is that we should set targets of monetary growth and other policies which appear to be appropriate to achieve as far as possible the twin goal of keeping inflation in check and assuring steady expansion; we should pursue these policies consistently and change them when the domestic situation calls for a change, but we should let the exchange rate take care of the balance of payments; the tail should not be allowed to wag the dog.

Of one thing we can be sure. The current-account deficit will be seized upon by special interests as an argument for import restrictions. These pressures must be resisted. Only if extensively used would import restrictions have an appreciable effect on the current balance, and to the extent that restrictions do improve the balance they have the same inflationary effect as a devaluation. At the same time, import restrictions invite retaliation, disrupt the international division of labor, and thereby reduce overall efficiency and output. Economists are virtually unanimous that the problem of protectionism should not be confused with the problem of balance of payments adjustment.

Nor should the balance of payments problem be conjoined with energy policy as it is so often done. Even a much more efficient energy policy than the one now under consideration—a policy that is to say which stimulates production by deregulation, would not influence the volume of imports for a long time to come. It is altogether a basic mistake to link the balance of payments, which is largely a monetary phenomenon, with particular imports such as crude oil, coffee, or what not, however important these commodities might be.

(4) The seven "leaders" assembled at the London Economic Summit declared: "We reject protectionism—it would foster unemployment, increase inflation and undermine the welfare of our people." This is fine but the next paragraph says: "In this field [that is, in "multilateral trade negotiations"], *structural changes in the world economy must be taken into account.*" According to news reports, the italicized clause was a concession the American administration had to make to the French who wanted to reserve the right to support their ailing steel industry by restrictive measures. The official appendix to the communiqué is more explicit. It says: "Such progress [in eliminating trade barriers and 'avoidance of new barriers in the future'] should not remove the right of individual countries under existing international agreements to avoid significant market disrup-

tions."[8] What this turgid phrase means has been vividly revealed by American actions. The ink of London summit declarations was hardly dry when the imports of shoes, largely from less-developed countries, and of color television sets from Japan were drastically slashed by so-called voluntary quota agreements with foreign exporters.

There is much confusion about the nature of these "voluntary" export restraints forced on foreign producers, or Orderly Marketing Agreements (OMA) as they are deceptively called. Thus, under the headline "Carter's Trade Policy Is Marked by Aid at Home, No Protectionism," the New York Times (May 5, 1977) wrote the "new trade policy. . . tilts towards liberalism while satisfying the most urgent needs of import-injured workers." This description could be applied to the policy of trade adjustment assistance, a policy which tries to help business firms and workers who have been injured by imports to shift to other lines of production. However, the Times article refers to OMA and does not mention trade adjustment policy. OMA cannot be described as a liberal policy. On the contrary, most economists agree that it is one of the worst methods of import restriction because it forces foreign exporters to organize themselves as effective monopolies in restraint of trade and in exploitation of the American consumer. A 40 percent restriction of imports of color TV sets from Japan and 25 percent reduction of shoe imports from South Korea and Taiwan is equivalent to a sharp increase of import duties. While under the tariff method of import restriction the proceeds from the higher prices that the consumers have to pay flow into the coffers of the U.S. Treasury, under the OMA system the money goes to the foreign exporters. That is the reason why this method finds less resistance abroad than tariff increases. OMA is, in effect, a method of bribing foreign exporters to accept restrictions of trade at the expense of the American consumer and taxpayer.[9]

The OMA system has been very aptly described as "part of a pattern of creeping cartelization." According to the New York Times[10] administration spokesmen argue that "the selectivity and time limitations of the agreements erase the cartel-like features."

---

[8] Official Communiqué, IMF Survey, May 16, 1977, pp. 152 and 154.

[9] Depending on the precise administrative arrangements and on the haggling of the interested parties, some of the windfall profits may go to the domestic importers. It is one of the distasteful features of quantitative restrictions (as distinguished from import duties) that they eliminate competition, create windfall profits and thus open the door for bribery and corruption. Importers, as distinguished from producers and final consumers, are usually the most vocal and effective opponents of protectionist measures. Quantitative restrictions often tend to mute this opposition by letting importers participate in the spoils.

[10] New York Times, June 3, 1977.

These excuses are unconvincing. That the method is applied selectively—that is to say, to the principal supplier countries only—does not change the fact that the exporters in those countries are forced to organize themselves as a monopoly. In addition, selectivity is apt to distort trade by diverting imports to less-productive foreign sources. That the arrangements are supposed to be temporary is not much of a consolation, for experience has shown that such arrangements are extremely difficult to eliminate. Indeed, they are more difficult to eliminate than import duties because, in this situation, unlike in the case of duties, foreign exporters have a vested interest to keep their monopoly position. The OMA system establishes a de facto conspiracy of protectionist interests at home and monopolistic exporters abroad.

Economists in the administration are aware of the dangers of the OMA system. Thus Secretary Blumenthal was very apologetic about the shoe and television restrictions, excusing them as necessary to ward off more protectionist measures and expressing the hope that the system would not spread to other industries.[11]

The strength of protectionist sentiments in the United States was highlighted by a speech of the secretary of labor, Ray Marshall, to the Convention of the International Ladies Garment Workers Union on June 2, 1977. Secretary Marshall wants a global minimum wage imposed around the world—he mentioned South Korea and Taiwan as examples of low wage countries—to check the importation of cheap textiles into the United States. According to the *New York Times* the secretary committed the Carter administration to a campaign in the International Labor Organization, the IMF, and other international organizations to establish a "living wage" for everyone everywhere as part of President Carter's commitment to universal protection for human rights.[12]

There is hardly a chance that foreign governments will be foolish enough to seriously damage their economies and jeopardize their development by following the American example of imposing minimum wages which in the United States have greatly contributed to the shockingly high rate of unemployment among teenagers, espe-

---

[11] Report on press conference, *Washington Post*, June 3, 1977.

[12] *New York Times*, June 3, 1977. While the secretary did not mention a concrete figure for the global minimum wage, the *Times* suggested $1.00 an hour. According to Secretary Marshall the ruling wage is 41 cents an hour in the apparel industry in Taiwan and 32 cents in South Korea. In an editorial on June 5, 1977, the *Times* quickly threw its support to Secretary Marshall's preposterous protectionist proposals "before he is laughed off stage as some kind of international demagogue." Such is the economics dispensed in one of America's leading newspapers!

cially blacks, and other underprivileged workers. Therefore the probable consequence of the proposed American campaign would be the spread to other industries of the pernicious policy of "voluntary" export controls which Secretary Blumenthal hopes to avoid.

(5) The London Economic Summit was preceded by a meeting of the Interim Committee of the IMF in Washington, April 28-29, 1977. This committee, too, discussed "the world economic outlook" and reached the same conclusion as the economic summit. "The Committee expressed concern . . . about the persistence of higher levels of unemployment" but stressed the importance of "measures to combat inflation . . . [which] will make for a better record over time in terms of growth and employment."[13] How to wind down inflation and reduce unemployment at the same time was not indicated.

As far as the work of the Fund is concerned, the committee reached two important decisions. It decided to increase the lending capacity of the Fund by creating "a supplementary arrangement of a temporary nature called the emergency or Witteveen facility." A significant feature of the new facility is that "access to assistance . . . should be subject to adequate conditionality."[14] In practice this will probably mean that loans under the new facility will normally be part of a comprehensive stabilization plan. If many countries are willing to submit to IMF guidance and supervision the new facility could significantly enlarge the area of financial stability and thus stimulate more rapid growth in the world economy, provided, of course, that the Fund continues to sponsor sound financial policies.

The other decision of the committee was to accept the executive directors' proposal to establish "Principles of Fund Surveillance over Exchange Rate Policies." These principles will supersede, after the amended charter has gone into effect, the existing "Guidelines for the Management of Floating Exchange Rates," which were discussed earlier in the present paper.[15]

The new guidelines implement the provision of the amended charter that "the Fund shall exercise firm surveillance over the exchange rate policies of members." They apply "to all members whatever their exchange arrangements," not just to those whose currencies are floating. The new guidelines are on the one hand much more comprehensive than the old ones, but, on the other hand, are less detailed and leave much more scope to the judgment of the Fund.

---

[13] Official Communiqué, *IMF Survey*, May 2, 1977, p. 130.

[14] Ibid., pp. 130 and 133.

[15] See "Text of Executive Directors' Decision on Exchange Rate Policy Surveillance," *IMF Survey*, May 2, 1977, pp. 131-32.

There is no mention of "target zones" or "aggressive interventions," but "among the developments . . . [that] might indicate the need for discussion with a member" about the member's exchange rate policy are the following: "Protracted large scale intervention in one direction in the exchange market; an unsustainable level of official or quasi-official borrowing . . . or lending, for balance of payments purposes of restrictions on, or incentives for, the inflow or outflow of capital."[16]

All in all, the new proposals seem to offer a much more realistic approach to the problem of surveillance over exchange-rate policies than the old guidelines did. There are to be annual consultations with all members about their exchange-rate policies, and the managing director may at any time "initiate and conduct on a confidential basis a discussion with a member" about the member's exchange-rate policy, if, "taking into account any views that may have been expressed by other members," he finds that "there is a question of the observance of the principles."[17]

The new regulations would seem to imply a lot of work for the Fund. But since there are now annual consultations with all members anyway, the additional work should be manageable. And if abuses of exchange-rate management ("dirty floating" and "competitive depreciation or appreciation") are prevented or corrected, the additional effort will be well spent.

Postscript to the Postscript

Well after the preceding parts of this paper had been written, the administration again shifted its position. In contrast to the Treasury's relaxed attitude, Assistant Secretary of Commerce Frank Weil sounded the alarm about the large U.S. trade and current-accounts deficits. "The trade deficit problem could get out of hand," he said, and "something has to be done." He flatly rejected protectionist measures and is evidently afraid of protectionist pressures (*Journal of Commerce*, June 23, 1977). Then Secretary Blumenthal recanted his earlier relaxed statements: According to the *Wall Street Journal* (June 29, 1977) he emphasized his personal concern about the U.S. deficits and conceded that "the Treasury has been remiss in failing to underline the necessity for reducing the deficits." How is the deficit to be reduced? Import restrictions are ruled out. Export promotion is the answer. Mr. Blumenthal said, "We have to do everything to push our

---

[16] Article IV, Section 3 (a) of the amended charter of the IMF.
[17] "Text of Executive Directors' Decision," p. 132.

exports." Mr. Weil mentioned "vigorous" Export-Import Bank activity, retention of the DISC export tax incentive, a "revitalized" Commerce Department export promotion and marketing program, attempts at the Geneva trade talks to scale down foreign tariff and nontariff barriers to trade, et cetera (*Journal of Commerce*, June 23, 1977). Some of these measures are unobjectionable, though, as regards the balance of payments, ineffectual or only marginally effective. But outright subsidization of exports, even in the form of cheap special credits and tax advantages, could provoke retaliatory or countervailing measures abroad.

Strong-currency, low-inflation countries are again being urgently requested to expand faster, that is to say, to risk higher inflation rates, and/or to let their currencies appreciate. Foreign exchange markets strongly reacted by depressing the dollar, especially vis-à-vis the mark and yen. This, in turn, caused apprehension and led to central bank interventions both in the United States and abroad to strengthen the dollar. It must be doubted that scare talk followed by countervailing interventions in the exchange market is the right method of managing the float. The market if left alone would do a better job. As Edward Bernstein recently said: "If nothing is done," that is to say if the mark and yen are not pushed up by official interventions, "the exchange market will recognize that the dollar is overvalued. It will respond by shifting funds from the United States to other countries. That will bring down the rate of the dollar." [1] The market will probably conclude that the mark and yen are undervalued (vis-à-vis most currencies) rather than that the dollar is overvalued (vis-à-vis most currencies).

---

[1] Edward M. Bernstein *The U.S. Trade Deficit and the Floating Dollar*, Washington D.C., June 30, 1977 (mimeograph).

COORDINATION AND MANAGEMENT OF THE INTERNATIONAL ECONOMY: A SEARCH FOR ORGANIZING PRINCIPLES

Marina v. N. Whitman

Summary

The international economic system is at present in a state of disorder and transition, resulting from developments of the past few years that have created a break with the arrangements and institutions of the post-World War II era. The system of the future, like those in the past, will be based on some combination of four organizing principles: automaticity, hegemony, supranationality, and regionalism (pluralism). But it will be a mixture quite different from that of the Bretton Woods system, which was characterized by a foundation in economic liberalism and universalism, supported by strong American leadership, and by the unprecedented prominence of international economic institutions that are partly pluralistic and partly genuinely supranational.

Today, the concept of a liberal international economic system— one that is basically market-oriented and neutral in intent—is under serious challenge. Among the reasons are the reduced hegemony of the United States, the major supporter of this view in recent years, and the broadened economic responsibilities of governments in the industrialized nations, including an intensified concern with economic security and distributional equity. These concerns, and the increased government intervention in the domestic economy that has accompanied them, have given rise to severe tension between the vulnerability associated with international market integration and increased interdependence and the demand for national autonomy as regards the domestic economy. The third major factor is the increasing prominence and activism of the developing countries, which reject liberalism and reciprocity as bases for international economic arrangements and insist that a "new international economic order" must take the international redistribution of income as an explicit and primary goal.

The major focus of the industrialized nations at present is on the international organization of macroeconomic relationships, the management of interactions among national stabilization policies and aggregate levels of economic activity. The shift in the exchange-rate regime from pegged rates to managed floating was successful in introducing greater automaticity into the payments adjustment mechanism. But much of the operational asymmetry of the Bretton Woods system, arising from the key-currency role of the dollar, remains. And the insulation flexible rates provide against external disturbances is more limited than many had anticipated. Thus, interest in dampening the international transmission and magnification of economic disturbances has persisted, even intensified, and the development of international criteria for the conduct of exchange-rate policies has merged into efforts to develop mechanisms for the coordination of stabilization policies among those major industrialized nations that are active participants in managed floating.

Beneath the widespread agreement that more macroeconomic coordination is essential lie confusion and disagreement about what the phrase means. To some, it means simply intensified consultation, enabling each country to take account in its own macroeconomic planning of what its major partners are planning to do and what the results of their intended policies are likely to be. To others, it appears to imply that nations should modify their domestic aims and policies to conform to international requirements, as suggested by the current proposition that the strongest industrialized democracies—West Germany, Japan, and the United States—should gear their stimulative policies toward leading economic expansion for the rest of the world. Because views differ widely on whether a Phillips curve trade-off between inflation and unemployment actually exists or not, and because there may be a genuine conflict of interest between strong and weak countries if both believe that export-led growth is less inflationary than that arising from domestic stimulus, agreement on common criteria for the conduct of national stabilization policies will be difficult at best. Because of these fundamental difficulties involved in institutionalizing macroeconomic coordination while preserving scope for diversity among nations in their domestic objectives, such efforts are likely to be pursued primarily in the informal and pluralistic context of "summit" discussions at the political level among a relatively few major industrialized nations.

The organization of microeconomic relationships, involving international movement of goods, services, and factors of production, affects a much larger group of countries, indeed, potentially, all of them. Throughout most of the postwar period, the thrust of international trade arrangements has been the restoration of greater automaticity or scope for operation of market forces. Currently, however, the trade-liberalizing, nondiscriminatory approach of the GATT is under severe pressure. The reasons include the decline in the economic hegemony of the United States, the proliferation of preferential trading arrangements among regional blocs, and increased government intervention in both industrialized and developing countries. Trade relations between the two groups are complicated by confusion between the concept of economic development, involving structural change, elimination of barriers to market access, and potential for mutual gain, and that of pure income redistribution, which is inevitably a zero-sum game. At the same time, tariffs are being replaced as the major trade-distorting mechanism by nontariff barriers utilized by industrialized nations as part of their agricultural policies, their efforts to minimize economic adjustment costs against a background of domestic stagflation, or their efforts to correct for market failure in such areas as the maintenance of environmental quality. Because commercial policies and domestic policies are frequently inextricably intertwined where nontariff barriers are involved, traditional efforts to liberalize trade by reducing barriers "at the border" are ineffective, and cooperative market management is required to reduce trade distortions.

Unlike trade, international investment—involving the transfer of both capital and technology—is not supported by any consensus regarding the economic benefits it confers. In particular, the divergent views of industrialized and developing nations make the creation of international ground rules governing the operation of multinational enterprises and their treatment by governments highly unlikely at present. In any case, while agreed rules of behavior might give developing countries expanded access to factor markets, income redistribution via unrequited transfers can occur only as the result of government action. Such transfers can occur either indirectly, as in the case of price-raising commodity agreements (which involve efficiency costs and are likely to have an arbitrary distributional impact) or directly, through official development assistance or, potentially, through international "revenue-sharing" of the scarcity rents derived from competitive exploitation of the mineral resources of the seabed. But, along with the decline of American leadership in the sphere of foreign assistance, the American-bred rationale for such assistance has also fallen victim to disillusionment; nor, ironically, does continued American financial dominance enable this country to exert effective leadership in creating an institutional framework for both private and public transfers of capital and technology.

In sum, the various pressures operating to shape a new combination of organizing principles for the international economy confront us with several major challenges. One is the need to maintain U.S. leadership in and a sense of responsibility for creating a viable international economic system in the face of a diffusion of power such that many countries can today thwart effective international action but none alone can insure it. Second, current pressures of economic nationalism mean that supranationality, in the form of international agreements and institutions, is today required to preserve automaticity, that is, to insure room for the operation of market forces in the international arena, while also incorporating concerns with economic security and distributional equity. Third, while regional arrangemments are clearly an essential aspect of the international economy, there is an urgent need to reverse their present inward-looking drift toward discriminatory mercantilism. Finally, the absence of a hegemonial power and the enlargement of the international economy to encompass a much larger and widely divergent group of nations make the emergence of a formal, comprehensive international economic "constitution" unlikely. Rather, the development of a viable framework for organizing, managing, and coordinating international economic relations is likely to occur on a more informal and piecemeal basis than was the case at Bretton Woods.

Introduction

The first half of the 1970s marked a watershed in the international economic system, the framework for international transactions and economic relationships among sovereign nations. The formal termination of the international monetary system under which the world had functioned for a quarter-century after World War II; the OPEC-created international petroleum crisis and the spectre that it raised of proliferating commodity cartels; the worldwide transmission and intensification, first of virulent inflation and then of global recession; the strident rhetoric of the developing countries' demands for a "new international economic order"—all these developments created a discontinuity, a sense of sharp break with the postwar era. They created also a sense of confusion and crisis, of a disturbing lack of order in the international economy, of the breakdown of a system and inability to create a successor.

The welfare costs associated with this generalized sense of disorder need not be dwelt on at great length. If the state of confidence has a significant impact on the levels and growth rates of real economic variables (and there is considerable and mounting evidence that it does), then the present sense of uncertainty must inevitably be manifesting itself—negatively—in global levels and growth rates of income, investment, employment, and economic activity. Although the United States remains the largest and most self-sufficient of the non-Communist economies, recent events detailed above have impressed on us the extent to which developments abroad affect not only our trade and payments balances but also levels of prices, employment, and output in this country, and thus the connection between a well-functioning international economic system and a healthy domestic economy. Without a clear sense of framework, the probability of incurring the efficiency costs of a general retreat into autarchic or mutually frustrating behavior increases. Even greater potential costs lie outside the economic sphere. Without any ground rules, criteria for what constitutes acceptable behavior and mechanisms for reconciling divergent national economic interests, the cumulative irritations of particular disputes are certain, sooner or later, to spill over into the political arena and poison the well of international relations.

An understanding of the organizing principles most likely to serve the international economy effectively in the foreseeable future is important for at least two reasons. First, recent history gives repeated evidence that the United States will inevitably have to assume a leadership position if the international economic system (or systems) is to evolve and be refined, in whatever form, as the result of a conscious and deliberate process, rather than simply being shaped by the interaction of drift and exogenous disturbances. Second, as the line separating domestic from foreign economic policy continues to erode, an understanding of how the international economic system functions is an increasingly essential input into the process of formulating economic policy at home.

Analytically, one can conceive of at least four "pure types" of organizing principle for the international economy. One is automaticity: a system such as universal free trade, a pure gold standard, or freely flexible exchange rates, subject to some absolute and self-regulating discipline of the marketplace. A second is hegemony: the generally accepted dominance of a country or group of countries that plays one or more special roles in the system, enjoys unique privileges, and in turn takes on special responsibility for the viability and successful operation of the system. A third is supranationality: collective adherence to the decisions of one or more supranational institutions which would utilize some mixture of rules and the discretionary judgments of international civil servants to make the system operate effectively, much as national governments do today. The final mechanism is variously referred to as pluralism or regionalism. Here, the system consists of a complex of special regional relationships (themselves often hegemonial in nature), reconciled via the repeated hammering out of compromises among the divergent interests of roughly equal groups of participants, with the intensity of economic relationships being generally greater within rather than among groups.

Obviously, no actual international system ever functioned solely according to one of the "pure types" just listed. Indeed, it would be more accurate to talk not in terms of a single world economic system, but of a network of interrelated systems, each associated with one particular area or aspect of economic relationships among nations. Today, for example, the search for improved mechanisms of economic organization or coordination is focused mainly on the macroeconomic sphere. There is an intense interest in finding ways to mitigate the international transmission and magnification of national economic disturbances and to organize the macroeconomic interactions among national economies in such a way as to reduce global instability in prices and levels of real economic activity.

It is generally agreed, however, that such macroeconomic co-ordination, however it is defined and implemented, is likely to be confined to a relatively small group of the major industrialized countries. For a much wider circle of nations, the major issues are more traditional ones, having to do with the organization of microeconomic relationships among nations—international movements of goods, services, and productive resources—in such a way as to minimize friction, distortions, uncertainty, and resort to mutually frustrating beggar-my-neighbor policies to solve domestic problems. Here, again, the question of how to organize the system can be viewed at two levels: one, the articulation of ground rules for economic intercourse among the traditional participants in the global economic system—the industrialized nations of the non-Communist world; the other, the formulation of a framework for relationships between this group and the newer participants in the global economy, particularly the developing countries.

Organizing Principles: A Historical Perspective

Most judgments regarding the current organization of international economic relationships have as their reference point, either explicitly or implicitly, one of two historical eras: the pre-World War I period of the gold standard (1880–1914) and the post-World War II Bretton Woods era (1945–1971). A brief discussion of the particular mixtures or combinations of organizing principles that prevailed during those reference periods, and some understanding of the ambiguities and differences of opinion that surround such characterizations, even with the benefit of hindsight, may serve as a useful prelude to any attempt to analyze the present or predict the future in terms of the analytical taxonomy just presented.

The Gold Standard Era. The traditional view of the gold standard era stresses the very high degree of automaticity that prevailed in international economic relationships. Freedom of international trade and capital flows presumably allowed the principle of comparative advantage to operate relatively unfettered, moving both goods and factors of production from where they were cheap to where they were dear and maximizing world output, as traders sought to maximize profits and investors, rates of return. On the monetary side, "one sees the system . . . as simply an aspect of the market, guided by the unseen hand, owing allegiance to no authority. Central banks exercised no discretion. Their behavior was wholly determined by market forces and, perhaps, by certain customary rules." [1]

The contrasting view of the gold standard era stresses the strong elements of discretion and conscious governmental control involved in the operation of the system.[2] Within this general outlook are two subcategories. One stresses the strongly hegemonial aspects of the pre-1914 system, noting that patterns of trade, migration, and capital flows were determined far more by the existence of colonial relationships—particularly those of the British Empire—than by the operation of purely economic incentives. On the monetary side, this view stresses the role of discretionary monetary policy exercised by central banks in making the gold standard work and, in particular, the central role played by the Bank of England. Primarily because of the widespread use of the pound sterling as international money, "the influence of London on credit conditions throughout the world was so predominant that . . . by modifying the terms on which she was prepared to lend—the Bank of England could to a large extent determine

---

[1] Harold van B. Cleveland, "The International Monetary System in the Interwar Period," in Benjamin M. Rowland, ed., *Balance of Power or Hegemony: The Interwar Monetary System* (New York: New York University Press, 1976), p. 12.

[2] This view was advanced in the pioneering work of Arthur Bloomfield, *Monetary Policy Under the International Gold Standard, 1880-1914* (New York: Federal Reserve Bank of New York, 1959).

the credit conditions prevailing elsewhere."[3] Gold flows served, in this view, less as the engine of adjustment described in Hume's price-specie-flow mechanism than as a signal to central banks in major countries to adjust their own policies in an equilibrating direction. Furthermore, it is argued, the gold standard system was able to function successfully only because Britain ameliorated the harshness of the textbook adjustment process by substantial capital flows that financed the current-account deficits of her trading partners.[4] As the leader of the world economic system, Britain provided, in fact, a number of important public goods including, in addition to counter-cyclical capital flows, a market for distress goods guaranteed by free trade, the coordination of macroeconomic policies and exchange rates via the rules of the gold standard, and a lender of last resort in the Bank of England.[5] Britain was able to exercise such hegemonial leadership in an apolitical and almost invisible manner, it is argued, because of the general acceptance of the doctrine and practice of laissez-faire, which made other central banks willing to "follow the market" rather than attempting to exercise independent national monetary policies oriented toward domestic economic goals.[6]

The second variant of the "discretionary" view of the gold standard system holds that it was plural rather than hegemonic, that it "was composed of a number of currency blocs, within each of which a particular reserve currency held sway." The Bank of England was at most "primus inter pares" in "a multilateral system designed to preserve equilibrium among a few powerful centers," each autonomous and roughly equal to the others.[7] In sum, not only was the gold standard system a combination of three of the four pure types of organizing principles listed above—automaticity, hegemony, and pluralism—but there is substantial disagreement among economic historians as to which element dominated the mixture.

The Bretton Woods System. The international economic system that prevailed roughly from the end of World War II until the beginning

---

[3] John Maynard Keynes, *A Treatise on Money* (1930), in *The Collected Writings of John Maynard Keynes* (London: Macmillan, 1971), vol. 6, p. 274.

[4] Robert J. A. Skidelsky, "Retreat from Leadership: The Evolution of British Economic Foreign Policy, 1870-1939," in Rowland, ed., *Balance of Power or Hegemony*, p. 162.

[5] Charles P. Kindleberger, "Systems of International Economic Organization," in David P. Calleo, ed., *Money and the Coming World Order* (New York: New York University Press, 1976), p. 32.

[6] Cleveland, "The International Monetary System," p. 57.

[7] David P. Calleo, "The Historiography of the Interwar Period: Reconsiderations," in Rowland, ed., *Balance of Power or Hegemony*, pp. 240 and 256.

of the 1970s represented a quite different mixture, one characterized by the unprecedented prominence of a number of international economic institutions: the General Agreement on Tariffs and Trade (GATT), the International Monetary Fund (IMF), the World Bank (IBRD), and the Organization for Economic Cooperation and Development (OECD), to name only the most prominent. Indeed, the Bretton Woods system took its name from the place where several of these institutions were created. But they were supplemented, or in some cases threatened, by a variety of regional arrangements and relationships. Furthermore, the effectiveness of these institutions has been less in formulating rules or promulgating administrative decisions for members to obey than in providing a framework and an agreed set of procedures within which their disagreements could be discussed, negotiated, and minimized. "The institutions were seen, in other words, as an adjunct to the ordinary processes of diplomacy, not as a substitute for them." [8]

Compared with the world of the gold standard, the Bretton Woods system depended far less on automaticity and gave greater scope for the exercise of national discretion as regards both the use of commercial policies and the manner and timing of international adjustment in the monetary sphere. Although the system did incorporate some pressures for balance-of-payments adjustment, these operated almost exclusively on deficit countries, leaving surplus countries essentially exempt, and substantial payments disequilibria did in fact persist for considerable periods. There was no effective limitation, furthermore, on the freedom of countries to decide unilaterally when—and whether—to change their exchange rates.

Completing the mixture was a strong dose of hegemonial leadership by the United States. This country placed its unmistakable stamp on each of the international institutions listed above, imbuing each of them with a strong foundation in economic liberalism and multilateralism or nondiscrimination in trade and payments (contrasting, in the American view, with the discriminatory Imperial Preference System of Great Britain). In addition, the United States enjoyed substantial (although by no means unlimited) leadership in the management of economic relationships within the framework provided by these institutions. The hegemonial position of the United States, grounded at Bretton Woods on the wartime dependence of the Allied

---

[8] See Andrew Shonfield, "International Economic Relations of the Western World: An Overall View," in Andrew Shonfield, ed., *International Economic Relations of the Western World 1959-1971* (London: Oxford University Press for the Royal Institute of International Affairs, 1976), vol. 1, p. 126.

nations,[9] was later maintained partly by our substantial economic dominance throughout most of the postwar period and partly by the security umbrella that this country spread over her allies as a bulwark against Communist aggression.

This hegemonial position had two aspects. It meant that the United States took some special responsibility for maintaining the international economic system; we were frequently willing to subordinate our short-term economic interests, narrowly conceived, to the long-term political and economic advantages of strengthened economies in other free-world nations and of a viable trading and monetary system linking those nations. Other countries, in turn, were willing to accord the United States certain special privileges (primarily that of printing international money) as a concomitant of the special responsibilities we undertook for the military security and economic stability of the non-Communist world.[10]

Just as the gold standard system is subject to varying interpretations regarding the organizing principles that characterized it, so, too, is there a variety of opinion concerning the particular mixture of organizing mechanisms that underlay the Bretton Woods system. In part, confusion may have been engendered by the contrast between the formal symmetry of the Bretton Woods system and the very substantial degree of asymmetry that characterized its actual functioning. The Articles of Agreement of the International Monetary Fund are based on the principle of legal symmetry or equality in the rights and obligations of member countries. But in practice, one country, and one currency, assumed a variety of special functions from the very beginning, and the system moved rapidly toward reliance on a single key currency, the dollar, thus enabling the United States to finance its payments deficits by printing international money but effectively eliminating this country's freedom to change its own exchange rate without bringing the system down.[11] And, while in the trade sphere the United States pushed hard for universal tariff reduction and quota elimination through the GATT, it long tolerated one-sided bargains

---

[9] Many scholars place the beginning of American leadership back in the interwar period, stressing particularly the leading role of the United States in the Tripartite Monetary Agreement of 1936. See, for example, Cleveland and Skidelsky in Rowland, ed., *Balance of Power or Hegemony.*

[10] See Marina v. N. Whitman, "Leadership Without Hegemony: Our Role in the World Economy," *Foreign Policy*, no. 20 (Fall 1975), pp. 138-60.

[11] For a discussion of these functions, see Marina v. N. Whitman, "The Current and Future Role of the Dollar: How Much Symmetry?" *Brookings Papers on Economic Activity*, no. 3, 1974 (Washington, D.C.: Brookings Institution, 1974), pp. 539-83.

in which its own barriers were reduced far more than those of Europe and Japan.

This contrast between formal symmetry and operational asymmetry raises questions about the fundamental nature of the Bretton Woods institutions. Are they best regarded, as some observers hold, simply as agents of American hegemony, embodying American views of how the international economy should operate and serving to universalize American economic interests? Do they, in contrast, embody elements of true supranationality, imposing on all participants in the system, including the United States, certain rules of behavior and constraints on national policies? Or are they, finally, simply convenient loci for negotiation and compromise among a number of roughly equal powers or power blocs?

The problem of choosing among these alternative interpretations is exacerbated by the dual nature of the international institutions themselves. At the very top level, their structure is pluralistic rather than supranational: the governors and the executive directors of the IMF and the World Bank, for example, are the representatives of particular countries (or groups of countries) to whose political leadership they are responsible.[12] Yet these institutions are staffed by a corps of international civil servants, whose influence and expertise impart a genuine supranational element. The interactions among these two groups contribute to the subtlety and complexity of relationships between these institutions and their sovereign member states, particularly since nations may often be guided informally by criteria or judgments whose constraints they would never formally acknowledge.

Closely related to this question of the true nature of the international institutions is the question of when American hegemony began to wane significantly. Clearly, the ascendancy of the United States was great during the prolonged period of transition, which lasted throughout most of the 1950s, until the European countries resumed limited currency convertibility, the IMF and World Bank undertook full-fledged lending operations, and the system began to function more or less as had been envisaged at Bretton Woods.[13] In those early years the United States, its economy alone intact among those of the major industrialized countries, became both lender and exporter to the world, countenancing discrimination against its own

---

[12] There is also a significant hegemonial element at this level, since weighted voting gives the United States (and, more recently, the EEC nations as a group) veto power over major decisions in both institutions.

[13] See Alfred E. Eckes, Jr., *A Search for Solvency* (Austin and London: University of Texas Press, 1975), chapter 8.

goods in an effort to relieve the worldwide dollar shortage. During the first decade or so after Bretton Woods it was the United States, rather than the IMF, that made the bulk of loans to member countries in balance-of-payments difficulties and took the lead in urging other nations to adopt policies to stabilize their payments positions, including the substantial devaluations of most major currencies against the dollar in 1949. The World Bank, heavily dependent for resources on the U.S. capital market and inadequate to the task of financing European reconstruction, relinquished that task to the American Marshall Plan. The Organization for European Economic Cooperation (OEEC) and its successor organization, the OECD, were byproducts of the Marshall Plan, and the European Economic Community (EEC) came into being with strong American encouragement. During this period, the universalism envisaged at Bretton Woods was displaced by a variety of asymmetrical regional arrangements, each led or supported by the United States.

As the decade of the 1950s drew to a close, the transition period finally ended and the Bretton Woods system and institutions began their long-delayed full operation. In one view, this shift marked the institutionalization of American hegemony in an international system grounded in American principles of economic liberalism and non-discrimination and the conviction that expanded international trade and investment would serve as a major vehicle for both global economic progress and world peace. In this view, the regionalism embodied in the EEC was simply a vehicle for the ultimate multi-lateralization and integration of the world economy. In contrast, other observers argue that the end of the transition also heralded the decline of American hegemony. A major element in the decline, in this view, was the shift from "dollar gap" to "dollar glut" as the U.S. payments position weakened, its reserves shrank, and its liabilities to foreign official institutions increased over the 1960s. The increasing independence of the World Bank from U.S. capital markets, the declining importance of American foreign aid and the deterioration in relations between the United States and the developing world, and the increasingly inward orientation of the EEC, creating mounting American frustration, are cited as further evidence of the declining U.S. position. And, finally, even after the American-financed post-war reconstruction had been completed, the economies of Europe and Japan continued to grow far more rapidly than that of the United States.

Whenever the decline in the U.S. position in the world economy began, it was clearly well under way by the late 1960s. Accelerating inflation, a large and persistent negative shift in the balance on goods and services, and a drastic drop in the U.S. international liquidity ratio all served to make manifest the instabilities inherent in the "gold dollar standard" system about which Triffin had warned at the beginning of the decade.[14] Increasing friction in trading relationships between the United States and her partners in the industrialized world made two things clear: first, that the trade policies of other major nations and groups were diverging increasingly from the liberal and nondiscriminatory ideal promulgated by the United States; and, second, that the United States itself, increasingly insecure about its position in the world economy, was subject to mounting protectionist pressures at home and was clearly no longer willing to tolerate perceived asymmetries in market access in order to make the trading system operate more smoothly.

Modern Political Economy: The Challenges Today

While the international economic system of the future will of course be based on some combination of the organizing mechanisms described earlier, it will not be the same mixture as before. But if the hegemonial element will inevitably be less than in the Bretton Woods system, the question arises, Which of the other organizing mechanisms will take up the slack? Academic analysts and policy makers alike seem to agree that international institutions will have to play an enhanced role. But this apparent agreement conceals an important divergence of views. One approach, which might be characterized as "the American position," holds that in the absence of a generally accepted hegemony, the reconciliation of divergent interests and thus the viability of the system can be ensured only by the discipline of universal rules: some combination of the self-enforcing disciplines of the marketplace and the general application of requirements of the various international institutions, accompanied by effective sanctions against members who evade the disciplines or break the rules. The Europeans are more skeptical of American legalism and dubious that sanctions can be effectively applied to sovereign states without endangering the survival of the system itself. They stress the need to develop and expand international institutions to support more effectively the negotiation of divergent economic interests, the development of modes for cooperative management of domestic and regional-

---

[14] Robert Triffin, *Gold and the Dollar Crisis: The Future of Convertibility* (New Haven: Yale University Press, 1960).

bloc policies so as to minimize distortions of international transactions, and the avoidance of retaliatory escalation of particular disputes.[15]

The question of whether the international economic system will evolve in the direction of true supranationality embodied in agreements and institutions or whether the international economic institutions will serve rather as convenient mechanisms for expediting pluralistic relationships among power blocs, is an important one. But even more fundamental is the question of what role will exist for markets, that is, whether a liberal international economic order can survive. Until relatively recently, it was taken for granted that the nations participating in postwar international trading and monetary arrangements concurred in the view that a system aimed at minimizing the distortions and uncertainties created by the existence of national boundaries would maximize both global income and international harmony, the latter by providing a framework for accommodating diverse national objectives and depoliticizing the distribution of economic gains both among and within nations. That is, the system was laissez-faire in its orientation and neutral in its intent. The characterization must not be pushed too far, of course. Each of the participants in the system practiced, in varying degrees, interventionist policies as regards particular aspects of their own economies, and the system proved relatively flexible in accommodating the international ramifications of those policies. Nor did the goal of neutrality prevent wrangles over whose interests the system was serving and efforts to bend its operation in favor of one nation (or group of nations) or another. But the liberal thrust of the system was nonetheless clear and generally accepted.

Today, however, these fundamental principles are under serious challenge. The reduced influence of the United States, successor to Great Britain as the major promulgator of economic liberalism, is one reason. Another is a shift in the domestic economic goals of most industrialized nations from a primary focus on efficiency and growth to an intensified concern with economic stability and distributional equity. This shift has been accompanied by greater government interventionism and the intensification of countervailing pressures against a laissez-faire international framework, directed toward promoting market integration. Finally, a significant challenge comes from the increasing prominence and activism of the developing countries. Despite their heterogeneity, most of these newcomers share a belief that the "neutrality" of postwar international economic arrangements has operated to their disadvantage and are firm in their insistence on

---

[15] Shonfield, "International Economic Relations of the Western World."

the construction of a "new international economic order" that takes the international redistribution of income as an explicit and primary goal.

International Interdependence and Domestic Goals. If there were no economic interdependence among nation-states, the need for principles by which to organize or coordinate international economic relations would not arise; the greater is such interdependence, the more important do the nature and effectiveness of such organizing mechanisms become to the economic welfare of both nations and individuals. In fact, the concept of increasing interdependence has in recent years received acceptance so universal as to elevate the phrase to the status of a cliché. Yet the realities underlying the concept are blurred by lack of clarity regarding both the definition of *interdependence* and the time horizon implied in the term *increasing*.

As generally understood by economists, the term *interdependence* refers to the sensitivity of economic behavior in one country to developments or policies originating outside its own borders. The quantitative evidence most frequently adduced in support of statements about interdependence, however, is some ratio of international to total transactions, in particular, the foreign trade ratio (the average of exports plus imports divided by GNP).[16] This ratio has indeed been increasing for most industrialized nations. For the United States, for example, it increased from 4.5 percent in 1950 to 9.1 percent in 1975. A similar pattern of increasing foreign trade ratios is observed for most other major industrialized countries, for the OECD countries as a group, and (to the extent that data are available) for the world as a whole, whether the base date used for reference is 1950, 1947–1949, or 1938.[17] But the trade ratios for these latter years reflect the aftermath of world war or worldwide depression. The 1929 trade ratios, in those countries for which they are available, were considerably higher. Indeed, if that earlier year is used as the reference base, it looks as if much of the postwar increase in trade ratios represented

---

[16] For measures that incorporate international capital flows as well as trade, see Marina v. N. Whitman, "Economic Openness and International Financial Flows," *Journal of Money, Credit, and Banking*, vol. 1, no. 4 (November 1969), pp. 727–41.

[17] Walter S. Salant, "International Transmission of Inflation," in Lawrence B. Krause and Walter S. Salant, eds., *Worldwide Inflation: Theory and Recent Experience* (Washington, D.C.: Brookings Institution, 1977), p. 180.

simply a return to pre-Depression levels.[18] However, the spurt that these ratios have taken during the mid-1970s may have brought them above their 1929 levels in a number of major industrialized countries.

More critical than variations in interpretation caused by differences in time horizon, however, is the nature of the implied link between the relative size of international trade and investment flows and the degree of international interdependence.[19] Although a positive relationship is intuitively plausible, the connection is neither rigorous nor precisely defined. A close logical link does exist between interdependence, defined as sensitivity to external developments, and the degree of responsiveness of international trade and capital flows to variations in key economic variables, that is, the size of price and income elasticities (or marginal propensities). But only to the extent that such marginal propensities coincide with the average propensities represented by trade and investment ratios, or at least move together over time or among nations, are the latter measures likely to serve as useful proxies for one aspect of interdependence. As regards price responsiveness, the link is much more tenuous, since theory suggests an *inverse* relationship between the trade ratio and the magnitude of the associated price elasticities. Despite all these difficulties, trade ratios will doubtless continue to be employed as measures of interdependence, simply because the data required to calculate them over time or among nations are far more easily available than is the information necessary for comparable calculations of income and price elasticities.

An alternative link is between interdependence and international integration, as measured by the dispersion of various kinds of prices in different national markets. Generally, the smaller the dispersion, the higher the degree of market integration. Contrary to what one might expect, a recent investigation found that the average dispersion in prices of fifteen world-traded commodities in different national markets nearly doubled from 1957–1959 to 1967–1969. The dispersion of their annual changes was about the same in these two periods but had increased dramatically by 1972, after the breakdown

---

[18] Data for earlier years, although not exactly comparable with those cited here, indicate that such ratios were even higher, for most major industrialized nations, in the period preceding World War I. See Simon Kuznets, "Quantitative Aspects of the Growth of Nations: Level and Structure of Foreign Trade: Long-Term Trends," *Economic Development and Cultural Change*, vol. 15, no. 2, Part 2 (January 1967).

[19] For a detailed discussion of the points mentioned in this paragraph, see Robert D. Tollison and Thomas D. Willett, "International Integration and the Interdependence of Economic Variables," *International Organization*, vol. 27 (Spring 1973), pp. 255–71.

of the Bretton Woods system.[20] At a more aggregative level, looking at general price indexes, the picture regarding trends in the dispersion among national rates of inflation is somewhat ambiguous.[21] Some studies have shown no clear trend in such dispersion over the postwar period spanned by the Bretton Woods system. Others, utilizing different price indexes, time periods, or country samples have found some degree of convergence—that is, reduction in dispersion—for the period from the mid-1960s through the early 1970s as compared with the earlier postwar years before about 1963 or 1965. Most of them, however, have found some increase in the dispersion among national inflation rates beginning somewhere between 1971 and 1973—that is, after the end of the Bretton Woods monetary arrangements in mid-1971 or, in some cases, after the move to generalized floating early in 1973, though even here, the evidence is not free of ambiguity. The findings for interest rates in major industrialized countries have been similar.[22]

Even if empirical evidence does not substantiate unambiguously the widespread perception of a long-run secular increase in interdependence, there is no question that the complexities of managing interdependence have increased significantly. This is because of the very significant increase in the degree of government intervention in, and responsibility for, the domestic economy of the nation-state. This virtually universal development has created increasing tension between the vulnerability associated with interdependence (and its efficiency gains) and the political imperative of national economic autonomy.

Because this tension is a critical factor in evaluating the combination of organizing principles most conducive to the maintenance of a viable international economic system, it is worth examining briefly the changing and broadening criteria for economic welfare that underlie it.[23] The traditional criterion for judging an economic

---

[20] Salant, "International Transmission of Inflation," pp. 176-78.

[21] For detailed references see, Marina v. N. Whitman, "International Interdependence and the U.S. Economy," in William Fellner, ed., *Contemporary Economic Problems, 1976* (Washington, D.C.: American Enterprise Institute, 1976), note 34.

[22] Dennis E. Logue, Michael A. Salant, Richard J. Sweeney, "International Integration of Financial Markets: Survey, Synthesis, and Results," in Carl A. Stem, John H. Makin, and Dennis E. Logue, eds., *Eurocurrencies and the International Monetary System* (Washington, D.C.: American Enterprise Institute, 1976), pp. 91-137 and Salant, "International Transmission of Inflation," pp. 169-79.

[23] For a similar but much more detailed discussion of these criteria, see: C. Fred Bergsten, Robert O. Keohane, and Joseph S. Nye, "International Economics and International Politics: A Framework for Analysis," in *World Politics and International Economics*, ed. C. Fred Bergsten and Lawrence B. Krause (Washington, D.C.: Brookings Institution, 1975), pp. 26-36.

system or set of arrangements is, of course, in terms of its micro-economic efficiency—whether it promotes the most efficient allocation of a given stock of factors of production. Even here, long-recognized sources of divergence between the most efficient and the market-determined outcome have received increasing emphasis in recent years: the existence of market power or of external economies or diseconomies calling for government intervention to eliminate distortions. Much more important, of course, is the postwar emergence of the Keynesian or macroeconomic concept of efficiency in terms of full employment and price stability and the view that the workings of the marketplace must be supplemented by government stabilization policies if this aspect of efficiency is to be maximized. The exercise of active national monetary and fiscal policies directed toward these domestic goals renders the "automatic" adjustment mechanism of the gold standard unworkable and sets up pressures to insulate a country against those integrative forces which might reduce the effectiveness of such policies in achieving the goals for which they were established. The tension thus created reflects a divergence between the requirements of microeconomic and macroeconomic efficiency. The former calls for integration of national economies, the latter (in the absence of a world central bank and fiscal authority) for autonomy of national stabilization policies. In addition, national macroeconomic efficiency may be pursued via beggar-my-neighbor policies that reduce global economic welfare.

In addition, economic security and income distribution have been added to the economic criteria by which modern governments are judged, with distributional equity defined in some cases as the provision of a minimum living standard for all and in others as a reduction in income inequalities at all levels. Most recently, the "quality of life" (or the need to internalize external diseconomies associated with the growth process) has joined national security as a major "noneconomic" goal.

Each of these concerns impinges importantly on the way governments formulate their policies regarding international transactions, and thus affects the optimal combination of organizing mechanisms for the international economy. Because changing patterns of international trade and investment are a highly visible source of disturbance to the domestic economy, governments may intervene to reduce the instabilities and adjustment costs thus created. Similarly, because transactions affect different individuals, industries, regions, and factors of production differently, governments may alter the environment in which they take place in the interest of achieving or maintaining particular domestic distributional goals. Concern with national security may lead governments to favor high-cost but low-risk sources of supply, or more expensive self-sufficiency, in particular areas, or to undertake international arrangements that will enhance the economic strength of allied nations, even if they entail economic costs. And, finally, concerns about the quality of life and, particularly, different levels of concern in different nations, may alter worldwide patterns of production, trade, and investment and create an additional source of potential conflict among nations.

In sum, the broadened concerns of governments have created countervailing pressures against a laissez-faire international framework directed solely toward promoting market integration. To look at the issue somewhat differently, the weight of public goods appears to have increased relative to that of private goods in the welfare function of the modern citizen. And, whereas the optimal domain for transactions in private goods is the world, the situation vis-à-vis public goods is more complicated. Here the efficiency losses generally associated with fragmentation must be set off against the welfare gains that arise from accommodating differences in national preferences or demands for such goods. And such differences can be accommodated only if national governments have autonomy in the provision of such public goods—that is, in the establishment of stabilization, distributional, and regulatory goals. This trade-off, and the tensions it creates, is fundamental to any evaluation of the international economic system.

Instability and Transmission in the World Economy. Under ordinary circumstances, international economic integration can be expected to have a stabilizing impact on individual national economies. That is, if the shocks that cause economic fluctuations were generated by a random process, the risk-pooling involved in large numbers (which underlies any form of insurance) would lead us to expect that the relative magnitude of fluctuations in the global economy would be smaller than the average magnitude experienced by individual countries. This suggests, in turn, that increased integration should, on average, reduce the magnitude of national fluctuations.

In recent years, however, a competing view of the relationship between stability and integration has come to the fore. Economic disturbances, in this view, are systematic rather than random, and therefore the damping effects of the risk-pooling argument do not apply. Rather, asymmetries in economic behavior or policy responses cause the international economic system to transmit economic disturbances from one country to the other in a manner that magnifies them in the transmission process. If this is so, then interference with international market processes may be called for on the grounds of promoting domestic macroeconomic stability.

Empirical verification of a positive relationship between interdependence and instability has generally been approached through efforts to demonstrate that business cycles in industrialized countries have been increasingly synchronized in recent years. This is so despite several weak links in the chain of reasoning involved. Convergence can occur for reasons other than increased international transmission; increased interdependence might, under certain circumstances, produce less observed synchronization rather than more, and the degree of synchronization is not the only, nor necessarily the most important, determinant of global economic fluctuations.[24] Even leaving these caveats aside for the moment, the empirical evidence regarding changes in the degree of dispersion of cycles in real economic activity is fraught with ambiguity. For one thing, there is a wide variety of potential proxy variables to choose from, each with its own technical weaknesses. The fact that such cyclical fluctuations take place around underlying growth trends, which themselves differ among countries, also complicates interpretation of the results.

The notion of increasing international synchronism is not a new one; such a long-term trend was noted, and its roots in interdependence analyzed, by the father of modern business cycle analysis in 1927.[25] Among the empirical investigations of this question for the postwar era, most have found no long-term secular trend in the dispersion of real GNP growth rates, changes in industrial production, or "potential output gaps" among major industrial countries.[26] The most detailed and exhaustive of the empirical studies did, however, discern the sort of changes in dispersion among the potential output gaps of twelve major industrialized countries that had been anticipated a priori. That is, the evidence presented there indicates some decline in the dispersion—or increase in the synchronization—of real cycles between 1952–1957 and 1964–1970, presumably as the result of increasing integration, and then a decrease in synchronization between

---

[24] For discussion of these points, see Charles Pigott, Richard Sweeney, and Thomas D. Willett, "Aggregate Economic Fluctuations and the Synchronization of Economic Conditions among the Industrial Countries," U.S. Department of Treasury Discussion Paper, 1976, paper presented at Department of Treasury Seminar on Exchange Rate Flexibility, February 26-27, 1976.

[25] Wesley C. Mitchell, *Business Cycles: The Problem and Its Setting* (New York: National Bureau of Economic Research, 1927), pp. 446-47.

[26] Pigott, et al., "Aggregate Economic Fluctuations" and references cited there.

the latter period and 1971–1974.[27] This decrease in synchronization, which would be expected to occur as the result of the shift from pegged to flexible exchange rates, apparently prevailed despite the impact of a major exogenous shock common to all the countries in the sample; the oil embargo and price increases of 1973–1974. This last piece of evidence suggests that, whether or not there was any consistent trend toward increased synchronization during the Bretton Woods era, the change in exchange-rate regime that occurred in the early 1970s is likely to promote reduced rather than increased synchronization in the future.

Finally, the degree of international synchronization would determine the magnitude of world economic fluctuations only if the size of fluctuations in individual countries were constant. In fact, some recent research suggests that the size of fluctuations in individual countries, and particularly in the United States, has been the major factor determining the amplitude of world cycles over the period 1956–1974.[28] This same study, contrary to widespread perceptions, found no statistical evidence that economic volatility, as measured by the variability of quarterly industrial production (both levels and changes), has risen secularly over the past two decades. The data indicated that, for the OECD nations as a group, such volatility has indeed increased in recent years (1968–1974) as compared with the mid-1960s (1962–1968), but that it was no higher in the more recent period, and perhaps lower, than in 1956–1962. This evidence, while it should be regarded as tentative rather than definitive, lends credence to the view that the extreme fluctuations in economic activity the world has suffered from in recent years are attributable to a series of unusually severe and highly correlated exogenous shocks rather than to long-run shifts in the structure of the world economy that are likely to persist into the future.

New Actors and Changing Roles. In addition to the significant developments in political economy just outlined, any discussion of the organizing principles of the international economic system must take account of the changing cast of characters involved. At Bretton Woods, the United States was clearly the dominant force, with Great Britain and, to a lesser extent, the Soviet Union (which ultimately failed to ratify the Bretton Woods agreements), playing important but

---

[27] Duncan Ripley, "Cyclical Fluctuations in Industrial Countries" (International Monetary Fund, 1976; processed). In contrast, the Pigott et al. study, based on earlier work by the OECD, found relatively high synchronization in 1971 and 1974.

[28] Pigott, et al., "Aggregate Economic Fluctuations."

distinctly subordinate roles. And, with some relatively minor modifications, it was the American blueprint, grounded in American views about how the international system should be organized, that became the basis for the postwar international framework. Since that time, the number of nations participating in the system has vastly increased, power relationships have altered, the bases of power have become more diffused and complex, and a number of entities other than individual nations have emerged as significant factors to be reckoned with.

This reduction in the economic leadership of the United States has recently been spurred by the diffusion of the bipolar focus created by the Cold War, but it has its roots also in a much more gradual decline in the importance of the United States in the world economy over the past quarter-century. Although the United States remains the world's largest economy, with a GNP accounting for nearly half of the OECD total, its share in world GNP, world trade, international reserves, world production of such major industries as steel and motor vehicles, and world consumption of industrial raw materials have all declined significantly over the period. And, while in the immediate postwar period the United States was the richest country in the world by a substantial margin, today a number of countries equal—and a few even surpass—the United States in income per capita.

There are, of course, exceptions to this pattern of a declining world share: the United States is today a more important agricultural exporter than ever before, and it continues to hold well over half of the total direct investment claims of the world's major capital-exporting nations. Continued American dominance is most significant in the financial sphere, as evidenced by the leading role played by foreign branches of U.S. banks in the expanding Eurocurrency market, and by the fact that one unexpected result of the international monetary upheavals of the past few years has apparently been to place the world more firmly than ever on a dollar standard.

The increasing share of the "rest of the world" in the global economy has been accompanied by a significant increase in the openness of the United States, and therefore in its sensitivity to influences from abroad. The ratio of foreign trade in goods and services to GNP increased gradually from 1947–1949 to 1967–1969, and then nearly doubled, in nominal terms, between the latter period and 1974. This was a far larger percentage increase than was experienced by any other OECD country, albeit from a very small base. The share of foreign earnings in the profits of U.S. nonfinancial corporations has nearly tripled since 1950 and today accounts for about a quarter of total profits. The assets of foreign branches of U.S. banks have grown far more rapidly than those banks' domestic assets over the past fifteen years, and today international operations account for half or more of the total earnings of a number of the largest U.S. banks. The proportion of U.S. gross public debt held by foreign and international investors leaped from less than 10 percent over the period 1958–1970 to more than 20 percent in 1971–1973. Finally, the United States is becoming dependent on imports for more than half its supplies of an increasing number of vital industrial raw materials, thus enhancing its potential vulnerability if producer nations are successful in forming OPEC-like cartels to exploit their potential oligopoly power. Responding to these developments, the United States has come to view interdependence increasingly as a two-way phenomenon. The result is a growing concern with the impact on the domestic economy of foreign economic policies and developments abroad, along with an increasing reluctance on the part of the United States to subordinate its own short-term economic interests to the maintenance of a viable and effective international economic system.

Far more dramatic than the decline in the relative economic position of the United States has been the increase in the economic positions of two nations that were not even present at Bretton Woods because they were still at war with the Allied participants—Germany and Japan. The rapid growth of output and productivity in these nations, along with the strength of their international trade, payments, and reserve positions, has made them mini-economic superpowers, and many suggestions for the restructuring of the international economic system would move them into a tripartite leadership role together with the United States.[29] But for both economic and political reasons—in which the constraints imposed by their relationships with the United States and the Soviet Union doubtless play a major role—these two nations have proved reluctant recruits to leadership, making it clear that they have no intentions of allowing the mark or yen to become major international currencies, for example, and continuing to look to the United States for initiative in the global economy. Nonetheless, the emergence of West Germany and Japan into their present positions of economic prominence underscores a broader shift. In contrast to the immediate postwar situation, in which a single strong creditor nation, the United States, confronted a world of weak debtors, the industrialized world is now more evenly divided into "strong" and "weak" nations (the former including West

---

[29] A variant is the idea of trilateral leadership, exercised collectively by the nations of North America, Western Europe, and Japan.

311

Germany, Japan, Switzerland, and the United States; the latter, Italy, the United Kingdom, and, at present, France) with divergent roles in, and demands on, the international economic system.

At the same time, the role of the developing nations in the international economic system has increased significantly. A number of "middle income" developing countries—including Korea, Mexico, Singapore, and Taiwan, for example—have become significant producers and exporters of a variety of manufactured consumer goods. Others, some of them still relatively undeveloped, are gaining importance as sources of important industrial raw materials. These include not only the rich oil-producing nations of the Middle East but also nations up and down the income scale: Ghana, Jamaica, Nigeria, and Venezuela, to name only a few. Linked to the industralized countries by both the products they export and the investment capital they absorb, such nations are bringing to bear on the international economic framework pressures very different from those exerted by the developed countries. Finally, the Communist nations, initially cut off almost completely from economic relations with Western countries by the *cordon-sanitaire* of the Cold War, have gradually been rejoining the global economy. As trade and investment expand between Eastern and Western Europe (although so far not, on any significant scale, with the United States), increasing consideration is being given to ways in which the international institutions might be adapted to encompass some of these nonmarket economies.

Another important group of new participants are the multinational corporations themselves. Such enterprises both transcend the domains of the nation-state, serving as powerful agents of global economic integration, and at the same time are themselves frequently the source of friction between sovereign states or the vehicles employed by nations in efforts to appropriate for themselves a larger share of the fruits of the global economy. A second group of nonnational participants are the regional blocs or groupings of nations that have come into existence since World War II. These range all the way from the well-established and relatively comprehensive EEC, which had its beginnings as a customs union but has since become considerably more, to such single-purpose associations as OPEC and its less successful imitators, and to such broad and relatively diffuse organizations as the OECD, encompassing the industrialized nations, and UNCTAD, which is the forum in which the otherwise highly diverse developing nations have come together to express common economic concerns and demands on the international system. Finally, the Bretton Woods institutions themselves have become participants, shaped by their member countries and yet in turn affecting the policies and behavior of these members in significant ways.

The altered roles of various participants in the international economic system, as well as the advent of new non-national participants, have at least two broad implications for the functioning of that system. The first is that, because of both the reduced hegemony of the United States, the chief proponent of universalism and non-discrimination in the postwar economic system, and the emergence and proliferation of regional groups, special regional arrangements to deal with particular issues or problems will inevitably have to supplement global rules and institutions.[30] Some degree of regionalism would be desirable in any case, simply because of the high costs and increased complexity of involving large numbers of vastly unequal countries in the solution of issues of major importance to only a few. Rather than resisting regional arrangements, it would be more productive to try to ensure that they are consistent with a general framework of criteria for acceptable behavior or, where this is not possible at the outset, that they at least approach such consistency over time.

The second important point is that the system has far fewer "free riders" than it did in the early postwar years, when few nations other than the United States were—or felt—individually constrained in their behavior by its potential impact on the viability of the international system as a whole. Today, with economic power considerably more diffused, no country can guide the functioning of the system single-handedly, but many possess the capacity to prevent or interfere with its effective functioning. Instead of regarding themselves essentially as atomistic units in a competitive world, many nations now must evaluate their own actions in oligopolistic or game-theoretic terms, taking account of the impact on the system as a whole and on the resulting feedback to their own economies.[31]

Macroeconomic Management: Insulation and Coordination

The idea of macroeconomic coordination, in the sense of the management of international interactions among national stabilization policies and aggregate levels of economic activity, would have been an alien one in pre-Keynesian days, when such matters were left pri-

---

[30] See Ernest H. Preeg, *Economic Blocs and U.S. Foreign Policy* (Washington, D.C.: National Planning Association, 1974).

[31] Even the OPEC nations appear to have made this transition. Contrast their unconstrained approach to price-raising in 1974 with their much more cautious behavior in 1976-1977, following the plunge into global recession.

marily to the workings of the marketplace, at the national as well as the international level. Today, however, increased policy interdependence has combined with the stubborn persistence of stagflation in most industrialized nations to make such coordination the central focus of concern among this group, as evidenced, for example, by the primacy of this topic at the London summit discussions held in May 1977.[32]

It is in the macroeconomic arena, furthermore, that two of the most dramatic shocks to the international system have occurred: the apparently abrupt termination of the pegged-rate international monetary system and the worldwide transmission and magnification, first of virulent inflation and then of severe recession, in 1973 and 1974. The jolt that accompanied the first of these developments was particularly great because, of all the aspects of postwar international economic relationships, the international monetary arrangements drawn up at Bretton Woods came closest to qualifying as a formal system based on an explicit constitution (the IMF's Articles of Agreement).

Goals for the Monetary System. Three major goals underlay the shift in the international monetary system that took place in the early 1970s. They were: (1) the introduction of greater automaticity and flexibility into what had become a sticky and inadequate international payments adjustment mechanism; (2) the achievement of a greater degree of economic insulation among nations, thus enhancing national autonomy in the formulation of macroeconomic policy; and (3) a reduction in the operational asymmetry of the system arising from the key-currency role of the dollar.

(1) *Greater automaticity.* The change in the exchange-rate regime has indeed introduced greater automaticity into the payments adjustment process, in the form of greater flexibility of exchange rates, particularly among the major industrialized nations. This development has made possible a more realistic valuation of the dollar, whose ability to adjust vis-à-vis other currencies was severely inhibited by the key currency functions it served under the Bretton Woods regime. This substantial correction (some would argue, overcorrection) of the long-term overvaluation of the dollar led to improvement in the underlying competitive position of U.S. goods and services, thus making an important contribution to the neutralization

---

[32] This section and the one that follows make use of material taken from Marina v. N. Whitman, *The Viability of the International Economic System: Some Issues for U.S. Policy*, Essays in International Economics, no. 121 (Princeton, N.J.: Princeton University, International Finance Section, 1977), where some of the issues touched on here are discussed in more detail.

of growing protectionist pressures at home and to the political feasibility of continued U.S. support for a liberal international trading system. It has also helped to retard the growth of American direct investment abroad and to accelerate foreign direct investment in this country and thus may relieve pressure for curbs on such investment exerted, paradoxically, both by the EEC nations and by organized labor in the United States. Finally, the change in the exchange-rate regime has slowed the rapid—and inflationary—increase in world reserves associated with the very large U.S. deficits on the official reserve transactions basis in 1970–1972, and has also alleviated the very large flows of speculative funds across national boundaries, which created severe difficulties for the conduct of monetary policy in a number of countries in the early 1970s.

The shift toward greater automaticity in the international monetary system has also substantially alleviated the problem of controlling the aggregate volume of international reserves. This has *not* been accomplished through any progress toward the goal stated in the IMF's 1974 "Outline of Reform," and confirmed in the 1976 amendments to its Articles of Agreement, that "the SDR will become the principle reserve asset," [33] which would, by implication, make the IMF a world central bank in the sense of an issuer of international money. Of world reserves totaling more than SDR 220 billion at the end of 1976, less than 9 billion were in the form of SDRs, and dollars remained the primary vehicle of reserve growth. Nonetheless, global liquidity management is far less of a problem today than it was under conditions of pegged rates and the creation of apparently excess U.S. dollar liquidity in the waning days of the Bretton Woods system, culminating in the veritable explosion of dollar reserves in 1970–1972. In part, the advent of the OPEC countries as the major reserve-gainers, with their high average propensities to save and preference for dollar assets, eliminated the "dollar overhang" and reduced the inflationary potential of reserve increases. More fundamental, however, has been the introduction of consumer sovereignty as regards the size of a nation's international reserves. The move to managed floating made reserve-accumulation voluntary rather than mandatory; countries today have the alternative of allowing the foreign exchange rate to move to clear the foreign exchange market, without the political difficulties associated with official revaluations or devaluations under the Bretton Woods system. Floating today is managed rather than free, and a need for international reserves remains, but the

---

[33] International Monetary Fund, "Outline of Reform," in *International Monetary Fund: Documents of the Committee of Twenty* (IMF, 1974), p. 15.

advent of a more effective international adjustment mechanism has very substantially reduced, if not entirely eliminated, the need to provide supranational control of the volume of global liquidity.

The increased automaticity of the adjustment mechanism has had problems of its own, of course. In particular, floating rates initially displayed considerable short-term instability, more, in some cases, than appeared to be warranted by underlying economic factors. But the greater correspondence between changes in rate relationships and divergences among national economic trends over the past two years supports the view that the initial large fluctuations may have been attributable, not only to the intensity of the economic disturbances that affected the world economy in 1973–1975, but also to two other transitional factors: the "learning behavior" frequently associated with a period of transition from one environment to another and large one-time adjustments of portfolios as official and private asset holders attempted to correct the distortions produced by a prolonged period of cumulative disequilibrium in exchange-rate relationships.

Finally, it must be emphasized that the present exchange-rate arrangements, although more responsive to market forces than the pegged rates of the Bretton Woods era, are far from the fully automatic, freely flexible rates of the textbooks. For one thing, relatively few countries are actually allowing their currencies to float. In its 1975 *Annual Report*, the IMF noted that, of 122 member countries, only 18 were floating either independently or jointly.[34] These 18, however, represent 70 percent of the total trade of member countries; in effect, they are the major industrialized nations. Of the remainder, the great majority are pegging their rates to the U.S. dollar, a shrinking but still significant number to the pound sterling, some to the French franc, and some to the SDR or an alternative form of currency "basket."[35] Furthermore, those countries listed as "floating jointly" are the remnants of the EEC snake, effectively pegged to the West German mark. Thus, there is a strong element of regionalism, in formal or informal currency blocs, in today's international monetary arrangements. Finally, among the actual floaters, the system is one of managed floating, with some governments undertaking substantial intervention in foreign exchange markets.

(2) *Limited insulation.* The fact that floating is managed rather than free may help to account for the fact that the insulation afforded

---

[34] IMF *Annual Report* (Washington, D.C. 1975), p. 24.

[35] As of June 1974, the numeraire of the SDR was changed from monetary gold to a weighted "basket" of sixteen leading currencies. See *IMF Survey* (June 17, 1974), pp. 177-85.

by the new exchange-rate arrangements appears to be substantially more limited than had been widely anticipated or than is suggested by simple Keynesian economic models. For, as was noted earlier, while the change in the exchange-rate regime has apparently been accompanied by some increase in the dispersion of national inflation rates and, perhaps, of national fluctuations in real economic activity as well, a considerable common element remains. Among the possible explanations for this phenomenon is the fact that much of the continued synchronization may be due not to international transmission per se, but to the strength of the common shocks that struck all industrialized countries simultaneously in 1971–1974. Furthermore, certain institutional factors and policy responses common to most industrialized countries tend to serve as transmission channels for world inflation even under floating rates. Among these are the tendency of monetary authorities to "accommodate" imported inflation by preventing a fall in nominal incomes in the face of a real-income decline caused by worsening terms of trade and the demand-shift inflation caused by the uneven sectoral impact of a rise in foreign prices and the resulting change in the exchange rate.

Most fundamentally, the expectation of complete insulation under flexible rates is generated by models that ignore international capital flows. More complex models indicate that flexibility cannot be expected to abolish interdependence in a world of capital mobility. In fact, depending on the particular kind of foreign disturbance involved, the structural characteristics of the economies involved, and the type of stimulus to which capital flows are most responsive, the international transmission process could even, under some circumstances, be magnified rather than dampened by rate flexibility.[36] Thus, the fact that the international transmission of disturbances appears to have been reduced but not eliminated by the shift to managed floating should not be surprising.

(3) *Continuing asymmetry.* Finally, as regards a reduction in the asymmetry or dollar-hegemony associated with the Bretton Woods system, the results are mixed. In one sense, the world is more completely on a "dollar standard" than ever before, and the special functions performed by the dollar as a key currency remain essentially undiminished in most respects. At the same time, the abandonment of parity obligations has reduced certain increasingly troublesome

---

[36] For a survey of the vast literature on this subject, see Edward Tower and Thomas D. Willett, *The Theory of Optimum Currency Areas and Exchange-Rate Flexibility.* Special Papers in International Economics, no. 11 (Princeton, N.J.: Princeton University, International Finance Section, 1976), chapter 5.

asymmetries in the Bretton Woods system. In particular, it has modified the disproportionate impact exerted by U.S. monetary policy on the world money stock because of its reserve-currency role and the "automatic sterilization" of the effect of the U.S. payments deficit on its own money supply that occurred whenever other countries held their foreign exchange reserves in the form of U.S. treasury bills or deposits in U.S. commercial banks. The United States exerted such a strong influence on monetary conditions and prices abroad partly because funds that flowed out of this country as ordinary money entered other countries as "high powered money" (part of their monetary base) and partly because its reserve-currency role made it "the only country that did not (or could afford not to) care seriously about the effect of its price level on its external position." [37]

Today, however, with exchange rates more responsive than before to developments in commodity and asset markets, the situation is reversed: It is now a question of the degree to which the United States, as well as other countries, must worry about the effects of changes in its external position, reflected in changes in its exchange rate, on the domestic price level. And, despite the relatively small size of its foreign sector, the United States clearly does not feel immune to the impact of changes in its effective exchange rate on its domestic price level. Furthermore, although the dollar remains the major source of global reserve increases and automatic sterilization still occurs, it arises from the voluntary decisions of surplus-country central banks regarding the desired composition of their asset portfolios rather than as a byproduct of exchange-market intervention conducted in fulfillment of nations' parity obligations under the IMF Articles of Agreement.

Considerable asymmetry remains under managed floating, however. The developments of the past five years have borne out Cooper's initial prediction that many of the special functions of the dollar would persist in the new system, and that the creation of a genuinely symmetrical system would be extremely complicated and costly. [38] The dollar continues to serve, for example, as the world's principal intervention currency, which means that the value of the dollar in exchange markets can be affected—at times significantly—by devel-

---

[37] William D. Nordhaus, "The Worldwide Wage Explosion," *Brookings Papers on Economic Activity*, no. 2, 1972 (Washington, D.C.: Brookings Institution, 1972), p. 459.

[38] Richard N. Cooper, "The Future of the Dollar," *Foreign Policy*, no. 11 (Summer 1973), pp. 3-23 and "Eurodollars, Reserve Dollars, and Asymmetries in the International Monetary System," *Journal of International Economics*, vol. 2 (September 1972), pp. 325-44.

opments that have nothing to do with the United States. Although this asymmetry could be overcome by the substitution of some other intervention medium, any alternative system would have to overcome the very substantial margin of efficiency, convenience, and simplicity enjoyed by the mechanism of dollar intervention.

More generally, the dollar continues to perform a variety of special functions in both private and official international transactions, primarily because there is no attractive alternative. No other medium of exchange possesses the advantages the dollar derives from the economic size of the United States, the breadth and resiliency of its domestic capital markets, and its freedom from exchange controls. More recently, the dollar has also regained much of its traditional position as a guarantor of stability in asset values, now that the U.S. inflation rate is lower than that of most other industrialized nations and the effective exchange rate of the dollar has remained remarkably stable over the past two years or so.

In addition to the continuation of special functions performed by the dollar itself, continuing relative passivity by the United States as regards its own exchange rate would prove helpful—perhaps essential—to the functioning of the international monetary system. The apparent desire of most countries to run current-account surpluses poses a continuous threat of inconsistent exchange-rate targets, particularly in current circumstances, when the collective surplus of the OPEC countries implies that the oil-consuming countries must, as a group, run a corresponding current-account deficit. Were the United States to undertake an active exchange-rate policy in order to buttress its own current account against these pressures, the effect would be to exacerbate greatly existing strains on the international monetary system.

Clearly, the United States cannot undertake an unlimited commitment to passivity. In particular, it could not tolerate the effects on the domestic economy if any of its major trading partners were to use exchange-rate manipulation as a way of exporting cyclical problems of inflation or unemployment in the manner of the self-defeating competitive depreciations of the 1930s. This is another instance in which the operation of market forces and continued leadership by the United States require the support of a supranational framework of criteria for appropriate behavior. In view of the fact that the system of flexible exchange rates is and will remain a heavily managed one, some international criteria to guide such management are essential.

Guidelines and Coordination. Work on the development of such guiding principles has been under way for several years. As regards the relatively uncontroversial guideline regarding intervention "to counter disorderly conditions . . . characterized . . . by disruptive short-term movements in the exchange of [a] currency,"[39] an effective set of informal working arrangements appears to have been developed among the central banks of the leading industrialized countries. The development of criteria for the longer term has proved more difficult; the interim guidelines for intervention accepted by the IMF's executive directors in 1974 hinged on the concept of "target zones" for the exchange rates and/or reserve positions of member countries.[40] When the final guidelines were promulgated in April 1977, this concept had been abandoned in favor of the much more general principle: "A member shall avoid manipulating exchange rates or the international monetary system in order to prevent effective balance of payments adjustment or to gain an unfair competitive advantage over other members."[41]

More significantly, the emphasis shifted between 1974 and 1977 from a focus on guidelines for exchange-market *intervention* to principles governing IMF surveillance of members' exchange-rate *policies*, reflecting recognition of the fact that direct market intervention is only one of a number of mechanisms a government can use to affect its exchange rate. As the 1977 IMF document explicitly recognizes, the same results can be achieved indirectly by official foreign borrowing or lending, by the use of restrictions on or incentives to either current or capital account transactions, or by the conduct of domestic monetary policy. Thus, the use of such measures for balance of payments purposes is regarded, along with direct intervention in exchange markets, as a proper subject for IMF surveillance and consultation.[42]

The new IMF guidelines thus recognize explicitly that effective criteria for the conduct of exchange-rate policy in a world of managed floating must go beyond a narrow focus on direct intervention to encompass other policy mechanisms affecting the compatibility—or incompatibility—of national macroeconomic policies. Indeed, because even freely flexible exchange rates cannot eliminate the international transmission of economic disturbances in a world where capital is mobile, macroeconomic policy coordination would be useful in reducing the continuing tension between interdependence and the desire for economic sovereignty even if exchange rates were not managed at all.

---

[39] *IMF Survey* (May 2, 1977), pp. 131-32.
[40] IMF, "Outline of Reform," pp. 35-36.
[41] *IMF Survey* (May 2, 1977), p. 131.
[42] Ibid., p. 132.

What is coordination? There is widespread agreement at present on the proposition that more economic coordination is essential, but beneath that agreement lie wide differences in perception of what that phrase means. During the first quarter-century after World War II, the focus of international discussions and negotiations was on what might be termed negative coordination: the avoidance of explicit beggar-my-neighbor policies, in the form of manipulation of exchange rates or other types of limitations on or incentives to international transactions, in alleviating domestic economic problems. Today, however, as international concern with the macroeconomic policies of individual nations persists, even under floating rates, there is a widespread feeling that increased *positive coordination* is also essential, at least among the major industrialized countries which are currently the effective practitioners of managed floating.

Again, however, there is no clear consensus on an operational definition of that concept. At the lowest level, such coordination might imply simply that each country should take account in its own macroeconomic planning of what other countries are planning to do and what the results of their intended macroeconomic policies are likely to be. One of the factors that appears to have contributed to the severity of global economic fluctuations during the past five years or so is a collective indulgence by the industrialized nations in policy overkill, first on the stimulative and then on the contractionary side, as each nation failed to take sufficient account of what other nations were planning to do and what impact their policies were likely to have, not only on their own economies but on those of their economic partners as well. As a matter of common sense, in an interdependent world, macroeconomic policies should be set in a global rather than an isolated national framework, with as much consultation and exchange of information as possible regarding other nations' views and intentions.

The real question is whether one should go a step beyond intensified consultation; that is, whether there should be an effort initiated among a few major industrialized countries to plan jointly their broad macroeconomic targets and the general policies required to achieve them. The crux of the matter is: Should there be some modification of domestic aims and policies to conform to international requirements? This concept is not a new one, of course. The IMF has been requiring such adaptations for some time, as a requirement of borrowing in the higher credit tranches and in order to promote the adjustments required to make repayment possible. Nor has acquiescence under such conditions been confined to small or developing countries;

the IMF negotiations with the United Kingdom and Italy in 1976 revealed that these nations were prepared, in this particular context, to modify their domestic macroeconomic policies to conform to international criteria. Furthermore, the financing requirements imposed on oil-consuming countries by the OPEC price increases suggest that this aspect of the IMF's function is likely to expand in the future.

What is new is the proposition that such coordination should be extended to creditor as well as debtor nations and should be exercised continuously and cooperatively rather than intermittently and in situations of duress. Some of the difficulties and ambiguities associated with this proposition are illustrated by a current debate that was one of the major topics of discussion at the May 1977 summit meeting in London: the so-called "locomotive economies" argument. This is the proposition that the three largest and financially most secure industrialized democracies—West Germany, Japan, and the United States—should at present gear their macroeconomic policies toward leading economic expansion for the rest of the world, thus alleviating the balance of payments and exchange-rate pressures that the weaker industrialized nations would face if they attempted to reflate their economies on their own.

To what extent does this proposition go beyond the uncontroversial concept of intensified consultation and global information-gathering in the process of setting macroeconomic targets? At one level of analysis, it would appear, not very far. It can be convincingly argued that there is no genuine divergence between the optimal macroeconomic policy from the international and from the domestic points of view. In both cases, the goal should be to achieve the degree of economic stimulus that will maximize the real growth of the national economy over some reasonable time frame, say, the next three to five years. There can be, and generally is, a good deal of honest disagreement over the degree of stimulus most likely to achieve that goal. But if that is the target on which domestic macroeconomic policy is predicated, then a greater degree of stimulus would only serve to exacerbate inflation, internationally as well as domestically. If the major industrialized nations recognize that each should, in the process of setting its own goals and policies, take account of what others are likely to do, there need be no divergence, in this view, between the appropriate goals from the national and the global perspective.

Controversy and conflict. Probing further, however, this portrait of universal harmony is seen to have several major flaws or weaknesses. For one thing, the reasoning of the previous paragraph contains some highly controversial assumptions, in particular, an implicit denial that there exists, except perhaps in the very short run, a Phillips curve trade-off that enables a country to achieve higher rates of output and employment at the cost of tolerating a higher rate of inflation. This alternative view, that more inflation will over the longer term make the achievement of satisfactory rates of growth and employment more difficult rather than less, has gained considerable currency as the result of the experience of recent years, and it is in fact explicitly acknowledged in the April 29, 1977, communiqué of the Interim Committee of the IMF's Board of Governors.[43] The issue remains a controversial one, however, and it is likely to prove difficult for governments holding opposing views on this critical question to agree on common criteria for the conduct of national stabilization policies.

Apart from controversies regarding the optimal degree of stimulus in the aggregate, problems relating to the sectoral composition of demand growth may also cause divergences in view regarding the conduct of macroeconomic policy. At the core of the "locomotive economies" argument is the conviction that the three strongest industrialized nations should not allow their stimulative policies to be limited by the prospect of associated deteriorations in their current account balances, nor should they resist pressures for appreciation of their currencies, as Japan appears to have done, at least intermittently, during recent years. In fact, this argument continues, it is essential for the economic health of the rest of the oil-consuming world that the trade or current-account balances of these particular nations move either into deficit or into a smaller surplus position as recovery proceeds, a development that has occurred so far only in the United States.[44]

Again, the issues here may arise to some extent from inadequacies in consultation, exchange of information, and global forecasting. It would obviously be detrimental to global recovery for such large nations as West Germany and Japan to count on export-led expansion to lead their own recoveries when the financial and economic situations of their partner countries could not sustain significant increases in imports. But, to the extent that weak and strong nations alike regard expansion in the export sector as less inflationary than an equivalent increase in aggregate demand arising from domestic stimulus (and it is clear that many do; whether or not this belief has a solid analytical or empirical foundation would require more ex-

---

[43] Ibid., p. 130.

[44] A contrary view is presented in the essay by Gottfried Haberler in this volume.

tensive investigation than can be pursued here), a genuine conflict of interest may be involved. The weaker industrialized nations have won wide-spread support for their belief that their own expansions must be coordinated with, and in fact led by, expansion in the stronger countries if they are to avoid weakening balances of payments and accompanying exchange-rate deterioration that would both threaten their financial viability and exacerbate their domestic inflationary problems. If, at the same time, the stronger nations also prefer export-led stimulus to the home-grown variety (either because they believe it to be less inflationary or because of political pressure from a domestic export sector with underutilized capacity), an impasse may well result.

Such problems would not disappear, incidentally, if exchange rates were freely flexible rather than managed, since the particular mix of monetary and fiscal measures utilized in domestic stabilization policy directly affects exchange rates and thus the composition of demand. In particular, standard macroeconomic analysis indicates strongly that expansionary fiscal policy financed by bonds rather than by an increase in the money supply will raise domestic interest rates, reduce net capital outflows, and thus cause the exchange rate to appreciate and the current-account balance to fall, whereas monetary expansion will have the opposite effect.

Finally, problems arising from different views regarding the nature and existence of a Phillips curve interact with those arising from conflicts of interest regarding the optimal composition of demand expansion. To those who believe that a Phillips curve operates over the medium to long run, and that under present conditions the increased global utility to be derived from greater demand stimulus would outweigh the costs of any associated acceleration of inflation, export-led growth appears as a zero-sum game in global terms, while real growth originating in the domestic sector benefits one's neighbors as well as oneself. To those holding the alternative view, any efforts to stimulate domestic demand beyond the point of maximum real growth can only serve to exacerbate inflation, globally as well as domestically.

Obviously, in a world of complete information and perfect forecasting, such controversies would be resolved immediately and definitively. In the real world of uncertainty, however, estimates and forecasts are bound to be influenced by the particular biases of their originators, and differences based on inconsistent assumptions and inadequate information will inevitably shade over into differences based on perceived conflicts of interest. Thus, in defining macroeconomic coordination, the line between intensified consultation and the subordination of domestic economic goals to a necessarily controversial definition of international interests is bound to remain a fuzzy one. Partly because of these fundamental difficulties involved in institutionalizing macroeconomic coordination while at the same time preserving scope for nations to pursue legitimately different objectives for their domestic economies, the guidelines of the IMF in this area are likely to remain general and largely unimplemented, while more intensive efforts in this direction are pursued in the more informal and pluralistic context of "summit" discussions conducted intermittently at the political level among a relatively few major industrialized nations.

Such summitry is appropriate for another reason as well, in that it parallels the pluralism of managed floating, in which only those nations at the head of one or another of the informal currency blocs are active participants. In the wake of an enormous spate of literature delineating alternative criteria for an "optimum currency area,"[45] the nations of the world appear to be seeking, through an informal process of trial and error, to create their own groupings within the broad, potentially universal framework of the IMF system. However, in recognition of the fact that managed floating cannot by itself prevent the transmission of macroeconomic disturbances from one such area to another, intensive efforts to develop some workable concept of macroeconomic coordination among the nations whose currencies dominate these informal blocs are also proceeding, albeit in the face of the considerable conceptual and practical difficulties outlined here.

The Management of Microeconomic Issues

Whereas the current interest in coordinating international interactions among national macroeconomic policies and fluctuations in the aggregate levels of economic activity is largely a phenomenon of the post-Keynesian era, the organization of international economic relationships in the microeconomic sphere—having to do primarily with international movements of goods, services, and factors of production—is the traditional focus of international political economy. Of course, no airtight distinction can be made between macroeconomic and microeconomic issues. For the impact of national stabilization policies, of fluctuations in the aggregate level of national economic activity, and of the processes by which these disturbances are transmitted from one country to another inevitably falls unevenly on different industries, sectors, regions, and economic and social groups within each country.

---

[45] For a review, see Tower and Willett, *Theory of Optimum Currency Areas.*

In addition, the maintenance of macroeconomic stability is critical for the successful management of microeconomic issues. The effectiveness, as well as the likelihood, of achieving or maintaining liberal trade policies depends heavily on the existence of healthy economies to serve as markets for the exports of others; agreements regarding international investment will have little meaning in the absence of adequate funds for foreign investment in the home country and opportunities for profitable investment in the host country. Above all, the domestic structural adjustments caused by changes in relative prices when international patterns of production, trade, and investment shift in response to market forces may be socially and politically manageable in the context of stable growth overall, but totally intractable if imposed on an economy suffering from stagnation or severe fluctuations in its level of economic activity. Fundamentally, improved management of macroeconomic problems and an effective framework for dealing with microeconomic issues in the international economy are complementary: success in the former will make the achievement of the latter both more probable and more meaningful, while progress on the latter will help to realize the potential opportunities for mutually beneficial international economic transactions created by dynamic stability in the world economy.

The Organization of Trade Relations. Through most of the postwar period, the thrust of international trading arrangements has been toward restoring greater automaticity, in the sense of increasing leeway for the operation of market forces, to a world in which trade had been initially severely limited by the interplay between economic devastation and governmental restrictions. The focus of these developments has been the periodic rounds of multilateral trade negotiations conducted under the auspices of the GATT, the latest of which has been under way for some three years in Geneva with little visible progress. More broadly, a variety of challenges currently stand in the way of further progress toward a liberalized international trading system, and even threaten to produce backsliding into protectionism.

The guiding principles of the GATT have traditionally been to achieve "freer and fairer trade": the substantial reduction of tariffs and other explicit barriers "at the border" and the elimination of discriminatory treatment in international commerce. Actually, these two principles of multilateralism and trade liberalization are mutually reinforcing. By ensuring that trade barriers are applied in a nondiscriminatory manner, the most-favored-nation (MFN) principle minimizes the inefficiencies and distortions they create, as well as avoiding trade diversion and thus injury to third parties as a by-product of negotiated selective reduction of trade barriers. Furthermore, it increases the scope of multilateral GATT negotiations by ensuring that any trade concession negotiated between two or more countries will be promptly extended to all member countries.

The major challenge to the global MFN approach is, of course, the proliferation of a great variety of preferential trading arrangements among regional or other special groups of countries. The GATT specifically exempts (Article 14) full customs unions and free trade areas from MFN obligations, in the expectation that the growth-stimulation and trade-creation they engendered would greatly outweigh any trade-diversion in their trade with nonpartner nations. And, indeed, throughout much of the Bretton Woods period, regional trade groupings did appear to assist gradual progress toward liberalized trade by greatly increasing the scope for the operation of market forces *within* each bloc. But concern about the erosion of MFN, which had cropped up periodically during the 1960s, intensified in the early 1970s, as regional arrangements that clearly met the GATT criteria, such as the EEC and EFTA, were increasingly supplemented by a variety of looser preferential arrangements, in particular the association agreements reached between the EEC and a growing number of developing nations [46] and the projected special trading arrangements between the enlarged EEC and those EFTA countries "left behind" in the enlargement. Because such arrangements are partial and selective, trade-diverting effects that restrict and distort international trade are far more likely to outweigh the trade-creating effects of enhanced efficiency and growth than they are in the case of full customs unions or free trade areas.

The tension between the global approach to trade-liberalization favored by the United States and the proliferating variety of special preferential arrangements undertaken by the EEC promises to persist, and a frontal attack on such arrangements is almost certain to be unproductive. Rather, efforts to minimize the distorting and disintegrative effects of such arrangements should focus on two areas. One is the establishment of more effective multilateral surveillance of regional arrangements, provided for in Article 24 of the GATT but never adequately implemented. The second is continued progress on multilateral trade-liberalization, which would reduce the discriminatory trade effects of preferential arrangements.

---

[46] Many of these arrangements were consolidated in the 1975 Lomé Convention entered into by the EEC and forty-six African, Caribbean and Pacific (ACP) countries.

Some of the intensified challenges currently faced by the market-oriented, prohibitory approach to trade expansion, focused on tariff reduction, have already been touched on: the decline in the economic hegemony of the United States, the major supporter of this approach; the broadening of the international trading system to incorporate newer participants, particularly Japan and the developing nations, with stronger traditions of government intervention in the economy; and the proliferation of economic goals in the Western industrialized democracies, thus increasing the pressure for interventionism in this basic nucleus of nations as well.

Market access and economic development. At present, the most overt challenge to the GATT system comes from the developing nations, with their explicit rejection of its liberal principles and their insistence on exemption from any commitment to reciprocity in international trade relationships. One of the reasons for their demand for a new international economic order may be the fact that they played no role in the formation of the old one. The Bretton Woods system and its implementing institutions were organized by the industrialized nations and were focused on the conduct of economic relations among them. The developing countries, many of which had not yet become independent nations at the time these institutions were established, were regarded, and in fact regarded themselves, as *"objects,* not *participants* in the world economy."* [47]

A major contributor to misunderstanding has also been a fundamental confusion between the concept of economic development, centered on a process of structural change in the economies of developing nations themselves that carries a potential for gains to all participants, and questions involving the redistribution of the world's existing stock of income or wealth, obviously a zero-sum process in which some participants can gain only if others lose. Actually, in the context of *international* economic relationships, the essential distinction is between measures that would eliminate existing market distortions, thus increasing potential output and income, and those that would have a purely distributional impact. Obviously, international conflict will be minimized to the extent that progress can be made in the first category, where positive-sum outcomes are possible and all participants can gain, although a strong case should be made on equity

---

[47] Lawrence B. Krause, "Development Assistance: The Problems of A Large Donor. The United States," in Leslie V. Castle and Sir Frank Holmes, eds., *Co-operation and Development in the Asia/Pacific Region: Relations between Large and Small Countries* (Tokyo: JERC, 1976), p. 168.

grounds for insuring that the lion's share of the benefits goes to the developing countries.

In fact, many opportunities for mutually beneficial changes do exist, particularly in the realm of increasing the access of developing countries to the markets of the industrialized world. Despite the heavy emphasis on commodity trade in current discussions, the most promising trade opportunities for many developing countries appear to lie with manufactured goods. Over the decade 1963–1973, the share of manufactures in total exports of the developing countries increased from 15 to 25 percent, and the aggregate rate of increase of such exports was higher for developing than for industrialized nations. The ratio of U.S. exports of manufactures to developing countries to its imports of manufactures from the same group fell from 3.2 in 1967 to 1.6 in 1973.

Such expansion has occurred in the face of formidable handicaps, however. The "cascaded" tariff structures maintained by the United States and most other industrialized nations militates against the expansion of export-oriented processing and manufacturing activities in the developing countries, thus depriving them of the benefits of substantial increases in value added.[48] Even more important than cascaded tariff structures are nontariff barriers (in the form of import quotas, tariff quotas, or negotiated "voluntary" export restraints) maintained by most industrialized countries against products (such as shoes and textiles) characterized by relatively simple standardized production processes and correspondingly low skill intensities, in which developing countries clearly have a long-run comparative advantage.

The domestic adjustment problem caused for importing nations by the rapid expansion of exports of such products by a handful of fast-growing developing nations, despite restrictions on access, cannot be ignored, particularly since the industries in which newly industrializing nations can compete most effectively are precisely those that employ large numbers of the lowest-paid and least mobile segment of the labor force in the older industrialized nations. Increased emphasis on domestic adjustment assistance and the introduction of credible self-destruct mechanisms into the protective provisions of temporary "safeguard" programs of import-restriction may help to prevent these relatively short-run problems of adjustment from

---

[48] The generalized systems of tariff preferences introduced in recent years by major industrialized nations are aimed at alleviating this situation, but they are riddled with limitations and exceptions and frequently vitiated by nontariff limitations on LDC manufactured exports.

eclipsing potential gains from such trade expansion to producers in the developing countries and consumers in the industrialized world. The fact remains, however, that market-access, market-expansion, and market-stability for the products of LDC exporters are likely to depend most heavily of all on the achievement and maintenance of high employment and steady, noninflationary growth in the industrialized countries.

Nontariff barriers. Less strident than the challenges posed by the developing nations, but just as threatening to the survival of a liberal international trading system, are the issues posed by the broadened scope of government responsibilities for and intervention in the economies of the industrialized nations. One factor making further progress on trade liberalization increasingly difficult is, ironically, the success of previous negotiating rounds: those tariffs that have survived at restrictive levels are likely to be ones whose removal is perceived to be particularly politically troublesome or socially disruptive. More important, however, the most significant remaining barriers to trade are so-called nontariff-barriers (NTBs). The definition and measurement of reciprocity, the cornerstone of the GATT approach to trade-liberalization, difficult enough in the case of tariffs, is infinitely more complicated in the case of NTBs. And, with the exception of quantitative import restrictions and explicit export subsidies, the major types of NTBs tend to be associated with some domestic social policy and deeply embedded in domestic law. With domestic policy and commercial policy thus inseparable, efforts to reduce trade-distortions by negotiating reductions in barriers "at the border" will inevitably be ineffective.

The area in which the obstacles to the international operation of market forces have proved most intractable within the GATT is that of agricultural policy. Virtually every nation, including the United States, has long-established policies of government intervention in agriculture. Thus, we are confronted with a paradox: the need for cooperative international "market management" to mitigate the distortions created by national policies and allow more room for the operation of market forces. As regards the Common Agricultural Policy (CAP) of the EEC, for example, efforts to force modifications in its substantive provisions in order to bring them closer to conformity with GATT rules are certain to prove unavailing, inasmuch as the CAP represents a carefully negotiated package reconciling the divergent goals of member governments and is also regarded as one of the main bonds holding the EEC together. Rather, focus must shift from issues of principle to more pragmatic issues relating to implementation of the CAP provisions: the height of specific support levels, the degree of self-sufficiency in particular products, et cetera. Furthermore, our concern with increasing the efficiency benefits of agricultural trade cannot ignore the widespread desire for stability in frequently unstable agricultural markets. Despite limitations on the workability of buffer stocks and commodity agreements suggested by technical considerations and past experience, some type of national or international arrangements to increase such stability for both producers and consumers are almost certain to be part of any successful effort to reduce protection and distortions in global agricultural markets.[49]

In recent years, efforts to relieve the twin pressures of stagflation have intensified demands in industrialized countries to impose trade-distorting policies in a broader range of economic sectors. On the one hand, export controls have been utilized for a variety of purposes, including improving a country's terms of trade or protecting the domestic economy from physical shortages or rapid price increases. In a world where the international transmission of inflation has become as much a matter of concern as the transmission of unemployment, restrictions on supply access, against which the GATT provides no effective limitations, can be as great a source of trade-distortion and global instability as restrictions on market access, the major focus of the GATT framework.[50]

At the same time, pressures on governments of industrialized nations to provide high employment, economic stability, and distributional equity have made them insistent on cushioning the domestic impact of abrupt changes in trade patterns against a background of stagflation. Regarding the "escape clause" provisions of the GATT as too restrictive, most have developed import-restricting safeguard mechanisms of their own that either fail to conform to GATT requirements or short-cut them by taking the form of "voluntary export restraints" negotiated with the major supplying nations. Such arrangements are generally defended as being less restrictive than unilaterally imposed restrictions would be, although their potential for distorting resource-allocation and raising prices is at least as

---

[49] It should be noted, however, that stabilization of commodity *prices* will not always produce stabilization of *earnings* from commodity exports. The whole issue is further complicated at present by the widespread belief that the major purpose of proposed commodity agreements is not to simply stabilize either prices or earnings but rather to raise and hold commodity prices above competitively determined levels.

[50] For an excellent discussion, see: C. Fred Bergsten, *Completing the GATT: Toward New International Rules to Govern Export Controls* (British-North American Committee, 1974).

great. If they are indeed temporary, such actions may even be justified (as second-best policies) on efficiency grounds: in the face of congestion in labor markets, it can be shown that individuals' income-maximizing decisions to move out of contracting industries will not be socially optimal, creating an external diseconomy that may justify government intervention to slow down the market-determined adjustment process.[51] The great danger is, of course, that such temporary provisions will become a disguised form of permanent protection, of creeping cartelization. To minimize this danger and reduce the potential for friction inherent in such "orderly marketing" arrangements, the United States has for some time urged the development of a multilateral safeguard system that would subject such measures to internationally agreed criteria and provisions for multilateral surveillance and review.

The global commons. A third group of issues relating to the interface between national policies and international trade has been created by recent concern for the management of the "global commons." The recognition that the environment and the oceans are not free goods, as they have traditionally been regarded, but scarce in the economic sense, and the associated efforts by governments to internalize in various ways the costs associated with their use and maintenance, are raising a host of issues for international economic relations. By definition, the resolution cannot simply be left to the marketplace, since these issues are defined by the presence of market failure, the existence of external economies or diseconomies.

Even in cases where the environment can be regarded as a national rather than an international public good (that is, where *transnational* pollution is not involved), national policies relating to the environment affect the operation of the international marketplace. Even if all countries had identical preferences regarding environmental quality, required the same degree of effort to meet the desired standards, and utilized the same policy instruments to do so, increased pollution-control efforts would still affect patterns of production and trade by raising the cost of pollution-intensive processes or products. In fact, of course, substantial differences among nations as regards public preferences, environmental assimilative capacity, and the types of instruments utilized generate an intensified impact on relative

---

[51] See A. E. Lapan, "International Trade, Factor Market Distortions, and the Optimal Dynamic Subsidy," *American Economic Review*, vol. 66 (June 1976), pp. 335-46 and James Cassing and Jack Ochs, "International Trade, Factor Market Distortions, and the Optimal Dynamic Subsidy: Comment," Working Paper no. 51, Department of Economics, University of Pittsburgh, 1977; processed.

prices, patterns of production, trade, investment, the terms of trade, balances of payments, and exchange rates as the proportion of available resources devoted to maintaining or improving the environment increases.[52] The most persistent effects on comparative advantage in this regard are likely to occur between industrialized and developing countries, partly because the present assimilative capacity of the latter is likely to be greater, and partly because their desired environmental standards are likely to be lower, on the assumption that clean air and water are luxury goods, with an income-elasticity of demand exceeding unity.

One resolution frequently suggested to the issues posed above is the international harmonization of environmental standards to minimize the "distortions" just described. Different standards may, however, reflect a legitimate diversity of preferences (or ineradicable differences in assimilative capacities); in such cases, harmonization would not only infringe on sovereignty but also lower total welfare. Where transnational pollution is not involved, the focus should be less on positive coordination through eliminating differences in standards than on negative coordination by ensuring that such differences do not become the basis for restrictions on or interference with international trade and investment. Such interference is likely to take one of two general forms. First, unless nondiscriminatory treatment of domestically produced and imported products is assured, environmental regulations can become a nontariff barrier limiting trade, as has occurred in such related areas as health and safety requirements, industrial standards, and packaging and labeling regulations.[53] Second, as environmental controls influence international competitiveness and trade and investment flows, pressures will inevitably build to minimize the resulting adjustment costs by establishing "countervailing duties or other special charges to offset competitive advantages of foreign suppliers operating under less stringent environmental standards."[54] Such arguments are akin to the "sweatshop labor" arguments for protection based on differences in labor costs and will have similar efficiency costs.

Economic issues that, unlike those just discussed, actually involve international public goods (the global commons) do require

---

[52] The term *environmental assimilative capacity* is used in a detailed discussion of the points mentioned in this paragraph in: Ingo Walter, "Environmental Management and the International Economic Order" in C. Fred Bergsten, *The Future of the International Economic Order: An Agenda for Research* (Lexington Mass.: Lexington Books, 1973), pp. 293-346. See also Ingo Walter, *International Economics of Pollution* (New York: John Wiley and Sons, 1975).

[53] Walter, "Environmental Management," p. 308.

[54] Ibid., p. 310.

some type of internationally agreed criteria for behavior, perhaps supplemented by institutions to administer and enforce these criteria. Examples of such issues are transnational pollution, nuclear proliferation, and fishing rights in international waters. Indeed, it is frequently suggested that the external economies and diseconomies associated with such problems should be internalized or controlled at the highest or most universal international level, in order to reap the efficiencies of centralized decision making and assure that all the externalities are fully captured. In fact, however, such a universal approach may be neither possible nor even efficient, in the sense of maximizing economic welfare.

The difficulties associated with efforts to delineate and enforce universal standards of behavior vis-à-vis the global commons are of three general types. The first has already been noted: the welfare costs associated with lost diversity, which have their practical reflections in assertions of national sovereignty, that are likely to stand in the way of universal solutions.[55] The second is what d'Arge terms the concept of "implicit entitlement": just because the oceans and the environment have long been regarded as free goods, no precedents exist for the definition of ownership rights. The institutionalization of universal regulations or standards of behavior would inevitably involve moving from implicit to explicit entitlements, a process sure to be fraught with tensions, disappointed expectations, and demands for distributional equity.[56] Finally, particular problems involving international public goods vary enormously in terms of the number of countries involved, the magnitude of costs involved, and the ease with which costs and benefits can be identified and liabilities assigned. This diversity suggests "that an overriding general principle for solving such problems is not only unlikely, but also inefficient."[57] Instead, many such problems might be dealt with more effectively by regional or special-purpose criteria and institutions encompassing only those nations with a sufficient stake in limiting a particular type of "free riding" (resulting in excessive pollution, overfishing, or whatever) to be willing to yield sovereignty and accept assignment of entitlement in a particular, limited area.

Government intervention and international rulemaking. A cen-

---

[55] It is ironic, for example, that the main result so far of the law of the sea negotiations appears to have been the unilateral assertion of 200-mile coastal economic limits by a number of countries.

[56] Ralph C. d'Arge, "Transfrontier Pollution: Some Issues on Regulation," in Ingo Walter, ed., *Studies in International Environmental Economics* (New York: Wiley Interscience, 1976), p. 260.

[57] Ibid., p. 254.

tral theme of this discussion of the organization of international relationships in the trade sphere has been that the operation of the marketplace must in the international arena be undergirded by effective mechanisms of international rule making. This apparent paradox is not a new one; as we have seen, even those who stress the high degree of automaticity associated with the gold standard era acknowledge the role of "customary rules" in allowing the marketplace to function relatively unimpeded. Today, however, greater government responsibility for and involvement in the domestic economy has created at least two significant differences. One is that an informal, unwritten code of customary behavior has been replaced by a more formal framework of international agreements and institutions. A second is that the most significant distortions of international trade can no longer be reduced simply by the elimination of explicit barriers at national borders, but require, in many instances, more complex international arrangements.

Given these conditions, the most orderly way of organizing economic relations might seem to be to create a comprehensive framework of universal rules of behavior by filling in the major "gaps" in the current GATT rules, extending their coverage to such matters as export controls, the use of trade restrictions for balance of payments purposes,[58] the multilateralization of safeguard schemes, and the management of trade issues associated with the global commons. In fact, however, progress on these issues is likely to be made in a much more fragmented and pluralistic fashion.

One reason for this prediction is the present diffusion of power and leadership where international trade is concerned. This is an area in which American hegemony was most limited, even in the earlier postwar years, and declined most rapidly. Furthermore, whereas international coordination in the macroeconomic sphere will doubtless be the concern of a relatively few countries for the foreseeable future, the management of trade issues must necessarily involve a much larger number of countries. This is true particularly in view of the need to gradually incorporate the developing nations as full-fledged members of the international trading system. This means avoiding the permanent incorporation of preferential treatment for these countries into the structure of the system. Rather, the ultimate aim should be, as it was for the European nations in the long period of

---

[58] The GATT has an escape-clause provision allowing quantitative restrictions for this purpose, predicated on the assumption of a world of pegged exchange rates that would have to be supported in the face of payments disequilibriums arising from domestic full-employment policies. The recent move to managed flexibility affords a promising opportunity to limit the use of such restrictions.

postwar transition, that increased assumption of responsibilities and willingness on the part of these nations gradually to adhere to the same international rules as everyone else should advance in parallel with their increased participation in international decision making.[59]

All this implies, of course, a continuation of the already great increase in the number of countries participating actively in the international system, with huge discrepancies among them in economic size and characteristics and in degree of interest and involvement in particular issues. Taken together with the increased importance of preferential regional arrangements, these developments suggest that, on issues of general concern, the ideal of universal nondiscriminatory rules can be approached only via negotiations among economic blocs and efforts to minimize the distorting effects of such regional arrangements. They suggest too that, as regards many issues in the trade area, the most effective form of international management will not be the codification of universal and comprehensive standards and implementing institutions but rather the construction of a number of more limited agreements and arrangements, with participation restricted to those countries with a significant interest in the particular issues involved.

International Transfer of Factors of Production. International investment—involving the transfer among nations of both capital and technology—has grown even more rapidly than international trade over the postwar period, while both have grown faster than world output. But, whereas international transfers of goods and services are generally acknowledged to be a source of important economic benefits, even by those who would limit them in particular instances or for particular purposes, investment across international boundaries is supported by no such consensus. The Europeans have generally tended to be skeptical about the American view that freedom of international capital movements is as important to the maximization of world income and world welfare as is freedom of commodity movements, while the views of developing nations on foreign private investment have ranged from ambivalence to unalloyed hostility. This absence of consensus on international investment is reflected in the asymmetry

[59] Not only is such exemption from the rules and procedures of international agreements inconsistent with the concept of "sovereign equality among nations" (Richard N. Cooper, "A New International Economic Order for Mutual Gain," *Foreign Policy* no. 26 [Spring 1977], p. 113), it is also likely to be counterproductive. Because the LDCs were not expected to lay anything on the table in the GATT multilateral trade negotiations, for example, products in which they were interested tended to be ignored.

[60] Regrettably, freedom of international labor migration has an even smaller constituency than does unrestricted capital migration.

of the IMF's *Articles of Agreement*, which stress the avoidance of restrictions on current-account transactions but are silent on the subject of capital-account restrictions.

Attitudes toward international investment are inseparably intertwined with those regarding multinational corporations, the major vehicle for such investment over the postwar period and the primary instrument of increasing interdependence. No other economic agent poses such a conspicuous threat to national economic sovereignty, nor is so effective in creating the efficiency benefits of international market integration. Indeed, much of the concern about multinationals has been based on the fear that they are eroding national economic sovereignty, that because their scope transcends any single national jurisdiction they can undermine or evade the tax, regulatory, and other legitimate functions of sovereign states.[61] More recently, a contradictory but no less urgent concern has been voiced: that the multinationals are becoming the pawns of national governments, hostages that can be used by a powerful parent country like the United States to extend its jurisdiction beyond its own boundaries, or by either home or host countries to alter the international distribution of income in their own favor, as in the case of the OPEC countries' utilization of the multinational oil companies to enforce their 1974 petroleum embargo and subsequent price increases.[62] Finally, it is frequently argued that the characteristics of multinational corporations, with their considerable market power and their heavy use of intrafirm rather than arms-length transactions, are so different from the assumptions underlying the neoclassical competitive model as to vitiate the efficiency arguments for freedom of international trade and investment based on that model. Although proponents of this view generally fail to explain how restrictions on international transactions would reduce existing deviations from a competitive solution, it is nonetheless invoked frequently to support limitations on international transfers of capital and technology.[63]

Paralleling the lack of international consensus regarding the

---

[61] This concern is reflected in the title of a well-known book by Raymond Vernon, *Sovereignty at Bay* (New York: Basic Books, 1971).

[62] For a somewhat alarmist view of such developments, see C. Fred Bergsten, "Coming Investment Wars?" *Foreign Affairs*, vol. 53, no. 1 (October 1974), pp. 135-52.

[63] What frequently underlies such arguments for restricting multinational investment is concern that the domestic adjustment costs created by foreign direct investment are likely to fall most heavily on labor, the least mobile factor of production. For a "scorecard" on the costs and benefits of foreign direct investment, see: Robert O. Keohane and Van Dorn Ooms, "The Multinational Firm and International Regulation," in Bergsten and Krause, eds., *World Politics and International Economics*, pp. 169-86.

benefits of international investment, particularly in its direct or controlling form, is the absence of any institutional framework or set of international ground rules governing the operation of multinational enterprises and their treatment by national governments. Initially, the "grand design" for the postwar international economic order provided for three major institutions: the International Trade Organization (ITO) was to provide the ground rules for both international trade and private investment; the IMF was to establish a framework for the international monetary system; and the World Bank was to coordinate the mobilization of capital, primarily from private sources, for the tasks of economic reconstruction and development. But the ITO was stillborn in the face of U.S. congressional opposition (partly because of objections to provisions regarding the rights of host countries to control foreign investment within their borders), leaving as its legacy the GATT, a partial and in many ways inadequate substitute that does not cover international investment.[64]

Ideally, the existing vacuum would be filled by some institutional framework, analogous to the GATT in the trade and the IMF in the monetary sphere. Ideally, furthermore, the international ground rules established by this framework would be symmetrical, governing both the behavior of multinational firms in relation to their home and host countries and the policies of national governments vis á vis such firms. A welcome first step in the direction of such a framework has been taken by the OECD's 1976 *Declaration in International Investment and Multinational Enterprises*, which calls for national treatment, "transparency," and cooperation as regards incentives and disincentives to international investment and consultation and review procedures. An annex sets forth guidelines for multinational enterprises, stressing the need for such enterprises to operate in conformity with the policy objectives of the countries in which they operate and spelling out a number of specific aspects of behavior relevant to this general criterion. But, despite the high level of generality of this document, and the large number of substantive and procedural gaps it leaves unfilled, it is doubtful that the developing countries outside the OECD would find such a framework acceptable.

Expanded access and unrequited transfers. Such wide differences in points of view, and the mutually conflicting efforts of developing nations both to expand the inflow of capital and technology and to regulate the terms on which they are transferred, complicate the problem of reducing market imperfections that limit the access of these

[64] The OECD's Code of Liberalization of Capital Movements, promulgated in 1961, remains nothing more than a very general statement of intent.

nations to such resources. Internationalizing antitrust provisions and mandating the disclosure of information on certain intrafirm transactions might help, by increasing the competitiveness of the multinationals' environment in return for reducing the uncertainty of that same environment arising from host governments' behavior. In addition, governments in capital-exporting countries can, and do, use the tax system, regulation, guarantees, and joint participation to stimulate —or discourage—the flow of privately owned resources in particular directions. But experience suggests that risk-sharing schemes have not effectively catalyzed private funds on a significant scale and that insurance generally cannot offset a basically hostile climate for direct investment.[65] Risk-sharing arrangements between public and private capital may in fact hold considerable promise, but they are most likely to be effective under the aegis of the international lending institutions and should probably be focused on private capital markets for portfolio funds rather than on direct investment by multinational firms.

More fundamentally, given the absence of any broad international consensus regarding international investment and the extreme sensitivity of many governments on such issues, attempts to create any formal universal institutional framework are probably premature. Indeed, relations between multinational enterprises and national governments, particularly in developing nations, are in a state of dynamic evolution at the moment and, given the adaptability of multinationals, new forms of resource and technology transfer (such as management contracts, licensing arrangements, and other arrangements involving reduced ownership and control) may evolve more effectively in the absence of a specific set of ground rules based on existing institutional structures. For the moment, the most important issues affecting LDC's access to capital and technology may well be negative ones: the avoidance of measures, such as a generalized moratorium on LDC debts, that would probably limit further their access to private capital markets; and avoidance of restrictions on the international transfer of technology for reasons other than military security. Such technological protectionism, which has recently surfaced in the traditionally laissez-faire United States in response to concern about its own international competitive position,[66] is not

---

[65] Experience over the period 1946-1963 is evaluated in Marina v. N. Whitman, *Government Risk-Sharing in Private Investment* (Princeton, N.J.: Princeton University Press, 1965).

[66] See, for example, U.S. Department of Defense, *An Analysis of Export Control of U.S. Technology—A DOD Perspective: A Report of the Defense Science Board Task-Force on Export of U.S. Technology* (Washington, D.C.: Office of the Director of Defense Research and Engineering, February 4, 1976).

only likely to prove ultimately self-defeating, but would risk depriving other nations of one of the most critical factors in the development process.

Whereas expanded access to factor markets can be achieved via the elimination of existing restrictions and distortions, pure income redistribution via *unrequited* transfers cannot, by definition, be achieved through the marketplace (where both parties to a transaction must gain, or at least not lose) but only via unilateral government actions or negotiations among nations or blocs. Proposals involving such transfers have generally fallen into one of two categories: price-raising commodity agreements (including commodity-price indexing) and official development assistance, either bilateral or multilateral.

The aim of price-raising commodity agreements is, of course, to turn the terms of trade in favor of commodity producers and against consumers, thus combatting what is widely believed—although never conclusively demonstrated—to be a long-run tendency for the terms of trade to turn against producers of primary commodities and in favor of producers of manufactured goods. Apart from the global efficiency costs of such arrangements, they would "generate a quite arbitrary distribution of gains and losses among both developed and less developed countries," [67] since most primary production is, in fact, located in high-income countries, and many developing nations are commodity importers who would suffer significant income losses.

For these reasons, indirect resource transfers through price-raising commodity agreements are inferior, on both efficiency and equity grounds, to direct transfers via some form of official assistance (foreign aid). However, as the leadership once exercised by the United States in this area has waned (although this country remains the single largest source of foreign aid, its share of the total has declined from more than one-half in the early 1960s to less than a third), the American-bred rationale for such assistance has also fallen victim to disillusionment, at home as well as abroad. There are several reasons. First, the postwar experience suggests that, on average, the relationship between the magnitude of foreign assistance received by a country and its pace of development has been essentially random, although such aid clearly has made a significant difference for particular countries. Second, it is chimerical to expect substantial international transfers with no strings attached; as Cooper notes, "while intergovernmental transfers *within* countries are common, they usually

---

[67] Cooper, "A New International Economic Order," p. 96.

carry with them strong implicit or explicit conditions." [68] And insistence on conditions for aid, whether they relate to economic, mutual security, or even humanitarian goals, is today generally regarded as undue interference by developing nations.

Although a role remains for special-purpose bilateral aid, in the current environment the aid-giving process is likely to be less troublesome and more effective if it continues to be channeled to an increasing extent through multilateral institutions. A considerable expansion of the lending facilities of the IMF has already occurred, largely in the form of new facilities designed to meet the needs of developing countries and supported by a recently approved one-third increase in quotas. Such lending is all conditional, of course. The developing countries continue to press for the unconditional funds that would be afforded by an SDR-aid link. Since, however, no new SDR allocations are likely to take place until the international monetary system has settled down and worldwide inflationary fears have receded, a more immediate issue is the need for increased capital (quotas) for the World Bank and its associated International Development Agency, to permit an expansion of longer-term development lending to complement the increased short- and medium-term facilities of the IMF. Since U.S. approval and support is a prerequisite for general agreement to increase quotas, and the U.S. share of the industrialized countries' contributions to these institutions is about one-third, each dollar provided by the United States toward increased capital subscriptions would be accompanied by the equivalent of two more from other industrialized nations.

Very recently, a new mechanism for transferring resources to developing nations has been advanced. It is frequently argued that, since seabed mineral resources are part of the "common heritage of mankind," their exploitation should be organized in such a way as to provide for such transfers. This proposition indeed appears attractive on distributional grounds, in that it would provide additional resources to poor nations without requiring the rich countries to give up anything to which they have traditionally had ownership rights. However, it is often mistakenly argued that acceptance of this principle would require limitation on access to the economic resources of the deep seabed by an international regulatory authority, perhaps even the prohibition of development of these resources by anyone other than that authority.

Such cartelization would involve the same efficiency costs and possibly arbitrary distribution of transfers as would price-raising

---

[68] Ibid., p. 111.

agreements for commodities derived from the land. Furthermore, as Tollison and Willett point out, the proposition involves a confusion arising from "the identification of those who physically exploit a resource with those who obtain the benefits from exploitation.[69] Far preferable to any cartelization schemes would be arrangements that provided for the assignment to the poor countries of rents from exploitation of ocean resources in a manner consistent with the competitive operation of the marketplace. Specifically, the U.S. proposals for free access and auctioning of competing claims (to drive returns down to competitive levels) would preserve efficiency, while the assignment of the auction revenues to a revenue-sharing pool would make it possible to assign part or all of the scarcity rents associated with such exploitation to the poor nations.[70]

International investment, like international trade, continues to expand rapidly despite the countervailing pressures of defensive economic nationalism. But, beyond this basic similarity, there are some significant differences in the way international relationships are organized in the two areas. Whereas in international trade the predominant role of the United States has been steadily declining, this country remains the major source of international investment funds and the parent country of a majority of major multinational corporations and Eurocurrency financial institutions. Paradoxically, this continued financial dominance appears to reduce the ability of the United States to exert leadership in the creation of an effective international framework (because of the fear and suspicion with which U.S.-based investment is regarded by many host countries) without enhancing the leadership capacity of any other nation or regional group.

In fact, regional blocs have played a much less important role here than in the trade sphere, as evidenced by the relatively limited effect of the EEC in integrating the capital markets of its member countries and the apparent lack of success so far of several Latin American efforts in this direction. And, whereas in the trade sphere the problem is one of adapting, expanding, or supplementing existing international institutions to minimize the tensions and distortions created by national boundaries, in the sphere of international transfers of capital and technology the problem is rather to create an institutional framework essentially from scratch. And, given the absence of any broad consensus regarding the role of private inter-

---

[69] Robert D. Tollison and Thomas D. Willett, "Institutional Mechanisms for Dealing with International Externalities: A Public Choice Perspective," in Ryan C. Amacher and Richard J. Sweeney, eds., *The Law of the Sea: U.S. Interests and Alternatives* (Washington, D.C.: American Enterprise Institute, 1976), p. 93.
[70] Ibid., pp. 92-97.

national investment, the criteria and mechanisms for international income redistribution through transfers of capital and technology, or the functions that an institutional structure for such relationships should perform, its creation is likely to be a long, slow, and difficult process at best.

The International Economy: Organizing Principles and Paradoxes

This essay began by noting that the international economy would be organized in the future, as it has been in the past, on the basis of some combination of automaticity, hegemony, supranationality, and regionalism, but that it would not be the same mixture as before. Rather than summarizing here the various pressures operating to shape new combinations of organzing principles or the way the pieces are likely to fit together in particular areas, I will simply note some basic paradoxes that currently confront efforts to build an effective framework for international economic relations.

The reduced hegemony of the United States, the diffusion of power among the industrialized nations, and the growing activism of the economically emergent developing world all imply a need for collective leadership, focused in the macroeconomic sphere on the trilateral ties among the United States, the EEC (particularly West Germany), and Japan, but extending to include broader and shifting groups of nations where microeconomic issues are involved. At the same time, other countries have made it quite clear, both in international organizations and in a series of more informal "summit" discussions, that they look to the United States as a primary source of, as well as solution to, their own economic problems. The decline of American military and economic dominance over the past quarter-century has made the continuation of U.S. leadership in, and a sense of responsibility for, maintaining a viable international economic system more difficult but no less urgent in a world where many can prevent effective international action but none alone can insure it.

A second paradox is that supranationality is today apparently required to preserve automaticity, to insure room for market forces to operate in the international arena. Customary rules and implicit agreements are no longer sufficient for this purpose, nor can economic liberalism look simply to American hegemony for its preservation. The broadened economic responsibilities of democratic governments, the continuing tension between international economic interdependence and the desire of national governments for domestic economic autonomy, and the increasing importance in the international economy of nations with interventionist traditions have intensified countervailing pressures of economic nationalism. This is so despite the fact that protectionism is generally a relatively inefficient and high-cost way to correct market failure or achieve nonmarket goals.

Among the advantages of the marketplace are not simply the promotion of economic efficiency but also the depoliticization of economic processes and thus the preservation of harmony amidst diversity. But, ironically, these benefits can today be achieved only to the extent that nations undertake explicit political commitments to be guided by international standards and procedures. However, the task of the international system and institutions is not to preserve a status quo determined by the marketplace. Rather, it is the vastly more challenging one of incorporating concerns with economic security and distributional equity, as well as new participants with widely divergent outlooks, while preserving basically liberal characteristics.

Whether such a synthesis is possible depends on a great many factors, many of them lying outside the economic sphere. But one is the critical importance of successful national macroeconomic management. Historically, it has been when high employment and reasonable price stability were absent that trade and investment problems became intractable, the monetary system faltered, and international economic relations deteriorated. And the profound distributional questions raised by the developing nations will be manageable, if at all, only in the context of stable economic expansion. This brings us to another paradox: that efforts to reduce global economic instability by positive coordination of national stabilization policies among major industrialized nations have intensified despite the shift to managed floating, intended to insulate national economies from external disturbances. The insights provided by more complex theoretical models and the intensity of the exogenous shocks to which the global economy has been subjected in recent years can explain this paradox, but the difficulties posed for macroeconomic coordination by conflicting views of the relationship between inflation and unemployment, conflicts of interest regarding the optimal composition of demand growth, and the need to preserve legitimate diversity in national economic goals are not so easily resolved.

Contrary to the universalism of economic theory and American tradition, regionalism is clearly here to stay. In view of the vast number of participants in the international economic system, the tremendous discrepancies in their size and other economic, political, and cultural characteristics, and their divergent interests, the existence of regional groups and special arrangements is not only inevitable but also essential to make the international system manageable. Such arrangements can operate, as they appeared to in the 1950s and early 1960s, as way-stations toward global liberalization in areas where universal nondiscriminatory treatment is the ultimate goal, and as supplements to broader international institutions in areas of major concern to particular groups of nations. Or they can move in a direction antithetical to internationalism and automaticity, becoming instruments of economic nationalism whose mercantilist policies are all the more distorting because they reflect economic power greater than that of any individual member nation. Increasing tendencies in this direction have been evident during the past decade or so. Reversing them is another of the significant challenges currently facing the international economic system.

Finally, the essential element of supranationalism is likely to take a somewhat different form than it did at Bretton Woods. The development of a relatively formal written constitutional framework for the international economic system during and immediately after World War II was made possible by an historically unique set of circumstances, particularly by the dominant role of the United States. Even so, the formal aspects must not be overemphasized. For the Bretton Woods institutions themselves have a dual nature, part supranational and part pluralistic. And they have operated at two levels; that of explicit contractual arrangements and the complementary one of more informal and flexible procedures for multilateral surveillance, consultations, and dispute settlement. The historical record suggests that these institutions have had a significant impact on the behavior of nation-states through the moral climate they create and the consultative mechanisms they generate, despite the sometimes disconcerting flexibility of international rules and the absence of effective international sanctions in many areas.

Today, the absence of a hegemonial power and the enlargement of the international economic system to encompass a much larger and more widely divergent group of nations, including some for whom national sovereignty is a recent acquisition and a particularly sensitive issue, make the further development of a comprehensive formal international economic "constitution" unlikely for the foreseeable future. There are indications that, in many instances, countries will be willing to commit themselves informally to limitations on their own behavior which, if formalized, would be politically unacceptable. Thus, while efforts at international institution-building must be persistent, they must also recognize that progress in this direction will be marked by piecemeal, informal, evolutionary developments as well as by occasional ratification of formal documents.

THE INCOME TRANSFER SYSTEM: IMPACT, VIABILITY, AND PROPOSALS FOR REFORM

Barry R. Chiswick

Summary

This paper examines the distribution of income and the incidence of poverty in the United States. It also analyzes the effects of the major income transfer programs that are targeted to the poor or to those who incur an involuntary decline in income. The two primary objectives of the income transfer system are, first, to alter the distribution of income so as to reduce family income inequality and the incidence of poverty, and, second, to make the system financially, economically, and politically viable over the long term. Financial viability refers to the actuarial soundness of the social insurance programs, such as social security. Economic viability refers to the proportion of the nation's resources that the system transfers. Political viability refers to the response of society to the net redistribution impact, through taxes and transfers, that is inherent in the system.

The differences between the current set of welfare programs and a negative income tax (NIT) are considered in some detail. The chapter also analyzes the impact and the short-term and long-term viability of the largest—and perhaps most important—income transfer program, the social security system.

The first section examines the official data on the level and inequality of income and the incidence of poverty. During the last three decades (1947–1975), average family income, expressed in constant dollars, has increased at an average annual rate of 2.1 percent, but the growth rate has varied considerably. Growth was 3.1 percent during the 1960s and was negligible in the first half of the 1970s. Family income inequality has, however, been remarkably stable, although there is a tendency for inequality to increase in a recession and decline in an expansion.

The growth in average income brought a reduction in the number of people at or below the poverty level from 40 million in 1959 to 23 million in 1973. As a result of the subsequent recession, the number of people in poverty rose to 26 million in 1975. The rise in poverty from 1973 to 1975 is somewhat smaller than would have been expected on the basis of historical experience, given the severity of the recession. Rising real wage rates and social security benefits, however, have changed the composition of the poor segment of society. Relatively few of today's low-income families are two-parent families with an adult worker. The poor are predominantly aged widows or families headed by a woman or a disabled man.

The second section of this paper examines the characteristics and recent developments of the seven major cash and in-kind transfer programs—including their responsiveness to swings in the business cycle. Of the $140 billion in federal, state, and local government expenditure for benefits under these programs in fiscal year (FY) 1976, one-half ($71 billion) was for social security. Unemployment compensation ($18 billion in FY 1976) is the most important counter-cyclical program. The maximum duration of unemployment benefits was temporarily extended to an unprecedented sixty-five weeks, and coverage was temporarily extended to all wage and salary workers.

Aid to Families with Dependent Children (AFDC) is the largest cash welfare program ($10 billion in FY 1976). Because of large increases in benefits for participating families, AFDC grew rapidly in the 1960s but as average real benefits have been stable its growth has been slow in the 1970s. Substantial expansion of the present small program that provides benefits for families with an unemployed father may be generated by a 1975 Supreme Court decision permitting eligible unemployed fathers (UF) to choose between unemployment compensation and AFDC-UF in states where the latter program exists. Supplemental Security Income ($6 billion in FY 1976), the latest federal welfare program, replaced the state programs for the aged, blind, and disabled in 1974.

The food stamp program ($5 billion in FY 1976) is the equivalent of a mini-negative income tax, although the benefits are in the form of food vouchers. It is the most cyclically sensitive income transfer program after unemployment compensation. Presidents Ford and Carter have proposed differing legislation to increase the program's efficiency and decrease participation by families that are not really poor. If adopted, President Carter's proposal to remove the minimum stamp purchase requirement for participating families would soon result in the "cashing-out" of the food stamp program (replacing food vouchers by cash benefits).

The third section examines the effects of the underreporting of cash income and the impact on income distribution of taxes and the transfer system, including transfers in cash and in kind. Correcting the official data for the underreporting of cash income raises the figures for the income of the poor and reduces the figures for the incidence of poverty. The transfer system is found to have a far more substantial redistribution effect than the tax system. Because of its enormous scale, social security has the greatest impact in reducing income inequality and the incidence of poverty. Cash public assistance (welfare) benefits are received almost exclusively by the very poorest of families. The programs for transfers in kind, particularly food stamps, Medicare, and Medicaid, appear to be important in reducing income inequality and poverty, but their effects are difficult to quantify. A study of the full impact of the transfer system needs to consider the effects on work effort, savings, and family composition.

Family income inequality as officially measured in the past three decades has been roughly stable. However, the analysis indicates that if these data were corrected for underreporting of cash income, and if they included the cash equivalent value of transfers in kind, which have grown rapidly in the last decade, a time series would show a decline in income inequality. These adjustments would also indicate a steeper decline in poverty than the official statistics show.

The paper next compares the current set of categorical welfare programs with a negative income tax (NIT) and discusses President Carter's twelve goals for welfare reform. The current set of programs differs from an NIT in two major respects: it is more costly to administer because several agencies are involved, and the programs and benefits for which a family is eligible depend on the family's specific characteristics (demographic differentiation). The fragmentation of administration may be wasteful. Demographic differentiation, on the other hand, saves program costs while providing work incentives for families from whom work effort is expected. The benefit structure implicit in Carter's goals does not have this feature, and in fact some of his goals may be inconsistent with others. The goals also imply that for families with children the federal government is to be an employer of last resort for at least one adult in the family.

The next section analyzes the social security system. Coverage has been expanded and eligibility for benefits eased; in addition, real social security benefits have increased faster than real earnings. For *male workers retiring at age sixty-five, social security replaced about 30 percent of real preretirement earnings during the 1950s and 1960s, after which the replacement rate increased, reaching 43 percent by 1976. The social security system has encouraged earlier retirement. The unfunded spouse benefit (which automatically entitles a wife to an amount equal to at least one-half of her husband's benefit) creates a disparity between families where the wife does not work and all others. This could be corrected by reducing the automatic entitlement and allowing nonworking women to contribute to the system to create their own benefits.*

The social security trust funds are on the verge of bankruptcy, and several short-term solutions are discussed. In the long run the system as now formulated will not be viable; the aging of the population and a quirk in the 1972 legislation, called double indexing, will in fifty years (by 2030) result in aggregate social security payment obligations equal to 26 percent of aggregate taxable earnings in covered employment (as defined in current law). The two major procedures proposed for "decoupling" (ending the double indexing of benefits) are wage indexing and price indexing.

President Carter's recent social security proposals include increasing the maximum taxable earnings (particularly for the employer's component of the tax) to solve the short-term problem, and wage indexing to achieve decoupling. If wage indexing were adopted, by the year 2030 social security benefits would be 19 percent of taxable earnings (as defined in current law). Under price indexing they would be 12.5 percent. If the age at retirement were gradually increased by three years and price indexing were adopted, benefits in 2030 would be 11 percent of taxable earnings—not very different from the current tax rate of 9.9 percent.

The Distribution of Family Income

Public policy should be concerned with the level and distribution of the economic well-being of the population. This concept is neither easy to define nor easy to measure. Economic well-being or "full income" is determined by money income, income in kind (such as home production or the rental value of owner-occupied dwellings), and the quantity and quality of leisure. It is difficult to estimate the cash-equivalent value to a family of income in kind and its consequent impact on income distribution. One set of estimates of the effect of income in kind is discussed in detail below in the section on transfers, taxes, and redistribution. Even more difficult is measuring the value of leisure, yet leisure is an important aspect of a family's economic well-being. If two families are the same size and have the same income in money and in kind, but only one person works full time in family A while two members work full time in family B, then family A enjoys more leisure (nonmoney income) and has a higher level of full income.

It is also difficult to define the relevant recipient unit. The family is generally viewed as the most relevant unit since individuals within families (people living in the same household who are related by blood or marriage) tend to pool their money and nonmoney income. There are, however, important unrequited interfamily transfers of money and nonmoney income. In addition, the size and characteristics of a family change over the life cycle and change with economic circumstances. The incentives built into public transfer programs can result in changes in household composition that, using conventional measures, appear to exacerbate the conditions they are designed to correct. For example, by enabling many low-income aged persons to live by themselves rather than with adult children, the social security system may have increased the number of aged persons living in low-income family units.

Public policy is concerned with several analytically distinct dimensions of the distribution of family income. These include the average level of income (mean and median),[1] the inequality of income around the average level, and the proportion of the population below a given income defined as the poverty level. The policy instruments designed to alter these three dimensions of income distribution are sometimes viewed as independent of each other. In practice, however, they are often related.

Overall or average income is generally viewed as the primary target of macroeconomic monetary and fiscal policy. Yet by promoting a recovery of income from a recession, these policies also reduce income inequality and poverty. On the other hand, policies that promote more rapid long-term (secular) economic growth may generate an increase in income inequality.[2]

Policies specifically designed to reduce income inequality are usually microeconomic and may focus either on the upper end or on the lower end of the income distribution scale. Gift and estate taxa-

---

[1] If families are ranked by their income, the income level that divides them into two groups of equal size is the median income. The mean is the arithmetic average.

[2] See, for example, Barry R. Chiswick, "Earnings Inequality and Economic Development," *Quarterly Journal of Economics*, vol. 85, no. 1 (February 1971), pp. 21-39.

Table 1

DISTRIBUTION OF AGGREGATE INCOME AMONG FAMILIES, 1947–1975

| Year | Percent Distribution of Aggregate Income | | | | | | Mean Family Income (in constant 1975 dollars) | Unemployment Rate, Males 25-54 |
	Lowest fifth	Second fifth	Middle fifth	Fourth fifth	Highest fifth	Top 5 percent		
1947	5.1	11.8	16.7	23.2	43.3	17.5	8,592	—
1948	5.0	12.1	17.2	23.2	42.5	17.1	8,250	2.6
1949	4.5	11.9	17.3	23.5	42.8	16.9	8,094	4.6
1950	4.5	11.9	17.4	23.6	42.7	17.3	8,568	4.0
1951	4.9	12.5	17.6	23.3	41.8	16.9	8,744	2.2
1952	4.9	12.2	17.1	23.5	42.2	17.7	9,124	2.1
1953	4.7	12.4	17.8	24.0	41.0	15.8	9,535	2.2
1954	4.5	12.0	17.6	24.0	41.9	16.4	9,440	4.4
1955	4.8	12.2	17.7	23.4	41.8	16.8	10,070	3.2
1956	4.9	12.4	17.9	23.6	41.1	16.4	10,660	3.0
1957	5.0	12.6	18.1	23.7	40.5	15.8	10,485	3.1
1958	5.0	12.5	18.0	23.9	40.6	15.4	10,359	5.6
1959	4.9	12.3	17.9	23.8	41.1	15.9	11,035	4.2

Year								
1960	4.8	12.2	17.8	24.0	41.3	15.9	11,317	4.2
1961	4.7	11.9	17.5	23.8	42.2	16.6	11,642	5.1
1962	5.0	12.1	17.6	24.0	41.3	15.7	11,868	4.0
1963	5.0	12.1	17.7	24.0	41.2	15.8	12,302	3.8
1964	5.1	12.0	17.7	24.0	41.2	15.9	12,729	3.2
1965	5.2	12.2	17.8	23.9	40.9	15.5	13,142	2.7
1966	5.6	12.4	17.8	23.8	40.5	15.6	13,922	2.1
1967	5.5	12.4	17.9	23.9	40.4	15.2	14,187	1.9
1968	5.6	12.4	17.7	23.7	40.5	15.6	14,960	1.7
1969	5.6	12.4	17.7	23.7	40.6	15.6	15,528	1.6
1970	5.4	12.2	17.6	23.8	40.9	15.6	15,394	2.8
1971	5.5	12.0	17.6	23.8	41.1	15.7	15,393	3.5
1972	5.4	11.9	17.5	23.9	41.4	15.9	16,242	3.1
1973	5.5	11.9	17.5	24.0	41.1	15.5	16,498	2.5
1974	5.4	12.0	17.6	24.1	41.0	15.3	15,828	3.1
1974[a]	5.5	12.0	17.5	24.0	41.0	15.5	16,056	3.1
1975[a]	5.4	11.8	17.6	24.1	41.1	15.5	15,546	5.7

[a] The procedures for reporting income were revised in 1974.

Source: U.S. Department of Commerce, Bureau of the Census, *Money Income in 1974 of Families and Persons in the United States,* Current Population Reports, Series P-60, no. 101 (January 1976), and *Money Income and Poverty Status of Families and Persons in the United States: 1975 and 1974 Revisions,* Current Population Reports, Series P-60, no. 103 (Advance Report, September 1976).

tion and high marginal tax rates on income are generally viewed as the instruments for reducing the net income at the upper end of the scale. Policies designed to raise directly the incomes of those at the lower end of the scale—that is, policies designed to reduce poverty— include income transfer and manpower training programs. Yet these policies may also influence the *average* level of income. Investments that increase the skills of the untrained at a low cost and hence have a high rate of return would decrease poverty and inequality and raise average real income. On the other hand, programs that supplement the income of the poor and reduce the economic incentives for work may decrease average real income.

The Level and Inequality of Family Income. Data on the distribution of family income and the incidence of poverty over time are usually expressed in terms of current money income. The most useful data are from the annual March supplement to the Current Population Survey (CPS).[3] The data refer to money income (before payroll and income taxes) received in the previous calendar year from wages, salary, self-employment, rent, interest, dividends, and public and private unrequited transfer payments. Excluded are income in the form of capital gains, imputed rent from owner-occupied dwellings, and the cash-equivalent value of public transfers in kind (such as food stamps, Medicare, and Medicaid).

Data on the average level and dispersion of family income from 1947 to 1975, as reported in the CPS, are presented in Table 1. The mean income is deflated by the consumer price index (CPI) to facilitate the comparison of real incomes. The share of income received by each quintile of the distribution is used to show relative income inequality. To facilitate comparisons over the business cycle, the table also reports the unemployment rate for adult men aged twenty-five through fifty-four inclusive, which is a useful cyclical indicator.[4]

Secular behavior. During the period since World War II there has been a dramatic rise in average family income. Mean family income, measured in 1975 dollars, increased by about 84 percent from nearly $8,600 in 1947 to over $15,000 in 1975, or at an annual rate of 2.1 percent. The rate of increase has not been uniform. After growing at an annual rate of 2.8 percent in the 1950s, real family income increased at an annual rate of 3.1 percent in the 1960s and

---

[3] There are currently about 47,000 households in the monthly CPS.

[4] This measure is preferable to the overall unemployment rate, which is sensitive to changes in the demographic characteristics (age and sex distribution) of the labor force.

did not grow from 1970 to 1975 (after adjusting for the revision in procedures). These differences from one decade to the next largely reflect the business cycle, with real family incomes rising more slowly —at times even declining—during recessions.

As became apparent in the recent presidential election, there is much confusion about the income of the "average" family. Mean family income in 1975 was $15,546—$17,513 for four-person families. Because some families have very high incomes, mean income is higher than median income. The median family income in 1975 was $13,719, and $15,848 for four-person families. A great fortune is not needed to place a family in an upper income group. A family with a total money income of $22,038 or more was in the upper 20 percent of families in 1975, and an income of $34,144 or more placed a family in the top 5 percent.[5]

Data on the dispersion or inequality of family income are frequently presented, as in Table 1, through the share of aggregate income received by each quintile of the distribution. A rise in the proportion of income received by the low-income families and a decrease for the high-income families constitutes a decline in inequality. Perhaps the most striking feature of inequality in family money incomes in the United States in the past thirty years, as reported in the CPS, is the relative absence of change: the average income in each quintile has risen by approximately the same percentage.[6] Thus the large increase in real income has been widely shared.

[5] In 1975, the upper limit of income for each quintile and the lower limit for the top 5 percent were:

	Limits ($)				
	Lowest Fifth	Second Fifth	Middle Fifth	Fourth Fifth	Top 5 Percent
Families	6,914	11,465	16,000	22,037	34,144
Unrelated individuals	2,320	3,760	6,150	10,025	17,100

Source: U.S. Department of Commerce, Bureau of the Census, *Money Income and Poverty Status of Families and Persons in the United States: 1975 and 1974 Revisions*, Current Population Reports, Series P-60, no. 103 (Advance Report, September 1976), Table 5.

[6] Focusing on the extremes of the distribution, there was some movement toward less inequality. The share of income received by the lowest quintile increased from 4.7 percent in the years 1950-1954 to 5.5 percent in 1970-1974. Moreover, the share received by the highest income families—the top 5 percent—declined from 16.8 percent in the period 1950-1954 to 15.6 percent in the years 1970-1974. However, this appearance of a reduction in inequality is exaggerated. The share of

To some, the failure of measured family income inequality to decline in the past three decades seems paradoxical, given the impressive rise in the average level of income and training (including schooling) and the rise in the share of gross national product (GNP) devoted to income transfers.[7] On closer examination, there may be no paradox. It has been shown elsewhere that income inequality is affected less by changes in the average level of income than by inequality in the possession of human and nonhuman assets.[8] Although the level of training has increased among adult men, for example, there appears to have been little change in the disparity of their schooling or of their labor market experience. Moreover, rates of return to schooling do not appear to have declined in response to the rise in the level of schooling, perhaps because much of the growth in schooling was stimulated by the increased demand for skill in the economy. In the analysis of the income transfer programs below, arguments will be presented which suggest that if allowance is made for the manner in which income is measured, for the distribution of benefits in income transfer programs, and for the effects of the programs on family structure, work effort, and savings, the paradox may be more apparent than real.

Cyclical behavior. In most recessions there is a tendency for the share of money income received by the lowest income groups to decrease. For example, from 1974 to 1975, when the overall unemployment rate increased from 5.6 percent to 8.5 percent, the share of income received by the lowest 40 percent of income recipients declined by 0.3 percentage points and the share received by the next 55 percent increased by 0.3 percentage points. This arises because the reduction in the length of the work week and the rise in unemploy-

---

income received by the second quintile declined slightly, while the share increased for those in the top quintile but not in the top 5 percent.

These distributions refer to family income in a particular year. There is substantial mobility of families among the quintiles from year to year. This is due partly to life-cycle changes in earnings and employment, and partly to the "random" component in income in any one year.

[7] The view that higher levels of income are associated with less income inequality has emerged largely from comparisons of developed countries with some less-developed countries in Latin America and Asia. In many of the poorest countries, however, there is very little inequality of income (for example, in Chad or Upper Volta).

[8] See, for example, Barry R. Chiswick, *Income Inequality: Regional Analyses within a Human Capital Framework* (New York: NBER, 1974) or Barry R. Chiswick and Jacob Mincer, "Time Series Changes in Personal Income Inequality in the United States since 1939, with Projections to 1985," *Journal of Political Economy, Supplement,* vol. 80, no. 3, part 2 (June 1972), pp. 34-66.

ment (reduction in the number of weeks worked) in a recession are not shared uniformly by all income groups.

The cyclical sensitivity of employment varies by occupation, industry, age, and race. Employment is more cyclically sensitive for unskilled than for highly skilled workers, for blue-collar than for white-collar workers, for younger (less-experienced) workers than for prime-age workers, and for blacks than for whites. As a result, the earnings, and hence the family incomes, of lower-income groups (less-skilled, young, black) are more cyclically sensitive than the incomes of the middle- and higher-income brackets.

The share of income received by the top 5 percent of families shows greater year-to-year variability than the share received by any of the quintiles, with the exception of the lowest. This arises in part from the smaller sample size—by definition there are four times more families in a quintile than in the top 5 percent of families. Another factor, however, is the greater variability of business profits in the form of self-employment income and corporate dividends, which are relatively more important in the incomes of the top 5 percent.[9]

Poverty. There is no single definition of poverty. It is usually measured as the percentage of the population living in families with incomes below a particular threshold. The income concept and the relevant threshold (which changes over time) determine the proportion of the population living in poverty in a given year.

Definition and measurement. The United States government's official poverty statistics are based on money income as reported in the CPS and on a poverty threshold derived from an index developed by the Social Security Administration in 1964 and revised by a federal interagency committee in 1969. The rationale for the threshold is that it is based on the Department of Agriculture's 1961 Economy Food Plan, which was intended to produce a nutritionally adequate diet and to reflect the differing consumption patterns of families according to size, composition, and residence, defined as farm or nonfarm. It was determined from the Department of Agriculture's 1955 survey of food consumption that families of three or more spend approixmately one-third of their money income on food. Hence the poverty threshold for those families was set at three times the cost of the economy food plan.[10]

---

[9] Capital gains are not counted as income in the CPS.

[10] A higher factor was used to compensate for the larger fixed expenses of smaller families and people living alone. U.S. Department of Commerce, Bureau of the Census, *Characteristics of the Population below the Poverty Level: 1974*, p. 143.

The poverty threshold is increased each year by the percentage increase in the overall consumer price index.[11] The official poverty threshold is therefore a measure of a given amount of real income and the threshold does not vary with changes in average real income. The poverty thresholds for 1975 are reported in Table 2.

Secular and cyclical behavior. The data in Table 3, columns (1) and (2) report the number of people and the percentage of the population living in poverty according to the official statistics. The data show a sharp decline in poverty from 40 million people in 1959 to about 23 million people in 1973. After 1973 poverty increased.[12] Be-

Table 2
POVERTY THRESHOLDS BY SIZE OF FAMILY, 1975

Size of Family Unit	Nonfarm		Farm	
	Male head of family	Female head of family	Male head of family	Female head of family
1 person	$2,851	$2,635	$2,396	$2,224
14 to 64 years	2,902	2,685	2,466	2,282
65 years and over	2,608	2,574	2,216	2,187
2 persons	3,515	3,460	2,963	2,834
Head, 14 to 64 years	3,636	3,530	3,086	1,933
Head, 65 years and over	3,260	3,237	2,772	2,770
3 persons	4,317	4,175	3,652	3,480
4 persons	5,502	5,473	4,697	4,616
5 persons	6,504	6,434	5,552	5,595
6 persons	7,322	7,270	6,230	6,105
7 persons or more	9,056	8,818	7,639	7,647

Note: The thresholds are weighted by the presence of children and hence are average poverty thresholds. The actual poverty count is based on a more detailed set of 124 poverty levels that explicitly account for differences in the number of children in a family of a given size.

Source: Department of Commerce, *Money Income and Poverty Status of Families and Persons in the United States*, Table 16.

---

[11] Before revisions in 1969, the threshold was revised each year by changes in the cost of the food in the economy food plan. During the 1960s food prices were rising less rapidly than the CPI. When the CPI was retroactively adopted as the price index, measured poverty increased. The change in the price index (using 1963 as the base) together with a minor change in the differential between farm and nonfarm income increased the poverty population in 1967 by 1.6 million people, or 0.8 percent of the total population.

[12] Revised procedures for recording income in 1974 resulted in a decline in reported poverty by 900,000 people and in the poverty rate by 0.4 percentage points. To keep the series comparable, the data in this paragraph assume the revision did not occur.

Table 3
PERSONS IN POVERTY, ACTUAL AND PREDICTED, 1959–1975

Year	Actual		Predicted Percentage of Population [a]	Actual Minus Predicted Percentage of Population
	Number (in millions)	Percentage of population		
1959	39.5	22.5	22.7	−0.2
1960	39.9	22.2	22.2	0.0
1961	39.6	21.9	22.2	−0.3
1962	38.6	21.0	20.6	−0.4
1963	36.4	19.5	19.7	−0.2
1964	36.1	19.0	18.4	0.6
1965	33.2	17.3	17.0	0.3
1966	28.5	14.7	15.3	−0.6
1967	27.8	14.2	13.7	0.5
1968	25.4	12.8	13.1	−0.3
1969	24.1	12.1	12.3	−0.2
1970	25.4	12.6	12.5	0.1
1971	25.6	12.5	12.6	−0.1
1972	24.5	11.9	12.1	−0.1
1973	23.0	11.1	10.8	0.3
1974	24.3	11.6	11.5	0.1
1975	—	12.7 [b]	12.8	−0.1
1974 [c]	23.4	11.2	11.1	—
1975 [c]	25.9	12.3	12.4	—

[a] Predicted from the regression equation in Table 4.

[b] Actual value computed by adding 0.4 percentage points to the 1975 poverty rate published by the Bureau of the Census which uses the revised procedures.

[c] Using 1974 revision of procedures.

Source: Department of Commerce, *Money Income and Poverty Status of Families and Persons in the United States*, Table 17; U.S. Department of Commerce, Bureau of the Census, *Characteristics of the Population below the Poverty Level: 1974* (1975), Table 1.

cause the population has increased, the decline in the *proportion* of the population in poverty was even more dramatic: from 23 percent in 1959 to 11 percent in 1973, with a rise to 13 percent in 1975. The change in poverty over time can be related to changes in statistical measurement and to both cyclical fluctuations and secular trends.

The official poverty rate can be explained statistically by a simple econometric equation (Table 4).[13] Whether a person is classi-

---

[13] This and the following four paragraphs are based on Barry R. Chiswick and Michael C. McCarthy, "A Note on Predicting the Poverty Rate," *Journal of Human Resources*, vol. 12, no. 3 (Summer 1977).

Table 4
REGRESSION ANALYSIS OF POVERTY RATE, 1959–1975

Variable	Slope Coefficient	t-Ratio
Intercept	13.074	3.17
Disposable personal income per capita	−2.568	−2.84
Unemployment rate	0.546	6.15
Time dummy[a]	−0.861	−2.19
Percent of employment in agriculture	1.57	6.10
Adjusted R square		0.9923
Durbin-Watson statistic		2.80
Standard error of regression		0.37
Number of observations		17

[a] Variable equals unity for 1967 and subsequent years, zero for years prior to 1967.

Source: Barry R. Chiswick and Michael C. McCarthy, "A Note on Predicting the Poverty Rate," *Journal of Human Resources*, vol. 12, no. 3 (Summer 1977).

fied as being in poverty is determined by the real money income of his family. Thus, the official poverty rate is a function of both the mean level of money income and the dispersion (inequality) in its distribution. Real disposable personal income per capita (measured in thousands of constant 1972 dollars) is a measure of the mean level of income and reflects secular developments. Family income inequality increases in a recession and declines in a cyclical expansion, so the unemployment rate is used as an indicator of cyclical changes in overall family income inequality, and hence in poverty.

The poverty threshold differs for farm and nonfarm families and unrelated individuals to reflect what the Bureau of the Census presumably believes to be differences in the cost of living and in non-money income.[14] For persons at the poverty threshold, if the shift out of agriculture resulted in an increase in income greater than the difference in the poverty thresholds, the poverty rate would decrease. Some of the increase in measured income as families shift from farm to nonfarm employment is due to differences in the accuracy with which money income is reported. It will be shown below (Table 9) that in the aggregate, cash wages, salaries, and nonfarm self-employ-

---

[14] In 1975, the poverty threshold for a four-person family with a male family head was $5,502 for nonfarm residents and $4,697 for farm residents.

ment income are accurately reported, but that only about one-half of farm self-employment income is reported in the CPS. The variable, "percent of employment in agriculture," is found to have a significant positive correlation with the poverty rate. It is not clear, however, whether this reflects a real or a measurement effect.

Because of a change in the methodology used for processing income data and several changes in the CPS questions relating to unemployment, there may be a break in the comparability of data at around 1967. To account for these measurement effects, a dichotomous variable has been included in Table 4 which takes the value of zero before 1967, unity for 1967 and thereafter. This variable is statistically significant, and the magnitude of its coefficient is consistent with the estimate for 1967 of the difference in the poverty rate when both sets of procedures are applied to the family income data. Given these variables, experiments revealed no significant time trends, nor did the inclusion of time variables make any of the other variables insignificant.

From 1959 to 1975 the poverty rate declined by 10.2 percentage points (Table 3). This decline can be broken down among the explanatory variables. The increase in real per capita disposable income (in 1972 dollars) from $2,700 in 1959 to $4,000 in 1975 was responsible for a decline in the poverty rate of 3.3 percentage points. The relative decline in farm employment from 8.6 percent to 4.0 percent of total employment was associated with a 7.2 percentage point decline in poverty. The changes in statistical procedures in 1967 and in 1974 appear to be responsible for declines in the measured poverty rate of 0.9 percentage points and 0.4 percentage points, respectively. On the other hand the increase in the unemployment rate from 5.5 percent in 1959 to 8.5 percent in 1975 tended to increase the poverty rate by 1.6 percentage points.

The apparent strong positive correlation between farm employment and the poverty rate is in part a reflection of the substantial underreporting of farm income. The associated decline in farm employment and in poverty may, however, also be measuring the effects of other developments in the rural economy. The proportion of employment in agriculture may not continue to decline, but further increases in real per capita disposable income can be expected to bring a further long-term decline in the poverty rate.

The sharp rise in the measured poverty rate in the recent recession has attracted considerable attention. From 1973 to 1975, the poverty rate increased by 1.6 percentage points. The regression analysis in Table 4 can indicate whether the increase is consistent with the severity of the recession. With the rise in the unemployment rate and the decline in real per capita disposable income, historical experience (as expressed by the regression equation) would suggest an increase of 2.0 percentage points. Although the observed increase from 1973 to 1975 of 1.6 percentage points is less than the predicted increase, the difference is not statistically significant. Thus the recent sharp rise in the measured poverty rate appears to be consistent with the severity of the downturn in the economy. As the economy recovers from the recession and real family income grows, the poverty rate can be expected to resume its decline.

The changing composition of the poor. The sharp decline in the number and proportion of families in poverty since the start of the official series in 1959 has not been uniform among demographic groups (Table 5). The poor are now far less likely than they were in the past to be in families with a working member or to be aged.

Of the 8.3 million families in poverty in 1959 (not counting unrelated individuals as a family) 28 percent were headed by a man age twenty-five to sixty-four who worked all year (fifty to fifty-two weeks) and another 19 percent were headed by a man twenty-five to sixty-four who worked only part of the year, primarily because of unemployment. By 1974, a year with a similarity to 1959 in its overall unemployment rate (5.5 percent), only 14 percent of the 5.1 million families in poverty were headed by a man aged twenty-five to sixty-four who worked all year and 13 percent were headed by a man who worked part of the year. This decline in poverty among families headed by a working male under age sixty-five was not directly due to income transfer programs, as these families are generally not eligible for cash transfers other than unemployment compensation.[15] This suggests that the decline in poverty for these families was largely due to the increases in real earned family income, resulting from the increase in real wage rates and the increase in the labor force participation of wives.

From 1959 to 1974 families in poverty headed by a person aged sixty-five or over fell sharply both in number and as a proportion of poor families. While 1.8 million such families were in poverty in 1959, only 0.7 million were in poverty in 1974. This decline was primarily due to the expansion in the coverage and benefit levels of

---

[15] There may have been an indirect effect, however, to the extent that such programs as AFDC encouraged marital breakup or discouraged remarriage, producing families headed by a female and an unrelated adult male. See Marjorie Honig, "AFDC Income, Labor Supply and Family Dissolution," *Journal of Human Resources*, vol. 9, no. 3 (Summer 1974), pp. 303-22.

social security, as discussed later in this chapter. Rising real wage rates have also had the effect of removing some aged persons from poverty, but many others were included due to the decline in labor-force participation.

The number of families in poverty headed by a woman age twenty-five to sixty-four increased from 1.4 million in 1959 to 1.8 million in 1974, and from 17 percent to 35 percent of the families in poverty. The number of such families in which the female head worked at any time during the year showed little change over the period. On the other hand, the number who did not work increased by 300,000 to 1.0 million. This is in contrast to the number of families headed by nonworking men twenty-five to sixty-four years old, which remained static at approximately 400,000 during the entire period.

Among families headed by young women under twenty-five, the number in poverty increased from 100,000 to 500,000 during the fifteen-year period, increasing their proportion among all poor families from 2 percent to 9 percent. Women in this group have young children and work very little during the year. Income transfers, including AFDC, food stamps, and Medicaid, are a very important source of income for these families.

Hence the composition of poverty families has changed. In 1959 they consisted predominantly of working low-income families under sixty-five (62 percent)[16] or aged families (22 percent), while by 1974 these groups were relatively less numerous in a smaller poverty population (47 percent and 15 percent, respectively). Among family heads under sixty-five who do not work (or who are in a group with a very low rate of employment)[17] the absolute number in poverty and the proportion among the poor has increased: from 1.2 million families and 15 percent of the poor in 1959 to 2.0 million families and 39 percent of the poor in 1974.

Poverty among unrelated individuals (that is, persons age fourteen or older not living in a multi-person family) is also largely associated with not working.[18] Of the 4.8 million unrelated indi-

---

[16] From Table 5, the sum of families with a male head under twenty-five, a male head twenty-five to sixty-four who worked all year or part of the year, a male head in the armed forces, and a female head twenty-five to sixty-four who worked all year or part of the year.

[17] From Table 5, the sum of families with a male head twenty-five to sixty-four who did not work, those with a female head twenty-five to sixty-four who did not work, and those with a female head under twenty-five.

[18] Department of Commerce, *Characteristics of the Population below the Poverty Level: 1974*, Tables 7 and 12.

Table 5

FAMILIES IN POVERTY, BY SEX, AGE, AND WORK EXPERIENCE OF HEAD, 1959–1974

Head of Family[a]	Millions of Families				Percentage of all Poor Families			
	1959	1969	1973	1974	1959	1969	1973	1974
Male Head	6.4	3.2	2.6	2.8	77.0	63.5	54.6	54.0
Under 25	.5	.3	.3	.3	5.7	5.3	5.9	5.6
25-64	4.4	1.9	1.7	1.9	52.8	38.0	35.5	36.3
Worked all year	2.3	.9	.7	.7	27.9	17.4	14.1	14.0
Worked full time	2.1	.8	.6	.6	25.4	16.0	13.0	12.6
Worked part year	1.6	.6	.6	.7	19.0	12.3	11.9	12.6
Unemployed	1.0	.2	.3	.4	11.3	4.8	5.4	7.0
Other	.6	.4	.3	.3	7.7	7.5	6.5	5.6
Didn't work	.4	.4	.4	.5	4.6	7.7	9.4	9.5
Ill, disabled	.3	.3	.3	.3	3.1	5.8	6.7	6.7
Other	.1	.1	.1	.1	1.5	1.9	2.7	2.8
In Armed Forces	.1	b	b	b	1.3	.6	.1	.1
65 and over	1.5	1.0	.6	.6	18.5	20.2	13.2	12.1

Female Head	1.9	1.8	2.2	2.3	23.0	36.5	45.4	46.0
Under 25	.1	.3	.4	.5	1.8	5.3	8.1	8.8
25-64	1.4	1.3	1.6	1.8	17.3	25.9	33.3	34.5
Worked all year	.3	.2	.2	.3	3.2	4.3	4.2	5.0
Worked full time	.2	.1	.1	.2	2.2	2.7	2.8	3.3
Worked part year	.4	.4	.4	.5	5.3	8.2	9.4	9.3
Unemployed	.1	.1	.1	.2	1.0	1.0	2.1	2.8
Other	.3	.3	.3	.3	4.3	7.2	7.3	6.5
Didn't work	.7	.7	1.0	1.0	8.8	13.4	19.7	20.2
Keeping house	.6	.5	.7	.7	7.7	10.6	15.0	14.3
Ill, disabled	b	.1	.2	.2	b	2.1	3.4	4.1
Other	b	b	.1	.1	b	.6	1.3	1.8
65 and over	.3	.3	.2	.1	3.9	5.3	4.0	2.8
All Poor Families	8.3	5.0	4.8	5.1	100.0	100.0	100.0	100.0

a Unrelated individuals, persons not living in a family, are excluded.

b Fewer than 50,000 families or less than 0.05 percent.

Source: U.S. Department of Health, Education, and Welfare, Social Security Administration, *Social Security Bulletin, Annual Statistical Supplement, 1974* (1976), p. 44, Table 9.

viduals in poverty in 1974, one-third were women sixty-five and over, one-third were women under sixty-five, one-twelfth were men sixty-five and over, and the remaining one-quarter were men under sixty-five. Among unrelated individuals in poverty, 65 percent did not work at any time during the year, most of them (about 88 percent) because of ill health, disability, retirement or "keeping house." Going to school and inability to find work were minor reasons for not working (2.3 percent and 4.2 percent, respectively, of the poor unrelated individuals). Although 35 percent of the unrelated individuals in poverty worked at some time in 1974, only half of these worked at least part time in more than twenty-six weeks in the year. Only 6 percent of the unrelated individuals in poverty worked full time (thirty-five hours or more per week) for at least fifty weeks.

Rising real wages and the expansion of coverage and real benefits under social security have gone far to solve the poverty problems of many, but among nonworking family heads under sixty-five and aged widows, measured poverty is still substantial. The statistical procedures, however, exaggerate measured poverty, particularly for these groups. Much of the cash income of the nonworking population under sixty-five and aged widows is in the form of income transfers, such as AFDC social security widows' benefits and disability benefits, and general assistance, which (as is shown below) are subject to substantial underreporting in the CPS. The most important changes in the income transfer system in the past fifteen years have been the introduction of programs for assistance in kind, particularly food stamps, Medicare, and Medicaid, which are not included in income for the computation of the incidence of poverty. Food stamps and Medicaid are important sources of real income for low-income families headed by women, and these programs as well as Medicare are available to families headed by disabled men and aged widows. The characteristics of the income transfer programs are discussed in the next section of the chapter. In a later section it is shown that reported poverty is substantially reduced when the CPS data are corrected for the underreporting of cash income and the exclusion of transfers in kind.

The Income Transfer System: Characteristics, Recent Developments, and Cyclical Behavior

In FY 1976, federal, state, and local government expenditures for the seven major income transfer programs exceeded $140 billion, excluding administrative expenses. These programs transfer resources to persons or families who actually experience, or are presumed to experience, low income or a decline in income for a variety of involuntary reasons. These reasons include old age, disability, unemployment, and the absence from the family of a working father. The programs were enacted at different times; they vary substantially in their basic characteristics and in their impact (Table 6). This section summarizes the basic characteristics of the income transfer programs and describes some recent developments.[19] It also considers the response of program participation and costs to the recent recession and subsequent economic recovery.

The income transfer programs played an important role in the recent recession and during the subsequent recovery. They helped to maintain aggregate demand by rapidly transferring purchasing power to people who experienced a decline in income, thus to some degree fulfilling their function as built-in stabilizers. At the same time they appeared to be fulfilling their second important function, promoting a more equal sharing of the burden resulting from the unequal impact of unemployment during a recession.

For the seven major income transfer programs, the total quarterly benefit payments in cash, in vouchers, and in services (expressed at an annual rate) increased from $108 billion in the fourth quarter of 1974 to $135 billion in the third quarter of 1975, after which it grew more slowly, reaching $147 billion in the fourth quarter of 1976 (Table 7). Real expenditures were substantially higher in third quarter 1975 than in the recession trough because of the 8 percent automatic cost-of-living increase in social security benefits in June. The differential changes in program sizes from fourth quarter 1974 to fourth quarter 1976 reflect different cyclical sensitivities and legal, administrative, and judicial changes in the programs.

The Cash Transfer Programs. As a result of the Social Security Act of 1935, three cash assistance programs were created, Old Age and

---

[19] For a study of the growth over time of the income transfer system, see Herbert Stein, this volume. For more detailed analyses of program characteristics and impacts see Barry R. Chiswick and June A. O'Neill, eds., *Human Resources and Income Distribution: Issues and Policies* (New York: Norton, 1977); see also Kenneth W. Clarkson, *Food Stamps and Nutrition* (Washington, D.C.: American Enterprise Institute, 1975), Karen Davis and Roger Reynolds, "The Impact of Medicare and Medicaid on Access to Medical Care," *The Role of Health Insurance in the Health Services Sector*, ed. Richard Rosett (New York: National Bureau of Economic Research, 1976), and Rita R. Campbell, *Social Security* (Stanford: Hoover Institution Press, 1977). For a review of the literature on the effect of unemployment compensation on the unemployment rate, see Phillip Cagan in this volume.

Table 6
ASPECTS OF THE MAJOR FEDERAL INCOME
TRANSFER PROGRAMS, FY 1976

Program	Federal Department	Year Program Enacted	Basis of Eligibility
Social Security (OASDI)	HEW	OASI, 1935; DI, 1957	Age, disability, or death of parent or spouse; individual earnings
Supplemental Security Income (SSI)	HEW	1972	Age or disability; income
Aid to Families with Dependent Children (AFDC)	HEW	1935	Certain families with children;[b] income
Food Stamp	Agriculture	1964[c]	Income
Unemployment Compensation	Labor	1935; SUA and FSB, 1974	Unemployment[d]
Medicare	HEW	1965	Age or disability
Medicaid	HEW	1965	Persons eligible for AFDC or SSI, and in some states the medically indigent; income
Total			

Note: The acronyms not explained in the table, going down the columns from left to right stand for: OASDI, Old Age, Survivors, and Disability Insurance; HEW, Department of Health, Education, and Welfare; DI, Disability Insurance; SUA, Special Unemployment Assistance; and FSB, Federal Supplementary Benefits.

a Expenditures by federal, state and local governments; excludes administrative expenses.

b Families with children deprived of support because of death, absence from home, or incapacity of parent, or in some states, in certain circumstances, unemployment of father (AFDC-UF).

c Started as a pilot project in a few counties in 1961, it became a regular program with the Food Stamp Act of 1964. The program spread among the counties and, as a result of 1973 legislation, it became nationwide as of July 1974.

Sources of Funds	Form of Aid	FY 1976	
		Expenditures[a] (in billions of dollars)	Beneficiaries (monthly average, in millions of people)
Federal payroll taxes on employers and employees	Cash	71.4	32.1
Federal revenues (some state supplementation)	Cash	6.0	4.3
Federal, state, local revenues	Cash and services	9.8	11.4
Federal revenues	Vouchers	5.3	18.6
For permanent programs, state and federal payroll tax on employers for SUA and FSB, federal revenues	Cash	18.3	12.5
Federal payroll tax on employers and employees	Subsidized health insurance	16.9	25.1[e]
Federal, state, local revenues	Subsidized health services	14.7	9.1
		141.4	[f]

[d] Involuntary separation from employment or voluntary separation for good cause.

[e] Estimated number of enrollees with hospital insurance and/or supplementary medical insurance.

[f] The total number of beneficiaries is less than the sum of program beneficiaries because of multiple program participation.

Source: U.S. Department of Health, Education, and Welfare, U.S. Department of Labor, and the Food and Nutrition Service, U.S. Department of Agriculture.

Table 7

INCOME TRANSFER PROGRAMS, 1974–1976

(Not seasonally adjusted)

Program	Unit	1974 IV	1975 I	1975 II	1975 III	1975 IV	1976 I	1976 II	1976 III	1976 IV
Unemployment										
Total number of persons	Millions	5.6	8.3	8.0	7.8	7.2	7.9	6.9	7.3	7.0
Unemployment Compensation										
Beneficiaries										
Total	Millions[a]	2.3	5.1	5.5	5.3	4.8	5.2	4.3	3.9	3.6
Permanent programs	Millions	2.3	4.7	4.6	4.0	3.5	4.1	3.2	2.8	2.8
FSB and SUA[b]	Millions		.4	.7	1.3	1.3	1.1	1.1	1.1	0.8
Benefit payments[c]										
Total[d]	Billions of dollars[d]	7.8	17.3	19.0	18.4	17.6	20.6	16.0	13.3	14.0
Permanent programs	Billions of dollars	7.8	16.2	16.7	14.7	13.2	15.6	12.2	11.1	11.2
FSB and SUA	Billions of dollars		1.1	2.3	3.7	4.4	5.0	3.8	2.2	2.8
Food Stamp Program										
Beneficiaries	Millions[e]	15.9	18.6	19.2	18.6	18.5	18.8	18.2	17.3	17.2
Benefit payments	Billions of dollars[d]	4.0	4.9	5.0	5.2	5.1	5.6	5.4	5.1	5.0
Aid to Families with Dependent Children										
Beneficiaries										
Total	Millions[e]	10.9	11.3	11.3	11.3	11.4	11.5	11.3	11.2	11.2
Unemployed fathers	Millions	.4	.5	.5	.5	.6	.7	.7	.6	.6
Benefit payments[c]	Billions of dollars[d]	8.4	8.9	8.9	9.3	9.8	10.1	9.9	10.0	10.0

Old-age, Survivors, and Disability Insurance										
Beneficiaries Total [f]	Millions [e]	30.7	31.1	31.1	31.5	31.9	32.3	32.4	32.6	32.9
Retired workers and dependents	Millions	19.6	19.8	19.9	20.1	20.3	20.5	20.5	20.6	20.9
Disabled workers and dependents	Millions	3.9	4.0	4.1	4.2	4.3	4.4	4.5	4.5	4.6
Benefit payments [g]	Billions of dollars [d]	56.8	60.6	63.0	67.1	68.3	69.4	71.4	75.3	76.8
Medicaid										
Beneficiaries	Millions [e]	8.2	8.8	9.0	8.7	9.0	9.4	9.3	9.1	8.9
Benefit payments	Billions of dollars [d]	11.9	13.4	14.3	13.7	14.6	15.3	15.3	15.8	15.8
Medicare										
Benefit payments	Billions of dollars [d]	13.7	14.9	15.4	15.5	16.5	17.3	18.3	18.6	19.4
Supplemental Security Income										
Beneficiaries	Millions [e]	4.0	4.1	4.2	4.3	4.3	4.3	4.3	4.3	4.3
Benefit payments	Billions of dollars [c, d]	5.5	5.6	5.6	5.9	6.0	6.0	6.0	6.2	6.2
Total benefits										
Current dollars	Billions of dollars	108.1	125.6	131.2	135.1	137.9	144.3	142.3	144.3	147.2
Real dollars (base 1976 IV) [h]	Billions of dollars	121.8	139.0	143.0	144.1	144.8	150.1	146.2	145.9	147.2

Note: Benefits are quarterly expenditures expressed at an annual rate. Program participants are those actually receiving benefits in that quarter.

a Weekly average.
b Federal Supplemental Benefits (FSB) and Special Unemployment Assistance (SUA).
c Includes state as well as federal payments.
d Annual rate.
e Monthly average.
f Total also includes recipients of survivors benefits.
g In current payment status.
h Deflated by the consumer price index.

Source: U.S. Department of Agriculture, U.S. Department of Health, Education, and Welfare, and U.S. Department of Labor.

Survivors Insurance (OASI, more generally referred to as social security), unemployment compensation, and Aid to Families with Dependent Children (AFDC). The disability insurance component of social security was created in 1957. Social security is the largest of the cash income transfer programs and is the only one that is exclusively federal. Unemployment compensation and AFDC are administered by the states, within broad federal guidelines. Supplemental Security Income (SSI), which came into effect in 1974 to replace the separate state programs, is a federal cash income transfer program for the aged, blind, and disabled low-income population, but it includes state supplementation of benefits.

Social security and unemployment compensation were viewed as social insurance programs to be financed through payroll tax contributions, levied on the employer and employee for social security, and levied solely on the employer for unemployment compensation. A pension for a company's aged workers (and for its workers' widows and orphans) and compensation for its workers' unemployment were to be viewed as part of the cost of doing business. Because these programs are viewed as insurance, their benefits increase with the worker's earnings and the length of his employment and do not depend on a means test to prove economic hardship. Over time, the proportion of paid wage and salary employment (and self-employment for social security) covered by these programs has expanded to the point where there is now virtually universal coverage for workers in the private sector of the economy.

Social security (OASDI). The social security system is examined in some detail below. This section reviews only the recent countercyclical adjustments made in the program. Since the reasons for participation are old age, disability, or the death of a worker, the cyclical sensitivity in the social security system is not very significant in relation to its size. Participation and total benefits in the social security system do, however, tend to rise in a recession (Table 7). Unemployed aged workers in most states can receive both social security and unemployment compensation benefits; unemployment compensation is not counted in the social security earnings test. Participation in the disability insurance component of social security is more cyclically sensitive than the retirement and survivors' component, in spite of the five-month waiting period after the onset of total disability.[20] Partici-

---

[20] See Mordechai E. Lando, "The Effect of Unemployment on Application for Disability Insurance," *American Statistical Association, 1974 Proceedings of Business and Economics Statistics Section* (1975), pp. 438-42.

pation in the disability insurance program increased by 10 percent in 1975, compared with 7 percent in 1976, while participation in the retired workers' and survivors' program increased by about 3 percent in each of the two years.

Unemployment compensation. By design, the most cyclically sensitive of all of the income transfer programs is unemployment compensation. Aggregate transfers under the program rise automatically as unemployment from job layoffs increases. The total number of beneficiaries under the permanent program more than doubled from fourth quarter 1974 to second quarter 1975 (Table 7). Participation was further increased by two emergency programs enacted in December 1974: Federal Supplemental Benefits (FSB) for people who exhausted their benefits under the permanent programs and Special Unemployment Assistance (SUA) for wage and salary workers not in covered employment.[21]

The permanent programs include the regular programs in the states and the federal government's programs for its civilian employees, ex-servicemen, and railroad workers. These generally have a maximum duration of benefits of twenty-six weeks. Legislation enacted in 1970 created the permanent countercyclical Federal-State Extended Benefit Program which provides benefits for up to an additional thirteen weeks (for a maximum of thirty-nine weeks) for people exhausting their regular benefits, if they are in a "high" unemployment state or if the national rate of unemployment is "high." Over time the unemployment-rate tests determining whether or not extended benefits will be granted ("triggered") in a state have been made more lenient.[22] Under current legislation, Federal-State Extended Benefits are authorized in a state: either if that state's insured-unemployment rate (insured unemployment under the regular state program as a percentage of covered employment) in the most recent

---

[21] For analyses of the characteristics of participants and the impact on employment of FSB and SUA see Walter Corson et al., *A Study of Recipients of Federal Supplemental Benefits and Special Unemployment Assistance*, Mathematica Policy Research, Inc., January 1, 1977, mimeo; and Barry R. Chiswick, "The Effect of Unemployment Compensation on a Seasonal Industry: Agriculture," *Journal of Political Economy*, vol. 84, no. 3 (June 1976), pp. 591-603.

[22] The duration of benefit entitlements has gradually been increased. Since World War II there has been a recurrent pattern, starting with enactment of a temporary emergency extended-duration program during a period of high unemployment. Over time the temporary measure becomes permanent, and the conditions for long-term benefits are gradually eased. Temporary emergency benefits of thirteen weeks' duration beyond the basic twenty-six-week program were enacted in the recessions of 1957-1958 and 1969, and were made a permanent countercyclical program in 1970.

thirteen-week period averages at least 4.0 percent and is at least 120 percent of the rate during the same period in the previous two years; or if the state enacts legislation to permit the benefits when the state's thirteen-week rate averages at least 5.0 percent; or if the seasonally adjusted state insured unemployment rate nationwide averages at least 4.5 percent for the most recent thirteen-week period.[23] Federal-State Extended Benefits were paid in every state in the first half of 1977 because the nationwide insured unemployment rate averaged over a thirteen-week period exceeded 4.5 percent. As the insured unemployment rate has been declining, it is likely the national trigger for benefits will turn "off" in the second half of 1977. However, because of the state triggers, these benefits are likely to continue in several states.[24]

FSB provides additional benefits to people who have exhausted their entitlements under the regular programs and the Federal-State Extended Benefit Program. As a result of March 1975 amendments, benefits under the federally funded FSB program could extend for at most twenty-six weeks, for a maximum duration of benefits under all programs of sixty-five weeks. The FSB program was in effect in all states in 1975 but in 1976 either one or both of its two thirteen week components triggered off in states with lower insured unemployment rates. Although it was due to expire at the end of March 1977, FSB has been extended by 1977 amendments to the end of the year, but it will provide only thirteen weeks of benefits for a maximum duration of benefits of fifty-two weeks. The state trigger for FSB is a thirteen-week state insured unemployment rate of at least 5 percent. The House of Representatives passed an amendment that

---

[23] The provision that the state insured unemployment rate in the most recent thirteen weeks be at least 120 percent of the rate in the same period in the previous two years was included to keep the program countercyclical and to adjust for state differences in the level of unemployment. This provision could be waived at state option under the 1974 amendments, but the waivers expired March 31, 1977.

[24] The state insured unemployment rate (the number of persons receiving regular state unemployment compensation benefits as a percent of the number of workers in covered employment) is lower than the overall unemployment rate from the CPS:

Unemployment Rates	1970	1971	1972	1973	1974	1975	1976
State insured	3.4	4.1	3.5	2.7	3.5	6.0	4.5
CPS	4.9	5.9	5.6	4.9	5.6	8.5	7.7

Source: Council of Economic Advisers, Economic Report of the President, 1977, Tables B29 and B31.

would make FSB available in high unemployment local areas even if the state unemployment rate were low, but this did not survive the House-Senate conference committee.

SUA provides benefits for up to thirty-nine weeks (the initial twenty-six weeks were extended to thirty-nine weeks in June 1975) for those not covered by a regular state or federal program because part or all of their wage and salary employment was in a sector not covered by a regular program. It thus provided coverage for 12 million wage and salary workers, largely state and local government workers, domestics, farm workers, and employees of small nonprofit firms. Under 1976 amendments, 9 million of these workers are to be brought under coverage by the state programs by 1978, at which time SUA is scheduled to expire. Some domestics and farm workers, who work few hours per week or work for small farms, as well as U.S. citizens working in the United States for international organizations, make up the bulk of the 3 million wage and salary workers who will still not be covered by a regular state or federal program.

With the economic recovery and the expansion in employment, and particularly with the recall of workers on a job layoff, the number of people receiving unemployment benefits declined more rapidly than did overall unemployment. By fourth quarter 1976 there were 2.8 million recipients under the permanent programs, 0.5 million more than two years earlier. In addition, however, there were 0.5 million FSB and 0.3 million SUA recipients.

Total participation in FSB and SUA showed little change from third quarter 1975 to third quarter 1976, in spite of the recovery in the economy, but declined sharply in fourth quarter 1976. By late 1975 and 1976 some workers who became unemployed in the downturn had experienced a very long spell of unemployment or several shorter spells that led to the exhaustion of their benefits under the permanent programs (regular and extended benefit), and hence they joined FSB. In addition SUA rolls grew as employers and employees learned of the availability of benefits for jobs not previously covered by unemployment compensation.[25]

SUA provides unemployment compensation benefits for employees of state and local governments. These include school employees, but not teachers during the summer recess if they have a contract for the following year. Some teachers, in addition to other government educational-sector workers (bus drivers, crossing guards, cleaners, cafeteria workers, aides, and so on), apparently were among

---

[25] See, for example, Chiswick, "The Effect of Unemployment Compensation on a Seasonal Industry."

the 500,000 additional SUA beneficiaries in the summer of 1976 (240,000 in May; over 700,000 in July and August; 300,000 in October).[26]

By fourth quarter 1976 the summer swelling of SUA rolls had passed and FSB and SUA participation had declined. Expanded employment opportunities attracted workers from FSB and SUA. One or both components of FSB benefits were triggered off in states with falling unemployment rates, and some workers with very long durations of unemployment exhausted all of their entitlements. Yet FSB and SUA enrollments were still substantial.

AFDC. Aid to Families with Dependent Children is a welfare program for children living in low-income families without a working father because of death, disability, or separation or, in some states, unemployment (see Table 6). AFDC is state administered within broad federal regulations and with a sharing of costs between the federal and state governments. The poorer the state, the larger the federal contribution. As a result of legislation in some states (for example, New York) a portion of the state share of the program benefits, as well as the administrative costs, are paid by the local governments.

The AFDC program grew rapidly from 1965 to 1970 but its growth has been moderate since then (see Table 8). The rapid growth in the late 1960s was partly due to the sharp rise in real benefits, the increase in marital instability in the society, and the easing of AFDC eligibility requirements. The spread of information about the program and the apparent decline in the welfare stigma due to the efforts of welfare rights organizations contributed to the increase in participation. In addition, because of the increase in the provision of services, including child care and training, and automatic eligibility for Medicaid (1965) and food stamps (which became available in more counties after 1965) the value of the total package of benefits

---

[26] There was a similar increase in the CPS unemployment rate during the summer months for people in the educational-services sector. The following table gives the rates of unemployment as a percentage of the labor force (not seasonally adjusted) for this sector:

	Jan.-Apr.	May	June-Aug.	Sept.	Oct.-Dec.
1970-73	1.8	1.4	3.9	3.0	1.9
1974	1.6	2.1	4.2	3.9	2.5
1975	2.3	2.7	5.4	4.3	2.8
1976	2.9	2.8	6.3	4.2	—

Source: U.S. Department of Labor, Bureau of Labor Statistics.

Table 8
PARTICIPATION AND CASH BENEFITS IN THE
AFDC PROGRAM, 1950–1976

	AFDC Beneficiaries			Cash Benefits	
		Number of families			
Year	Number of persons (in thousands)	(in thousands)	(percentage of all female-headed families with children)	Annual total (in millions of current dollars)	Monthly average per recipient (December 1975 dollars) a
1950	2,233	651	51.3	547	46
1960	3,073	803	38.3	994	53
1965	4,396	996	40.2	1,644	57
1970	9,659	2,394	81.8	4,857	70
1975	11,300	3,395	77.8	9,349	72
1976	11,248	3,408	b	b	71

Note: AFDC is Aid to Families with Dependent Children. Excludes families in the unemployed fathers (UF) program.

a Data are for December of each year except 1976, when they are for June. Figures in the last column deflated by the CPI.

b Data not available.

Source: U.S. Department of Health, Education, and Welfare, and U.S. Department of Commerce, Bureau of the Census.

available to AFDC participants increased by far more than the cash benefits.

The Council of Economic Advisers (CEA) estimated that in 1972, for a hypothetical female-headed family of four, consisting of a mother and three children, the average cash AFDC benefit and the food benefits available to the family (food stamp and child nutrition) would be the equivalent of about $4,100 in taxable earnings.[27] Adding only $400 for the cash equivalent value of Medicaid benefits (this is just over half of the average Medicaid payment of $770 per AFDC family), the CEA estimated the equivalent taxable earning to be about $4,560. Because of benefit increases in AFDC and food stamps the CEA estimated the benefits in 1974 (excluding housing subsidies and child-care services) to be the equivalent of about $5,350 in taxable earnings. In the same year, women with the same educational distribution as AFDC mothers but who worked full time all year earned an average of $6,175. The high ratio of benefits (viewed as a pack-

[27] Council of Economic Advisers, *Economic Report of the President, 1976*, p. 96. The magnitude of the AFDC benefit, however, varies substantially among the states.

age) to potential earnings is a significant financial deterrent to seeking employment for women currently in or potentially eligible for the AFDC program.

The number of beneficiaries in the AFDC program increased by 400,000 from fourth quarter 1974 to first quarter 1975, partly because of a typical seasonal increase, but primarily because of the sharp increase in unemployment (see Table 7). Participation increased by 200,000 in the next four quarters, and then declined. However, if we deduct participants in the unemployed fathers component of AFDC, participation in the regular AFDC program increased by about 300,000 in first quarter 1975 and was unchanged over the next four quarters, after which it declined. By the end of 1976 participation was at roughly the same level as before the economic downturn, suggesting a continuation of what may be a recent trend toward declining participation. The relatively weak cyclical sensitivity of the AFDC program is due to the fact that many of the beneficiaries are in families with low rates of employment, and what employment they do have is primarily in the service sector. They are therefore largely immune to the adverse effects of a recession on employment or income.

AFDC-UF. At the option of the state concerned, AFDC benefits have been available since 1961 to families with an unemployed father if the families satisfy the other conditions of eligibility (AFDC-UF). Currently available in twenty-eight states which elected to participate, the AFDC-UF program is still very small, with about 700,000 participants (150,000 families) in the average month in 1976. Benefits are available if the father has been unemployed for at least thirty days, has had sufficient work experience to satisfy a minimum requirement, is seeking and available for work, and is unemployed or working less than 100 hours per month. In June 1975 the Supreme Court declared unconstitutional another requirement, that if the father was eligible for federal or state unemployment compensation benefits the family was categorically ineligible for AFDC-UF. Largely as a result of this requirement, the AFDC-UF program had been small, as it was effectively limited to families headed by a man who had worked in a sector not covered by unemployment compensation or who had exhausted his benefits.

The June 1975 decision enables a family to choose between AFDC-UF and unemployment compensation. For a family with no other earners, with few assets, and with several dependents, the package of benefits available from AFDC-UF participation could substantially exceed that available under unemployment compensation.

In the first half of 1976, cash benefits to AFDC-UF families averaged $325 per month, about the same as the *average* monthly unemployment compensation benefit. For those who tend to have low earnings when they work, however, the unemployment compensation benefit is below this average.[28]

As workers exhausted their unemployment compensation entitlement and as low-wage workers learned of the greater benefits under AFDC-UF, program participation increased.[29] Because overall unemployment and long-duration unemployment were declining, participation in AFDC-UF declined in the second half of 1976. However, as an increasing proportion of male-headed families learn of the greater benefits and get accustomed to participating in AFDC-UF, long-term program growth can be anticipated. Not all of this growth will be a net increase in AFDC rolls. During the period of ineligibility for AFDC-UF benefits some of the participating parents may have separated and the woman and children may have enrolled in the regular AFDC program.

Supplemental Security Income. The major new federal program in the 1970s is Supplemental Security Income (SSI). As of January 1974, federal assistance to states for providing welfare to low-income aged, blind, and disabled persons (ABD) was discontinued and replaced by a federally administered and financed program, SSI, which is the responsibility of the Social Security Administration. The purpose of the program was to provide a uniform nationwide minimum income guarantee for these three demographic groups which, in general, could not earn a sufficient income on their own. For many participants in the state ABD program, particularly in low-income states, the introduction of SSI significantly increased income transfer benefits. When it was enacted an important feature of SSI was that it was to "cash-out" (replace by cash) the food stamp subsidy and make SSI recipients categorically ineligible for food stamps. However, this restriction was quickly removed and SSI participants are now automatically eligible for at least the minimum food stamp subsidy. The federal SSI benefit as of July 1977 for those with no money income

---

[28] Moreover, although both AFDC-UF and unemployment compensation beneficiaries can participate in the food stamp program, the former have categorical eligibility and are thus automatically entitled to at least the minimum subsidy. AFDC-UF families can participate in the Medicaid program, but two-parent families receiving unemployment compensation can participate only in some states, and then only if they are "medically indigent," that is if they have very large medical expenses relative to their income and assets.

[29] The number of families in AFDC-UF increased from 112,000 in June 1975 to 146,000 in June 1976.

is $178 a month for an unrelated individual and $267 a month for a married couple. The federal benefit increases automatically each July at the same rate as the consumer price index.

SSI is not an exclusively federal program. At state option, SSI will administer a state supplementation of the federal benefit. Thus SSI benefits vary among the states, with recipients in higher-income states generally receiving larger benefits.[30] The state supplementation program has substantially increased administrative costs, as the regulations and qualifications for these additional benefits vary among the participating states. Of the 4 million SSI recipients in fourth quarter 1974, 3.6 million received federal SSI payments and 0.4 million received *only* state SSI. Of those receiving federal SSI, 1.2 million were getting state supplementation and 2.4 million were not. In fourth quarter 1974, benefits were paid at a rate equivalent to $5.5 billion a year, of which 76 percent was from federal revenues and 24 percent was state supplementation.

Participation in the SSI program increased by about 8 percent from fourth quarter 1974 to third quarter 1975, presumably reflecting the sharp rise in unemployment and delays in the start of benefits, particularly for new claims on the basis of blindness or disability, for which verifications take time. Since then, however, the number of participants has been stable.

The Programs for Transfers in Kind. The major programs created during the 1960s, food stamps, Medicare, and Medicaid, provide income in kind rather than in cash. Yet these programs provide benefits that are closer to cash (that is, provide greater flexibility in consumer choice) than the systems they replaced, which comprised the direct distribution of surplus food commodities and free medical care in county or charity clinics and hospitals. The new programs resulted in a substantial increase in coverage and program benefits per recipient.

Food stamps. The food stamp program is the second most cyclically sensitive of the income transfer programs, after unemployment compensation (Table 7). Program participation increased by 2.7 million people (17 percent) from fourth quarter 1974 to first quarter 1975, in part because of the extension of the program to all counties

---

[30] The amount of supplementation varies substantially among the states that offer it. In California in 1977 the maximum monthly supplement for an unrelated individual was $108 and for a couple $270, if they have no money income other than SSI. Thus the maximum federal and state SSI cash benefit in California is $286 a month for an unrelated individual and $537 a month for a couple.

in the fifty states and Puerto Rico, but also because of the increase in unemployment and the shortening of the work week which reduced the incomes of some families. After reaching a peak of 19.2 million people in second quarter 1975, participation declined to 17.2 million in fourth quarter 1976, roughly in proportion to the fall in unemployment.

The benefits under the food stamp program increase in proportion to the rise in the price of food consumed by low-income families. Hence as food prices increased at a slower rate in 1976 than in 1974 and 1975, the rate of growth in benefits per recipient (in current prices) slowed in 1976.[31] As a result of the decline in the number of beneficiaries and the slow growth of benefits per recipient, expenditure for the program declined by nearly 10 percent from first quarter 1976 to third quarter 1976, when it was the equivalent of $5.1 billion a year. The more rapid rise in food prices in late 1976 and 1977 can be expected to increase dollar benefits per recipient in the coming year.

The food stamp program started as a pilot project in 1961 and became a regular program in participating counties as a result of the Food Stamp Act of 1964. Over time many counties switched from the Food Distribution Program to the Food Stamp Program,[32] and as

---

[31] The consumer price index for food (1967=100) in recent years has been:

Year	CPI (Food)
1973	141
1974	162
1975	175
1976	181

Source: U.S. Department of Labor, Bureau of Labor Statistics.

[32] Participation in the Food Distribution Program for Needy Families and the Food Stamp Programs, 1950 to 1975, was:

	1950	1960	1965	1970	1975
Participants (average monthly number in millions)					
Food distribution	0.2	4.3	5.8	4.1	0.3
Food stamps	—	—	0.4	4.3	17.1
Total	0.2	4.3	6.2	8.4	17.4
Federal cost (millions of dollars)					
Food distribution	6	59	227	289	36
Food stamps	—	—	35	550	4,396
Total	6	59	262	839	4,432

Source: U.S. Department of Agriculture, Food and Nutrition Service.

a result of 1973 amendments, federal law mandated the Food Stamp Program in all counties and territories (including Puerto Rico) as of July 1974.[33] The benefits are financed by federal revenues, while the administrative costs are shared with the states that administer the program under federal regulations concerning eligibility and benefit levels.

Under the food stamp program a family of a particular size is assumed to consume a certain dollar amount of food in a month. Twice a month the participants buy vouchers for half of this amount, which is referred to as the *purchase requirement*. The lower the income of the family, the smaller the purchase price for the monthly allotment of vouchers; for the very low-income family the purchase price is zero. The difference between the purchase price and the face value of stamps is the "bonus" or subsidy. The stamps can be used only for food for humans to be eaten at home, not for alcoholic beverages or tobacco. The purchase requirement is apparently an important deterrent to participation, particularly for those who would receive only a small bonus or subsidy.

Although food stamp benefits are not in cash, they are nearly the equivalent of cash.[34] The stamps can be used to purchase a very wide variety of foods and need not be expended in the month they are received. The subsidy releases money income from the purchase of food and thereby enables the recipient family to consume more non-food items.

Unlike the other income transfer programs, the food stamp program does not require that participants be in a particular demographic category. Families or unrelated individuals with low current income (because of unemployment, illness, a strike, or other reason) and with few assets are eligible for the program if they satisfy a work test: those participants who are not employed, aged, disabled, or required at home for child care are required to register for and accept suitable employment. The food stamp program is therefore virtually the equivalent of a negative income tax.

The benefits per recipient family in the food stamp program are not large. As of July 1977 a four-member family could purchase vouchers worth $170 a month. For families with no "net income," the subsidy equals the face value of the coupons. The purchase price increases (and hence the subsidy declines) by 30 cents for each dollar

---

[33] From July 1974 to July 1976 the number of food stamp participants in Puerto Rico increased from 30,000 to 1.5 million, about half of the island's population.

[34] For an analysis of the effects of the program on food purchases and estimates of the cash equivalent value of the subsidy, see Kenneth W. Clarkson, *Food Stamps and Nutrition* (Washington, D.C.: American Enterprise Institute, 1975).

of net income. A family's net income is its gross cash income from work, property, and transfers less deductions. The deductions include federal, state, and local income taxes; social security taxes; retirement contributions; union dues; medical expenses in excess of ten dollars per month; child care when needed for work; fire, theft, and disaster-related expenses; expenses for school tuition and fees; alimony paid out; and payments for rent, utilities, and mortgage that exceed 30 percent of net income (after all other deductions have been subtracted). A family is excluded from participation if its liquid and certain other assets exceed $1,500 ($3,000 if the family includes a person age sixty or over). However, the equity value in an owner-occupied home, one automobile per worker, and any other personal effects are not counted in the asset test. The procedures for calculating income and assets mean that families who are not poor may participate, and may get larger subsidies, if their income fluctuates over the year and if they have a preference for private schools and for expensive owner-occupied housing (high mortgage payments, equity not included in assets).

Proposals for food stamp reform. To remedy these and other inequities the Carter administration, in April 1977, proposed a revision of the food stamp program.[35] The major reforms proposed would include: replacing the itemized deductions with a standard deduction; lowering the ceiling for income of participating families; eliminating the purchase requirement; and removing automatic (categorical) eligibility for participation by AFDC and SSI recipients. These changes would move the food stamp program closer to the concept of a negative income tax. The proposal also includes several features to tighten administration and reduce fraud. The Carter administration estimates that the proposal will result in little net change in program costs.

Under the Carter proposal the complex set of itemized deductions would be replaced by a monthly standard deduction of $80 per household plus 20 percent of earned income (in lieu of the itemized deduction for taxes and work-related expenses). The standard deduction would not vary with family size. As of April 1977 a four-person family would be ineligible if its gross money income exceeded $537 a month (equivalent to $6,444 per year) if none of the income were earned and $673 a month (equivalent to $8,075 per year) if all

---

[35] For a summary of the Carter administration's proposals see Robert Bergland, secretary of agriculture, statement before U.S. Congress, House of Representatives, Committee on Agriculture, April 5, 1977, or "Plan to Change Food-Stamp Aid Offered by Carter," *Wall Street Journal*, April 6, 1977, p. 4.

of it were earned. The flat standard deduction would be increased every six months in proportion to the rise in the price of nonfood items in the CPI. The new standard deduction would be somewhat larger than the current average deduction but would reduce administrative costs, reduce the incentives to shift consumption toward deductible items, and allocate benefits more equitably among families.

In addition, under the Carter proposal the net income limit for program eligibility would be reduced to the poverty level, currently $5,500 a year for a family of four. This would be a reduction of more than $1,000 per year from the current eligibility level. The poverty level cutoff would create a "notch"—a sharp discontinuity in the benefit structure as earnings rise. Such notches in transfer programs generate strong work disincentives for families near the notch, but they have the advantage of saving on program costs.

Some AFDC and SSI participants, though ineligible for food stamps because of their income or assets, are now categorically eligible (that is, automatically eligible because they receive AFDC and SSI benefits) for the minimum food stamp subsidy. The purchase requirement had discouraged many of them from participating in the food stamp program. With the elimination of the purchase requirement, the inequity of categorical eligibility would be far more glaring. Hence, the Carter proposal to remove the categorical-eligibility provisions.

The proposed elimination of the purchase requirement would end the need for the participants to have the cash in hand to buy two weeks' worth of stamps. The subsidy would, however, still be received in the form of food stamps. This would increase the participant's discretion in allocating the family's resources and thereby increase the value of the program to them. The Carter administration estimates that 2.5 to 3.0 million new participants would enter the program if the purchase requirement were eliminated.

From the inception of the food stamp program, the purpose of the purchase requirement has been to encourage greater food consumption among the poor by subsidizing the price of food. Food consumption would be increased, however, only if the face value of the food stamps received by a family exceeded what the family would spend on food if all of its income were in the form of cash. Otherwise, dollars rather than stamps would be spent on food at the margin, and these dollars could easily be diverted to other purposes. If the purchase requirement is removed, food expenditures will exceed the face value of the stamps received (that is, the subsidy) for all participating families, except possibly the very poorest. Because money is fungible there would be no increase in food expenditures from the program, other than what would arise from the increase in family income.

Even without a purchase requirement, the food stamp program will still require much of the administrative expense of using stamps, but will have little or no effect on the pattern of food consumption of the poor, except perhaps the very poorest. It would appear to be more efficient to eliminate the stamps and provide the subsidy directly in cash, and it is likely that this will in fact soon occur. The real policy choice at the present time is between the food stamp program with a purchase requirement and an all-cash program which would be consistent with most versions of a mini-negative income tax. (The difference between the current set of categorical welfare programs and a negative income tax is discussed below.) The intermediate step of a food stamp program without a purchase requirement clouds rather than clarifies the policy choices.

The Ford administration attempted to reform the food stamp program in 1975.[36] Many of the features proposed were quite similar to those in the Carter proposal: a standard deduction to replace the itemized deductions; denial of benefits to families with incomes (net of the standard deduction) that exceed the poverty line; increased administrative stringency; and a more stringent work requirement. The Ford proposal differed from the Carter proposal in two major respects. It did not propose eliminating the purchase requirement. However, it proposed what may be a more effective procedure for dealing with the problem of participation by nonpoor families with temporary low income: it recommended changing from the prospective to retrospective accounting and averaging income for three months rather than using income for a single month.

This proposal was designed to disqualify families with sufficiently high incomes that declined in only one month, since these families were likely to have assets or access to credit to finance consumption in that month.[37] Retrospective accounting was designed to make the program more rational. Benefits are now based on prospective accounting of what claimants report will be their income and deductions in the coming month. They can seek a refund on the

---

[36] For a summary of the Ford administration's proposed 1975 National Food Stamp Program Reform Act, including cost estimates, see Council of Economic Advisers, *Economic Report of the President, 1976*, pp. 104-05.

[37] The Ford administration's proposal for averaging income over three months was often misinterpreted to imply low income in *each* of three months before benefits could be received.

purchase price of the stamps if they overestimate their income or underestimated their deductions. If the opposite occurs, a higher purchase price should have been charged. The difficulties in monitoring a prospective accounting system and collecting from clients when the estimated purchase price is too low raise program costs by about 5 percent. Three-month retrospective accounting was endorsed to improve program efficiency and to make treatment of families with stable and fluctuating incomes more equitable.

As a result of both congressional inaction and court injunctions to bar administrative changes in regulations, the Ford administration's proposals did not take effect. The fate of the Carter administration's proposals remains to be seen.

Medicare and Medicaid. Although they were both created by the 1965 amendments to the Social Security Act and are often confused, Medicare and Medicaid are quite different programs (see Table 6). Medicare is a federal program which provides uniform benefits to the aged and disabled covered by social security and to persons with end-stage kidney disease. There is no means test for program participation, as it is viewed as an extension of the OASDI system. The hospital insurance (HI) component of Medicare is financed through the social security payroll tax (0.9 percent of taxable earnings paid by both employer and employee) and has its own trust fund. Under Medicare, there is a "deductible" for hospital care that must be paid by the client ($104 in 1976). Otherwise, Medicare pays for the first sixty days of hospitalization in any year, and shares the cost for hospitalization exceeding sixty days. The Supplemental Medical Insurance (SMI) program of Medicare provides for the reimbursement of physician fees, with a deductible clause and a coinsurance clause, and is partly financed by participant premiums. In 1976 Medicare expenditures were $18.4 billion, about 13 percent of total expenditures for medical care in the United States.

Medicaid, on the other hand, is part of the welfare system. It is administered and financed by the states within federal guidelines and with federal contributions varying among the states from one-half to three-quarters of program costs. Program benefits and population coverage vary among the states. Participants in AFDC are categorically eligible for Medicaid, as are most of the aged, blind, and disabled in the Supplemental Security Income program (SSI). Many states have also extended coverage to the "medically indigent," but the definition of this group varies widely among the states. Participation in the Medicaid program has increased rapidly, as have program costs. The more than 9 million participants in the average month in 1976 cost the program about $1,700 per participant per year. The $15.5 billion in federal and state Medicaid expenditures in 1976 were about 11 percent of total medical expenditures in the United States.

Participation in Medicare and Medicaid is not very cyclically sensitive because their primary target populations experience little cyclical variation in employment and income. The main exception is the case of two-parent families with low income and few assets (the "working poor") who experience large medical expenditures and hence can be classified as medically indigent under Medicaid. From fourth quarter 1974 to second quarter 1975 Medicaid participation increased by 0.8 million persons to 9.0 million, and although participation fluctuated thereafter, it was about the same level at the end of 1976. The increase in the combined Medicare and Medicaid payments by 40 percent from an annual rate of $26 billion in fourth quarter 1974 to one of $35 billion by fourth quarter 1976 reflected not only the increase in participation and the growth in real benefits per participant, but also the rise in the price of medical care (the medical care component of the CPI increased by 21 percent in the two-year period).

Transfers, Taxes, and Redistribution

The data on the distribution of income and the incidence of poverty discussed in the first part of this paper are based on money income as reported in the Current Population Survey. The data from the CPS are subject to substantial conceptual difficulties and errors in the measurement of money income. In particular, there appears to be systematic underreporting of money income, varying according to the type of income.[38] Furthermore the income data ignore income in kind and do not remove taxes from income.

This section considers the accuracy with which income is reported in the CPS. It then examines the effects of alternative definitions of income on measurement of family income inequality and the incidence of poverty. This facilitates an analysis of the extent to which cash transfers, transfers in kind, and taxes alter these two dimensions of the income distribution. The procedures used in this calculation do not account for family composition or for labor-supply

---

[38] This issue is analyzed in detail in Dorothy S. Projector and Judith Bretz, "Measurement of Transfer Income in the Current Population Survey," in *The Personal Distribution of Income and Wealth*, ed. James D. Smith (New York: National Bureau of Economic Research, 1975), pp. 377-448.

responses to the transfer system. Therefore, they do not permit quantitative estimates of what the income distribution would be in the absence of these programs.

If the official income data included transfers in kind and were adjusted for the underreporting of cash income and for the changes in family composition in response to the transfer programs, the data would more closely approximate the full income of the families in the population. If this were done, the number of low-income families would be much smaller. The stability of family income inequality in the official statistics for the past three decades in spite of the rise in public transfers in cash and in kind is not a paradox, but rather a consequence of the manner in which family income is measured. If the data were adjusted for underreporting and for transfers in kind they would show a decline in the inequality of family incomes in the period since World War II. In addition, they would show a decline in poverty much more rapid than that shown in the official series.

Underreporting of Cash Income. Table 9 compares aggregate money income by type as reported in the CPS with the corresponding estimates made by the Census Bureau from independent sources. For example, the extent of social security and railroad retirement income reported in the CPS is compared with the aggregate benefits disbursed according to the administrative records of the Social Security and Railroad Retirement Trust Funds. Overall, for 1973, income estimated from the CPS was 89 percent of income estimated from independent sources.[39] However, the proportions vary substantially by type of income, from a high of more than 97 percent for wage, salary, and nonfarm self-employment income to a low of 44 percent for property income (dividends, interest, and so on). Money transfer payments whether for the poor (public assistance) or the unemployed are substantially underreported. Income is most underreported for the types received by the high-income groups (property income) and the low-income groups (transfers). This tends to lower the aggregate income reported in the CPS and increase the extent of measured poverty. Inequality is increased in the lower half of the income distribution and decreased in the upper half; but the effect on the overall inequality of income is not clear a priori.

Assuming that the quality of the reporting of income by source has not deteriorated over time, it is possible to make inferences about

---

[39] The underreporting of income in the CPS in Table 9 is, of course, relative to the independent source. If the latter overestimates the income received by families, the extent of underreporting in the CPS is smaller than indicated.

Table 9

CPS AND INDEPENDENT ESTIMATE OF AGGREGATE
MONEY INCOME OF FAMILIES BY SOURCE, 1973

Source of Income	CPS (in billions of dollars)	Independent Estimate[a] (in billions of dollars)	CPS as a Percentage of Independent Estimate
Wages and salaries	656.7	676.3	97.1
Nonfarm self-employment	55.5	56.0	99.1
Farm self-employment	15.6	32.3	48.4
Social security and railroad retirement	44.7	50.0	89.4
Dividends, interest, net rental, and royalties	36.7	83.0	44.2
Public assistance and welfare	8.2	11.0	74.5
Unemployment compensation, workers' compensation, government employee pensions, and veteran payments	19.8	34.2	57.9
Total money income	854.1	957.1	89.2

Note: CPS stands for Current Population Survey.
[a] Adjusted to CPS income concepts.
Source: U.S. Department of Commerce, Bureau of the Census, *Money Income in 1973 of Families and Persons in the United States,* Current Population Reports, Series P-60, no. 97 (January 1975), Table A-8.

the effects of the reporting errors and omitted forms of income on time series data for measured inequality and poverty. The sources of income that have increased most rapidly in relative importance in the past three decades are public transfers—social security and government pensions, unemployment compensation, and public assistance in cash and in kind. As a result of the secular increase in transfer payments—which are underreported—the growth in the money income of the low-income population has probably been underestimated. A correction for this error would tend to reduce the measured inequality of income and poverty, with a larger reduction for more recent years.

Effects on Income Inequality. Several studies have attempted to estimate the extent to which the income transfer system and the tax system alter the distribution of income.[40] The studies vary in their assumptions, data, and methodology, making comparison difficult; but in their conclusions there is substantial agreement. The discussion here will focus on the recent Congressional Budget Office (CBO) analysis, *Poverty Status of Families under Alternative Definitions of Income.*

The CBO used simulation analysis to adjust the Current Population Survey data for the underreporting of money income and to allocate taxes and income in kind among families. The CBO analysis includes people living in Puerto Rico and other outlying areas not included in the CPS reports. This inclusion increases the degree of family income inequality and increases the proportion of all U.S. families living at or below the official poverty threshold. Although not directly comparable with the CPS figures, the data are helpful for examining the sensitivity of reported income distribution and poverty to changes in measurement concepts and for evaluating some of the difficulties in such an analysis.

Cash transfer programs. The CBO classified families (including unrelated individuals as one-person families) on the basis of their pretax, pretransfer income, that is, on the basis of their labor-market earnings and property income (see Table 10). On this basis the lowest quintile received 0.3 percent of aggregate income and the highest quintile 50.2 percent. The bottom quintile's share in total income (on the basis of pretax, pretransfer income) is increased by 3.3 percentage points by the cash social insurance programs (social security, unemployment compensation, workers' compensation, government pensions, and some veterans' benefits) but is increased only 0.9 percentage points by the cash public assistance programs (AFDC, SSI, state general assistance). Social insurance programs raise the second-lowest quintile's share by 2.2 percentage points, while cash transfers have a trivial effect on its share.

It might seem surprising that the social insurance programs have a greater role in redistribution income to low-income groups than the public assistance programs, as the latter are targeted to the poor while many people who are not poor receive social insurance benefits. The distribution of income from public assistance is more pro-

---

[40] See, for example, Council of Economic Advisers *Economic Report of the President, 1974,* chapter 5, "Distribution of Income"; Projector and Bretz, "Measurement of Transfer Income" and Benjamin Okner, "Individual Taxes and the Distribution of Income," in *Distribution of Personal Income and Wealth,* ed. James D. Smith, pp. 5-74; Congressional Budget Office, *Poverty Status of Families under Alternative Definitions of Income,* Background Paper No. 17 (Revised, June 1977).

Table 10

POVERTY AND INCOME DISTRIBUTION ESTIMATES USING
ALTERNATIVE DEFINITIONS OF INCOME, FY 1976

(in percentages)

	Income before Taxes and Transfers	Income after Social Insurance[a] but before Taxes and other Transfers	Cash Income[b] before Taxes but after Transfers	Income in Cash and in Kind[c]	
				Before taxes but after transfers	After taxes and transfers[d]
Families classified by income before taxes and transfers					
Lowest quintile	0.3	3.6	4.5	6.1	7.2
Second quintile	7.2	9.4	9.6	10.1	11.5
Third quintile	16.3	16.3	16.2	16.0	16.6
Fourth quintile	26.0	24.5	24.2	23.6	23.4
Top quintile	50.2	46.2	45.5	44.2	41.3
Total	100.0	100.0	100.0	100.0	100.0
Families below the poverty level	27.0	15.7	13.5	11.3[e] / 8.1[e]	11.5[e] / 8.3[e]

Note: Unrelated individuals are included as one-person families. Detail may not add to total because of rounding.

a Social insurance includes social security, unemployment compensation, workers' compensation, government employee pensions, and some veterans' benefits.

b Includes cash transfers through public assistance programs such as AFDC and SSI.

c Includes transfers in kind such as food stamps, child nutrition, Medicare, Medicaid, and housing allowances.

d Removes from income federal and state personal income taxes and federally mandated payroll taxes.

e The upper row excludes medical transfers from income, the lower row includes them in income.

Source: U.S. Congress, Congressional Budget Office, *Poverty Status of Families under Alternative Definitions of Income*, Background Paper No. 17 (Revised, June 1977), Tables 3 and A-4.

gressive than the distribution of income from social insurance, which in turn is more progressive than the distribution of income from work and property. The bottom 40 percent of families, classified on the basis of income before taxes and transfers, received 7.5 percent of the aggregate income from work and property, 60.3 percent of the income from social insurance, and 82.0 percent of the cash assistance income.[41] The redistribution impact of social insurance programs is much greater than that of public assistance because social insurance payments are sevenfold larger—$124 billion in fiscal year 1976 compared to $18 billion for cash public assistance.

Programs for Transfers in Kind. The inclusion of transfers in kind (food stamps, child nutrition, Medicaid, Medicare, housing assistance) also has a strong redistributive effect, although the impact is substantially exaggerated by the CBO procedures. The CBO estimated the increase in income to the family from transfers in kind as equivalent to the cost to the government of providing the transfer.[42] Government expenditure is an appropriate measure for estimating the cost to the public of a program for transfers in kind; but for evaluating the income distribution impact it is the cash equivalent

---

[41] The percentages for the bottom *quintile* are even more striking: 0.3 percent of the aggregate income from work and property, 31.9 percent of the aggregate income from social insurance, and 61.5 percent of the aggregate income from cash public assistance. CBO, *Poverty Status of Families under Alternative Definitions of Income*, Table 2, p. 4, and Table A-4, p. 24.

[42] The Congressional Budget Office's simulated number of beneficiaries and program costs for transfers in kind in fiscal year 1976 were:

	Beneficiary Units [a] (in millions)	Simulated Benefits (in billions of dollars)	Benefits per Beneficiary Unit (in dollars)
Food stamps	7.7	5.3	688
Child nutrition	26.0	2.0	78
Housing assistance	2.0	2.3	1,107
Medicare: Hospital Insurance	5.7	12.3	2,152
Medicare: Supplemental Medical Insurance	13.3	4.7	351
Medicaid	23.5	14.9	634
Total	[b]	41.5	[b]

[a] Families, except for Medicare and Medicaid under which the beneficiary unit is the individual.

[b] Does not add to total because of multiple program entitlements.

Source: Congressional Budget Office, *Poverty Status of Families under Alternative Definitions of Income*, Table A-2, p. 22.

value to the recipient of the transfer in kind that is relevant. The cash equivalent value of a transfer in kind is the dollar cost to the participant of acquiring equivalent goods or services, or the cash income the participant would be willing to forgo in exchange for the transfer, whichever is the smaller. Placing a low-income family in luxury housing and charging them the rent for low-cost housing would be an expensive housing subsidy program but would have no meaningful income distribution effect if the low-income family placed no value on the additional luxury of its residence.[43]

The CBO's procedure for estimating income in kind is perhaps most accurate for the food stamp program, where there is reason to believe that the subsidy is nearly the equivalent of cash. It is less accurate for housing assistance. There are also difficult conceptual problems in estimating the income distribution impact of the Medicare and Medicaid programs. Medicare provides health insurance for social security recipients and for people with end-stage kidney disease. Medicaid provides subsidized health care for the poor (AFDC and SSI recipients, and the medically indigent). Rather than the public cost of providing a given family with health services in a year, a more appropriate measure of the value to the recipient family of these programs would be the value of the health insurance coverage they provide. The premium cost of an insurance package that would provide the same coverage is a measure that averages the fluctuations in a family's medical expenditures from year to year. It is superior to the CBO's procedure, which is based on the assumption that a family's well-being is increased by $10,000 in a year when Medicaid pays for an operation costing that amount and by nothing in a year when there is no illness in the family.

The actuarially fair insurance premium for the services received by Medicaid participants would overestimate the value of the insurance if the participants place less value on the provisions in the insurance package than the cost of these provisions. For example, the value they place on having access to a hospital bed in a semiprivate room instead of a ward may be less than the additional insurance cost of this extra service. It would be useful if future negative income tax experiments gauged what the recipients perceive to be the cash-equivalent value of income in kind, particularly housing and medical services.

The programs for transfer of income in kind included in the CBO analysis are all means-tested and targeted to the poor, with the ex-

---

[43] The income distribution effect would exist if the low-income family could, without restrictions, rent or sell its entitlement to the luxury housing.

ception of the child nutrition program, which provides some subsidy for children in higher-income families. Other government spending on transfers in kind may benefit mainly the middle- or upper-income groups—for example, public subsidy for higher education. It is likely that an analysis of all programs for transfers in kind would reveal a smaller redistribution impact than is found in an analysis limited to the means-tested programs.

Taxes. The CBO also analyzed the effect of subtracting from income the money paid in federal and state income tax and federally mandated employee payroll taxes. The purpose was not to assess the distribution of the tax burden, but to determine the distribution of family income net of taxes. Using simulation analysis, it was found that taxes are slightly progressive relative to income from work and property,[44] and somewhat more progressive relative to full income including transfers in cash and in kind.

Deducting taxes from income results in a further narrowing of income inequality (see Table 10). The resulting relative increase in the share of income is greatest for the lowest quintile, presumably because so little of its cash income is subject to taxation. The income share also increases for the second quintile and to a smaller extent for the third quintile. Only the top quintile shows a substantial decline in its proportion of aggregate income when taxes are deducted.

Summary. In summary, using income before taxes and transfers —that is, wage, salary, self-employment, and property income—as the base for determining the quintile distribution of families, the Congressional Budget Office analysis shows a substantial redistribution effect from the income transfer system, with a much smaller

---

[44] The upper-income groups pay a larger proportion of the taxes than their share in income. Simulated share of income and taxes of families classified by income before taxes and transfers, FY 1976:

	Quintiles					
	Lowest	Second	Third	Fourth	Top	Total
Income before taxes and transfers (percentage of total)	0.3	7.2	16.3	26.0	50.2	100.0
Taxes (percentage of total)	0.3	3.3	13.1	24.5	58.8	100.0

Note: Detail may not add to total because of rounding.
Source: Congressional Budget Office, *Poverty Status of Families under Alternative Definitions of Income*, p. 4, Table 2 and p. 24, Table A-4.

effect from the tax system (see Table 10). The transfers substantially increase the income shares of the lowest and second-lowest quintiles. Social insurance and the sum of cash public assistance and transfers in kind are of approximately equal importance for the lowest quintile, with the adjustment for taxes having a smaller effect. For the second quintile, social insurance and the adjustment for taxes have important effects, while cash public assistance and transfers in kind (with the exception of Medicare) have little impact. The income share of the third quintile is essentially invariant with the definition of income— their share of the transfers and taxes is about the same as their share of wage, salary, and property income.

The share of income received by the top 40 percent of families declines when income is adjusted for taxes and transfers. The decline is small for the fourth quintile and occurs mainly when the large social insurance income is included. For the top quintile both the inclusion of social insurance and the adjustment for taxes substantially reduce their income share.

Effects on Poverty. On the basis of earnings and income from property (that is, income before taxes and transfers) the CBO estimates that 27.0 percent of families, including unrelated individuals as one-person families, would have been at or below the official poverty level in FY 1976 (see Table 10). Including social insurance income (primarily social security) reduces the proportion of families in poverty by nearly half, to 15.7 percent. Cash public-assistance payments reduce poverty even further, to 13.5 percent of families. Including nonmedical transfers in kind (that is, food stamps, child nutrition and housing allowances) reduces the family poverty rate to 11.3 percent. Removing tax payments from income has a small effect on the poverty rate because few people with income just above the poverty threshold have much taxable income.

The CBO estimates that medical transfers in kind have a large poverty-reduction effect, about 3.2 percentage points. However, as noted above their procedure for treating income in kind substantially overestimates the value to many families of the medical insurance and housing transfers. On the other hand, for families that have access to the medical insurance coverage but make no use of the service during the year, the CBO procedure underestimates the value to the family of the medical insurance. It is not clear a priori whether a more accurate estimate of the value to low-income families of these transfers in kind would result in more or fewer families crossing the poverty threshold.

Feedback Effects of the Transfer Programs. The distribution of wage, salary, self-employment, and property income as computed by the CBO, and by others, is *not* the distribution of income that would exist in the absence of transfers in cash and in kind. Work effort, the savings rate, and the distribution of persons among family units would all be different if there were no transfer system or if the system were smaller in scope. The transfers apparently increase the number of family units (including one-person households) by providing financial incentives that encourage marital instability or, perhaps more often, discourage remarriage among AFDC mothers and social security recipients.[45] The rise in real social security benefits has increased the real income of the current aged population, thereby enabling more aged persons to maintain separate households rather than live with relatives, whether aged or not. The increase in the number of family units headed by women or aged persons due to these programs increases the number of low-income families. This tends to increase the inequality of family income and the proportion of the population in poverty because the statistical procedures assume a reduced pooling of income within the family.[46]

The income transfer programs tend to reduce work effort and investment in assets that produce money income. As a result they tend to increase the inequality of income as well as the incidence of poverty as measured in the CPS. By providing assurance of a minimal level of income, even if there is no current work or past savings, the programs tend (via the income effect) to reduce work effort and undermine lifelong saving habits. In addition, program benefits are reduced when there are earnings or property income, thereby discouraging (via the substitution effect) both work and saving. While the benefit reduction rate (the reduction in benefits for each dollar of nontransfer income) under each program sepa-

---

[45] Although the effects of AFDC on marital status have attracted much attention, it is less well known that several features of the social security system, including the widow's entitlement to 100 percent of her husband's benefit compared with the 50 percent spouse benefit, also discourage remarriage. To the extent that these programs enable people to avoid unhappy marriages, there is presumably a gain in social welfare.

[46] See Lenore E. Epstein, "Measuring the Size of the Low-Income Population," in *Six Papers on the Size Distribution of Income and Health*, ed. Lee Soltow (New York: National Bureau of Economic Research, 1969), pp. 157-97. Even if two families are both at the poverty threshold, marriage can result in a reduction in the poverty rate. If a nonfarm woman head of family with two children marries a nonfarm male with no children the combined poverty threshold (1975) declines from $7,026 ($4,175 plus $2,851) to $5,502 (Table 2). If an aged nonfarm man and woman marry the combined poverty threshold declines from $5,182 to $3,260.

rately may not be very large, many low-income recipients receive a package of benefits, and the sum of the marginal benefit-reduction rates may be substantial. For an aged person receiving social security and food stamps, for example, the combined benefit reduction from working an extra day may be 65 percent of that day's earnings. This would result from a 50 percent benefit reduction for social security and a 30 percent benefit reduction for food stamps on the combined social security and labor income, not allowing for payroll and income taxes and possible reductions in Medicaid, housing, and other benefits. Similarly, for a female-headed family with young children the reduction in AFDC benefits, the food stamp subsidy, and Medicaid entitlements, can also result in very high benefit-reduction rates.[47]

Since the public assistance programs (AFDC, food stamps, SSI, and Medicaid) all have asset tests, low-income families or families that anticipate low income in the future have little incentive to save. The transfer programs provide incentives for such saving as does take place to be in the form of consumer durables rather than assets, such as savings accounts, that produce money income. Since the asset tests discourage income-producing investments that would be measured, although imperfectly, in the CPS, they increase the measured incidence of poverty and the inequality of income before taxes and transfers.

The Elusive Paradox. There may not be any paradox in the observation that measured family income inequality has hardly changed in the last three decades in spite of the substantial growth in public transfer programs, particularly in the last fifteen years. Cash-transfer income is poorly reported in the CPS. As benefits under the transfer programs have increased over time, the reporting problem has underestimated their importance in reducing inequality in more recent years. The programs that have grown most rapidly since the mid-1960s provide assistance in kind and the value of these subsidies to recipients has not been well estimated or included in conventional estimates of income inequality.

The official income data are for income before income and payroll taxes. Even if taxes have not become more progressive in the

---

[47] Most studies of benefit-reduction rates are program-specific—they estimate the rate for particular transfer programs. What is relevant for the family, however, is the overall change in income in cash and in kind from additional earnings or transfer income from property. Thus, the relevant benefit-reduction rates are family-specific and should include increased taxes as well as the reduced benefits from the package of programs in which the family participates.

past three decades, the rise in the proportion of income paid in taxes would imply a narrowing of after-tax income inequality.

The transfers have feedback effects on family composition, work effort, and investments that by themselves tend to widen the inequality of family income as it is conventionally measured. Yet if the low-income population is responding rationally to the incentives, the behavior that lowers the family's reported income may actually be increasing its overall well-being.

The largest component of the transfers is social insurance, including social security and unemployment compensation. Their target populations, the aged and the unemployed, are predominantly not in the lowest income brackets.

If the income data were corrected for such measurement problems as underreporting of cash transfers, omission of transfers in kind, and failure to deduct taxes, and if allowance were made for the change in the composition of the recipient units as a result of the programs, a time series would show a decline in family income inequality in the past three decades.[48]

Categorical Welfare Programs vs. the Negative Income Tax

The current system of categorical welfare programs is an administrative nightmare. At the federal level some welfare programs are administered by the Social Security Administration (SSI, and AFDC if the recently announced administrative reorganization comes into effect), others by the Food and Nutrition Service in the Department of Agriculture (food stamps and other food subsidy programs). For all of the major welfare programs there are varying degrees of federal-state cooperation and coordination.[49]

From the client's perspective, benefits under different programs are combined in packages (see Table 11). Multiple program participation means several applications, several different sets of regulations concerning eligibility and benefit levels, and several different agencies to notify if there is a change in status or income, if checks are lost, or the like.[50] Fragmentation facilitates welfare fraud, resulting

---

[48] For some preliminary estimates see Edgar K. Browning, "The Trend Toward Equality in the Distribution of Net Income," *Southern Economic Journal*, vol. 43, no. 1 (July 1976), pp. 912-23.

[49] Of the major social insurance programs, social security and Medicare are exclusively federal and unemployment compensation is a joint federal-state program.

[50] Major components of the additional cost to clients from participating in several categorical programs are the additional time and transportation expenses. Time has economic value even for low-income persons who are not working.

Table 11

BENEFIT PACKAGES AVAILABLE TO THE LOW-INCOME POPULATION

Characteristic of Family Head	Programs for which Family May Be Eligible	Combined Marginal Benefit Reduction Rates for Earnings[a]	Combined Benefit Guarantee[b]
Aged	Social security, SSI, Medicare, Medicaid, food stamps	High[c]	High
Disabled	Social security, SSI, Medicare, Medicaid, food stamps[d]	High	High
Woman with children	AFDC, Medicaid, food stamps[e]	High	High
Adult living with spouse and children;	Food stamps	Low	Low
If unemployed	Unemployment compensation, and in some states AFDC-UF, Medicaid	High	High
Other adult;	Food stamps	Low	Low
If unemployed	Unemployment compensation	High	High

Note: Only the federal and federal-state programs summarized in Table 6 are considered here.

[a] The combined marginal benefit reduction rate, the decrease in benefits for each dollar of earned income, is designated as high if it will often exceed 50 percent and as low if it is generally less than 50 percent.

[b] The benefit guarantee is the transfer income received if the family has no other income. The combined benefit guarantees are designated as high or low in comparison to each other.

[c] Under social security there is a 50 percent marginal tax rate on earnings in excess of $3,000 per year (1977).

[d] Also AFDC if there are dependent children in the family.

[e] Also social security if she is a widow.

[f] Adults who are not aged or disabled and do not have dependent children in the family.

Source: U.S. Department of Health, Education, and Welfare, U.S. Department of Labor, and U.S. Department of Agriculture, Food and Nutrition Service.

in excessive welfare benefits for some. Many low-income people are poor because they have difficulty coping in a modern labor market. These same people have difficulty coping with a complex welfare system, and as a result receive smaller benefits than they are legally entitled to.

For these reasons there has been much discussion in recent years of the advantages of replacing our current set of categorical welfare programs with a uniform negative income tax (NIT).[51] Other advantages of an NIT are that it would give the poor greater freedom of choice in consumption, since it would be an all-cash system, and that it would reduce the extent to which welfare investigators harass the low-income population.

This section reviews some of the principles of the NIT and the current set of categorical welfare programs. It identifies differences that are substantive and alleged differences that have little or no substantive content.

Work Incentives. Several parameters are relevant for an analysis of any welfare system, whether it is a set of categorical programs or a negative income tax added on to the current positive income tax system. These parameters are:

(1) *benefit guarantee*—the benefit a family would receive if it had no other income,

(2) *benefit reduction rate*—the rate at which benefits decline as earned income rises,

(3) *break-even income*—the earned income at which benefits are reduced to zero,

(4) *demographic differentiation*—differences in the benefit guarantee and the benefit reduction rate that apply to different demographic groups, and

(5) *program cost*—the aggregate benefits paid to participants.

As indicated in Table 11, the current welfare system includes demographic differentiation; the various demographic groups have different benefit guarantees and benefit-reduction rates. The poor who are aged, disabled, or in families headed by women caring for

---

[51] For a review of the economics and politics of a negative income tax see Daniel P. Moynihan, *The Politics of a Guaranteed Income* (New York: Random House, 1973) which focuses on the Nixon administration's proposed Family Assistance Plan (FAP).

small children can receive a package of benefits with a high guarantee and a high benefit-reduction rate. Other families participate in a limited number of programs and have a low benefit guarantee and a low benefit-reduction rate.[52] When the guarantee and the benefit-reduction rate are both high, work is discouraged; in a system in which both are low it is not discouraged.

A substantive difference between a system of categorical welfare programs and a negative income tax is that the former facilitates demographic differentiation in eligibility criteria, benefit guarantees, and benefit-reduction rates. In most NIT proposals program features would differ little among demographic groups.

Demographic groups may differ in labor-supply (wage rate and income) elasticities, and hence in their work response to the benefit-reduction rate and the benefit guarantee. Perhaps more important, society's attitude toward work effort by the low-income population varies according to the demographic characteristic of the recipient. Low rates of employment among aged persons, the disabled, and women without husbands who are caring for small children are viewed differently than low rates of employment among adults not disabled or aged, who are living by themselves or in two-parent families. If the benefit guarantee and the benefit-reduction rate are to be uniform among demographic groups, society must decide whether it is more averse to work disincentives for able adults than it is to low-transfer income and strong work incentives for the aged, the disabled, and women who head families with small children.

Like the current set of categorical welfare programs, an NIT would presumably include a work-test—a requirement that an adult who is not working and does not have good cause for not seeking a job engage in a job search and accept a suitable job offer. A work-test becomes a more essential feature the higher the benefit guarantee and the higher the benefit-reduction rate. However, while it is not always easy for a person seeking a job to find one, it is quite easy for a person who does not want to work to make certain he does not receive a job offer. The benefit structure and the "pull" of job opportunities may be stronger than the "push" of a work-test in encouraging employment.

---

[52] The main exception occurs when a family member is eligible for unemployment compensation. There is a work-test to receive welfare and unemployment compensation. However, unemployment compensation differs from the welfare programs in that benefit levels and duration are positively related to previous earnings and employment and the duration of benefits is limited, while welfare benefits are means-tested on the basis of current income.

Consider an NIT scheme with a high benefit guarantee, a low benefit-reduction rate, and the same benefit schedule for all families of a particular size. A high guarantee and a low benefit-reduction rate mean that the program has a high break-even income and reaches far up into the income distribution.[53] Program costs escalate rapidly, partly because of the larger benefit per participant in each income group, but primarily because of the sharp increase in the number of families eligible for benefits when the break-even income moves closer to the median income. The objective of having an economically and politically viable welfare system then becomes very difficult to attain.

There would be substantial opposition to any welfare reform measure that involved large increases in welfare expenditures. Political constraints also make a welfare program with a low benefit guarantee unrealistic for the poor from whom substantial work effort is not expected—the aged, the disabled, or women caring for young children. A high benefit-reduction rate for these groups is acceptable in that it saves on program costs. Similar political constraints require programmatic incentives to encourage work by able adults not caring for young children or in two-parent families. To be effective, this requires a low benefit guarantee and a low marginal benefit-reduction rate, supplemented by a work-test. These various constraints cannot be satisfied in an NIT unless it involves significant demographic differentiation in the benefit guarantee and the benefit-reduction rate—a differentiation that results in a lower guarantee and a lower benefit-reduction rate the greater society's concern with encouraging work by members of the group.

---

[53] There is a simple relation between the break-even income (BEI), the benefit-reduction rate (T), and the benefit guarantee (BG):

$$BEI = \frac{BG}{T}$$

The break-even income can be computed for each of six combinations of the benefit guarantee and the benefit-reduction rate:

Benefit Reduction Rate	Benefit Guarantee	
	$3,000	$5,000
.3	$10,000	$16,667
.5	6,000	10,000
.7	4,286	7,143

Median family income in 1975, the latest year reported, was $13,719. In 1977, median family income is likely to be about $15,700.

Administration. Many of the costly administrative features of the categorical welfare programs would necessarily exist under a negative income tax. The reported income, assets, and family composition of the low-income population would have to be verified to reduce fraud. This function is now performed by the various welfare agencies. It is largely ignored by the Internal Revenue Service (IRS) because of the small additional income tax revenues that would be forthcoming from a more intense examination of the taxable income of the low-income population. If an NIT were merged into the positive income tax system, IRS would presumably take over the verification function.

It is likely that a negative income tax would include a work-test to supplement whatever work incentives existed in the benefit structure. To have any effectiveness a work-test needs to be enforced. This would presumably be done under the auspices of the Department of Labor which, in conjunction with state agencies, administers the unemployment compensation system and its work-test. Coordination among IRS, the Department of Labor, and state employment service agencies would be required.

The frequency of benefit payments and the frequency of reporting income and assets could not be reduced under a negative income tax. Current welfare programs make monthly or semimonthly payments.[54] Because the target population of an NIT has low income and few assets their economic well-being is sensitive to small changes in earned income and benefit levels and to changes in the composition of the family. If, for example, payments were placed on a quarterly basis there would be a tendency for some low-income families to consume their quarterly benefits in two months and then file a supplemental claim for benefits for the last month. Denying all such claims would create unfair hardships for some, while paying all such claims would eventually bankrupt the system. To prevent such abuse of the NIT, monthly or semimonthly benefit payments would still be required.

For the working-poor participants, frequent reporting of income (for example, monthly) might be as important a feature of an NIT as it is in the current categorical programs, although it might be less important for aged and disabled participants. The earnings of the working poor often vary substantially from month to month. The positive income tax system can rely on annual accounting because payroll deductions vary directly with earnings in the pay period and

---

[54] This is essentially the same frequency with which payroll deductions are made for wage and salary workers in the positive tax system, even though the accounting is done once a year.

the number of exemptions claimed by the worker. Moreover, workers who are not poor are presumed to have enough assets to pay the difference between their total payroll deductions and their tax liability. If annual accounting were used for an NIT, however, the collection of overpayments from the low-income population might be administratively costly and politically difficult.[55]

State Differences in Benefits. Under the current system of categorical welfare programs, benefit levels vary from state to state. This is a result of differences in state supplementation of SSI, in benefits under AFDC and Medicaid, and in the small state general-assistance and emergency-assistance programs.[56] These differences are partly offset by the food stamp program, since AFDC, SSI, and the other cash benefits are counted as income, and out-of-pocket medical expenses are deductible in determining net income for the computation of the food stamp subsidy.

To some, the variation in benefits by state is a virtue of the current system. In principle, it permits the benefits to reflect differences in the cost of living and in the style and standard of living from state to state.[57] To others, the geographic variation in benefits is one of the sins of the system. Why should two low-income families in the United States be treated differently simply because one lives in a state with a larger proportion of low-income families? Moreover these benefit differences may encourage migration of the poor to states that provide high real benefit levels.

An important substantive question regarding the welfare system is the extent of state differences in benefit levels. It would appear difficult, if not unconstitutional, to prohibit a state from providing extra benefits to its own low-income residents. The major issue then becomes the level of the federal guarantee. The minor issue is whether the federal programs will administer state supplementation. These issues, however, are independent of whether there is a set of categorical welfare programs or an NIT. The federal government could mandate uniform state benefit levels for programs in which it provides some or all of the benefits, as is currently the case for food

---

[55] Recall the difficulty noted above in collecting overpayments in the food stamp program because monthly reporting is prospective rather than retrospective.

[56] Among the social insurance programs, state differences in benefits exist in unemployment compensation but not in OASDI or Medicare.

[57] An extreme example of the effect of eliminating state differences in benefit levels is found in the food stamp program which has the same benefit schedule nationwide. About 8 percent of the population of the fifty states participated in 1976, compared with 50 percent of the population in Puerto Rico.

stamps. Alternatively, state supplementation could be allowed in a federally administered NIT, just as it is currently allowed in SSI.

Cash Benefits vs. Benefits in Kind. The difference between an NIT and the current set of categorical welfare programs is sometimes described as the difference between a cash program and one that provides benefits both in cash and in kind. On closer examination, this does not appear to be a telling difference.

The food stamp program is the largest nonmedical program for transfers in kind. Food stamp coupons are a close substitute for cash, and the subsidy could be given in cash while maintaining the current set of categorical programs.[58] Alternatively, an NIT would not preclude giving some of the benefits in the form of food vouchers. Either way, the food stamp program is unique in the United States in being essentially a mini-NIT.

Although it may be possible and perhaps desirable to "cashout" food stamps and housing subsidies (that is, replace them by cash benefits), it is not likely that this would be feasible in the case of subsidized health services for the poor. If the poor did not use the funds intended for health coverage to buy health insurance, society would still provide medical services when an illness or injury threatened serious disability or death. Hence the low-income family would have a weak incentive to use cashed-out Medicaid funds for health insurance. However, it would seem that the poor could be provided with health insurance vouchers to give them greater flexibility in the choice of medical insurance, and hence in the type of medical care they receive.

One particularly pernicious feature of Medicaid is that physician services and drugs can be reimbursed only if the fee is less than or equal to the scheduled Medicaid fee. The Medicaid client is therefore denied the ability to supplement the public subsidy if he prefers the services of a physician who charges higher fees than the Medicaid schedule or prefers to buy a higher quality drug or to buy from a more expensive pharmacy. As a result there is a tendency toward two "classes" of medical providers and hence of medical services.

Summary. The current system of categorical welfare programs differs from most conceptions of a negative income tax in two major respects. These are the coordination of administration and demographic differentiation in program benefits.

---

[58] See above discussion of President Carter's proposals for reform, especially p. 385.

The current, largely uncoordinated, welfare system is complex. The public's and the participants' resources are wasted through duplication of administrative efforts. Failures of coordination enhance the possibilities for fraud, and the sheer complexity of the system results in some people receiving smaller benefits, and others receiving larger benefits, than they are entitled to.

Society often seeks to achieve a large number of objectives through a smaller number of policy instruments. The objectives of the welfare system include a high benefit guarantee for people who are not expected to be able to provide for their own support, strong work incentives for those from whom work may be expected, and tolerable total costs to society. It may be possible to satisfy these objectives only if another objective is sacrificed to provide the same benefit structure for all demographic groups. With demographic differentiation, the greater society's concern with promoting work effort from the demographic group, the lower the benefit guarantee and the benefit-reduction rate. A fully coordinated categorical welfare system may differ in name only from an NIT that includes demographic differentiation in the benefit schedule.

Welfare Reform Principles of the Carter Administration. In May 1977, President Carter announced his administration's principles for welfare reform.[59] After an examination of the welfare system, he had concluded that the current categorical welfare programs "taken together, still do not constitute a rational, coherent system that is adequate and fair for all the poor. They are still overly wasteful, capricious and subject to fraud. They violate many desirable and necessary principles."

It may be too much, however, to expect any nationwide federal program to be "adequate and fair for all the poor." The relevant question is whether a more fair and less wasteful and arbitrary system can be developed.

President Carter announced twelve goals or principles that will be the basis of his future welfare reform recommendations. The twelve principles point to a fully coordinated national welfare system with no differences in real benefit levels among the states. The basic difficulty which has retarded welfare reform, and which is not explicitly recognized in the twelve principles, is that several objectives are mutually inconsistent. The goals may be grouped under the headings cost limitation, benefit structure, administration and federal-state relations, and public sector job creation (see Table 12).

---

[59] See "Text of Carter Welfare Remarks," *New York Times*, May 3, 1977, p. 34.

Table 12

CARTER'S TWELVE GOALS FOR WELFARE REFORM

Cost Limitation: Goal 1

Goal 1—"No higher initial cost than the present systems."

Benefit Structure: Goals 3, 5, 6, 7, and 8

Goal 3—"Incentives should always encourage full-time and part-time private sector employment."

Goal 5—"A family should have more income if it works than if it does not work."

Goal 6—"Incentives should be designed to keep families together."

Goal 7—"Earned income tax credits should be continued to help the working poor."

Goal 8—"A decent income should be provided also for those who cannot work or earn adequate income, with Federal benefits consolidated into a simple cash payment, varying in amount only to accommodate differences in costs of living from one area to another."

Administration and Federal-State Relations: Goals 9, 10, and 11

Goal 9—"The programs should be simpler and easier to administer."

Goal 10—"There should be incentives to be honest and to eliminate fraud."

Goal 11—"The unpredictable and growing financial burden on state and local governments should be reduced as rapidly as Federal resources permit."

Public Sector Job Creation: Goals 2, 4, and 12

Goal 2—"Under this system, every family with children and a member able to work should have access to a job."

Goal 4—"Public training and employment programs should be provided when private employment is unavailable."

Goal 12—"Local administration of public job programs should be emphasized."

Note: The goals are direct quotations from President Carter's statement, but they are presented here in a different order.

Source: "Text of Carter Welfare Principles," *New York Times*, May 3, 1977, p. 34.

Goal 8 implies a unified all-cash welfare system. The earned income credit for low-income families, introduced in 1975 legislation, would be retained (Goal 7). Although it is not mentioned, for the reasons discussed above it is unlikely that Medicaid would be cashed-out. The benefit-structure goals imply a welfare system that would provide a high benefit guarantee (Goal 8) and a low benefit-reduction rate (Goals 3 and 5) and would presumably provide essentially the same benefit-structure for one-parent families with young children as for intact two-parent families (Goal 6). If a welfare system is not to create incentives for separation, or disincentives for the first marriage or remarriage of women with young children, it must give the two-parent family with one working adult a benefit almost equivalent to their combined benefits if separated—that is, to the combined benefits of an adult unrelated individual who works and a one-parent family with children and no worker in the family. As discussed above, a program that includes a high benefit guarantee and a low benefit-reduction rate for all families, including intact families, would cover a much larger proportion of the population than the current welfare system. As a result it would be more costly and would appear to violate the initial goal of maintaining the cost of the welfare system at its current level (Goal 1).

Moving from the current set of largely uncoordinated categorical cash and in kind programs to a consolidated cash system (Goal 8) would go far in satisfying Goals 9 and 10, but one should not expect the elimination, perhaps not even a substantial reduction, of the welfare bureaucracy. Frequent reporting of the income and assets of the participants will still be needed. Because of the large number of recipients receiving relatively small benefits, the incentives for petty fraud exist and are administratively expensive to reduce. In addition, as indicated above, it is not likely that Medicaid, an administratively complex in kind transfer program, would be cashed-out.

Goals 2 and 4 imply that through federally funded manpower training and direct public job creation programs the federal government will assume the role of an employer of last resort for able adults with children in the family. Training programs have been used in the past as an antipoverty measure (for example, the Job Corps and the AFDC-Work Incentive Program), but in the era since World War II public service employment and public works employment for adults have been viewed as countercyclical programs rather than as explicit antipoverty or welfare instruments. The availability of public jobs might discourage workers from taking a regular private sector job. If so, it would be inconsistent with Goal 3 which seeks to encourage private sector employment.

As in the current Comprehensive Training and Employment Act (CETA) programs, the public jobs would be initiated and administered at the local level, although within broad federal guidelines (Goal 12). Thus far, public jobs programs have apparently been of limited usefulness.[60] The jobs have had to pay the prevailing wage, rather than a low wage, thereby increasing the cost per job created and reducing the incentive of the participants to continue to seek private sector employment. Rather than selecting people who would have the greatest difficulty finding a private sector job, public works and public service employment programs tend to hire workers with more favorable employment characteristics. These features would tend to make the public jobs program inconsistent with Goals 1, 3, and possibly 4. In addition, the net job-creation impact of public employment programs has been small, as state and local governments tend to use the funds for job slots that would otherwise have been funded out of their own resources.

The public job goals in the Carter welfare reform message represent a new departure in public policy. Since they are beyond the scope of this chapter, and since only general principles have been announced, they have been only very briefly discussed here. As the specific details of these programs take shape, they will warrant more intensive analysis.

Social Security

The largest governmental income transfer program is Old Age, Survivors and Disability Insurance (OASDI), more commonly known as social security (see Table 6 for a summary of program characteristics). In FY 1976, the average monthly number of recipients was 32 million, 15 percent of the population. The $71.4 billion in benefits was 20 percent of federal expenditures and 4.2 percent of gross national product (GNP). The program has undergone extraordinary growth in recent years through the aging of the population, the expansion of coverage of the labor force, new program features (for example, the introduction of disability insurance in 1957) and the rise in the real level of benefits (see Table 13). Social security has been an important feature in the sharp decline in poverty among the aged. In addition, the social insurance program, and social security in particular, have a very large income redistribution impact, greater

---

[60] For analyses of manpower training and public jobs programs, see Chiswick and O'Neill, *Human Resources*, chapter 8; Alan Fechter, *Public Employment Programs*, (Washington, D.C.: American Enterprise Institute, 1975); George E. Johnson and James D. Tomola, "The Fiscal Substitution Effect of Alternative Approaches to Public Service Employment Policy," *Journal of Human Resources*, vol. 12, no. 1 (Winter 1977), pp. 3-26; Dave M. O'Neill, *The Federal Government and Manpower* (Washington, D.C.: American Enterprise Institute, 1973) and Thomas Ribich, *Education and Poverty* (Washington, D.C.: Brookings Institution, 1968).

Table 13
SOCIAL SECURITY (OASDI) COVERAGE, BENEFICIARIES, AND BENEFITS, SELECTED YEARS, 1950–1976

Coverage, Beneficiary, or Benefit	1950	1960	1965	1970	1974	1975	1976
Coverage							
Percentage of employed workers [a]	65	88	89	90	90	90	90
Number of beneficiaries (millions) [b]							
Total beneficiaries	3.5	14.8	20.9	26.2	30.9	31.9	33.0
Retired workers, dependents, and survivors	3.5	14.2	19.1	23.6	26.9	27.6	28.3
Retired workers	1.8	8.1	11.1	13.3	16.0	16.5	17.1
Disabled workers and dependents		.7	1.7	2.7	3.9	4.3	4.7
Annual cash benefits (in billions of dollars)	1.0	11.3	18.3	31.9	58.5	67.1	75.7
Average monthly benefits (in dollars)							
All retired workers	44	74	84	118	188	207	225
All retired workers (in 1976 dollars) [c]	104	142	151	173	217	218	225
Maximum to men retiring at age 65 [d]	45	119	132	190	305	342	387
Maximum to women retiring at age 65 [d]	45	119	136	196	316	360	403
Minimum to persons retiring at age 65 [d]	10	33	44	64	94	101	108

[a] Employed workers defined as wage and salary workers and the self-employed.
[b] As of December of each year.
[c] Deflated by the consumer price index.
[d] Assumes retirement at beginning of year. For 1974–1976, as of June.

Source: For 1950–1974, *Social Security Bulletin, Annual Statistical Supplement, 1974;* for 1975 and 1976, Social Security Administration; for the CPI (all years), U.S. Department of Labor, Bureau of Labor Statistics.

than that of the cash welfare programs. The viability of the social security system has, however, been questioned. The original objective of financial viability (actuarial soundness) was abandoned long ago. Even its viability as a pay-as-you-go system is now threatened by rising benefit payments per recipient and by a rise in the ratio of program recipients to workers.

This section examines several aspects of the growth, equity, and viability of the current social security system. Some of the characteristics of the original program and important amendments introduced in 1939 are discussed. One of the latter was the introduction of the spouse benefit, that is, the automatic entitlement to benefits for married women who did not work and who therefore do not have benefit entitlements in their own name. Recent court decisions have changed several other program features that involved sex discrimination. The section then discusses the effects of expanded social security coverage and the growth in real benefit levels on program participation and the labor supply of older persons. Earlier retirement tends to reduce the viability of the program by simultaneously reducing social security tax yields and raising aggregate benefits paid out.

The social security trust funds are now operating on a very thin margin. In the near term, the adverse effects of the recent recession and of earlier retirement, particularly in the disability insurance program for persons under age sixty-five, threaten the trust funds. In the long term, the aging of the population and the rapid growth in future benefits currently built into the social security system ("double-indexing") threaten to make the entire social security system an unbearable burden on the work force. This section closes with a discussion of the viability of the trust funds and of some measures to keep the share of the social security system in the economy at roughly its current level.

Payroll Tax Rates, Covered Employment, and Replacement Rates. Although legislated in 1935, social security tax payments started in 1937 as 2 percent of the worker's earnings, contributed equally by the employer and employee, up to a maximum of $3,000 taxable earnings.[61] This $3,000 in 1937 dollars was equivalent to approximately $12,600 in 1976 dollars.

The tax rate and tax base for the Old Age and Survivors Insurance program (OASI) has increased to 8.75 percent of the first $15,300 of earnings in 1976, and to $16,500 in 1977. As a result of the introduction of the disability insurance (DI) program in 1957

---

[61] There is some evidence that although half of the social security tax is paid directly by the employer, its burden is shifted to the workers in the form of lower wages. See John A. Brittain, *The Payroll Tax for Social Security* (Washington, D.C.: Brookings Institution, 1972), chapters 2 and 3. For a historical series of the social security tax rate, maximum taxable earnings, and coverage, see U.S. Department of Health, Education, and Welfare, Social Security Administration, *Social Security Bulletin, Annual Statistical Supplement,* 1974 (1976), pp. 30-33 and p. 66.

and the hospital insurance (HI) component of Medicare in 1965, the total OASDHI tax rate increased by 1.5 percentage points and 1.8 percentage points, respectively, to 11.7 percent of taxable earnings. The self-employed pay a total tax of 7.9 percent of their taxable earnings for the OASDHI program. Since 1975 the maximum for taxable earnings has been indexed to changes in average wages in covered employment, so it will rise automatically with wages. The three components of social security, OASI, DI, and HI, have separate trust funds.

Periodic changes in legislation, as well as the changing composition of employment (primarily the decline in self-employment and farm employment), have increased the proportion of the work force covered by social security. In 1940, 58 percent of those in paid employment (wage and salary earners including members of the armed forces and the self-employed) were covered by social security. This increased to 65 percent in 1950, 88 percent in 1960, and 90 percent in 1966, at which level it has since remained.

Of the 8.7 million in paid employment not covered by social security in 1974, 2.5 million were federal civilian employees, and 1.1 million were nonfarm self-employed workers or domestics earning less than the required minimum. Most of the remaining 5.1 million were state and local government workers, self-employed farmers, or employees of nonprofit organizations for whom coverage is authorized but not mandated. The federal civilian employees and most of the state and local government workers not under mandatory coverage have their own pension plans. Because of substantial job mobility, many of the workers not covered by social security in any one year will have social security credits when they retire.

In addition to the growth in social security coverage, there has been an increase since 1970 in the replacement rate—the ratio of a worker's social security benefits to his earnings before retirement. Replacement rates have been calculated for men who retire at age sixty-five and who had median earnings in the year before retirement.[62] Adjusting for price differences in the two years, the replacement rate generally fluctuated between 29 percent and 33 percent from 1953 to 1970. Since 1970, however, the replacement rate has increased continuously from 31 percent to 43 percent in 1976.

The 1939 Amendments. The Social Security Act of 1935 envisioned a program that would be self-financing, using payroll taxes on em-

---

[62] U.S. Congress, Congressional Budget Office, *Issues in the Financing of Social Security*, April 1977, Table 4, p. 12 (mimeo).

ployers and employees in covered employment, and that would be more or less actuarially sound. Individual benefits were to be closely related to the tax contributions made into the system, except that preferential treatment would be given to people at the minimum benefit level. The 1939 amendments made two program modifications that fundamentally changed the nature of the social security system. Only one of these was intended to have a long-term impact.

The amendments provided that covered workers retiring early would receive benefits substantially larger than the actuarial value of their taxes. This was, in principle, only a short-term violation of the actuarial soundness of the program until the system matured—until enough time had passed that workers at retirement age would have been contributing to the system for most of their working lives. Since then, however, even the pretense that benefits would be scheduled on an actuarially sound basis has been dropped. The second change, which was intended to be long-term, was the creation of the unfunded spouse benefit.

Spouse Benefits. The spouse benefit has become a major issue in discussions of the social security system. It provides that if a worker has an aged wife, his retirement benefit is to be increased by 50 percent or by the difference between 50 percent and his wife's own social security entitlement, whichever is larger. The spouse benefit was introduced at a time when married women had very low labor-force participation rates; it was an attempt to overcome the objection to the social security benefit structure that two could not live as cheaply as one. As coverage by the spouse benefit required no increase in taxes, inequities were created between married men with a nonworking wife and all others.

The inequities have become far more complex in the modern world. With a rise in the labor-force participation of women, an increased proportion have social security entitlements of their own, and at retirement many are entitled to benefits that exceed 50 percent of their husband's benefits. As a result there is little or no additional social security benefit for the aged couple at retirement from the wife's contribution to the system.[63] That is, for couples with the same combined pattern of lifetime family earnings and tax contributions, benefits are substantially larger if the wife did not work in the labor

---

[63] For estimates of rates of return from social security contributions by sex, marital status, earnings, and work history, see June A. O'Neill, *Returns to Social Security*, paper presented at American Economic Association Annual Meeting, September 1976, Atlantic City, New Jersey.

market than if both husband and wife worked. This has led to the charge that the social security system discriminates against working women. A more accurate description is that the system discriminates *in favor* of couples in which the wife does not work in the labor market and discriminates against single men, single women, and two-worker couples.

There are several avenues for reforming the spouse benefit inequities. However, because work histories and retirement plans have been partly based on the expectation of the spouse benefit, no solution offers immediate relief. One solution for future retirees would be to gradually reduce the automatic entitlement proportion for the spouse from the current 50 percent. Hence, as time passes the unfunded spouse credit could be phased out.

To permit an explicit recognition that women who are not working in the labor market are productive in the home and to reduce opposition to the phasing out of the unfunded spouse benefit, a plan could be created in which nonworking women, or women during nonworking years, could voluntarily contribute to the social security system and increase their own entitlement. As there is no explicit measure of the taxable earnings of the nonworking wife, this could be assumed to be equal to the husband's taxable earnings or some fraction thereof. (Implicit in the current system is that the wife's "earnings" are equivalent to one-half of the husband's.) Contributions for the spouse credit would be equivalent to the employer and employee components combined, so that at retirement the same taxes would have been paid for persons receiving the same benefits, regardless of whether the person was in the paid labor force.[64] Because of the difficulties of measuring disability for persons in home production, it may not be feasible to include the disability insurance program in this scheme.

Tying the wife's entitlement to her *own* social security record would separate her benefits from her marital status. A divorced woman is now entitled to the spouse benefit only if the marriage to her latest husband lasted at least twenty years. Moreover, social security contributions cannot be made on income from alimony. Hence some divorced women are in effect denied social security benefits. This problem would not exist if contributions made for a nonworking wife were tied to her social security record and if, on a voluntary basis, alimony income could be treated as a basis for social security contributions.

---

[64] Using the same reasoning, there is an inequity in the self-employed receiving the same benefits as wage and salary workers for a smaller total tax contribution.

A program of this type would remove the inequity favoring the nonworking wife and provide her with an entitlement of her own. The plan should, of course, be nondiscriminatory so that a nonworking husband with a working wife could also participate in the program and increase his social security entitlement.

Sex Discrimination and "Double Dipping." The social security system has had many sex discriminatory features that have been successfully challenged in the courts in the last few years. Most of the sex discrimination arose from the 1930s stereotype of the family: the husband works, the wife does not work, and the husband dies several years before the wife. In two separate decisions in March 1977 the Supreme Court ruled unconstitutional the differential treatment of widows and widowers and the differential application of the spouse benefit according to the sex of the spouse. Previously, a widow was entitled to survivor's benefits without having to prove dependency, while a widower had to prove he was dependent on his wife at the time of her death for at least one-half of his support. The spouse benefit also required a dependency test for a man to receive 50 percent of his wife's entitlement if this exceeded his own entitlement. The removal of the dependency test for survivors benefits and for spouse benefits is expected to raise total benefits by $200 million per year and $300 million per year, respectively.[65]

Most of the nondependent men who are affected by these decisions have little or no social security entitlement because their employment was primarily in a sector of the economy exempt from mandatory coverage. These include civilian federal government workers, some state and local government workers, farm and domestic workers, and some self-employed persons. The federal employees' retirement system and, where they exist, state and local government pension plans provide benefits for the workers concerned. The maintenance of several public systems enables some workers and couples who have worked in more than one system to receive benefits from two or more public pension systems ("double dipping") and hence receive larger benefits than other persons who have made equal contributions into one system. The larger benefits for the same dollar contributions arise from the automatic spouse benefit in social security and from the progressive social security benefit structure—after satisfying minimum requirements for benefit entitlement, the lower the level of contributions (either because of low-wage rates, few weeks worked per year, or few years in the

---

[65] *Wall Street Journal*, March 22, 1977, p. 4.

system), the larger the benefits relative to contributions. Double dipping increases program costs and raises issues of equity. With the long planning horizon for pensions, coordination of public pension systems to reduce double dipping is likely to provide few economies in the short term, even though the long-term increases in equity and reductions in program costs may be substantial. The problem would also be alleviated if the automatic spouse credit in social security were phased out and the spouse entitlement were made contingent on the spouse's own contributions to the system.

The Age at Retirement. The average age at retirement has an important impact on the social security system. Earlier retirement means smaller tax contributions and a longer benefit period. In the coming decades, because of the changing demographic structure of the population, the increase in the aged population relative to the working-age population will increase the burden to the economy of financing the social security system. The burden will be reduced to the extent that the decline in the age at retirement slows or is reversed.[66]

The purpose of the social security system is to replace the earnings lost through death of a spouse or retirement arising from old age or disability. Because the system is treated as an insurance against lost earnings, ownership of assets or income from property, pensions, or other sources except earnings from employment for those less than seventy-two years of age do not disqualify beneficiaries. The earnings test for aged recipients is intended to strike a balance among considerations of program cost, work incentives, and equity. In 1977 recipients could earn $3,000 a year without any reduction in benefits, but for each dollar of annual earnings in excess of this amount, annual benefits were reduced by fifty cents.[67] The social security system has apparently had an effect on work incen-

---

[66] The OECD has estimated that "the potential savings for an average country could be in the order of 0.3 percent of GDP for each one year by which the pensionable age was postponed." Organization for Economic Cooperation and Development, *Public Expenditure on Income Maintenance Programs* (Paris: Organization for Economic Cooperation and Development, 1976), p. 85.

[67] Since 1975 the amount of earnings that can be received before benefits are reduced has been indexed to average earnings in covered employment. The effective marginal tax rate on earnings for those in the range of the 50 percent benefit-reduction rate actually exceeds 50 percent because earnings are subject to payroll and income taxes, while social security benefits are exempt from taxation. The employee's share of the contribution to the social security system is taxed as part of earnings, while the employer's share is treated as a business expense of the employer but not as a fringe benefit to the employee, and is not treated as part of the employee's taxable income.

tives, and enrollments in the system are apparently responsive to overall employment opportunities in the economy.[68]

The effect of the social security benefits on work effort can be seen in an examination of the labor-force participation rates of aged persons. During the 1940s there was a moderate increase in the proportion of all aged men eligible for social security benefits, but real benefits declined. During this period the labor-force participation rate of men age sixty-five to sixty-nine was unchanged at about 60 percent (Table 14). In the following two decades, however, both coverage and real benefits increased sharply, and the labor-force participation rate of older men fell from 60 percent in 1950 to 39 percent in 1970. In 1961 men age sixty-two to sixty-four became eligible for social security at reduced benefit levels. The labor-force participation rate of men age sixty-two to sixty-four varied between 75 and 78 percent in the three census years 1940, 1950, 1960 and fell sharply to 68 percent by 1970. For men age sixty to sixty-one, the participation rate fell only slightly, from 82 percent between 1940 and 1960 to 80 percent in 1970. The sharper decline in labor-force participation for the age group sixty-two to sixty-four during the 1960s was apparently a consequence of the change in eligibility for retirement.

The expansion of social security coverage and the rise in real benefits per recipient, including the widow's benefit, have also tended to reduce labor-force participation among aged women. The labor-force participation rate of women age sixty-five and over increased slightly from the end of World War II to 1960 and then declined, while the participation rate among younger women increased throughout the period, but particularly after 1960.[69] It should be noted that

---

[68] For econometric studies see, for example, Michael J. Boskin, "Social Security and Retirement Decisions," *Economic Inquiry*, vol. 15, no. 1 (January 1977), pp. 1-25, and Mordechai E. Lando, "The Effect of Unemployment on Application for Disability Insurance," *American Statistical Association, 1974 Proceedings of Business and Economic Statistics Section* (Washington, D.C.: American Statistical Association, 1975), pp. 438-42.

[69] The labor-force participation rates of women from 1950 to 1975 were:

	Age Groups	
	25 to 34 Years	65 Years and over
1950	34.0	9.7
1960	36.0	10.8
1970	45.0	9.7
1975	54.6	8.3

Source: U.S. Department of Labor, Employment and Training Administration, *Employment and Training Report of the President, 1976*, Table A-2, p. 214.

Table 14

LABOR-FORCE PARTICIPATION AND SOCIAL SECURITY
ELIGIBILITY AND BENEFITS FOR MEN OVER FIFTY-NINE,
SELECTED YEARS, 1940–1975

Age Group	"Census of Population" Data				"Current Population Survey" Data	
	1940	1950	1960	1970	1970	1975
Percentage of men in the labor force[a]						
60-64 years	79.0	79.4	77.8	73.2	75.0	65.7
60-61 years	81.7	81.8	82.0	80.3	78.7	75.2
62-64 years	77.0	77.7	74.7	67.9	69.8	58.8
65-69 years	59.4	59.7	44.0	39.3	41.6	31.7
70 years and over	28.4	28.3	21.9	16.6	17.7	15.1
70-74 years	38.4	38.7	28.7	22.5	25.2	21.2
75 years and over	18.2	18.7	15.6	12.1	12.0	10.2
Percentage of men eligible for social security benefits[b]						
62-64 years	[c]	[c]	[c]	93.8	—	96.4
65 years and over	10.9[d]	32.4	80.7	91.0	—	92.5
Average monthly primary social insurance benefit for men filing for benefits in given year:						
In current dollars	23.26	31.88	92.03	146.99	—	263.53
In 1975 dollars[e]	89.81	71.80	168.24	205.12	—	263.53

[a] The data are for the noninstitutional population in April of each year.

[b] Based on the number of people eligible at the beginning of the year.

[c] Not eligible for social security benefits. Eligibility was extended to this age group in 1961.

[d] The figure is for 1941.

[e] Deflated by the consumer price index.

Source: U.S. Department of Commerce, Bureau of the Census; U.S. Department of Labor, Bureau of Labor Statistics; and U.S. Department of Health, Education, and Welfare, Social Security Administration.

in 1961 the social security widow's benefit was raised from the 75 percent of her husband's entitlement that had been in effect since 1939 to 82.5 percent, and in 1972 this was increased to 100 percent.

The social security system is only one of several factors that influence the decision to retire.[70] The rise in real incomes over time has increased the economic demand for leisure. People now work fewer hours per day and fewer days per year, in addition to retiring earlier. Tax incentives for private pensions have also encouraged earlier retirement. As the self-employed tend to retire later than wage and salary workers, the decline in self-employment is partially responsible for lowering the age at retirement. The increase in mandatory retirement provisions may have resulted in earlier retirement for some; yet this may simply be the institutionalization of other economic incentives.[71]

On the other hand, there are factors which would have tended to encourage later retirement. In general, white-collar jobs are less physically demanding than blue-collar jobs, and the relative increase in the importance of the latter should have encouraged later retirement. Investments in training (schooling and postschool training) have the effect of lowering nonhuman assets during the training period and raising the relative value of the person's working time (wage) thereby encouraging more work, including later retirement.[72] Although the effects of schooling on age at retirement need not be the same over time as in the cross-section, this does suggest that the rise in the average level of schooling and training should have tended to raise the retirement age, other things being equal.

---

[70] See for example, Lowell E. Galloway, *The Retirement Decision: An Exploratory Essay*, Research Report No. 9, Social Security Administration, Division of Research and Statistics, 1975.

[71] A mandatory retirement provision in a firm can compel a worker to retire from that firm earlier than he would choose but by itself cannot compel him to retire from the labor force.

[72] It has been estimated that men with higher levels of schooling retire at a later age and have a somewhat shorter length of working life:

Years of Schooling	Estimated Average Retirement Age	Estimated Length of Working Life
8	65	45
9-11	66	47
12	67	47
13-15	67	45
16	68	45
17 or more	70	45

Source: Jacob Mincer, *Schooling, Experience and Earnings* (New York: National Bureau of Economic Research, 1974), pp. 8-9.

The Trust Funds. The social security system operates on a pay-as-you-go basis. Current tax receipts are used to finance current benefits. This is done through trust funds: contributions are made into the funds and benefits are paid from them. Originally the trust fund was to be actuarially sound; contributions to the fund were to be large enough so that the size of the fund at any time would equal the present value of outstanding liabilities. This principle, which is essential for the financial survival of a private pension plan, is not essential for a public program that may have access to general revenues if the trust fund is depleted. Starting with the 1939 amendments that granted pensions to retirees substantially larger than the value of their contributions, the principle of actuarial soundness has been increasingly violated. At the start of 1976 the combined OASDI trust fund was equivalent to only 57 percent of the benefits distributed in that year, a decline from 186 percent in 1960.[73] The DI trust fund was 71 percent of annual benefits in 1976, whereas it had been 304 percent in 1960. The OASI trust fund was 55 percent of annual benefits, compared with 180 percent in 1960.

The size of the trust fund responds to economic and demographic factors and to the characteristics of the social security system. For example, since 1970 there has been a slower growth in annual earnings than in benefits per recipient. This is the result both of a slowdown in economic growth, in part due to the recession, and of legislated rapid increases in real benefit levels. In addition, the high unemployment rate since 1975 has encouraged earlier retirement in the old age and disability insurance programs.

The Congressional Budget Office has estimated the size of the trust funds from now to 1985 using current program characteristics and tax rates and various forecasts as to the macroeconomic performance of the economy.[74] By 1980 the disability insurance trust fund will be depleted, while the OASI trust fund is likely to cover about 26 percent of annual benefits. The OASI trust fund will be depleted by 1983 or 1984, and the combined OASDI trust accounts will be depleted by 1983.

The DI trust fund—an immediate problem. The disability insurance trust fund will soon be depleted because of the rapid and unexpected growth in program participation (see Table 15). The disability insurance (DI) program was established in 1957 to provide benefits

---

[73] U.S. Congress, Congressional Budget Office, *Issues in the Financing of Social Security*, Table 5, p. 14.

[74] Ibid., pp. 15-18.

Table 15
BENEFICIARIES UNDER THE SOCIAL SECURITY PROGRAM, SELECTED YEARS, 1940–1975
(in thousands)

Year	Type of Insurance			Total OASDI
	Retirement	Disability	Survivor	
1940	77	—	36	113
1950	1,918	—	1,094	3,012
1955	5,443	—	2,097	7,540
1960	10,310	543	3,446	14,299
1965	13,918	1,654	4,681	20,253
1970	16,870	2,573	6,369	25,812
1974	19,409	3,712	7,197	30,318
1975	20,015	4,142	7,302	31,459

Source: 1940 to 1974, *Social Security Bulletin Annual Statistical Supplement, 1974,* Table 14; 1975, U.S. Department of Health, Education, and Welfare, Social Security Administration.

for disabled persons age fifty to sixty-four who are covered by social security, after a waiting period of six months following the onset of the disability. The requirement that recipients be at least fifty years of age was removed in 1961 and the waiting period was reduced to five months in 1973. The number of beneficiaries has increased from 1.7 million in 1965 to 4.1 million in 1975. The rapid increase in DI program participation in the past decade appears to be greater than the growth that could be attributed to the higher rate of unemployment or the rise in the ratio of social security disability benefits to average wages.[75] The rapid program growth in the early 1960s may be largely due to its absorbing the existing stock of disabled people under sixty-five and to the public's gradually learning of its existence.

The program's growth in the last decade may, in part, be due to the increase in the total package of benefits available to disability insurance beneficiaries. Disability insurance beneficiaries are eligible for Medicare (enacted in 1965). Those with few assets and little other income are eligible for Supplemental Security Income (established 1974) and, as a result, for Medicaid and food stamps.[76] It has

---

[75] Lando, "The Effect of Unemployment on Application for Disability Insurance," finds that, controlling for these factors, there has been a strong secular trend in applications for benefits.

[76] In December 1974, 1.7 million people under sixty-five received SSI benefits for the blind and disabled, and 2.3 million recipients were age 65 or over.

also been alleged that the standards of disability needed to qualify have been eased, but this is difficult to measure.

In spite of its rapid growth, the disability insurance program is only a small part of the overall social security system. To prevent bankruptcy of the DI trust fund, the contributions to the fund could be increased either by raising the tax rate or maximum taxable earnings above currently scheduled levels, or by using general revenue financing. However, payroll tax increases at this time are likely to be viewed as undesirable because of the continued high level of unemployment.

There is also much opposition to direct general-revenue financing of the social security system. The prevailing view, or perhaps more accurately the prevailing myth, is that the social security system is an insurance; that is, that retired people are entitled to benefits because of their past contributions through payroll taxes. This view differentiates social security from welfare, the former being considered a right and the latter tainted with the stigma of public charity. Were it not for this myth, it would be far more difficult politically to justify the current system, which does not have a means test and which provides higher benefits to persons who had higher earnings when they worked.

Merging the DI and OASI trust funds might be one short-term solution to the problem of financial viability for the disability insurance trust fund, but not for that of the social security system in general. As noted above, current projections indicate that the combined trust fund would be depleted by 1983. To merge the two would provide time for a more careful and less hurried analysis by policy makers of the role of the social security system in our society.

Long-term problems: double indexing and decoupling. Under current legislation the social security system will become an increasing burden on the economy over the next few decades primarily because of two problems, one legislated, the other demographic. The legislated problem—"double indexing" of benefits for future retirees —is recent in origin, will not develop vested interests for several years, and could be readily corrected. The demographic problem is the rise in the proportion of aged persons relative to the working age population.

From the inception of the social security system, benefits have been increased periodically on an ad hoc basis by legislation. After each benefit increase, real benefits would decline for a few years until the next legislated increase raised real benefits above the previous peak level. Hence the aged experienced temporary downward variability in real benefits and uncertainty as to when benefit increases would occur.[77] The 1972 amendments to the Social Security Act sought to maintain the real purchasing power of the benefits to retirees by tying future increases in their benefits to changes in the consumer price index (CPI).

Apparently by inadvertence, the legislation coupled the benefits for future retirees to real benefit levels for those already retired. Inflation creates a rise in nominal wages and in maximum taxable earnings, as well as in the most common measure of inflation, the CPI. As inflation increases nominal wages, workers move higher up in the benefit schedule. The dollar benefit for each step in the schedule is, however, linked to the CPI. Hence, inflation now has a double effect on the benefit entitlements of future retirees—they move higher up in the schedule, and the nominal dollar value of their place in the schedule is increased. This is analogous to walking up a moving up-escalator. The double effect, referred to as double-indexing, means that many future retirees will have social security benefits at retirement close to or even in excess of their preretirement earnings!

Removing the double-indexing, referred to as "decoupling," is clearly necessary to prevent taxes from having to rise to excessively high levels to support such a generous system. The Social Security Advisory Council estimated that under current legislation, assuming a 2 percent annual growth in real wages, a 3 percent annual increase in the CPI, and a fertility rate of 2.1 births per woman (a rate ultimately consistent with zero population growth), by 2030 social security benefits would equal 17.6 percent of the taxable payroll, as taxable payroll is defined under current law.[78] The social security trustees' median forecast used somewhat less optimistic, but perhaps more realistic, assumptions (1.75 percent annual growth in real wages, 4 percent rate of inflation, fertility rate of 1.9 births per woman) and estimated that the expenditures in year 2030 would be about 26 percent of taxable earnings.[79] Neither the Advisory Council report nor

---

[77] Benefit increases tended to be more frequent in periods of high inflation. From September 1950 to June 1974 there were eight legislated benefit increases: in 1950, 1959, 1965, 1968, 1970, 1971, 1972, and 1974. Automatic increases started in June 1975. From September 1950 to June 1975 the cumulative minimum percentage increase in OASDI primary insurance benefits was 190 percent, while the CPI increased 130 percent. The average annual rate of growth of real benefits for the twenty-five-year period was 1.9 percent.

[78] Report of the Advisory Council of Social Security, 1975, Washington, D.C., 1975, pp. 119-20 (mimeo).

[79] 1976 Annual Report of the Board of Trustees of the Federal Old-Age and Survivors Insurance and Disability Insurance Trust Funds, Washington, D.C., May 1976 (mimeo), p. 91, Table 26. The Board of Trustees consists of the secretaries

the trustees' report takes explicit account of the probable effect of high benefits relative to earnings on earlier retirement, which would raise program costs even further. In comparison, the current tax rate for OASDI is 9.9 percent of taxable earnings and is scheduled to rise by the year 2011 to 11.9 percent of taxable earnings.

While there is widespread agreement that decoupling is required, there is less agreement on the procedure or formula. The main issue is whether, before retirement, benefit entitlements should rise with the CPI or with the growth in average wages in covered employment.[80] If the benefits associated with each step in the schedule increased with the average wage (wage indexing), and if a worker's position (step) in the schedule were determined by his real wages, social security replacement rates for the average retiring worker would remain constant over time.[81] If the benefits associated with each step in the schedule increased solely with the CPI (price indexing) and if a worker's position in the schedule were determined by his real wages, the replacement rate would be constant for a given level of real earnings. In this situation, because the social security benefit structure is progressive (that is, social security replaces a larger proportion of preretirement earnings for low-wage workers), replacement rates decline over time for the average worker as average real social security benefits rise at a slower rate than average real earnings. Under either wage or price indexing, the real value of the social security benefit at retirement would be rising over time. The issue is the rate at which it would rise.

Social security benefits in the year 2030 can be calculated as a percent of taxable earnings if wage indexing or price indexing were adopted now.[82] Under the assumptions of a 1.75 percent annual growth in real wages, a 4 percent rate of inflation, and a fertility rate

---

of the treasury; labor; and health, education, and welfare. The commissioner of social security is secretary to the board.

[80] There appears to be widespread agreement that once a worker retires the benefits should increase in proportion to the rise in the consumer price index.

[81] With the current benefit schedule, replacement rates are higher for low-wage workers. As a rise in nominal earnings raise a worker's position in the benefit schedule, the replacement rate for the worker would decline, unless replacement rates within each step of the schedule were continuously increased. If there were growth in real earnings, the benefit schedule would have to be linked to average earnings to keep average replacement rates from declining over time.

[82] Wage indexing was proposed by President Ford in the Social Security Benefit Indexing Bill of 1976. Price indexing was proposed by an expert panel on social security appointed by Congress. See U.S. Congress, *Report of the Consultant Panel on Social Security*, August 1976, referred to as the Hsiao Report after the panel's chairman. Thus far, legislative action has not been taken on either measure.

of 1.9 births per woman, by 2030 benefits would be 26.0 percent of taxable earnings (as defined under current law) under the current double indexing system, 18.9 percent if wage indexing were adopted, and 12.5 percent under price indexing.[83] The longer the delay in changing the indexing procedure, the more costly the program once it is adopted.

The social security replacement rate—social security benefits as a percentage of earnings in the year before retirement, adjusted for price level differences in the two years—for the median worker retiring at age sixty-five in year 2030 would differ under wage and price indexing.[84] For wage indexing it would remain at the current level (about 44 percent) over the next fifty years, while under price indexing it would gradually decline to 25 percent by 2030. In contrast, a worker receiving real earnings equivalent to median earnings in 1976 would, at retirement in 2030, receive a replacement rate of 100 percent under wage indexing and the current replacement rate (about 44 percent) under price indexing.

The decision whether wage indexing or price indexing is to be preferred cannot be made in isolation, but rather requires an assessment of the role of social security in the entire pension and retirement income system and of the probable size of the social security population relative to the working population.[85]

Long-term problems: the aging of the population. The Social Security Advisory Council reported that there were about 6 beneficiaries for every 100 workers in 1950, about 30 beneficiaries for every 100 workers in 1975 and (projecting on the basis of the likely demographic composition of the population and likely labor-force participation rates) by 2030 there would be a peak of about 45 beneficiaries for each 100 workers in the economy.[86] The rise in the ratio of beneficiaries to workers from 1950 to 1975 is due partly to expansion in the sectors of activity covered by the system and partly to the maturation of the program; even in 1950 many aged persons had

---

[83] U.S. Congress, Congressional Budget Office, *Issues in the Financing of Social Security,* Table 12, p. 37.

[84] Ibid., Table 11, p. 35.

[85] As a result of the Pension Reform Act of 1974, minimum federal standards have been established for the investment of private sector pension funds in income-producing assets and for vesting in workers their contributions to pension plans. The law does not require that a firm provide a pension program for its workers. Federal law also provides tax incentives for creating individual retirement programs for the self-employed and for workers in firms where pension plans do not exist or do not satisfy minimum federal standards.

[86] *Report of the Advisory Council of Social Security, 1975,* p. 121. The Advisory Council assumed that the fertility rate will rise from the current 1.9 births per woman to 2.1 and indefinitely remain at that level (zero population growth).

insufficient work experience in covered employment to qualify for benefits. The system has now matured, and coverage has been widespread for many years. The rise in the ratio of beneficiaries to workers over the next half-century will be due primarily to the aging of the post-World War II baby boom population and to the lower fertility rates since the late 1950s.[87] Other things being equal, this demographic change would necessitate more than a 50 percent increase in the payroll tax rate.

Solutions to the Increasing Burden of Social Security. The increased burden of the social security system in the coming decades can be financed by substantially increased payroll taxes or by increased income taxation and general revenue financing for social security. Alternatively, the increasing burden on the working population can be mitigated.[88]

One means of reducing the relative burden is to permit a gradual decline for future retirees in the ratio of average benefits at retirement to preretirement earnings. If the current double-indexed system were replaced by wage indexing, average replacement rates would remain constant, that is, the ratio of average benefits to average preretirement earnings would remain at about the current 44 percent. If, however, price indexing were adopted—that is, replacement rates remained constant for a given level of real income—average replacement rates would gradually decline (to about 25 percent in 2030) as average retirement benefits increased at a slower rate than average wages. Under price indexing the real benefits of future retirees would be higher, yet the burden of the social security system on the work force would be reduced somewhat. In addition, lower taxes would mean a higher income after taxes, thereby giving workers greater discretion in allocating their resources between current consumption and investments (including private pension plans) that would provide income at retirement.

A second means of reducing the social security burden is to gradually increase the average age at retirement. Other things being equal, a later retirement age means more years of contributing to the social security system and fewer years in which benefits are received. With the reduction in the proportion of jobs that are physically demanding and the growth in the relative importance of training, there

---

[87] In recent years the fertility rate has been below 2.1, the level ultimately needed to maintain a stable population in the absence of immigration and emigration.

[88] Some potential solutions, such as government programs to increase the birth rate or to increase immigration of workers, are assumed to be politically unacceptable and are not considered here.

are economic incentives for extending the length of the working life. The Social Security Advisory Council has prepared estimates of the savings in benefits as a percentage of taxable earnings that would result from an increase in the retirement age by two months per year starting in 2005 and ending in 2023 (so that by 2023 the retirement age would be sixty-eight and early retirement at reduced benefits would be at sixty-five).[89] If this proposal were adopted, the resulting percent reduction in the ratio of benefits to taxable earnings would be as follows:

Year	Percent Reduction in the Ratio of Benefits to Taxable Earnings
2005-2014	1.6
2015-2024	4.9
2025-2050	9.3

If the age at retirement were gradually increased by three years in this manner, the social security tax in 2030 would be about 24 percent of taxable earnings if the current system were retained, 17 percent under wage indexing, and 11 percent under price indexing. A tax rate of 11 percent in 2030 is not very different from the current 9.9 percent (scheduled to rise to 11.9 percent in 2011) and would not represent a substantially increased burden on the payroll tax system.

Social Security Proposals of the Carter Administration. The Carter administration announced in May 1977 its proposal to ensure the short-term and long-term viability of the social security system.[90] The four major aspects of the proposal are: (1) raising the maximum taxable earnings for the employer's component of the tax, (2) shifting half of the scheduled hospital insurance (HI) tax increase to the disability insurance trust fund, (3) making contributions to the OASDHI trust funds from general revenues when the unemployment rate exceeds 6 percent, and (4) decoupling through wage indexing. There are apparently no recommendations concerning the unfunded spouse benefit or the age at retirement.

The Carter proposal would, in stages, raise the ceiling for maximum taxable earnings used to compute the employer's share of the payroll tax from $16,500 in 1977 to $37,500 in 1980; it would remove the ceiling in 1981. The maximum taxable earnings for workers

---

[89] *Report of the Advisory Council of Social Security, 1975*, pp. 146-47.

[90] "Statement by President Carter on Social Security Reform," White House press release, May 9, 1977, and "Social Security Financing Proposals" *HEW News*, press release, May 9, 1977.

would be increased only slightly, by $2,400, above the levels antici-
pated under current law. This proposal would raise payroll taxes,
but only for higher-income workers. Since under current law only the
contribution "made" by the employee is used to determine benefits
at retirement, future benefit entitlements would not be raised by
increasing the taxable earnings maximum for the employer's contribution but not the employee's. As was noted above, however, it appears
that even if they are levied on employers, payroll taxes are shifted to
workers in the form of lower earnings after taxes.

The hospital insurance (HI) program in Medicare is financed by
a tax of 0.9 percent of the taxable payroll, levied on both the employer and the employee. This tax rate had been scheduled to increase by 0.2 percentage points in 1978 and 0.25 percentage points
in 1981. Under the Carter proposal, about one-half of this increase
would be diverted to the disability insurance trust fund to help forestall bankruptcy. The viability of the hospital insurance trust fund
would then depend on the success of the administration's efforts to
slow the rise in hospital costs. Alternatively, additional general revenue financing would be needed to help finance Medicare.

In addition, the OASI and DI trust funds would effectively be
merged. The amount of revenue required to keep the DI trust fund
from running out of money would be transferred from the OASI
trust fund. Under the proposal, general revenue financing for social
security (OASDHI) would occur only to the extent that unemployment rates in excess of 6 percent deprived the trust funds of payroll
taxes. Although this is proposed as a five-year experiment, HEW
Secretary Califano indicated that the Carter administration would like
to make this a permanent feature of the program.[91] As noted above,
general revenue financing would appear to be inconsistent with a
program that is not means-tested, but that instead scales benefits
according to preretirement earnings.

The proposal to decouple through wage indexing would, as
noted above, keep average social security replacement rates at the
current level of about 44 percent. This is substantially above the 29
to 33 percent replacement rates that prevailed during the 1950s and
1960s. Because the changing age structure of the population will increase the ratio of social security beneficiaries to workers by 50 percent by the year 2030, under wage indexing the ratio of social security payments to taxable earnings (as defined in current law) would
be 50 percent larger than at the present time.

---

[91] "Califano Says Shift on Social Security Could Be Permanent," *New York Times*,
May 10, 1977, p. 1.

Cover and book design: Pat Taylor